GREAT GA

Bertil Lintner was a senior writer for the *Far Eastern Economic Review* for more than twenty years, covering Burma and related issues. He now teaches journalism in Burma and writes for international websites such as Yale Global Online and Asia Pacific Media Services. He is a recognized expert on Burmese issues as well as ethnic minorities, insurgencies and narcotics in Southeast and South Asia.

In 1985, the Swedish-born Lintner and his Shan wife from Burma headed out on an eighteen-month, 2,275-kilometre overland journey from northeastern India across Burma's northern rebel-held areas to China. They became the first outsiders in over four decades to cross that isolated area, which then was controlled by various ethnic insurgents. Lintner chronicled that epic trek in his classic *Land of Jade: A Journey from India through Northern Burma to China*.

Lintner is the author of six other books on Burma, among them *Burma in Revolt: Opium and Insurgency since 1948*, *Merchants of Madness: The Methamphetamine Explosion in the Golden Triangle* and *Aung San Suu Kyi and Burma's Struggle for Democracy*. He has also written a book about organized crime in Asia, *Blood Brothers: The Criminal Underworld of Asia*, and one about North Korea, *Great Leader, Dear Leader: Demystifying North Korea under the Kim Clan*. In his most recent book, *World.Wide.Web: Chinese Migration in the 21st Century – And How It Will Change the World*, Lintner examines modern, state-sponsored migration from China and what it means for the rest of the world. Lintner has been living in Asia since 1975, and in Thailand since 1980.

Praise for the book

'This book is as authoritative as it is intriguing.' —*Literary Review*

'This is a timely and important work that sheds light on the important geopolitical developments occurring in South Asia . . . If indeed we are in the Asian century, Lintner's *Great Game East* will be an important guide to our understanding of how this came about and what to expect in the immediate future.' —*Asian Review of Books*

'Lintner shines a bright light on one of the most obscure corners of Asia: the region of mountains and jungles in northeastern India that is surrounded by Bangladesh, Tibet, and Myanmar (also called Burma). What comes into view is a complex struggle between China and India for influence across the wide arc of land and sea that lies between them.' —*Foreign Affairs*

'The considerable historical background, the careful description of contemporary developments, and the deft analysis of both the roles of domestic and external players in the region makes this book a most useful contribution to a very small body of existing work.' —*Pacific Affairs*

'*Great Game East* is no armchair study but the result of hands-on experience . . . This is an area that policymakers need to watch, and *Great Game East* is a good place to start.' —*The American Interest*

'He points out that Coco Islands, which belongs to Myanmar and where China is reportedly building naval structures, are just a few miles north. The game, clearly, is not yet over.' —*DNA*

'This book should caution those in India who are enticed by the idea of linking Yunnan to India's North-east to end its isolation and enable its development in a regional context.' —*India Today*

'A grand survey of the frontiers that are shared by India, Burma and China and their often conflicting interests.' —*Millennium Post*

GREAT GAME EAST

India, China and the Struggle for Asia's Most Volatile Frontier

Bertil Lintner

HarperCollins *Publishers* India

First published in hardback in India in 2012 by
HarperCollins *Publishers* India

First published in paperback in 2016

Copyright © Bertil Lintner 2012, 2016

P-ISBN: 978-93-5106-995-9
E-ISBN: 978-93-5029-536-6

2 4 6 8 10 9 7 5 3 1

HarperCollins *Publishers*

A-75, Sector 57, Noida, Uttar Pradesh 201301, India
1 London Bridge Street, London SE1 9GF, United Kingdom
Hazelton Lanes, 55 Avenue Road, Suite 2900, Toronto, Ontario M5R 3L2
and 1995 Markham Road, Scarborough, Ontario M1B 5M8, Canada
25 Ryde Road, Pymble, Sydney, NSW 2073, Australia
195 Broadway, New York, NY 10007, USA

Typeset in 11.5/15 Garamond Regular at
SÜRYA

Printed and bound at
Thomson Press (India) Ltd

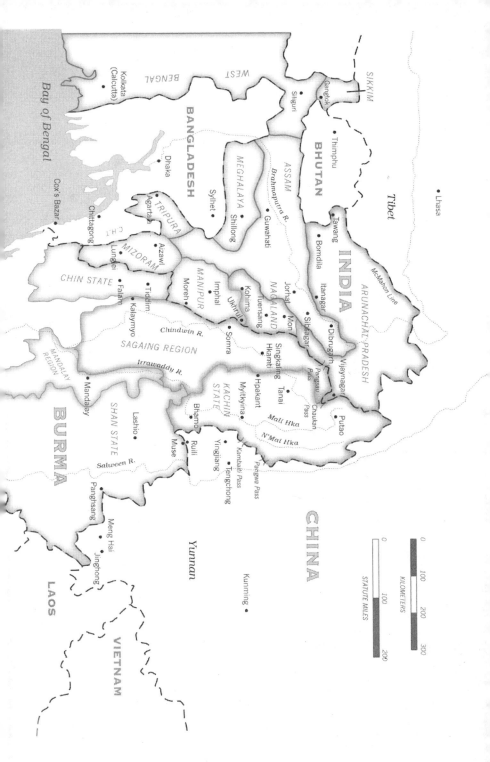

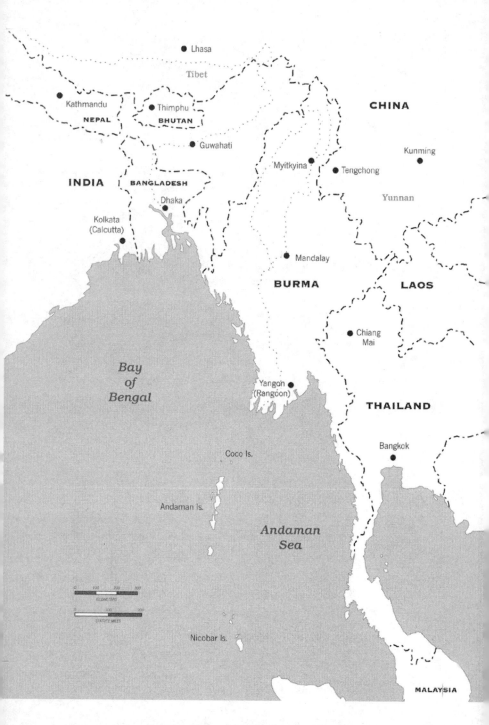

CONTENTS

INTRODUCTION

Few, apart from some Kachin hunters and other tribesmen make it to the windswept Pangwa Pass high in the rugged mountains, which separate northernmost Burma from China's Yunnan province. So the Chinese border guards were startled when, on a cold winter day in 1967, more than a hundred armed strangers suddenly appeared on the grassy high plateau. They were dressed in tattered fatigues and clutched Lee Enfield rifles and other weapons of World War II vintage. One of the border guards, an officer judging from his standing among the men around him, stepped forward.

And so did one of the strangers, a swarthy man in his early thirties. The officer pointed at the Mao badge he was wearing on his uniform. The young stranger said confidently: 'Mao Zedong.' The Chinese officer raised his thumb in an appreciative gesture. He then lowered his hand somewhat and looked at the young man, who replied: 'Lin Biao' – the number two in the Chinese hierarchy at the time. It was thumbs up again. The officer then put his hand somewhat lower still. 'Zhou Enlai,' came the answer. After that the tension eased and the leaders of the foreign militants were invited to the Chinese border post, where they were served tea and biscuits.[1]

A few days later, two Chinese schoolteachers, who had some basic English, arrived at the border post, which made it possible for the strangers to explain who they were and why they had come to China. The young man who knew the names of China's three top leaders was Thuingaleng Muivah, a Tangkhul Naga from Manipur and the general secretary of the Naga National Council, NNC, which for more than a decade had been fighting for independence from India. The slightly older military commander of the group, Thinoselie Medom Keyho, an Angami Naga from Kohima, was a high-ranking officer in the Naga rebel army who had been with the movement since the early 1950s. They had set out from the Naga Hills of Burma on 24 October 1966, and it had taken them three months and three days to reach the Yunnan frontier, trekking through the dense jungles and over the mountains of Kachin state.

They had had to fight their way through upper Burma, often sleeping in the daytime and marching at night to avoid Burmese Army patrols and, more importantly, hostile tribesmen along the way. Immediately across the border lay hundreds of kilometres of wild and largely unchartered territory, upper Sagaing division of Burma, home of tribes that the outside world also considered to be 'Nagas' but who were largely unaware of that fact. Many of them were still headhunters; it was like the Naga Hills on the Indian side of the border before the arrival of Christian missionaries in the nineteenth century. During the British time, Burma's Naga Hills were one of only four areas which were categorized as 'unadministered'; the other three were the equally wild Wa Hills – home of another tribe of headhunters – along the Chinese frontier, a swathe of land known as 'the Triangle' between the Mali Hka and Nmai Hka Rivers in the northern Kachin region, and the Somra Tract – a smaller Naga-inhabited area opposite Manipur.

Traversing the Naga Hills proved to be a formidable task, but the situation was not much easier when they had crossed the Chindwin into the Kachin-inhabited areas east of the river. Although not as steep as the Naga Hills on the Indian frontier, the Kachin country was densely forested. And there were no roads apart from the Ledo Road, which had been built by the British and the Americans during World War II to connect their bases in upper Assam and northern Burma, where local tribesmen, allied with the West, were resisting the Japanese Imperial Army.

That war was long over, but the Kachins, distant cousins of the Nagas, had been fighting a secessionist war against the Central government in Rangoon since 1961. But the NNC had at that stage no contacts with the Kachin Independence Army, KIA, which held sway over most of Kachin state. The Nagas ran into a group of KIA guerrillas somewhere east of the Chindwin, and managed to persuade them to act as guides. Communicating with them was not a problem; most KIA leaders were Baptist Christians like the Nagas, and fluent in English. One of the Kachin officers, a former headmaster of the Kachin Baptist High School in Myitkyina called Brang Seng, even escorted them all the way to the Pangwa Pass and the Chinese border.

The Nagas had not set out on this long and hazardous trek just by chance. Since the late 1950s, the Naga rebel movement had been tacitly supported by India's arch-enemy, Pakistan, and sanctuaries had been established in what was then East Pakistan, now Bangladesh. Many Naga leaders had also been flown to West Pakistan to meet high-ranking Pakistani military officials and intelligence operatives. One of the Nagas, Mowu Gwizan, a veteran of the Naga struggle, had stopped over in Karachi in June 1962 on his way to fly to London, where he was going to meet Angami Zapu Phizo, the exiled leader of the Naga independence movement. While in Karachi, Mowu's Pakistani hosts had introduced him to a 'Chinese friend', who promised them aid and military assistance.[2] China's interest in the Naga rebels grew after the war with India later that year and the subsequent redeployment of Indian troops previously based in the Naga Hills to the McMahon Line, the de facto border between India's North-East Frontier Agency, NEFA, now Arunachal Pradesh, and Chinese-occupied Tibet.

Relations between the two Asian giants were never going to be the same after India's crushing and humiliating defeat in the 1962 war, and the arrival of Thinoselie, Muivah and their contingent of Naga rebels on the Yunnan frontier on 27 January 1967 marked the beginning of China's involvement with ethnic rebel movements in India's volatile north-eastern region. Over the next decade, nearly a thousand Naga rebels made it through northern Burma to China, where they received military training and were sent back to India, equipped with assault rifles, machine guns, rocket launchers and other modern Chinese weapons. Almost the same number of Nagas tried to reach China, but for various reasons had to turn back or were captured by Burmese government forces.[3]

Inspired by the Nagas, Mizo rebels also began trekking to China in 1972. Several hundred fighters from the Mizo National Front, MNF, underwent similar training and received Chinese weapons that were used on north-eastern India's battlefields. A smaller group of Manipuri rebels made it to Tibet in 1976, where they received political and military training and became so inspired by their Chinese instructors that they even named their force the People's Liberation Army, PLA, which also is the common name for China's military. Following the death of Mao Zedong on 9 September 1976, China began to change politically and, especially economically, as a more moderate faction of Chinese communists led by Deng Xiaoping took over. Exporting revolutionary ideals to the rest of the world was no longer China's main foreign policy objective; Deng turned out to be precisely the kind of 'capitalist roader' his dogmatic Marxist–Leninist detractors has accused him of being while Mao was still alive. China began to modernise and diversify its economy, and Deng declared that 'being rich is glorious'.

When Deng died at the age of ninety-two in 1997, China was already an economic power that was expending its influence all over the world. In February 2011, it became official: China had surpassed Japan as the world's second largest economy. And it is still growing at a breakneck pace. Communism survives only in China's authoritarian political system. It remains a dictatorship where dissent is mercilessly crushed, as was seen during the bloody events in and around Beijing's Tiananmen Square in June 1989, and again in February 2011, when young dissidents who called for a 'jasmine revolution' were beaten up by the police in the streets of Beijing and Shanghai and led away in captivity. Not to speak of decades of brutal repression in Tibet.

And what Asia's pro-Chinese revolutionaries did not achieve on the battlefield in the 1960s and 1970s, China did through trade and diplomacy. The new ideology is business augmented with military cooperation, which in turn leads to political clout. China's influence in Asia today is stronger than at any time in modern history. China is a major trading partner of most Asian countries, and it has managed to establish military relationships with countries in the South and South-east Asian regions – such as Pakistan, Burma, Cambodia and even Bangladesh, Nepal and Sri Lanka – which could hardly be described as communist states. The estimated value of Chinese arms deliveries to other Asian countries from 2006 to 2009 totalled US$3.1 billion.

At the same time, China's long-standing suspicion of India has not diminished. These two Asian giants remain bitter rivals – a strained relationship that predates the 1962 border war and China's subsequent support for rebel movements among the Nagas, the Mizos and other ethnic communities in north-eastern India. It all began when, in 1950, China invaded Tibet. China's new communist rulers, who had come to power in Beijing the year before, saw it as their historical duty to 'unify' the country, which had been badly torn apart during the turmoil that followed the fall of the old Chinese Empire in 1911. And, according to the Chinese communists – and most other Chinese as well – Tibet was part of China.

The Tibetans saw it differently, however. While Tibet had paid tribute to Chinese emperors off and on down the centuries, few if any Tibetans would ever have felt that they belonged to some greater Chinese fraternity, let alone a Chinese state or empire. In fact, Tibet tended to have much closer religious and cultural ties with the kingdoms south of the Himalayas. Buddhism came from what today is India; the Tibetan alphabet is derived from the ancient Indian Brahmi script and bears no similarity or relationship with ideogrammatic Chinese characters. Tibetan belongs to the Tibeto-Burman family of languages and is related to Burmese, Bhutanese Dzongkha and various tribal languages in northern Burma and north-eastern India. There is no 'Sino-Tibetan' group of languages, as often claimed by ideologically motivated Chinese scholars. Some Chinese, and along with it some Chinese characters, were used in old Tibet, but only as a foreign language used in certain religious texts such as the Diamond and Lotus sutras. When British India was more firmly established in the nineteenth century, post and telegraph services as well as trade were usually conducted through Calcutta (now Kolkata), not any Chinese capital or city. And in all respects, Tibet was an independent country, largely isolated and having limited interaction with the rest of the world. It did, however, have its own government, flag, national anthem and a small and poorly equipped army, but still an army.

The 1950 invasion altered all that – and India did not protest. In fact, independent India's first prime minister, Jawaharlal Nehru, acquiesced and, in the Sino-Indian Agreement of 1954, Tibet was referred to, for the first time in history, as 'the Tibet Region of China'.[4] Sardar Kavalam Madhava Panikkar, the scholar and historian who was India's ambassador to Beijing from 1948 to 1952, had already, before the agreement was signed, stated rather fancifully, 'British and American intrigues against the interests of both China and Tibet were ripening and preparations were afoot to make Tibet a base against China and the Soviet Union . . . It was high time for China, in the interests of Tibet as well as her own safety, to take steps for the liberation of Tibet as it has done for the rest of the Chinese territory.'[5] Panikkar saw no reason why India should worry about the Chinese invasion of Tibet: 'I do not think there is anything wrong in the troops of Red China moving about in their own territory.'[6]

The three years following the 29 April 1954 agreement have been described as a Sino-Indian honeymoon. Under the Hindi slogan *Hindi–Chini Bhai–Bhai*, or 'Indians and Chinese are brothers', the friendship seemed to blossom and both countries viewed themselves as champions of the Third World that was emerging as old colonial empires ruled by the British, the French and other Western powers crumbled. The 1954 agreement based the relationship between India and China on the Five Principles of Peaceful Coexistence, or *Panch Shila*: Mutual respect for each other's territorial integrity and sovereignty; mutual non-aggression against anyone; mutual non-interference in each other's internal matters; equality and mutual benefit; and peaceful co-existence. Put forth by Nehru, these principles also came to form the basis of the Non-Aligned Movement, which was born when leaders from twenty-five mostly newly independent Asian and African countries met in the Indonesian resort city of Bandung in April 1955.

Between June 1954 and January 1957, Chinese premier Zhou Enlai paid four visits to India and was on each occasion given a warn welcome by Nehru, his Indian counterpart. But events in Tibet were soon to turn sour, and the Indians and the Chinese would no longer be brothers but bitter rivals. China's occupation of Tibet had been brutal and bloody. In his autobiography *Four Rivers, Six Ranges*, veteran Tibetan resistance fighter Gompo Andrugtsang writes that the Chinese had begun their programme of so-called 'liberation' in the countryside as early as 1953: 'Chinese collected large sums of money for taxes, locals were selectively arrested and publicly executed to arouse terror, monasteries were destroyed, and monks were imprisoned or executed without reason.'[7]

This led to an uprising among the Khampas, nomads of eastern Tibet who have always been fiercely independent. They struck back, ambushing Chinese Army convoys with whatever weapons they had. The resistance of the Khampas attracted the attention of the US Central Intelligence Agency, CIA, which was looking for any movement in the region that could undermine the growing power of communist China. The 1950–53 Korean War had brought an end to the relative peace that had prevailed since the end of World War II, and Mao's China, in the eyes of the United States, was the new, main enemy, even more dangerous than the Soviet Union, leadership of which had mellowed considerably following the death of Josef Stalin in 1953 and the ascendance to power of the more moderate Nikita Khrushchev. With the Soviet Union, the United States was able to achieve a balance of terror based on the fact that both were nuclear powers – and not willing to strike first. China, with its seemingly uncontrollable revolutionary fervour, was perceived as vastly different and much more dangerous.

The CIA was already working closely with Chiang Kai-shek's defeated regime that had fled to the island of Taiwan, where his 'Republic of China' lived on. Frogmen and other infiltrators were sent to infiltrate the mainland and carry out sabotage and intelligence missions. Several thousand defeated soldiers from Chiang's Guomindang (Kuomintang) Army had also retreated south, into the wild hills of northern and north-eastern Burma, which were not under the control of the government in Rangoon. Arms and ammunition were flown in from Taiwan to the Guomindang's bases in the eastern Burmese mountains, and an American consulate was set up in the city of Chiang Mai, across the border in Thailand, for the sole purpose of coordinating the effort. The Guomindang's 'secret army' on China's southern flank tried on no less than seven occasions between 1950 and 1952 to invade Yunnan, but was repeatedly driven back into the Shan states of Burma.[8] The Americans needed more allies in their 'secret war' against China.

The CIA made its first operative contacts with the Tibetans in the early 1950s. Its Far East Division had met Gyalo Thondup, the elder brother of the Dalai Lama, to discuss the situation in the

Chinese-occupied territory. In 1956, the CIA decided that the time was ripe to support the nascent Tibetan struggle against the Chinese.[9] The picturesque hill station of Kalimpong in northern West Bengal became the base for CIA-supported covert operations across the Himalayas. Arms were sent in to Tibet and the first airdrop took place in October 1957.[10] By then, Tibetan resistance fighters had also been flown to the US-held Pacific island of Saipan, where they received military training. Later, a more extensive training facility was established at Camp Hale in Colorado. The Rocky Mountains were more similar to the terrain in Tibet than the jungles of Saipan.

Then, in March 1959, an anti-Chinese uprising broke out in Lhasa. It was brutally crushed, with 10,000 to 15,000 Tibetans killed in only three days. The Dalai Lama, however, managed to escape and made it to India, where he set up a government in exile in McLeodganj, an old resort town in the hills overlooking Dharamshala in north-western India. The Chinese were furious, and the newly found Hindi–Chini Bhai–Bhai friendship with India was soon to pass into history.

In October 1962, China decided to 'teach India a lesson'. Thousands of Chinese troops stormed across the McMahon Line, which China had never recognized, thus claiming that the Sino-Indian border was undemarcated and disputed. When they had made their point, the Chinese withdrew unilaterally back to the McMahon Line – a typically Chinese military tactic that was to be repeated against Vietnam in February 1979, following the latter's invasion of China-supported Cambodia. Then too, the Chinese attacked across the border and retreated when enough damage had been inflicted on the adversary without actually capturing any territory. The difference though is that the 1979 'punitive action' against Vietnam was caused by that country's central authority's decision to take military action against Cambodia, whereas it is still an open question about whether Nehru and his government, although they had granted the Dalai Lama asylum, were fully aware of the CIA's machinations with the Tibetans in Kalimpong and elsewhere.

But that was not the end of China's animosity towards India – which was reflected in its subsequent support for Naga, Mizo and other ethnic, north-eastern insurgents. The Chinese had actually wanted to support the Maoist Naxalites, but their tiny organizations were torn apart by infighting and factional rivalries. Therefore, somewhat paradoxically, China's communist authorities decided to support the staunchly Christian tribesmen from the north-east. At least, they were better fighters and more useful for China's strategic interests in the region than the unruly and disorganized Naxalites.

When the Nagas, the Mizos and others began trekking through northern Burma to China, India set up a consulate in Chiang Mai in northern Thailand. The town does have a sizeable Indian population which no doubt needed consular services, but the main purpose of the new diplomatic mission was to establish contacts with ethnic minority rebels across the border in Burma, who could provide the Indians with useful intelligence about the movements of the Naga and the Mizo insurgents in northern Burma. With the US consulate in the same town already busy with their campaign against China, Chiang Mai became a hotbed of intrigue and espionage.

The Chinese no longer provide training for ethnic insurgents from India's north-east. In fact, the last attempts by the Nagas, Manipuris and Assamese to enter China from Burma in the late 1980s were rebuffed by the Chinese. Letters from the Nagas were returned unopened, and no one was allowed across the border into China for talks. But the north-eastern insurgents found another way. Using Bangladeshi passports they had acquired through their contacts with Bangladesh's Directorate General of Forces Intelligence (DGFI) they travelled by air from Thailand to Kunming, the capital of China's Yunnan province. Front companies were set up and weapons obtained on what euphemistically is called 'the Chinese black market', which in reality is more grey than black.

Former officers of the People's Liberation Army run their own private businesses, selling surplus weapons to whoever wants to buy them. In April 2004, a huge consignment of Chinese weapons were seized in the Bangladeshi port city of Chittagong, and the munitions were destined for Assamese and other insurgents in North-east India.[11]

At the same time, licit trade between India and China is booming. When Chinese premier Wen Jiabao visited New Delhi in December 2010, he and his Indian counterpart Manmohan Singh vowed to raise bilateral trade to US$100 billion by 2015, from US$60 billion in 2010, and 'called for a stronger partnership between Asia's two giants'.[12] Along the McMahon Line, Chinese and Indian soldiers meet regularly to play football, and exchange gifts and greetings.

Even so, the two countries remain deeply suspicious of each other, as Indian insurgents continue to have access to the 'grey' arms market in China, and India has no intention to restrict the activities of the Dalai Lama and his government in exile on Indian soil. Equally important is the fact that China has made considerable inroads into Burma over the past two decades. Burma, once proud of its neutralist stance between India, China and the rest of the world, has fallen into China's sphere of influence. In 1988, Burma was shaken by a massive, pro-democracy uprising that was brutally suppressed by the ruling military. Thousands of unarmed demonstrators were gunned down as the Burmese military moved in to reassert power. But the outcome was also international condemnation. Burma then turned to China, which was more than willing to provide it with generous loans, aid and arms to an estimated value of US$1.4 billion.

China's interest in Burma was mainly strategic. It needed an outlet to the sea for trade from its landlocked, south-western province of Yunnan. On 6 August 1988, the two countries signed a trade agreement – the first of its kind that a hitherto isolated Burma had entered into with a neighbour. It was especially significant because the agreement was signed at a time when Burma was in turmoil: two days later, millions of people in virtually every city, town and village in the country took to the streets to demand an end to army rule and a restoration of the democracy the country had enjoyed prior to the first military coup in 1962.

The Chinese, renowned for their ability to plan far ahead, had expressed their intentions, almost unnoticed, in an article in the official *Beijing Review* as early as 2 September 1985. Titled 'Opening to the Southwest: An Expert Opinion', the article, which was written by the former vice minister of communications, Pan Qi, outlined the possibilities of finding an outlet for trade from China's landlocked provinces of Yunnan and Sichuan, through Burma, to the Indian Ocean. It mentioned the Burmese railheads of Myitkyina and Lashio in the north-east, and the Irrawaddy River, as possible conduits for the export of Chinese goods – but it omitted to mention that all relevant border areas at that time were not under the control of the Central government of Burma.

That situation changed in 1989 with a mutiny within the hill-tribe rank-and-file of the powerful Communist Party of Burma, CPB, which China had built up in the 1960s and 1970s when it was Beijing's policy to support revolutionary movements in the region. The mainly Burman leadership of the CPB was overthrown, and forced into exile in China. Subsequent to the revolt, the CPB split along ethnic lines into four different regional armies, and all of them entered into ceasefire agreements with the government. By 1990, trade between the two countries was flourishing, and ties between Burma and China gradually gained strength. By 1990, Burma had become China's principal political and military ally in South-east Asia.

Chinese arms poured into Burma to help the survival of the extremely unpopular military regime. In view of the Rangoon massacre of 1988 and the Tiananmen Square massacre the following year, it is hardly surprising that the two then isolated, internationally condemned neighbours would feel a great empathetic bond. On 30 September 1989, Burmese intelligence chief, Gen. Khin Nyunt, said in an address to a group of Chinese engineers working on a project in Rangoon: 'We sympathize with the People's Republic of China as disturbances similar to those in Burma last year broke out in the People's Republic of China [in May–June 1989].'[13]

The strategic importance China placed on Burma soon became obvious. By late 1991, Chinese experts were assisting in a series of infrastructure projects to spruce up the poorly maintained roads and railways. Chinese military advisers arrived in the same year – the first foreign military personnel to be stationed in Burma since the Australians had a contingent there to train the Burmese Army in the 1950s. Burma was, in effect, becoming a Chinese client state. After crushing the 1988 uprising, and to prevent a recurrence of similar popular movements, Burma's military regime rearmed with Chinese-supplied weaponry and equipment, and it has more than doubled the size of its armed forces. The number of men in the three services increased from 186,000 in 1988 to 450,000 in 2010, and all three branches underwent significant modernization programmes.

While one of the reasons why China has decided to arm Burma may be to provide a military umbrella to protect new trade routes through potentially volatile territory, some analysts view the support in a more long-term perspective. Access, even indirectly, to the Indian Ocean gives China a strategic advantage. The Strait of Malacca is, for instance, a key transit point for the bulk of Japan's West Asian oil imports.

But it is India, not Japan, that has reacted in the strangest way to China's high-profile presence in Burma. Of particular concern has been the Chinese role in the upgrading of Burma's naval facilities – including at least four electronic listening posts along the Bay of Bengal and the Andaman Sea. Although China's presence there was limited to instructors and technicians, the fact that the new radar equipment is made in China – and was in the beginning most likely also operated at least in part by Chinese technicians – has enabled Beijing's intelligence agencies to monitor this sensitive maritime region. China and Burma have signed several agreements under which they have pledged to share intelligence that could be of use to both countries. The arrival of a Chinese submarine in a Burmese port also adds an important strategic element to Beijing's arms sales to Burma, indicating that they were much more than purely commercial deals.

In June 1998, India's defence minister George Fernandes caused great uproar when he accused Beijing of helping Burma install surveillance and communications equipment on islands in the Bay of Bengal. Burma denied the accusations, while China's foreign ministry expressed 'utmost grief and resentment' over the minister's comments.[14] New Delhi, however, had good reason to be concerned. In August 1994, the Indian coastguard caught three boats 'fishing' close to the site of a major Indian naval base in the Andamans. The trawlers were flying the Burmese flag, but the crew of fifty-five was Chinese. There was no fishing equipment on board – only radio communication and depth-sounding equipment. The crew was released at the intervention of the Chinese embassy in New Delhi. The incident was discreetly buried in the defence ministry files in New Delhi.[15]

But when China's designs became more obvious, the new and more alert government in New Delhi began to pay greater attention to developments in Burma. In March 1997, the China News Agency in Beijing reported that a Sino-Burmese expert group had 'conducted a study on the possibility of land and water transport, via Yunnan and into the Irrawaddy valley in Burma'. On 5 May that same year, the official Xinhua news agency reported that Beijing and Rangoon had reached an agreement on developing this route. Xinhua said this route would be 5,800 kilometres shorter than the older route of access to open waters, which linked the Yunnanese capital Kunming and the nearest port on China's east coast, Shanghai.

Long before that agreement was reached, however, China had begun to construct a railway from Kunming to Xiaguan near Dali, on its side of the Yunnan frontier. By now, the old Burma Road from Kunming to Ruili on the Burmese border has also been upgraded, and Chinese engineers have completed work on the last 120-kilometre stretch of the road from Ruili across the border to Bhamo on the Irrawaddy River in Burma's Kachin state. Bhamo is the northernmost port on the Irrawaddy that is navigable from the south. Intelligence sources in Burma say the plan was to use a fleet of barges to transport goods from there to Minhla, some 1,000 kilometres downriver and 280 kilometres north of Rangoon. From Minhla, a road is being built across the Arakan Yoma mountain range, running via An to Kyaukpyu on the coast. Kyaukpyu had been chosen as the site for a new deep-water port rather than the silted mouth of the Rangoon River. Plans for the project were finalized when Burmese Army chief General Maung Aye went to China in June 2000. By 2010, the construction of the new port was in full swing, and China has also begun laying a gas and oil pipeline from the Burmese coast, across the country to Yunnan.

In the beginning, India was quite sympathetic to the pro-democracy Opposition in Burma. India's prime minister at the time, Rajiv Gandhi, came out in open support of the movement and it was the stated policy that India would give shelter to genuine Burmese refugees. However, this was not for altruistic reasons alone; it was thought to have been India's way of countering China's influence in Burma. Then, around 1993, India began to re-evaluate its strategy out of concern that its policies had achieved little except push Burma closer to Beijing. The result was a dramatic policy shift aimed at improving relations with Burma's ruling generals; and they, in turn, were sending signals to New Delhi to take greater interest in bilateral relations to lessen their heavy dependence on China.

India's interests in Burma are quite obvious: it wants to make sure the north-eastern insurgents are deprived of sanctuaries and supply lines through the eastern neighbour and to keep Chinese influence there at bay. The rapidly expanding Indian economy also needs energy, and India has/shown considerable interest in buying oil and gas from Burma. Burma is also India's link to lucrative markets and trading partners in South-east Asia. In short, it wants to open a west–east corridor through Burma to protect its own strategic and economic interests. In September 2010, the New Delhi ambassadors of the Association of South-East Asian Nations, ASEAN, were taken on a tour of the Manipuri town of Moreh on India's border with Burma – India's gateway to South-east Asia.

But to accomplish this grand plan, India also has to rid Manipur and Nagaland of insurgents and establish permanent peace in the north-east. That task was made easier when Sheikh Hasina's pro-Indian Awami League took over the government in Bangladesh in December 2008. Her predecessor Khaleda Zia, and the Bangladesh National Party, BNP, had provided sanctuaries for insurgents from India's north-east, who moved about freely in Dhaka and Chittagong. In late November 2009, Bangladesh arrested Arabinda Rajkhowa, the chairman of the United Liberation Front of Asom, ULFA, and its deputy commander-in-chief Raju Barua along with eight other Assamese militants, and handed them over to India. In September 2010, Rajkumar Meghen, better known as Sana Yaima, the leader of the United National Liberation Front (Manipur), was arrested in Dhaka and unceremoniously handed over to India's security agencies. At about the same time, the main arms procurer of the Naga rebels and a frequent visitor to China, Anthony Shimray, was arrested at Kathmandu airport and also ended up in Indian custody.

India's strategy seems to be working, but it is far too early to say whether Burma can once again be more neutral between its more powerful neighbours, and if solely arresting the main leaders of the insurgencies can solve the ethnic problems in North-east India. Or if China would deprive the insurgents of access to the country's grey arms market as long as the Tibetans are maintaining their government in exile in India. The Chinese and the Indians are still far from re-establishing a fraternal bhai–bhai relationship – that was to be but a brief interlude for a few years in the 1950s.

In the nineteenth century, Arthur Conolly, an intelligence officer of the British East India Company's Sixth Bengal Light Cavalry, coined the expression 'the Great Game' to describe the strategic rivalry between the British and the Russian Empires for supremacy in Central Asia. More than any other objective, the Russians also sought access to the Indian Ocean. The idea of the Great Game was popularized and entered public consciousness through *Kim*, the 1901 novel by Rudyard Kipling, the grand guru of British imperialism. The story about the young Anglo-Irish orphan – who was recruited by the secret service of British India and travelled undercover along the Grand Trunk Road to India's remotest western frontiers during the heyday of the Western colonial empires – has captivated the imagination of generations in Asia and the West alike. But behind Kipling's highly romanticized version of the great spying game at the time lay what undoubtedly was then the main superpower conflict in Asia.

In recent years, 'the Great Game', or more often 'the New Great Game', has come to signify the conflict between the United States and other Western powers on the one hand and Russia and China on the other, over Central Asia's oil and other natural resources. By direct intervention, or acting through proxies, this conflict is now evident to everyone in the Central Asian republics of the former Soviet Union, in Afghanistan, Iran and Iraq.

But there is also another Great Game being played out in Asia: on the eastern fringes of the Indian subcontinent. The rivalry between India and China, and the resistance and uprisings in Tibet and North-east India, go back to the 1950s. Spies and agents from both sides have been active in each other's volatile frontier areas for decades. Spies from various other countries have also wanted to keep an eye on developments inside 'the forbidden area' in India's north-east, long out of bounds for foreigners and strategically located at the crossroads of the Indian subcontinent, China and South-east Asia.

The rebels, isolated in the remote mountains between India and Burma, have always tried to get support or sympathy from the international community, and many people from outside the region have all along taken an interest in the insurgencies (among the Nagas and the Mizos especially) for a variety of reasons. Some felt genuine sympathy for the 'tribal underdog' facing the might of the Indian military; others were fascinated by exotic tales of the Naga headhunters who had become 'Christian soldiers'. And then, of course, certain foreign countries – mainly Pakistan and China, and, more recently, Bangladesh – had, and still have, a vested interest in fomenting unrest in India's north-east. But it is also important to remember that China – or Pakistan or Bangladesh – did not invent the rebellions in Nagaland, Mizoram, Manipur and Assam, but simply took advantage of decades-old, and even centuries-old, ethnic conflicts. British colonialism brought with it a semblance of artificial peace, *Pax Britannica*, which froze the problems but did not solve them. After India's independence in 1947, many of these old conflicts flared anew; and without a proper understanding the complex histories of the North-eastern peoples and the evolution of their fractious rebel movements and fragile alliances, little headway can be made towards achieving peace in one of India's most volatile regions.

On the other side of the McMahon Line, there is Tibet, where a mystical, ancient theocracy now led by an exiled modern-day saint has captured the imagination of millions of Westerners from the earliest European explorers to people as disparate as a group of German Nazis who, in the 1930s, thought the high plateau in the Himalayas was the cradle of Aryan civilisation, Hollywood stars Richard Gere and Pierce Brosnan, and other present-day celebrities and human rights activists. There is no doubt that the Tibetans have suffered tremendously under Chinese rule and the Dalai Lama may appear godlike, but his men have also been working closely together with the US Central Intelligence Agency as part of a broader scheme to encircle China. And the fact that the government in exile that he leads is based in India is deeply resented by China, where the question of Tibet's status is seen as the main threat to the future unity of Asia's most populous country. In more recent years, the Great Game East has become a pressing regional issue in an entirely different setting, as China is seeking access to the Indian Ocean. Burma already has fallen under China's sway, and once China has upgraded the ports and naval facilities of India's eastern neighbour, there will be another major player in a maritime area that India has got used to thinking of as its own lake.

In 2011, however, there were signs indicating that Burma is seeking to lessen its dependence on China and chart a more independent foreign policy. Public discontent with China's exploitation of Burma's natural resources led to the new Burmese president Thein Sein's stunning announcement on 30 September that a massive US$3.6 billion hydroelectric power project in northern Kachin State would be suspended. The dam would have flooded more than 700 square kilometres of forestland – and around 90 per cent of the electricity generated by the massive power station was to be exported to China.

Equally significantly, Gen. Min Aung Hlaing, who was appointed commander-in-chief of Burma's armed forces in March 2011, took his first foreign trip in mid-November to Vietnam – Beijing's traditional adversary – rather than China. Burma and Vietnam share similar fears of their powerful northern neighbour and so it is reasonable to assume that Min Aung Hlaing had much to discuss with his Vietnamese hosts.

The United States was quick to exploit the nascent rift between Burma and China. On 1 December, US Secretary of State Hillary Clinton visited Burma, the first such visit by a high-ranking US official in decades. For years, Washington had been a fierce critic of Burma's military regime, but now Clinton praised what she termed political reform in the country. However, while paying lip service to human rights and democracy, China–Burma relations were high on Clinton's diplomatic agenda.

In the end, China's march to the Indian Ocean may not be as smooth and easy as Beijing's security planners had envisaged when they launched their new Burma policy in the late 1980s. But the struggle for control is far from over, and China is bound to do everything in its might to maintain its influence over Burma, which is still strong – and certainly stronger than India's.

Many stories in this book about foreign adventurers, odd personalities and curious events may appear parochially anecdotal, but nevertheless are meant to show that north-eastern India's insurgencies, like the much more widely publicized conflict in Tibet, did not occur in isolation. And the Great Game East is also about India's struggle to keep its ethnically diverse north-eastern states within the Union. Many Nagas, Mizos and Manipuris, and even Assamese, do not consider themselves Indians, and it is necessary to understand why they feel that way. For China, it is a determined effort to maintain its supremacy over Tibet, whose people definitely do not think they are Chinese.

It has been my desire to describe, in a journalistic manner because I am not an academic, the geopolitics of the region, and how seemingly localized ethnic conflicts fit into this bigger picture. And as an increasingly stronger and more self-confident India is beginning to challenge China's near-supremacy in the region, the Great Game East may well become Asia's most serious superpower rivalry in the twenty-first century. And although Tibet and north-eastern India will remain important in a strategic sense, it is in the Indian Ocean, not in the heights of the Himalayas as during the 1962 Indo-Chinese border war, that the main conflict of interests will be played out.

My own association with the region began when I, as a young man, travelled by bus, jeep and train through Sikkim, northern West Bengal, Assam, Meghalaya and Bangladesh in 1977. I returned to India's north-east in 1985, entering Assam – then a restricted area – illegally. My final aim was to reach rebel-held areas across the Indo-Burmese border in northernmost Burma, which had not previously been visited by any foreign journalist. Hunched under the canvas awning in the rear of a jeep, disguised with a wig and wearing dark sunglasses and a Naga shawl, I was smuggled into the even more forbidden territory of Nagaland. We – because I was travelling with my wife, who is a Shan from Burma – got stuck in Kohima for several months.

While we were in hiding in Kohima, our daughter Hseng Tai was born on 13 September 1985. Six weeks later, we emerged from our hiding place and all three of us did make it across the border into the wild Naga Hills of north-western Burma. We spent more than a year and a half trekking from the village of Longva on the Indian border, across Burma's Sagaing division and Kachin state and down to insurgent-controlled areas in Shan state – South-east Asia's fabled Golden Triangle – before we crossed the border into Yunnan, China, in April 1987. I described those years in rebel-held Burma in my book *Land of Jade*, which has been published in English, Danish, and to my great delight and pride, even in Manipuri. Evidently, even some people in the North-east found it worth reading. It is my hope that this book will shed more light on the origin of the ethnic problems in the North-east and thus contribute to a better understanding of these complex issues as well as their geopolitical implications. The Naga struggle has been longer, more complicated – and bloodier – than any of the other rebellions and as such deserves special attention. It is an issue that is not likely to go away easily.

Inevitably, we were blacklisted in India after undertaking our illegal journey to Nagaland and across the border into Burma. We had forged documents, overstayed our visas, entered a restricted area without permission, and then left the country on foot from a small village on the Indo-Burmese frontier, hardly an official border crossing. But I was nevertheless allowed to visit India a few times, with special permission to attend seminars and similar activities, before the statute of limitations for our transgressions finally expired in the early 2000s.

In December 2009, I returned to Nagaland – legally this time – equipped with a Protected Area Permit, as passes for foreigners are called. It was a fantastic feeling to be able to walk around Kohima, to explore a town I previously had only seen from behind a curtain in one of our hiding places, and then after dark. It had become a booming town, quite unlike the place where we were in hiding for several months twenty-five years before. But I managed to find the house where our daughter was born. At that time, it was located in an isolated area on the outskirts of Kohima. In 2009, it was still there – now in a state of disrepair and completely surrounded by new, concrete buildings. I took a few pictures, which I later sent to Hseng Tai, who is now twenty-five years old and works as an architect in South-east Asia. She is proud of the fact that her Swedish passport, for she is a Swedish citizen, states as her place of birth: 'Kohima, Nagaland, India'.

I have also been able to travel to Arunachal Pradesh, by jeep all the way to Tawang near the McMahon Line. And I have visited Manipur several times, including the Naga-inhabited district of Ukhrul. I travelled to Mizoram in October 2010, and, in January 2011, the Andaman Islands. In April 2010, I visited McLeodganj, the site of the Tibetan government in exile; I have also, on two occasions, in 1984 and 1993, met the Dalai Lama.

During my recent visits to the region I have been able to meet and interview local activists, journalists, analysts and security officials, thus supplementing and updating the thousands of pages of notes I took during our two-year sojourn in Nagaland and northern Burma during 1985–87, when I became the first Western journalist to interview Thuingaleng Muivah, Isak Chishi Swu, Shangwang Shangyung Khaplang and other leaders and cadres of the Naga underground on both sides of the Indo-Burmese border; Arabinda Rajkhowa, Paresh Barua, Pradeep Gogoi and others in the United Liberation Front of Asom, the notorious ULFA; Manipuri rebel supremo Sana Yaima; militants from the People's Liberation Army (Manipur); and the leaders of the Kachin Independence Army as well as the now defunct Communist Party of Burma.

Among my colleagues, I am especially indebted to my old friend Subir Bhaumik whose writings and reports I have followed for decades. No one knows India's north-east as he does, and he has always generously shared his information with me – and even put me up in his apartment during several visits to Kolkata. I have also benefited from the knowledge of Jaideep Saikia and Wasbir Hussain in Assam; Sagolsem Hemant, Pradip Phanjoubam, Nobokishore Urikhimbam, Chitra Ahanthem and others in Manipur; Neingulo Krome and his human rights activists in Nagaland; Aung Kyaw Zaw, a Burmese veteran resistance activist living in exile in Yunnan; and many, many others who for reasons of their own security cannot be named. The now retired commodore C. Uday Bhaskar provided useful background to the power plays in the Indian Ocean, and also put me in touch with naval officers in Port Blair, the Andaman Islands. In McLeodganj in April 2011, I interviewed several officials from the Tibetan government in exile, including the then chairman of the *kashag*, or Tibetan government in exile, Samdhong Rinpoche, Tibetan Youth Congress leader Tenzin Norsang, and Lhasang Tsering, a veteran of the Tibetan war of resistance against the Chinese. Legendary British film-maker Adrian Cowell shared his experiences from his foray into Tibet in 1964, when he, cameraman Chris Menges and journalist George Patterson accompanied a group of resistance fighters who ambushed a Chinese military convoy on the road to Lhasa.

I would also like to thank Shantanu Ray Chaudhuri of HarperCollins for his brilliant editing work, which has made this book a much better read.

I am grateful to all these sources, colleagues, friends and acquaintances for providing me with information and sharing their views of respective issues and problems. But any factual errors and other mistakes in this book are entirely my own, for which I am solely responsible.

Chiang Mai, Thailand
May 2012

CHAPTER ONE

WAR AND SPOOKERY IN THE HIMALAYAS

It was an ordinary Saturday evening, 6.30 to be precise, and Brigadier John Dalvi was relaxing in a bathtub at his quarter at the army base in Tezpur. He had just played a round of golf at the town's newly laid course and was preparing for an early night. He had a flight to catch at dawn the following day, and had even turned down an invitation from his general to watch a movie at the local Planters' Club. As commander of the 7th Infantry Brigade of the Indian Army, Dalvi was responsible for defence of the western sector of the North-East Frontier Agency, NEFA, and always took his duties seriously. But this evening he was tempted to ignore the phone that kept on ringing. He was sick of telephone calls and, besides, he was officially on leave from midday because it was weekend.

On the other hand, as he recalled much later: 'Some extrasensory intuition told me that I had better answer it as it was probably an emergency message. Very few people knew where I was staying and only someone who wanted me desperately would persist in contacting me.'[1] Brigadier Dalvi was right. It was an officer calling from the border town of Tawang high up in the snow-capped mountains of north-western NEFA. Six hundred Chinese soldiers had just crossed the Thagla Ridge and come down to the Indian

1

Army post at Dhola. The intruders had cut a nearby log bridge and were threatening the water supply to the post. The local commander was asking for immediate help, the local officer told Dalvi over a radiotelephone from the border.

It was the first serious incursion by Chinese troops into NEFA, and Dalvi was anxious to know what they were up to. He did not think it was an accident or a decision taken on the spur of the moment to cross the border: 'I have no doubt that the Chinese selected Saturday to ignite the Thagla incident as they correctly reasoned that, by the time information reached Delhi, it would be late evening or early Sunday morning . . . the Chinese must have known by 1962 that no Indian Commander had any initiative to act without consulting Government.'[2] And the government would not get its act together until Monday morning at the earliest. Dalvi concluded that the Thagla incident should not be treated as a 'petty border incident'. He reminded his commander that the post had been established in an area which the Chinese did not consider part of India: 'We should cater for a sharp and massive Chinese reaction. I told the GOC [General Officer Commanding] that the Chinese had the advantage of time and space and logistic support, while we suffered from grave administrative handicaps.'[3]

Dalvi's words turned out to be prophetic. The Thagla incident and a few ensuing skirmishes were only the harbingers of what was to come later that year, 1962. On 20 October the Chinese People's Liberation Army, PLA, launched a massive assault across the McMahon Line, the Himalayan watershed that India marks as its boundary with Tibet. China, on its part, does not recognize that border and claims not only Tibet but also most of NEFA as theirs. Tens of thousands of Chinese troops launched simultaneous attacks across the McMahon Line and into the Chip Chap Valley in Aksai Chin in Kashmir to the far west of the common border. The Indian Army, ill prepared for attacks of that magnitude, was routed. On 23 October, Tawang fell to the Chinese who continued to push south, towards the foothills of the Himalayas, reaching the plains and the outskirts of Dalvi's garrison town, Tezpur. Then, on 21 November, after a month of heavy fighting, the Chinese declared a unilateral ceasefire and withdrew to the McMahon Line. India had suffered a humiliating defeat. But there was also immense bravery. Not far from Sela Pass – the highest point on the road from Tawang down to the southern lowlands – rifleman Jaswant Singh single-handedly stopped the Chinese for three days before he was killed. A memorial to his honour was erected at the spot where he laid down his life, and today many travellers on the road to Tawang stop there to pay their respects to the brave young soldier who died defending India against an overwhelming enemy force. Many other Indian soldiers also died fighting in the freezing cold of the inhospitable heights of the Himalayas, often cut off from supplies from the lowlands. Casualties kept mounting, and soon more than a thousand Indian soldiers lay dead in the mountains. At least 700 Chinese soldiers were killed and many more wounded as well – but that did not stop them. Massive infantry attacks, or human waves, have been part of Chinese military tactics since the Korean War in the early 1950s.

It was not only the pride of the Indian Army that lay in tatters after the brief but fierce 1962 border war. It also had a devastating effect on Prime Minister Jawaharlal Nehru personally. He felt genuinely betrayed. There could be no more friendship with China, which he had nurtured throughout the 1950s. India's leftist defence minister, Krishna Menon, who had been critical of the West and dismissed the possibility of a war with China over the border issue, was sacked. Nehru died, a broken man, in May 1964. The Chinese had violated his trust and left India looking weak, feeble and vulnerable.

There were also other casualties of the 1962 war that hurt India's image as a strong democracy. More than 3,000 ethnic Chinese, many of them living in Assam at the time, were rounded up and sent to an internment camp in Deoli in Rajasthan. In 2010, survivors of the camp went public saying that they wanted a monument to be raised at Deoli as 'an acknowledgement of the persecution of the ethnic Chinese' forty-eight years before, and as a reminder of 'our loss of freedom'.[4] They were no 'fifth columnists' for China's communist government – nor were the tens of thousands of ethnic Chinese who then lived in Kolkata, worked as tanners, shoemakers and carpenters, and owned restaurants, beauty parlours, shops and small businesses. They had come during the British rule and now many of them chose to emigrate to Taiwan, Hong Kong, Canada, Australia and the United States. It was not until 1998 that ethnic Chinese were allowed to become naturalized Indian citizens.

India was not alone in targeting members of an entire ethnic community because their country of origin happened to be the enemy in an armed conflict. During World War II, more than 100,000 Japanese immigrants were interned in 'War Relocation Camps' in the United States. But that is hardly an excuse. People of Chinese descent in Assam, who were brought there as indentured labourers by British tea planters in the nineteenth century, were largely forgotten until Assamese novelist and activist Rita Chowdhury highlighted their plight in her novel, *Makam*: 'The least India can do is apologise to them for the misery inflicted by an insensitive state machinery for just being Chinese at an inconvenient time,' she said in an interview in 2010.[5]

The Chinese PLA may have withdrawn unilaterally after it had shown the world that it was capable of asserting its territorial claims if it wanted to, but the 1962 war also set in motion a chain of events which were to have a profound impact on the entire region and the stability of India's north-eastern frontier: Chinese support for the Nagas, the Mizos and the Manipuris; Western support for the Tibetan resistance; a massive military build-up in India and modernization of its armed forces; and the covert involvement of spies and intelligence operatives of all sorts in the theatre of conflict that stretched from north-eastern India to northern Burma and, eventually, even the Indian Ocean. India and China, once partners if not allies, and bound together under the slogan Hindi–Chini Bhai–Bhai, became bitter enemies. No one could any longer deny that there was a new Great Game in the East.

Devastating as it might have been – and to a large extent still is – for the Indian psyche, the 1962 war was not entirely unexpected, and cross-border espionage and regional rivalry did not begin with the Chinese attacks on NEFA and Aksai Chin. Diverging views on the status of Tibet, its border with India, and China's role in all this, pre-dated the war by several decades.

During the colonial era, a new concept was invented to describe the status of territories that were not really under the sovereignty of any power, nor recognized as independent by outsiders. It was called 'suzerainty' and was first used to describe the relationship between the Ottoman Empire and its outlying areas. Later, China was said to enjoy 'suzerainty' over countries such as Korea and Tibet. It is doubtful whether there is any word in the Tibetan language – or Korean – to describe something as fuzzy as 'suzerainty'. By using that term, Britain and other colonial powers could appease the Chinese by making them believe that it enjoyed some kind of overlordship of a certain territory, while the actual rulers of the same territory could interpret it as recognition of a more independent status.

George Patterson, a champion for the Tibetan cause, wrote shortly after the 1962 war: 'The confusion in boundaries which existed in the minds of the leaders of other nations was due to a variety of reasons, compounded by the geographical remoteness of Tibet, the indifference of the Tibetan government to outside affairs and the predilection of the Chinese government for extending the boundaries on their maps farther and farther westwards.'[6] Patterson also noted that throughout most of Tibet's history there was no war that could unite its many tribes against their common enemy,

China. They were busy fighting each other and if the proud and independent tribesmen were opposed to any higher authority, it would have been the central government in Lhasa.

The official Chinese version of the situation was outlined in a book published after the 1959 anti-Chinese uprising in Tibet and the subsequent flight of the Dalai Lama to India, and another which Beijing produced after the 1962 war. The former contained pictures of serfs in fetters and thumbscrews with which the 'former local government of Tibet' used to punish the people and safeguard the 'special minority privileges' of the oppressors – and then shots of Chinese soldiers helping smiling Tibetan peasants reaping highland barley, an important crop for the Tibetans, and Chinese Army officers presenting gifts to chubby-cheeked, happy Tibetan girls. The text assures the reader that 'friendly contacts between the Tibetans and China's other nationalities, mainly the Han nationality, began a long time ago.' The Tibetans seemed to love the Chinese regardless of what dynasty was in power, sending gifts to the emperors, and the Chinese reciprocated by sending emissaries to Tibet to invite important lamas to preach the Buddhist canons. Chinese princesses happily married Tibetan dignitaries and Chinese emperors conferred titles of honour on prominent Tibetan Buddhists.

Then came the 1911 Chinese revolution and the fall of the last imperial dynasty, the Manchu Qing, and 'the British imperialists lost no time in inciting their protégés, the reactionaries of the upper strata in Tibet, to stage a revolt.' The British imperialists, apparently, never ceased trying 'to undermine the normal relations between the Chinese central government and the local government of Tibet.' In the late 1940s, the British – and now also the US – imperialists 'tried in every way to thwart the peaceful liberation of the Tibet region of China.' But, naturally, 'the Tibetan people, along with other nationalities of the motherland, will advance from victory to victory under the leadership of the Chinese Communist Party and Chairman Mao Tse-tung.'[7]

The authors of the official Chinese publication also went on to criticize Nehru – three years before the 1962 border war: 'Mr. Nehru hopes that we "will win them [the Tibetans and others] to friendly co-operation". No doubt this is a good idea, though it was meant by Mr. Nehru as an indirect charge that we have not done so and are not doing so. In point of fact, only the revolutionary proletariat can find a thorough and correct solution to the nationalities question inherited from the past.'[8]

There is hardly a sentence in the propagandistic book that China produced in 1959 that could be considered even remotely convincing. But that has not prevented a stream of foreigners from supporting the Chinese version of their occupation of Tibet. The most notorious were Stuart and Roma Gelder whose *The Timely Rain: Travels in New Tibet* became a classic in left-wing circles all over the world. The British couple interviewed a former serf who had been blinded and mutilated for stealing two sheep from a landlord. They visited schools with happy children. The Gelders assured everyone that Buddhism was alive and well in Tibet, and that they did not witness any atrocities.[9] Their book carried a foreword by Edgar Snow, the author of *Red Star Over China*, and a close friend of the Chinese communist leadership.

Anna Louise Strong, an American journalist and activist who had lived in the Soviet Union before she settled in China in the 1950s, wrote the even more passionate *When Serfs Stood Up in Tibet*, which also depicted the Tibetans as a happy people in the great fraternity that is China.[10] In the same vein, Israel Epstein, a Polish-American journalist who later became editor-in-chief of the official publication *China Reconstructs*, wrote *Tibet Transformed*, which praised 'Tibetan revolutionaries, old and young' and wrote about 'the reactionary rebellion' in 1959.[11]

Han Suyin, half-Chinese, half-Belgian, also uncritically reproduced the official Chinese version in her *Lhasa, the Open City*.[12] Remarkably, Han visited Tibet in the mid-1970s, only a few years after the immense destruction that had taken place during the Cultural Revolution, but still saw nothing untoward.

Some South Asian writers were also taken in by the Chinese propaganda. Ratne Deshapriya Senanayake, secretary general of the Ceylon Writers' Association and president of the Ceylon Journalists' Association in the 1950s and 1960s, wrote *Inside Story of Tibet* in which he stated that the 1959 'rebellion was suppressed by the people of Tibet with the assistance of the People's Liberation Army.' The imperialists and reactionaries used 'religion as a camouflage . . . to mislead and deceive those who were not familiar with the true situation inside the Tibet region of China before liberation'.[13]

China's official version of the boundary question, as published in the 1962 book, at least tries to be more factual than the crude propaganda it spread about Tibet, and which was later accepted by all those foreign visitors on guided tours to Lhasa and other places on 'the roof of the world'. The book about the boundary, which was also published by the Foreign Languages Press in Beijing, contains official statements, letters from Premier Zhou Enlai to Nehru, and detailed maps of the areas claimed by China. But it also includes some hilarious statements such as, 'Indian troops eventually launched massive armed attacks all along the line of Chinese frontier guards on October 20, 1962.'[14]

At the heart of the problem are two issues: the status of Tibet and the McMahon Line, which was agreed upon by Britain and Tibet at Shimla in 1914 but rejected by China which did not recognize the right of the Tibetan government to conclude treaties with foreign powers. Named after Sir Henry McMahon, foreign secretary of British India, it follows the crest of the Himalayas and therefore could be considered a natural border between India and whatever name and status of the land north of it. The agreement also stated that, 'The Government of China engages not to convert Tibet into a Chinese province. The Government of Great Britain engages not to annex Tibet or any portion of it.'[15]

Zhou Enlai outlined his version of what happened when representatives of the three countries met at the summer capital of British India just before the outbreak of World War I in a 'Letter to the Leaders of Asian and African Countries dated November 15, 1962' – while fighting was still going on in the Himalayas:

In 1911 there occurred the revolution which overthrew the absolute imperial rule in China. Seizing upon this as an opportune moment to detach Tibet from China, British imperialism sought to negotiate China's sovereignty in Tibet by recognising merely China's so-called suzerainty there. It was against this historical background that the Simla [Shimla] Conference was convened in 1914. But even at the conference the British representative dared not openly demand that China cede large tracts of its territory. It was outside the Conference and behind the back of the representative of the Chinese Central Government that the British representative drew the notorious 'McMahon Line' through a secret exchange of letters with the representative of the Tibet local authorities, attempting thereby to annex 90,000 square kilometres of China's territory to British India. The then Chinese Government refused to recognise the illegal McMahon Line. So have all Chinese Governments since then. That is why even the British Government dared not publicly draw this line on its maps before 1936. The illegal McMahon Line was wholly imposed on the Chinese people by British imperialism.[16]

Those '90,000 square kilometres of Chinese territory' were, of course, China's territorial claims in today's Arunachal Pradesh, which basically cover most of the state except the south-eastern districts of Tirap and Changlang. Premier Zhou went on to claim that 'British imperialism, seeking a short-cut for invading the heart of Sinkiang [Xinjiang], laid covetous eyes on the relatively flat Aksai Chin in the eighteen sixties and dispatched military intelligence agents to infiltrate into the area for unlawful surveys. In compliance with the will of British imperialism, these agents worked out an assessment of boundary lines for truncating Sinkiang. The British Government did try at one time to alter according to its own wishes the traditional customary line in the western sector of the Sino-Indian border, but was promptly rebuffed by the Chinese government.'[17]

What Zhou was referring to would in more judicious English be the line proposed in 1865 by W.H. Johnson, a civil servant of the Survey of India, which put the entire Aksai Chin in Kashmir. But the British never bothered presenting the line to China. A revised version of the Johnson Line was proposed in 1897 by Sir John Ardagh, a British military officer, which suggested that the crest of the Kun Lun Mountains north of the Yarkand River should be the border. This line would be easier to defend than the original Johnson Line, and became known as the Johnson-Ardagh Line.

Ardagh's proposal came at a time when China and Britain were allies in the first Great Game. They shared a common interest in preventing the Russians from taking over Aksai Chin in its attempts to secure control over Central Asia and, eventually, reach the Arabian Sea. In 1899, when China began to show more interest in the remote and uninhabited high plateau north-east of Ladakh proper – which was definitely part of Kashmir – Britain proposed a revised boundary. Initially suggested by George MacCartney, the half-British, half-Chinese British consul general in Kashgar in Xinjiang, and presented to the Chinese by Sir Claude MacDonald, another British diplomat, it placed most, but not all, of Aksai Chin on the Chinese side of the boundary. Called the MacCartney-MacDonald Line, it corresponds roughly to the actual line of control today – but the Chinese did not at the time respond to MacDonald's note. The British, for some reason, interpreted this as Chinese acquiescence.[18]

The British left independent India with a legacy of confusion that could lead to different interpretations, at least in the Aksai Chin area. But that does not mean that China's claims have any validity. And judging from his letters to Nehru, it is evident that Zhou had not done his historical homework properly. The Shimla Conference was convened in October 1913, not in 1914. It was concluded on 3 July 1914 – after the Chinese delegate, Ivan Chen, or Chen Yi-fan, the special commissioner for foreign affairs in Shanghai, had left. The final agreement was signed by McMahon for the British side and Lonchen Shatra, the prime minister of Tibet.

Zhou's references to 'the Chinese Central government' and 'the local government in Tibet' would have been ludicrous in the context of the time when the conference was held. In 1913, the thirteenth Dalai Lama had issued a declaration which was not really a proclamation of independence, as it has been called by some historians, but more in the nature of a document reasserting the way in which the Tibetans always had viewed their relationship with their powerful neighbour:

> Tibet is a country with rich natural resources; but it is not scientifically advanced like other lands. We are a small, religious, and independent nation. To keep up with the rest of the world, we must defend our country. In view of past invasions by foreigners, our people may have to face certain difficulties, which they must disregard. To safeguard and maintain the independence of our country, one and all should voluntarily work hard. Our subject citizens residing near the borders should be alert and keep the government informed by special messenger of any suspicious developments. Our subjects must not create major clashes between two nations because of minor incidents.[19]

The impetus for the Shimla Convention, as it became called, was 'the British discovery that during the summer of 1912 the Chinese were making plans to invade Tibet. The Tibetan Government had already dispatched troops to eastern Tibet to ward off Chinese attackers from Sichuan and Yunnan.'[20] The British, on the other hand, had flexed their colonial muscle in Tibet, when Francis Younghusband, an army officer and explorer, had led an expedition to Lhasa in 1904. A hundred miles inside Tibet, the expedition was attacked by a Tibetan militia, consisting mostly of monks. The British response was fierce, as described by Tibetan historian Phuntsog Tsering:

> When the Tibetan soldiers had extinguished their fuses, the British soldiers opened fire with machine guns from the surrounding area. It was as if the heroic Tibetan soldiers had had their hands disabled, and they fell on the wasteland. The British invaders, having disabled the Tibetan soldiers, then savagely massacred them.[21]

Younghusband himself telegraphed back to his headquarters: 'Tibetans are bolting like rabbits.'[22] With the backbone of the Tibetan resistance broken, Younghusband, in full diplomatic regalia and followed by his mostly Gurkha soldiers, rode into the holy city of Lhasa on 1 August.[23] Eventually, however, Tibet got its revenge in its own way: Like many Westerners before him and after, Younghusband became mesmerized by Tibetan spiritualism and mysticism. After his return to England in 1910, Younghusband set out to preach free love and founded numerous outlandish societies, including one that claimed there were extraterrestrials with translucent flesh on a planet called Altair. Or, as British writer Patrick French put it decades later, Younghusband, 'the blimpish colonialist managed to end up as a premature hippy.'[24]

But before he went through that remarkable transformation, Younghusband did assert Britain's influence over Tibet, but he did not occupy it. A major objective was to make sure the Russians did not intrude into Tibet – and to keep the Chinese at bay as well. There was a plan to 'divide' Tibet into an 'inner' and an 'outer' area in the same way China and Russia had created an 'inner' and 'outer' Mongolia in the beginning of the twentieth century. In 'inner' Mongolia, China exerted more direct rule than in the more independent 'outer Mongolia'. The former is an 'autonomous region' of China and the latter the independent Republic of Mongolia.

'Inner Tibet' would comprise eastern Kham and Ando where Lhasa would retain control of religious matters only, while 'Outer Tibet' would comprise roughly the same area as today's Chinese 'autonomous region' of Tibet.

That plan never materialized and the status quo remained. China was too weak and divided internally after the fall of the last emperor and subsequent civil wars and warlordism and was in no position to assert its claim over Tibet. Britain did not interfere, and Tibet probably enjoyed one of the most tranquil periods in its entire history. It was, in every meaning of the word, a de facto independent country. The thirteenth Dalai Lama, who reigned until his death in 1933, the time of the Great Game between Russia and Britain, was a skilful politician. He managed to maintain Tibet's independence, restored discipline in the monasteries and increased the number of lay officials in his administration to curb the previous excessive powers of the monks. He also abolished amputations as a means of punishment of criminals and was generally seen as a reformer who could have brought Tibet into the modern world. No country formally recognized the independence of Tibet, but in 1936 Britain established a more permanent diplomatic mission in Lhasa headed by George Sherriff, a professional soldier, amateur botanist and skilled mechanic.[25] Tibet also maintained a trade office in Kalimpong near Darjeeling, where the country's only overseas representatives were stationed.

But the emergence of a more modern independent nation of Tibet was not to happen. World War II broke out and a new world power, the United States, entered the scene, ushering in an entirely new era in most of Asia. The United States in its war against Japan was closely allied with the Republic of China – which, like any Chinese state before it, claimed Tibet as part of its territory. The United States did send two reconnaissance specialists from the Office of Strategic Services, OSS – the forerunner to the CIA – to Tibet. They did not go there through China, but the Americans did not want to upset the sensitivities of their Nationalist Chinese allies; so OSS director William Donovan explained in a letter to President Franklin Roosevelt why he, in correspondence with the ruling fourteenth Dalai Lama, had carefully avoided mentioning Tibet's status: 'This letter is addressed to the Dalai Lama in his capacity of religious leader of Tibet, rather than in his capacity of secular leader of Tibet, thus avoiding any offense to the Chinese Government which included Tibet in the territory of the Republic of China.'[26]

While the United States never formally recognized Tibet as part of China – as claimed by successive Chinese governments – it did treat it as such so as not to upset its relations with its Chinese war allies. On 10 May 1943, Chinese nationalist leader Chiang Kai-shek asserted that 'Tibet is part of Chinese territory . . . no foreign power is allowed to interfere in our domestic affairs.'[27]

US attitudes changed somewhat when World War II was over – and the communists were making swift advances in China. In January 1949, when it was becoming obvious that the days of Chiang's Guomindang government were over, the US ambassador to India suggested to the State Department in Washington that a review of its Tibet policy would be appropriate. In particular, the ambassador proposed that if Mao Zedong and his communists succeed in taking control of China, the United States should be prepared to treat Tibet as independent: 'If the Communists gain control of China proper, Tibet will be one of the few remaining non-Communist bastions in Continental Asia. Outer Mongolia is already detached. Communist influence is strong in Burma and Communists are infiltrating Sinkiang [Xinjiang] and Inner Mongolia. Tibet will accordingly assume both ideological and strategic importance.'[28]

Once again, Tibet found itself a pawn in a Great Game for power in Central Asia. Russia was gone as a player in Tibet, but it was only a matter of time before a communist China would try to 'unify' the country after decades of misrule and civil war. On 1 October 1949, before hundreds of thousands of people who had gathered outside Tiananmen, the Gate of Heavenly Peace at the old Imperial Palace in Beijing, Mao Zedong proclaimed the People's Republic of China, saying: 'Never again will the people of China be enslaved!' And it was certainly his plan to bring in Tibet, Xinjiang and Inner Mongolia into his new 'dictatorship of the proletariat'.

About a year later, on 7 October 1950, communist troops crossed the Jinsha River and fought their first and perhaps most decisive battle with the tiny, ill-equipped Tibetan Army. About 5,000 Tibetan soldiers are believed to have died in the fighting, which amounted to wholesale slaughter. A captured governor, Ngapoi Ngawang Jigme, was sent to Lhasa to negotiate with the Dalai Lama. After several months of deliberations, on 23 May 1951 Jigme signed the seventeen-point agreement for 'the Peaceful Liberation of Tibet' in Beijing. It was the first time – long before Hong Kong reverted to Chinese rule in 1997 – that China promised a model based on 'one country, two systems'. The agreement affirmed China's sovereignty over Tibet, but according to point four: 'The central authorities will not alter the existing political system in Tibet. The central authorities also will not alter the established status, functions and powers of the Dalai Lama. Officials of various ranks shall hold office as usual.'[29]

Rather ominously, however, in late 1951 the PLA set up a base in Lhasa. The Chinese occupation had begun. And there were not going to be two systems under this arrangement. The 1959 propaganda book, published after the uprising and the Dalai Lama's subsequent flight to India, had no references to maintaining 'the existing political system in Tibet'. But it reproduced an editorial from the *Renmin Ribao*, or *People's Daily*, stating: 'To protect the unification of the country and national unity, Premier of the State Council Chou En-lai [Zhou Enlai] has ordered the dissolution of the local government in Tibet, which organised the rebellion . . . actively assisted by the Tibetan people, both ecclesiastical and secular, the People's Liberation Army had swiftly stamped out the rebellion in the Lhasa area and is mopping up rebel bandits in some other places in Tibet.'[30]

For the first time in history, Tibet was under direct Chinese rule. But from the very beginning in 1950, the United States also had to tread carefully because the old Republic of China lived on in the island of Taiwan, where Chiang Kai-shek sought refuge after his inevitable defeat. His government continued to represent China in the United Nations, including its Security Council, and remained a close US ally – now against the Chinese communists.

The intrigues that followed the Chinese invasion of Tibet, and the characters who were involved, put even the old Great Game to shame. As the Chinese were moving into Kham in the east and beginning to consolidate their grip on Tibet, the Americans began to take more interest in the Tibetan issue. In the spring of 1951, Larry Dalley, a young CIA officer at the US consulate general in Kolkata seeking information about China's designs for Tibet, contacted two young ladies in the city's diplomatic circuit. One of them was Pema Tseudeun, the older sister of the Crown prince of Sikkim, Palden Thondup. She was more commonly known in her social circles as Kukula, a stunningly beautiful Himalayan lady who was married to a Tibetan nobleman. During World War II, while still a teenager, she had befriended Ilya Tolstoy and Brooke Dolan, the two OSS reconnaissance specialist officers then stationed in Lhasa. She and her husband owned considerable property in Lhasa, but the Chinese incursions had forced her to return to Sikkim, and they moved on to Kolkata.[31]

The other early American contact was Kukula's younger sister, the equally stunning Pema Choki, or 'Kula' to her friends. She was also married to a Tibetan and her father-in-law had been a high-ranking official at the Tibetan trade office in Kalimpong. Dalley asked the sisters if they thought the Tibetans would need any American assistance, and a channel to the resistance on the other side of the Himalayas was opened. According to US researchers

Kenneth Conboy and James Morrison: 'In June 1952, Kukula approached the consulate with an oral message from Dalai Lama. She had just returned from a visit to her in-laws in Lhasa, and although she had not personally met the Dalai Lama, she had been given information from Kula's father-in-law, Yurok Dazza, who had been in Lhasa at the same time, circulating among senior government circles. Kukula quoted the Dalai Lama as saying that when the time was propitious for liberation, he hoped the United States would give material aid and support.'[32]

As discontent with the Chinese occupation was brewing throughout Tibet, the Dalai Lama was invited to visit Beijing in September 1954, ostensibly to lead a Tibetan delegation to an event that would celebrate the inauguration of the first constitution of the People's Republic of China. The young Dalai Lama, then only nineteen years old, met all important Chinese leaders of the time: Mao Zedong, Zhou Enlai and Deng Xiaoping. Pictures of a smiling Dalai Lama with these seemingly friendly Chinese hosts were published in the official media, but Mao insulted the spiritual leader of the Tibetans by telling him that religion was poison. Mao also told him that an entirely new body, the 'Preparatory Committee for the Autonomous Region of Tibet' was being created, effectively undermining the promises made under the seventeen-point agreement of 1951.

When the Dalai Lama returned home to Lhasa, he found that the Chinese had built new roads into Tibet. There were more PLA soldiers everywhere. He was distraught, realizing that whatever autonomy his beloved Tibet had enjoyed since the Chinese first entered Tibet would soon be gone. And, given the Chinese chairman's attitude to religion, the future of Tibetan Buddhism was definitely in jeopardy.

There was an opening when in late 1956 the Dalai Lama went on a pilgrimage to India. It was Buddha Jayanti, the birthday of the Buddha, and the Dalai Lama received an official invitation from

Nehru to attend the celebrations at Bodh Gaya, where the Mahabodhi temple had been renovated for the event. Dalai Lama and a fifty-five-man strong Tibetan delegation entered India through Sikkim – but to their astonishment, they found that Zhou Enlai was there as well on an official visit. The Tibet issue was discussed and Nehru invited the Dalai Lama to New Delhi. There would be no asylum for him in India, should he decide to escape from Chinese-dominated Tibet. India's newly won friendship with China was far more important, the Indian prime minister had concluded. The Dalai Lama returned to Tibet, advised to do so also by his two official soothsayers.[33]

It is not clear how much the Dalai Lama knew about the anti-Chinese resistance that was being formed – or if even Nehru was aware of what the CIA in Kolkata and their two royal Sikkimese lady friends were up to. In September 1952, the US consul general in Kolkata, Gary Soulen, went on a trek in Sikkim with Princess Kukula to survey the terrain. On his return to India, he contacted India's then spymaster, Bhola Nath Mullik, who was more steeped in the old colonial tradition than Nehru, a progressive politician. Contacts were made with two of the Dalai Lama's brothers then living in exile. The elder of the two, Thubten Norbu, already had CIA contacts through an obscure outfit called the Committee for a Free Asia. The younger, Gyalo Thondup, had settled in Darjeeling. Nearby Kalimpong, on the main line of communication between India and Tibet, became a hub of covert activity.

By 1956, the Khampa rebellion was sweeping across eastern Tibet, and a group of warlike Khampas had congregated in Kalimpong. Getting them out of India posed a major problem as Nehru and his government would have to be kept in the dark. But there was a way: across the narrow neck of Indian territory between Bhutan and East Pakistan. In 1956, Pakistan had become a close ally of the United States, and would be more welcoming than India to secret proposals from Washington. In 1954, Pakistan had joined the anti-communist defence organization SEATO, the South-East Asia Treaty Organization, which apart from the United States also included Australia, New Zealand, France, Thailand and the Philippines. In 1955, a parallel alliance had been formed in West Asia: the Central Treaty Organization, CENTO, which brought together Britain, Iran, Iraq, Turkey – and Pakistan.

To what extent the CIA actually helped the Dalai Lama flee to India in March 1959 is still an open question, but they were certainly aware that he had left Lhasa within days of his escape from the Tibetan capital in disguise. Up in the mountains, the Dalai Lama's party caught up with the CIA's Tibetan resistance fighters inside Tibet, who were equipped with radios. They keyed a message to Okinawa, the US base on the Ryukyu Islands, which had not yet been handed back to Japan after they were occupied during World War II. The CIA also knew that the Dalai Lama, while on his way to the Indian border, had repudiated the seventeen-point agreement for 'the Peaceful Liberation of Tibet'.[34]

These messages from the CIA-trained Tibetan radio operators prompted the Agency to ask India to grant the Dalai Lama asylum before he had even reached the Indian border. The CIA's station chief in New Delhi went straight to Nehru with the request. The prime minister agreed – cutting through layers of red tape to facilitate the process. Melinda Liu wrote in *Newsweek* in April 1999: 'A CIA-trained Tibetan even managed to film the odyssey with a 16-mm camera; it showed the spiritual leader, astride on a brown horse with richly embroidered saddlebags, and his retinue picking their way across Tibet's bleak hillsides, with the People's Liberation Army breathing down their necks.'[35]

On 30 March 1959, the Dalai Lama and his men crossed the last mountain pass in Tibet and rode into Tawang in north-western NEFA. From there, the Dalai Lama, weak from dysentery, continued down to Tezpur in the Indian plains, where a media frenzy awaited him. The twenty-four-year-old God King of Tibet had fled from communist China – and that was world news. He was then moved to the hill station of Mussoorie on the western foothills of the Himalayas, where he met Nehru and other Indian dignitaries. A new place was chosen for the Tibetan leader, the much smaller hill station of McLeodganj in today's Himachal Pradesh, which since 1960 has also been the site for the Tibetan government in exile.

With the Dalai Lama and his entourage safely settled in India, the CIA could step up its support for the Tibetan resistance. The abandoned airstrip at Kurmitola, north of Dhaka, which was built by the British during World War II, became the forward base for airdrops into Tibet, and from there Tibetan resistance fighters were also flown out to Okinawa, Clark Airbase in the Philippines, and the Pacific island of Saipan, the secret headquarters of the CIA's covert operations in the Asia-Pacific region. Nationalist Chinese, Korean, Lao and Vietnamese commandos were trained there – and now the Tibetans. The secret Tibetan operation was codenamed ST CIRCUS and its aerial portion ST BARNUM. According to Conboy and Morrison, because the planes would need to overfly Indian territory without permission, they had to factor in the radar at Kolkata. But the CIA had done their homework 'and knew that the Indian system had no compensation feature and could be defeated if the B-17 used the Himalayan massif as a radar screen. Flying north over Sikkim, the crew would go as far as the Brahmaputra [in Tibet] for the first drop, cut east across the Tibetan plateau to Kham for the second drop, then veer southwest through Indian territory back to East Pakistan.'[36] To conceal American participation in the scheme, in case one of the planes was detected or shot down, the pilots were all anti-communist Poles who had been given asylum in the United States.

Muslim guerrillas in Xinjiang also benefited from the CIA's largesse, as did Nationalist Communist soldiers in secret camps in northern Burma. A covert war on China was being launched, but as Conboy and Morrison point out, 'the agency had taken great pains to exclude ROC [the Republic of China] from its Tibetan operations.'[37] And it is doubtful whether the US was actually in favour of Tibetan independence; the limited scope of the operation seems to indicate that the main purpose was to annoy the Chinese and keep their armed forces occupied.

Whatever the case, when the special training facility was established at Camp Hale not far from Leadville in Colorado, a group of tightly knit CIA officers were in charge of the Tibetan programme, and they developed a fondness for the Tibetans that was rather unique. They would later reminiscence how the staunchly Buddhist Tibetans would carefully rescue flies which fell in their teacups, while expressing a deadly desire to kill as many Chinese as possible. At Camp Hale, the Tibetans were trained in guerrilla warfare as well as covert operations like spy photography, Morse code and minelaying.

Details about the training were not revealed until the 1990s, when it was all over. According to Melinda Liu's 1999 cover story for *Newsweek*: 'The training took place in utmost secrecy. US officers made up stories about a top-secret nuclear research project at Fort Hale, and guards deterred intruders with shoot-to-kill orders. In 1961 four dozen American civilians were temporarily detained at gunpoint when they inadvertently witnessed 15 Asians wearing camouflage fatigues being escorted onto a C-124 Globemaster with blacked-out windows. Defence secretary Robert McNamara personally intervened to persuade the *New York Times* to spike the story.'[38]

The American agents who were sent to train the Tibetans were all very young for the formidable task that lay before them: to destablize the most populous nation of earth. Some of them were smokejumpers from Montana, daring young men looking for adventure. After Tibet, many of them and a few others went on to take part in the CIA's secret war against the communist resistance in Laos. Among them was Thomas Fosmire, a former US Army sergeant in his late twenties who had also served as an adviser to the border police in Thailand and, after Laos, remained in Vietnam until the communists marched into Saigon in April 1975. Another CIA operative, a Chinese linguist and philosophy major at Stanford University, John 'Ken' Knaus, was less of a gung-ho fighter and later wrote a book about his experiences with the Tibetan guerrillas who underwent training in Colorado. He felt remorse for, in the end, letting the Tibetans down. He felt guilt 'over our participation in these efforts, which cost others their lives, but which were the prime adventure of our own'.[39]

There was also the colourful Anthony Poshepny, better known under the short version of his name: Tony Poe. A former US marine who was wounded on Iwo Jima during the last battles against the Japanese during World War II, he joined the CIA as a paramilitary officer in 1951. He fought behind enemy lines in Korea and, in the late 1950s, tried and failed to foment an uprising in Sumatra against the Indonesian president Sukarno. Outgunned and trapped on the island, he and one of his companions fled to a fishing trawler that took them away to a waiting US submarine. At Camp Hale, Poe trained Tibetan guerrillas and even accompanied them to the airfield in East Pakistan from where they were flown and parachuted into Tibet.[40]

After Tibet, Poe went straight to Laos to train anti-communist guerrillas, a secret army of tribesmen raised by him and other CIA operatives. In the mountains of northern Laos, he ran his own fiefdom, and soon became infamous for his brutality. He paid rewards for bringing in enemy ears, and higher remuneration if these were accompanied by a communist cap with a red star. He was also reported to decapitate his enemies and put their heads on spikes to boost the morale of his own soldiers. Mentally unsound, Poe became the model for the renegade Green Beret Colonel Kurtz in the 1979 Hollywood movie *Apocalypse Now* – as far as one could possibly get from the spiritual ideas of the Dalai Lama.

The CIA's cowboy operation with the Tibetans took on a new dimension after the 1962 border war. China no longer was India's friend. India was now on board and prepared to support the Tibetan resistance. In the early 1960s, the Tibetans who had been trained at Camp Hale in Colorado were transferred to India where, according to Tibetan historian Tsering Shakya, 'the Indians had established a secret Tibetan Army base near Dehra Dun at Chakrata, more commonly known to the Tibetans as Unit Twenty-Two.'[41] At the same time, Pakistan was beginning to drift away from its alliance with the United States and, in 1966, began receiving military assistance from China. The border war had prompted China to look for new friends among India's enemies.

But the main forward base for the resistance was not in India, but in Mustang in a remote corner of Nepal, adjacent to the Tibetan frontier. Mustang, ruled by a local feudal lord and sometimes described as 'a semi-independent Tibetan kingdom' inside Nepal, was surrounded on three sides by Chinese-occupied Tibet. It was sufficiently difficult to access by land, making it easy for the CIA to keep the operation secret. Soldiers from the regular Nepalese Army also guarded all the mountain trails and passes leading into Mustang.

There, the National Volunteer Defence Army, as the resistance force was called, set up bases from where it launched cross-border raids into Tibet. They were equipped with rifles, mortars and light machine guns, but their job was also to collect intelligence for the CIA on Chinese troop movements along the Xinjiang–Lhasa highway that ran through the mountainous terrain a few days march from the border. Weapons and other supplies were airdropped into Mustang from C-130 planes that had flown from Okinawa, which were refuelled at Takhli in Thailand, where more weapons were also loaded onto the aircraft. ST CIRCUS and ST BARNUM were the most secret of the many secret operations that the CIA at that time carried out in China's periphery. And after the 1962 border war, the Indians began to permit the Americans to fly through their airspace. It was no longer necessary to take off at night from some obscure airfield in East Pakistan.

Nepal's role in the operation was circumspect, to say the least. The country was strictly 'neutral' – which meant that it happily accepted assistance from anyone eager to get a foothold in the Himalayan kingdom with its strategic location between India and China. Nepal's first motorable connection with the outside world, the 200-kilometre, steep switchback from Birganj on the Indian border to Kathmandu, was built by India. Named after King Tribhuvan, who had died in 1955, it was completed the following year. Under an agreement signed with China in 1961, the Chinese built the Arniko or Kodari Highway from the Tibetan border to Kathmandu, which, if combined with the Tribhuvan Highway, provided the first overland link between China and India. In 1956, Nepal had signed a friendship treaty with China, recognizing Chinese sovereignty over Tibet, and began to accept assistance from Beijing. Meanwhile, the Soviet Union paid for part of the East–West Highway in the lowlands, connecting Birganj with towns to the east, just north of the Indian border.

The United States also built roads and paid for other development projects, which made the covert Mustang operation possible. No foreigners, apart from CIA operatives, ever made it close to the Tibetan resistance bases in Nepal – apart from three intrepid adventurers from Britain: Adrian Cowell, a China-born documentary film-maker who had driven a Land Rover from London to Singapore in 1956; Chris Menges, a cinematographer and film director who later earned worldwide fame for shooting and directing movies such as *The Killing Fields*, *The Mission*, *Michael Collins* and *The Boxer*; and George Patterson, a Scottish missionary and author who was fluent in the Khampa language.

Under the pretext of making a documentary on Nepal, they had made contact with the unofficial representative of the Tibetan resistance in New Delhi. Cowell, Menges and Patterson could not enter the heavily guarded Mustang area, but made it to a small Tibetan settlement in the narrow Dzeum Valley near the upper reaches of the Budhi Gandaki River. Carole McGranahan, an American academic, wrote a paper in which she claims the three men accompanied 'a resistance battalion' into Tibet and that 'the British government suppressed the footage, entitled "Raid into Tibet", for several years before it was publicly shown.'[42]

Cowell says this is nonsense.[43] He, Menges and Patterson followed a group of no more than nine Tibetan guerrillas with eight rifles between them into Tibet. Traversing a mountain pass at an altitude of more than 5,000 metres above sea level, they reached the heights overlooking the Kodari Highway, where the Tibetans ambushed a Chinese Army convoy. And their dramatic footage of the daring raid was not suppressed by anyone. On their return to Kathmandu, Patterson made the mistake of telling the British ambassador what they had done. The ambassador then told King Mahendra. The CIA thus learnt about it and instructed the Tibetans to recover the footage 'at any cost'. The Tibetans, unfortunately, interpreted that as killing the British team. However, Cowell, Menges and Patterson got away – only to be arrested on the Indian border as they were trying to leave Nepal. By then, all the film had been sent out through other channels, and all that the Nepalese got hold of was a recording that Cowell, who was also interested in ornithology, had made of a Himalayan cuckoo. The Nepalese policemen played the tape backwards and forwards, suspecting that the sound of the cuckoo contained some secret, coded message. Finding nothing, the three were released, and their documentary was shown shortly after that in Britain, the United States and some other countries.

Cowell provided the general public with the only independent assessment of the Tibetan guerrillas that exists, and his impression of them and their fighting skills was extremely favourable. The unit that Cowell and his two companions followed was armed with Springfield rifles of World War I vintage and similar weapons, which the Americans had supplied to disguise their support for the movement. But even with those antiquated weapons, the Tibetans managed to stop the Chinese convoy. Most guerrillas in other countries would have blocked the road with boulders or logs. The Tibetans did not. Excellent marksmen, they first shot the drivers of three of the four trucks moving along the road and then raided the convoy. Cowell's prediction was that the Tibetan resistance was going to cause the Chinese a lot of problems.

But the CIA's Tibetan programme did not become more than an irritant to the Chinese military. The Americans, not wanting to risk a large-scale war in the Himalayas, kept the operation small, and mainly focused on intelligence gathering. It is also dubious whether Mustang was an ideal place for the operation of a guerrilla force that was going to make a serious impact across the border in Tibet. During my most recent visit to the headquarters of the Tibetan government in exile at McLeodganj in April 2011, I met Lhasang Tsering, a veteran of the Mustang operation who now runs a small bookshop in the sprawling town in the mountains of Himachal Pradesh. Inspired by Cowell's film and the articles he also wrote, Lhasang, then living in exile in India, decided to join the resistance. It was in the early 1970s and he was twenty years old. 'When I arrived there,' Lhasang remembers, 'I thought this is the wrong place for a guerrilla base.'[44]

Mustang itself was barren and desolate, and there were almost no villages on the Tibetan side of the border where they could get food and other supplies – or organize an uprising against the Chinese. Lhasang, whose job was to carry messages between the various camps in Mustang, says there were sixteen of them spread out along the border with a total of 2,000–2,500 men. The operations were coordinated from a secret base in the Nepalese town of Pokhara, where there was an airport and relatively easy access to the rest of the country and beyond. The Annapurna Guest House in Pokhara – disguised as a tourist hotel – was built by the CIA for the Tibetans, and later became part of a 'rehabilitation effort' for the refugees.

By the time Lhasang reached Mustang, American support for the Tibetans was dwindling and ceased completely when Washington began to seek rapprochement with China in order to isolate the enemy that the US then shared with Beijing: the Soviet Union. Ideology has never been an important part of national security policies. Already in 1971, US Secretary of State Henry Kissinger went to China for talks with Zhou Enlai, paving the way for President Richard Nixon's historic visit to Beijing, Hangzhou and Shanghai in February 1972. Although it has never been formally admitted, it is widely believed in Tibetan circles that China agreed to normalize relations with the United States, provided it, among other things, agreed to stop all assistance to the Tibetan resistance.

That was not going to become a major problem. In January 1972, Nepal's King Mahendra had suffered a heart attack and died while hunting in the jungles of Chitwan in the country's southern lowlands. Although Mahendra had tried to steer a neutral course between India and China, his son Birendra, who succeeded him, wanted to improve relations with Nepal's northern neighbour. In December 1973, he visited China and it is certain that the Chinese expressed their displeasure over the Tibetan bases in his country. In order to maintain a more independent stance towards India, the traditional 'big power' in Nepal, Birendra was willing to listen. The Chinese reciprocated by giving generous aid to Nepal.

In May 1974, a trade agreement was signed in Kathmandu between the Chinese and the Nepalese governments. In July, the Nepalese military moved against the Tibetan camps in Mustang. The guerrillas surrendered and were disarmed without much resistance. The morale of the Tibetans had vanished almost completely after listening to a taped message from the Dalai Lama, urging them, probably on instructions from the Americans, to lay down their arms and leave Mustang. It had to be a recorded message, so the Tibetan fighters would be convinced that the message really came from the Dalai Lama and was not a fake. It was too much for several of the guerrillas to bear. A Khampa commander shot himself in the head when he heard the Dalai Lama's plea, and two guerrilla fighters threw themselves in the cold and swift waters of the nearest river. 'They had promised to fight to the death,' said Lhasang Tsering. 'And there was dignity only in death.'

Armed resistance against the Chinese occupation of Tibet was over, but the Dalai Lama continued his non-violent crusade for the rights of his people. In 1989, he was awarded the Nobel Peace Prize for his efforts, even as the Chinese government continued to spew vitriol over him and his followers. They branded him 'a wolf in sheep's clothing', a 'political leader, not the religious head of a minority; a globetrotting character who wants the world to support Tibet's secession and independence'.[45]

As long as the Dalai Lama is alive, he will remain a major worry for the Chinese, who will also never forget the fact that he is allowed to reside in India along with the Tibetan government in exile. And the border issue will remain a source of tension and an important part of the spying game between Asia's two giants. But it should also be remembered that espionage and covert operations across the Himalayas preceded the Dalai Lama's flight to India, the 1962 war and the secret mission to support the Tibetan resistance.

During 1949–50, a secret expedition led by Douglas S. Mackiernan trekked over 3,000 kilometres across Tibet in an attempt to arm the Tibetans and convince their leaders to seek international recognition for their country's independence. As the Chinese communists had emerged victorious from the civil war, it was only a matter of time before they invaded Tibet. Kathmandu-based writer Thomas Laird has chronicled Mackiernans's mission brilliantly in his *Into Tibet: The CIA's First Atomic Spy and His Secret Expedition to Lhasa*.[46] Only two of the five men who set out survived. Mackiernan was not among them. In fact, he was the first CIA agent to be killed in the line of duty, although that remained a secret until Laird uncovered the whole story in the 1990s.

Mackiernan had served as a cryptanalysis officer in the US Army during World War II and was trained in intelligence work long before the CIA was formed in 1947. In November 1943, he was sent, among all places in the world, to Urumqi in Xinjiang. He returned to the US after the War, but then was sent back to Urumqi in 1947. This time his assignment was more specific: espionage for the new spy agency that America has founded. The Soviet Union was no longer a US ally, and Urumqi was a good listening post for anything that could happen in Soviet Central Asia. And it did. In August 1949, Mackiernan informed Washington that he was opening detection for atomic explosions. On 29 August, the Soviet Union tested its first nuclear weapon at a site in Kazakhstan across the border from Xinjiang.

By early September, most of Xinjiang was under communist control after local Guomindang troops had switched sides, and Washington decided to close its consulate in Urumqi. Mackiernan could have flown out to Beijing and back home to the United States, but another route was chosen for him and some of his staffers: overland through Tibet to India. On 27 September, Mackiernan and Frank Bessac, a Fulbright scholar and, according to most sources, also a CIA agent, drove out of Urumqi without being stopped by its new communist overlords. The Americans' vehicle was laden with machine guns, grenades, radios, gold bars, navigation equipment and general supplies for survival in the harsh conditions of the mountains in Central Asia.

Mackiernan and Bassac linked up with three anti-communist Russians, left their vehicle and continued their journey on horseback and camel across the Taklimakan Desert towards Tibet. Along the way, they left some equipment with anti-communist Muslim guerrillas, who in this way received their first American-supplied weapons and radio equipment. But when the Americans and their Russian allies reached Tibet, nervous border guards opened fire. Mackiernan and two of the Russians were shot dead. The border guards realized that they had made a terrible mistake only after a message arrived from the Dalai Lama informing them about the arrival of some 'foreign friends'. The two survivors, Bessac and a Russian called Vasili Zvansov, proceeded to Lhasa, where they were received by the Dalai Lama. In July 1950, as Mao Zedong's forces were preparing to invade Tibet, Bassac and Zvansov floated south from Lhasa on a branch of the Tsangpo River in a yak-skin coracle.[47] They made it to India, and the contacts the two survivors of the CIA's first mission to Tibet had made provided useful information when the agency, encouraged by the Sikkimese princesses Kukula and Kula, later decided to support the Tibetan resistance.

The Indians also organized their highly unusual, covert operations 'on the roof of the world'. In 1955, marine archaeologist Sydney Wignall organized what he called 'the Welsh Himalayan Expedition' to climb the highest peak inside the Tibetan plateau, Gurla Mandhata. The expedition was going to be launched from the north-western corner of Nepal – and Wignall and two of his companions were on a much more secret mission than mountain climbing. In London, they had been contacted by an Indian intelligence officer, who had persuaded them to undertake the expedition. It would be, strictly speaking, an illegal undertaking as the peak was located across the border, and the Chinese, the new rulers of Tibet, would never allow a foreign team to climb one of 'their' mountains. 'Mr Singh', as the Indian intelligence officer called himself, wanted the Welshmen to report on Chinese military operations in newly invaded Tibet.[48]

The unlikely Indian spies managed to cross the border into Tibet where they were captured by the Chinese and released only after international pressure. After all, they were just mountain climbers, were they not? They made it back to India – battered, malnourished, suffering from frostbite and dysentery, and bringing with them news about a new highway that the Chinese were constructing from Xinjiang to Tibet. The road, as it turned out, was being built through Aksai Chin, Indian territory according to all maps made in India.

The news was received by the grateful mastermind behind Wignall's expedition, whose identity had been kept secret to the Welsh mountain climbers. Wignall learnt much later who he was: General Kodendera Subayya Thimayya, 'Timmy' to his friends, a World War II and Korean War veteran who, in 1957, became Indian Army chief of staff. 'Timmy' soon found himself at loggerheads with the left-leaning defence minister at the time, Krishna Menon. In 1959, 'Timmy' even briefly resigned because Menon refused to consider his plans for preparing the army for what he saw as a forthcoming conflict with China. Apparently, not everyone in the Indian establishment shared the government's enthusiasm over the official Hindi–Chini Bhai–Bhai policy. 'Timmy' retired in May 1961, seventeen months before the Chinese attacked across the Himalayas.

India's next covert operation into Tibet was a joint Indian–American espionage mission, involving the Intelligence Bureau, IB, and the CIA. In 1964, two years after the border war, China had stunned the world by conducting a nuclear test in the Xinjiang desert, long before the outside world knew that the Chinese had such capabilities. The mission was to scale Nanda Devi, a 7,816-metre peak in northern India, to install a terrestrial communications device, powered by a nuclear electrical generator, on the summit. The equipment, if it worked properly, would register any unusual seismological activity in Xinjiang and Tibet. China's sudden emergence as a nuclear power had caused alarm in the United States – and India.[49] Nehru had let the CIA in to assist India with intelligence gathering and to support the Tibetan resistance.

The generator, known as SNAP 19C – System for Nuclear Auxiliary Power – consisted of five elements: a hot fuel block, radioactive fuel capsules placed in its core, thermoelectric generators mounted around it, insulation material, and the block's outer casing.[50] It was not a bomb and could not explode unless equipped with a trigger. But it was a device powered by radioactive material, which could be harmful to humans who came too close to it, and it was not meant to be lost somewhere on a remote mountain top.

Because of bad weather, most of the equipment had to be abandoned during the first attempt to scale Nanda Devi, which had been made by experienced Indian mountaineers, intelligence officers, nuclear experts, radio operators and a virtual army of sherpas carrying the heavy equipment on their backs. When the sherpas, who had carried it up the mountain, returned the following year, it was gone. An avalanche had swept away the rock to which it had been secured. There was no trace of the generator. For several years after the loss of the device, the IB and the CIA would send search teams to find it. But it was never located. Meanwhile, the Chinese had carried out more nuclear tests, now with warheads mounted on missiles. Vinod K. Jose remarked wryly in a story for the December 2010 issue of the Indian monthly magazine *The Caravan*: 'After three consecutive years of searching for the missing nuclear device, the CIA and the IB decided it would never be retrieved. Today, 45 years later, the generator is still at large in the vicinity of Nanda Devi.'[51]

The 1962 war also prompted India to establish a more efficient administration in NEFA, which the Chinese continued to claim as theirs. But no Chinese government has ever ruled that area, and even if the claim could be seen as indirect via its claim to sovereignty over Tibet, it is a very liberal interpretation of history. Precisely defined borders, as we know them in a modern sense, did not exist in Asia before the arrival of the colonial powers. Thai scholar Thongchai Winichakul has examined the pre-colonial state of boundaries in his *Siam Mapped: A History of the Geo-Body of a Nation*: 'The boundary of a sovereign nation . . . could be defined without the agreement or ratification of another country. The boundary of a kingdom was of this kind, so it was not necessary to be joined to another – leaving the corridor border outside the boundaries belonging to neither . . . the sovereignty of . . . two kingdoms was normally set apart without interface.'[52] Boundaries were loose and flexible, as no proper maps even existed before the colonial powers felt a need to carve up and divide territories to avoid overlapping economic interests, usually between different colonial powers.

The north-eastern frontier of British India was never clearly defined until the 1913–14 Shimla conference. The area that became NEFA and later Arunachal Pradesh was populated by dozens of different tribal peoples who traded with Tibet and, more easily because of geographic conditions, the plains of Assam. Tibetan authorities collected tax in Tawang and a few other places in the high mountains, but never really ruled these. The British acquired Assam and neighbouring areas from the king of Burma through the 1826 Treaty of Yandabo but they also knew that the tribes of the north-eastern frontier were 'unruly savages' whom the Ahom kings had never managed to subjugate.[53] But soon after the conquest of Assam, the British felt a need to secure control over the northern mountains as well, and led several military expeditions into the area. Gradually, the Miris, the Apatanis, the Mishmis, the Adis, the Akas, the Tagins and other tribes came into contact with the British as well as Indians from the Brahmaputra plain. There were several wars with the tribes, who never had been ruled by any outside power. In the early twentieth century, the Chinese made a few attempts to penetrate the area, which prompted the British to convene a conference to establish, for the first time, a clearly defined north-eastern boundary. In 1910, China had tried to invade Tibet, so it was obviously a matter that required more serious attention than the previously relaxed attitude to the question of where the border actually was, or should be.

When representatives of British India, Tibet and the new republican Government of China met at Shimla on 6 October 1913, no consensus could be reached between the three powers. With China's refusal to accept the proposed McMahon Line – and its demand that Tibet should be recognized as an integral part of

China – there was little more to discuss. But the crest of the Himalayas became the de facto border, even if colonial maps could be somewhat ambiguous on that point.

As the Tibet issue had its cabal of pro-Chinese Western supporters, so did the Sino-Indian border dispute. Alastair Lamb, an Australian academic, and British journalist Neville Maxwell both have published books arguing for the Chinese claim. They base their findings mainly on the fact that some British maps placed the border at the foothills of the Himalayas, and that the text of the Shimla Convention of 27 April 1914 was not included in *Aitchison's Treaties*, a 1929 official publication. Lamb's scholarship is detailed, well researched and comprehensive, while it is not difficult to detect a clear anti-Indian bias in Maxwell's *India's China War*.[54]

Also in the 1960s, Maxwell went on to write a report for Minority Rights Group about the Nagas.[55] But Maxwell lost much of his credibility when he in the late 1960s wrote a series of articles for his newspaper, *The Times* of London, on 'India's Disintegrating Democracy'. He said, 'The great experiment of developing India within a democratic framework has failed. [Indians will soon vote] in the fourth – and surely last – general election.' Maxwell predicted that India would soon be ruled by the army. A commentary in *The Guardian* ridiculed those assertions Maxwell made before the 1967 election by mentioning how 'the Delhi correspondent of a British newspaper whose thundering misjudgements in foreign affairs have become a byword has expressed the view that Indian democracy is disintegrating', adding: 'My own view after three weeks travelling round the country and talking to all and sundry, is that Indian democracy is now for the first time coming fully alive.'[56]

As for the boundary question, India produced Chinese maps, which actually placed the border more or less along the McMahon Line.[57] The fact of the matter is that China had too many internal problems to deal with during the civil wars of the 1920s and 1930s to be bothered about a remote border in a remote corner of Tibet which it did not control. Only after the communist victory in 1949 and the invasion of Tibet in 1950 did it become an issue. And India, independent in 1947, also began to be more conscious about border demarcation. Two entirely different personalities are closely associated with that demarcation, and the emergence of NEFA: Verrier Elwin and Nari Rustomji. Elwin, a British missionary who had married a tribal woman from a village near Jabalpur in today's Madhya Pradesh, converted to Hinduism in 1935 and became an Indian citizen after independence. Rustomji, an Indian Parsi, was a product of the Indian Civil Service, who later became prime minister of Sikkim, adviser to the king of Bhutan and for ten years served as chief executive in the administration of the tribal areas of India's north-eastern frontier.

The mapping of NEFA, however, was done by Elwin who gave advice to his close friend, Prime Minister Nehru. It was first formed in 1951 and then reorganized in 1954. Elwin wrote in his autobiography: 'In NEFA I had to survey a vast tract of mountainous territory . . . and help to look after thirty or forty tribal groups. What I did, therefore, was to go out on tour for periods varying from three to six or seven weeks far into the interior, collect what sociological facts were possible, write reports on the general condition of the tribes and make suggestions to the Administration.'[58] Because of his efforts and unique knowledge of the area, he was appointed as tribal consultant to the NEFA administration in November 1953 with his headquarters at the then Assam capital, Shillong. In 1958, Elwin's book *A Philosophy for NEFA* was published with a foreword written by Nehru.[59]

Rustomji also travelled the length and breadth of NEFA: 'It was a time when, whether we liked it or not, we had no alternative but to walk to get from one place to another, as the hill tracks were not yet fit for even ponies or mules to negotiate. There were often stretches of the journey during which we had to get on all fours to make any progress.'[60] There could not have been many Indian civil servants who were forced to endure such unusual working conditions, but Rustomji did. After China's invasion of Tibet he felt a need for 'a heavier physical presence of the bureaucracy and of the engines of law and order in the very centre of the hills, and not merely at their extreme southern periphery as in the past.'[61]

With the help of Elwin and Rustomji, NEFA began to take shape as a functioning administrative entity, but it was the 1962 war that laid the foundations for what was to become Arunachal Pradesh. More aid from Delhi was poured into NEFA, new roads were built, political parties were formed and educational standards improved. In 1972, the Union territory was established, and, in February 1987, it became a state within the Indian Union. Arunachal is huge – 83,000 square kilometres, or bigger than Assam – but sparsely populated with only 1.3 million people. The name Arunachal Pradesh means 'Land of the Dawn' in Sanskrit – but the Chinese continue to refer to it as 'southern Tibet'. China protested both when its status was elevated to that of a Union territory and, more vigorously, when it gained statehood.

As late as in October 2009, China expressed strong dissatisfaction over a visit to the state by Prime Minister Manmohan Singh. 'We demand the Indian side address China's serious concerns and not trigger disturbance in the disputed region so as to facilitate the healthy development of China–India relations,' said Chinese government spokesman Ma Zhaoxu in a statement posted on the foreign ministry's website. 'China is strongly dissatisfied with the visit to the disputed region by the Indian leader disregarding China's serious concerns.'[62] Takam Sanjay, an Indian MP, who, unlike Ma's government, was democratically elected, responded: 'It is simply blasphemous on the part of China to oppose or express dissatisfaction over the visit of our prime minister to Arunachal Pradesh.'[63]

Arunachal Pradesh is very much a product of the Great Game in the east and it differs from other tribal states in the north-east in that it is populated by an abundance of different tribes who, furthermore, were never converted to Christianity, unlike, for instance, in Nagaland and Mizoram. There were no Christian missionaries who introduced a written language, a common creed and the sense of nationhood that often follows such an awakening. Apart from two French missionaries who tried to enter the area in the nineteenth century and were killed by the chief of a Mishmi tribe, no further attempts to convert the people there were made.

Substantial aid from the centre in New Delhi and a heavy military presence because of the proximity to China are other factors contributing to the absence of any tribal unrest in the state. Consequently, there has never been any ethnic insurgency in Arunachal Pradesh for the Chinese to take advantage of – unlike in Mizoram, Manipur, Assam and, especially, Nagaland.

CHAPTER TWO

THE NAGAS: CHALLENGING THE IDEA OF INDIA

Immediately after the arrival of the Naga contingent on the Chinese border in January 1967, the local border guards at Pangwa Pass had to confirm the credentials of Thinoselie Keyho and Thuingaleng Muivah with higher authorities in Kunming and probably also Beijing. But once that had been done, the Nagas were given red-carpet treatment. Including the two leaders, 132 Naga rebels had reached China, and a training camp was established for them at Tengchong not far from the Burmese border in western Yunnan. They received daily instructions in the use of Chinese weapons and were well looked after. Political lectures were also held, but most Nagas stuck to their Bibles. While Tibetan monasteries were being desecrated, ransacked and destroyed by hordes of Red Guards, and Buddhist monks forcibly disrobed and sent to do hard labour in the fields, the Chinese authorities let the Nagas practise their Christianity without interference. Christian hymns could be heard every Sunday morning from the simple, wooden church that had been built in the camp in Tengchong. The anti-religious fervour that swept across China during the Cultural Revolution did not affect the Nagas. The Chinese authorities did everything to please their new allies; their potential usefulness in the strategic conflict with India was seen as more important than any ideologically motivated notions.

Thinoselie and Muivah were soon taken to Baoshan, the nearest town with an airport, and flown to Kunming, the provincial capital of Yunnan. It was the peak of the Cultural Revolution, and Muivah remembers hearing gunfire, including artillery explosions, at night even in the city as hot-headed Red Guards were engaged in pitched battles with supposed 'counter-revolutionaries'. One morning, the two Nagas woke up to find all the windows in the guest house they were staying in shattered. 'Are you afraid?' one of the Chinese officers asked Muivah. 'No,' the young Naga replied curtly. He was probably more excited than scared; after all, he was a dedicated revolutionary, already familiar with the works of Karl Marx, Lenin and Mao Zedong, which he had read while still a student at St Anthony's College in Shillong.[1]

From Kunming, the two Naga leaders travelled to Beijing, where high-ranking foreign ministry officials met them at the airport. Meetings were held with other Chinese dignitaries and Muivah told them boldly: 'We have our rights too, even if we used to be half-naked savages. Tell us if we have the right to fight against India. If we don't, we can stop. Right now.' One of the courteous Chinese hosts replied: 'Continue your fight. We'll support you to the end. Our help is selfless and there are no strings attached.'[2] The Chinese gave the Nagas strong support, Muivah remembers: 'They were not like the Pakistanis, who had a domineering attitude. We felt even culturally much closer to the Chinese than the Pakistanis.'[3]

Muivah and Thinoselie were taken to see the Great Wall just north of Beijing, to Shanghai, Nanjing, Guangzhou, and to Yan'an, the revolutionary base of the Chinese communists during the civil war in the 1930s and 1940s against the Chiang Kai-shek's Guomindang regime. They participated in mass meetings in Beijing's Tiananmen Square among hundreds of thousands of Red Guards waving Mao's Little Red Book. They cheered as the chairman himself and Premier Zhou Enlai appeared on the balcony overlooking the square, waving to the crowds.[4] But the political situation in China at the time was extremely volatile, and it was sometimes hard to say who was in charge and of what. One of the highest-ranking Chinese military officers to receive Thinoselie and Muivah when they had first arrived in Beijing was Chen Yi, a famous marshal of the People's Liberation Army.[5] But later that same year, he was purged along with numerous other communist veterans, although not officially dismissed. It was only in 1971 that Chen Yi was rehabilitated, although not restored to his former position of power. In 1967, before he became one of many victims of the Red Guards, he was vice premier, foreign minister and president of the China Foreign Affairs University.

In November 1967, Thinoselie left China with the Naga guerrillas who had been trained at Tengchong. They reached Nagaland two months later, after an arduous trek through northern Burma. But even before he had arrived home, word had reached the Naga rebels that he and Muivah had been well received in China. In December 1967, another group of more than 300 men, led by the commander-in-chief of the Naga rebel army, Gen. Mowu Gwizan, and Isak Chishi Swu from the movement's political wing, the Naga National Council set off for China. Like Thinoselie and Muivah before them, they were also received with open arms and the troops were given military training at the camp in Tengchong, while Mowu and Isak were taken on a tour of 'historical and revolutionary sites' in China.[6]

The early treks to China took place when the Naga rebels and the Indian government actually had a ceasefire agreement, which had been negotiated in 1964 by a peace mission consisting of B.P. Chaliha, chief minister of Assam, social activist Jayaprakash Narayan and the Rev. Michael Scott, a British clergyman who had taken an interest in the Naga cause. But when the Nagas returned from China, equipped with modern Chinese weapons, the peace was shattered, and fierce battles erupted between the guerrillas and Indian government forces. In June 1968, the Indian Army encountered more than a hundred heavily armed Naga rebels near the village of Jotsoma, not so far from the state capital Kohima. More than a thousand Indian troops were thrown in, and casualties were heavy on both sides as the Nagas fired their newly acquired Chinese machine guns and rocket launchers. A month later, the Indian authorities decided that there was no point in maintaining the ceasefire, and the Naga war flared anew.

Chinese weapons were recovered at the Jotsoma battlefield, and New Delhi warned the Chinese that it would not 'tolerate interference of any kind in India's internal affairs.'[7] A lengthy protest note was handed over to the chargé d'affaires at the Chinese embassy in New Delhi in the morning of 19 June 1968. There was no response from the Chinese side, which continued to support the Naga rebels, and soon the Mizos and other ethnic rebels from north-eastern India were also to trek to China to get military aid and training.

Muivah, the youngest of the Naga leaders, remained in Beijing for more than three years as the unofficial representative of the NNC, first staying at the fabled Beijing Hotel near Tiananmen Square — which was originally built in 1900 and then proclaimed as 'the only deluxe hotel in the Far East' — and later at a special accommodation for PLA officers. In a country where press freedom was non-existent, he had privileged access to foreign publications. He regularly received copies of the *Far Eastern Economic Review*, the *Asian Survey* and the *Bulletin of Concerned Asian Scholars*. He travelled quite freely around China and was refused permission to visit only one part of the country: Tibet. However, he denies that he ever went to Hanoi, as reported in some parts of the Indian media.[8] But he and Thinoselie did travel by air from Beijing to Dhaka, East Pakistan and back again shortly after their arrival in China in 1967.[9] Contacts had to be cemented with the Naga rebels who had sought sanctuary in that country, because Thinoselie was going to return through Burma with all his men later that year.

When Mowu and Isak arrived in Beijing, Muivah met them there and enthusiastically told them about the gains of the Chinese revolution. Deeply impressed by China, he became a dedicated Maoist. But he could not give up his Christian beliefs; that would have antagonized most other Nagas, who remained deeply religious. The outcome was the curious blend of revolutionary socialism and evangelical Christianity, which became the hallmark of the National Socialist Council of Nagaland, NSCN, the group that he formed when he broke away from the NNC in January 1980. The quaintly jumbled manifesto of the new Naga organization, which was written by Muivah, quoted Mao Zedong emphasizing the importance of a revolutionary organization having correct policies, and went on to praise 'the Christian God, the Eternal God of the Universe' and say that 'to us the sovereign existence of our country, the salvation of our people in socialism with their spiritual salvation in Christ are eternal and unquestionable . . . we stand for socialism . . . we stand for the faith in God and the salvation of mankind in Jesus, the Christ, that is Nagaland for Christ.' The NSCN's manifesto also rejected the idea of a multiparty system, paraphrasing Maoist jargon: 'To achieve socialism, the dictatorship of the people through a revolutionary organisation is absolutely indispensible.' That organization was, of course, the NSCN, which promised to liberate the Nagas from 'the exploiting class . . . of reactionary traitors, the bureaucrats, a handful of rich men and the Indian vermin.'[10]

Muivah may have spent his politically formidable years in China during the Cultural Revolution, but the Chinese did not initiate the Naga rebellion, and played no part in it until the late 1960s. Like in the case of Western powers' support for the Tibetan resistance, they simply took advantage of an already existing ethnic conflict to gain and strengthen a fifth column inside a strategic adversary. The Nagas unwittingly became pawns in a much bigger game than their own struggle against India, which began in the late 1940s and escalated into a civil war in the 1950s.

According to a recent interview with Muivah, the Nagas were once a nation that was 'first divided by the British, then by India . . . were the Naga people asked when they divided our land between Manipur, Assam and Arunachal Pradesh?'[11] Therefore, all those Naga-inhabited areas have been united with the present state of Nagaland – and the Naga Hills of Burma – to form a united, independent nation called 'Nagalim'.

Historical realities, however, are not that simple. The people who are collectively known as Nagas speak numerous mutually unintelligible languages, and the origin of the various tribes is as obscure as the name of their nation. There are no written records of the Nagas' early history, and even their own folklore and oral traditions are erratic and often contradictory. Verrier Elwin, who in the 1950s was Jawaharlal Nehru's adviser for tribal affairs and has written extensively about the Nagas, recounts an early legend according to which God, in the beginning of time, gave men skins of deer to write their history on. But the hillmen, 'hungry and omnivorous, cooked and ate their writing material, with the result that they were unable to leave any records of their past'.[12] The story of 'the lost book', or records that have been lost in other ways, is common among many hill peoples in the South-east Asian region and is most probably the result of an inferiority complex that comes from a feeling amongst them that the people on the plains have books, so they must once have had such scriptures too. If they had existed, or if some animal ate the material on which they were written, or were going to be written, the people would not have lost their ability to write and replace whatever had been lost.

The only reasonably secure lead to the origin of the Nagas has been given by Visier Sanyu, a Naga historian of the Chakhesang tribe. According to oral history that he has collected, a man called Koza came from 'the east', and arrived along with a herd of *mithun*s –

a wild ox that is the Nagas' most prestigious animal and a symbol of wealth and power – at a place called Khezhakenoma in an area inhabited by a tribe now called the Chakhesang. He was blessed with many children, and that was the origin of the Nagas. He decided to settle down in Khezhakenoma. The settlement had a sacred stone which became a symbol of the origin of the Naga tribes, and Koza's sons began the practice of spreading rice on it to ensure good harvests – which, of course, was essential for the survival of his newly established community.[13] One day, however, Koza's sons began to quarrel over whose turn it was to spread rice on the stone. Koza's wife realized that the stone could become a bone of contention between her sons. She lit a fire under the stone and it exploded with a thundering sound. The power of the stone left it and went to Heaven, and the Nagas were scattered all over the eastern mountains.

This legend is not accepted by all Naga tribes, but a consensus has emerged that the Nagas must have migrated from the east into the highlands that today form the border between India and Burma. Those hills were rich in forest, fruit and wild animals, which must have attracted the first settlers to the area. Hunting appears to have played an important role in early Naga communities. It was also often associated with warfare, reflecting rivalries and competition between different villages. In the Angami Naga language, 'hunting' and 'war' are even synonymous: *chu-terhu*, literally 'hunting-war'.[14] The various Naga tribes, who in the early days were not really tribes but groups of villages, were constantly at war with each other – and with the politically and socially more advanced people of the Brahmaputra plain.

Today's Assam was in ancient times a kingdom, founded by the Ahoms, a Tai- or Shan-speaking people who migrated from upper Burma in the thirteenth century. The first Ahom prince, Seu Kan Hpa (Sukapha in modern Assamese) crossed the Patkai range, say the chronicles, with a following of 'eight nobles, 9,000 men, women and children, and two elephants and 300 horses'.[15] As all Tai peoples before them had done, they decided to settle in the most fertile river valley they could find. They cultivated the Brahmaputra Valley, established towns and villages, and founded a civilization that lasted for several hundred years.

While some Naga villages in the eastern hills appear to have owed allegiance to the Ahom throne, others raided the settlements on the plains – in search of heads. Most Nagas were headhunters, as it was believed that good harvests would follow if the blood of an enemy could be sprinkled over their fields. But, as Naga historian Asoso Yonuo states, there were also other reasons for taking heads: No one would be entitled for marriage, or a seat in the village council, if he had not chopped off an enemy head. British historian L.W. Shakespear wrote at the turn of the last century: 'All Nagas are headhunters, their women being the chief incentive to this pursuit, as girls will not look on men with favour who have not taken heads or been in raids.'[16] The preserving of severed heads of men killed in warfare was also proof of success over the enemies. Yonuo describes how this was done:

> First of all, all the able-bodied and strong warriors assemble together and decide on the enemy villages to be attacked and also whether the attack will be by surprise or by an open challenge. Appointed to command the party, the chief consults, before starting the sojourn for war, the usual omens in accordance with established custom and if proving propitious, a fowl is killed and cooked and all partake of it. Then they provide themselves with their usual war weapons – spear or javelin, *dao* (dagger), shield, occasionally a crossbow and arrows of pointed bamboo, sometimes poisoned with vegetable extract or venomous snakes. At times, they put on war dress, which consists of a number of odd contrivances to give them a fierce appearance. They carry food for about two days, which is wrapped in leaves . . . and set out for the village to be sallied out. If no straggling men can be intercepted when they lie in

ambush on vantage-ground, from dusk till dawn, they advance . . .
towards the village, set the houses on fire if it remains undefended,
kill men, women and children with utmost ferocity . . . (cut) their
heads, roll them in cloth and carry them home as trophies of their
victory . . . In some cases they keep the skulls in their houses for
five days, during which the warriors do not eat food cooked by
women. They cook themselves . . . and shall not have sexual
intercourse with their wives. The heads are kept or buried followed
by a great feast of pork and beef with rice beer.[17]

Heads could also be taken in more regular warfare between the
inhabitants of different groups of villages who were engaged in
traditional tribal disputes over land or women or both. The warriors
would then tear off the heads of dead enemies and bring those back
to their villages. Warriors who had taken such heads were entitled
to wear a collar round their necks, dyed in red and interlaced with
the long, flowing hair of the enemies they had killed. This was
considered, as Yonuo describes it, 'an insignia of honour'.

Generally, warring parties did not take prisoners of war, but
sometimes enemies who had been captured alive were brought
back as slaves. Slavery was common in the Naga Hills until the
British annexation in the late nineteenth century, and slaves could
also be thieves or people who had been unable to repay their debts
to a richer man. The people of the Ao Naga area especially were
great slave traders. Children were often kidnapped and sold, and so
were women who were kept as servants in larger households.
According to Naga historian Mashangthei Horam: 'A man was
considered really well-to-do if he possessed slaves, and each slave
added to his master's social prestige. When such a man died it was
customary for the Ao to put up symbols on his grave showing that
he had possessed slaves in his lifetime. For each slave owned a
symbol was erected.'[18]

In such a hostile environment, it is only natural that people
grouped together in large, fortified villages rather than risking their

lives in small, undefended settlements. All villages were surrounded by high stockades and their gates permanently guarded, and they were located on hilltops, from where approaching enemies could be easily spotted. Consequently, there was little or no interaction between the different village clusters, and each cluster retained its own language with virtually no outside influences. Large villages were divided into *khel*s, or sections, and people's loyalties and sense of belonging lay with the family, the khel, the clan and the village cluster. Thus, 'tribes' in a broader sense did not exist before the late nineteenth century when the British colonialists and American missionaries introduced new administrative structures and social values.

The arrival of Christianity in the Naga Hills, then one of the remotest and least accessible corners of the Indian subcontinent, has its roots, unlikely as it may sound, 200 years ago in Salem, Massachusetts. In 1810, the state's Congregationalists and Presbyterians succeeded in setting up the first American missionary society. There had been American missionaries before, but they had been attached to British religious orders. Now, the Christians of Massachusetts decided that with America having been independent for more than thirty years, the time was ripe for the new country to appoint its own missionaries and send them abroad. On 6 February 1821, the American Board of Commissioners for Foreign Missions called their followers to a historic service in the huge, barn-like Tabernacle Church in Salem.

It was one of the coldest days of the year, but upward of 2,000 people plodded and rode through the snow to attend America's first ordination of missionaries. Six members of the congregation were set aside 'for the sake of Christ and the promotion of His Kingdom in some Asiatic field.'[19] It was a tumultuous meeting and people were ecstatic. Many admired the missionaries and their determination. They were all young and included some women as well. One of them was only seventeen.

More than six thousand dollars – a huge sum then – was collected to support the undertaking. Members also donated food, including cartloads of New England gingerbread, for the missionaries to eat during their voyage to 'some Asiatic field' and to share with the 'heathens' they were going to encounter and convert. On 19 February, their ship, the *Caravan*, sailed from Salem harbour. The missionaries on board watched the snowy, rocky New England coast disappear behind them as they sailed around Cape Cod.

In mid-June, 'after nothing but sky and water for one hundred and fourteen days,' as a missionary on board wrote, they reached India. In Calcutta, they became guests of the British Baptists who persuaded them that Baptism ought to be only by immersion. The Americans gave up their Congregationalist allegiance, and were immersed in the baptistry of Kolkata's Lal Bazar Chapel on 6 September 1812. But political events across the oceans had unexpected consequences for the first American Baptist missionaries in India. In the same year, a war had broken out between Britain and its former American colonies. The British authorities in Kolkata now ordered the American missionaries either to return to America or face deportation to Britain. They had to leave India, and one couple – the Judsons – found a Portuguese ship sailing for Rangoon, then not yet a British colony. They ended up with the Karens, a tribal people in south-eastern Burma, who rapidly took to Christianity.

When the war was over, the Baptists in America had decided to sponsor the Judsons as their first missionary couple in Asia. The success of the Judsons encouraged the American Baptists to send more missionaries to this new 'Asiatic field'. The British attitude towards Americans also softened somewhat after the war, and in 1836, Captain Francis Jenkins, the commissioner and agent to the Governor General of Bengal in Assam, invited two American Baptist missionary couples from Burma to come to Sadiya in Upper Assam.

Ten years before, the British had fought a war with the Burmese king, who had been forced to cede the Tenasserim area in south-eastern Burma, where the Judsons were active, and Arakan, a coastal region bordering Bengal. The Burmese Army had also been forced out of Assam, which they had conquered after subduing the last Ahom king during 1816–19. All these territiories – Tenasserim, Arakan and Assam – became British under the terms of a treaty signed in 1826. But the Burmese hold over Assam and the smaller states of Manipur, Jaintia and Cachar had never been more than formal, amounting to mere military occupation without any functioning local administration. Assam had to be conquered anew by the British, who moved into the vast, green and fertile plain of the Brahmaputra Valley.

The valley was surrounded by rugged massifs inhabited by an abundance of Nagas and other fierce hill peoples, and the British plan was to subdue them as well in order to find a route to China from India via Assam. This also meant that they would have to expand their Burmese conquests from some coastal regions to the heart of the Burmese kingdom: the area surrounding the ancient capital of Mandalay in the north. Captain Jenkins evidently thought that a missionary presence in the hills east of Assam would make it easier for him (and the British) to implement this grand colonial scheme. Jenkins had found the Hkamtis, a Buddhist, Tai-speaking people who lived in Sadiya not only a 'nuisance', but 'treacherous and tricky demon-worshippers' as well. He thought, 'the only thing that will make them better is Christianity.'[20]

The two American Baptist missionary couples who came to Sadiya in May 1836 were Nathan Brown and Oliver Cutter with their respective wives. A year later, they were joined by Mr and Mrs Miles Bronson, and Jacob Thomas. Life was not easy in their remote outpost on the eastern fringes of the Assam plain. The Hkamtis attacked Sadiya in 1838, forcing them to flee to Jaipur just below the Naga Hills, where the British had established a garrison. By then, Jacob Thomas had already drowned in a river near Sadiya, and the Browns had lost one of their daughters, Sophia. But all these tragedies had not diminished their missionary zeal. They turned their attention to the Nagas, of whom the missionaries knew little more than that they were a wild people who frequently raided towns and villages on the plains, and which had prompted the British to send military expeditions into the hills to 'pacify' them.

The British had first encountered the Nagas after they had annexed the Cachar Hills in 1832. In the same year, Captains Jenkins and Pemberton, with a party of 700 soldiers and 800 coolies, or porters, had marched to Assam from the princely state of Manipur, which was also attracting the attention of the British. A.J. Moffatt Mills wrote in his *Report on the Province of Assam*:

The route pursued via Saengmae, Myung Khang, Mooram Khoohoo, Mohee Long, Yang, Papoolongmaie, Tiriamah, Sumooguding, Dhunseree river, Mohong Dejoa and Ramsah, which latter place they reached about the 23rd of January 1832. The whole party suffered much from the want of provisions, and in consequence were obliged latterly to march all day through a heavy dark forest until they arrived at Dejoa, where their wants were supplied. The party was opposed in its progress from Yang to Papoolongmaie by the Angami Nagas, and having no idea of the effect of firearms, their opposition was most determined. They rolled down stones from the summit of the hills, threw spears and did their utmost by yelling and intimidation to obstruct the advance of the force, but all in vain, the village of Papoolongmaie, consisting of 300 to 400 houses was occupied by the troops, and a constant firing of musketry was necessary to keep the Angami Nagas at a distance. A stockade was taken at the point of the bayonet. The village was burnt, some lives were lost and many wounded; cunning, treacherous, vindictive and warlike, the Angami Nagas had hitherto never encountered a foe equal to contend with them, and in utter ignorance of the effect of fire-arms, they vainly imagined no party could penetrate through their territory; luckily the force was well supplied with ammunition and overcame all opposition.[21]

From this very first encounter with the Nagas, the British realized that more force would be needed to secure the supply routes between their new conquests on the eastern fringes of the Indian subcontinent. But the missionaries, strangely enough, found the Nagas friendlier than other peoples they had met in eastern Assam. They could also communicate with some of them in broken Assamese. The old Tai-Ahom tongue had died out over the centuries, and a new, Indo-European and Sanskrit-based language had replaced it, which was not too difficult for the foreigners to learn. The Nagas living on the foothills closest to the Brahmaputra Valley, who traded with the plains people, had also picked up some rudimentary Assamese. More importantly, they discovered that Nagas were not Hindus, but worshipped in a rather rough and primitive manner a number of stone and animal spirits. The missionaries already knew how hard it was to convert the hopeless Hindus, who readily accepted the Christian God and Jesus by adding them to their own pantheon without changing their traditional beliefs.

On 10 May 1838, the Rev. Nathan Brown sent a letter to the Home Board in America, requesting support for a mission to the Nagas. Two years later, yet another American missionary couple arrived in eastern Assam: Cyrus Barker and his wife, who the Board had appointed for work among the Nagas. But it was not until the 1870s that missionary work in the eastern hills began in earnest with the conversion of Subongmeren, an Ao Naga from the village of Dekahaimong, who had come in contact with Godhula Rufus Brown, an Assamese evangelist. In 1871, Subongmeren was baptized at Sibsagar in Assam by Dr Edward Winter Clark, and then left for the hills with Godhula, and after some initial difficulties, more Nagas accepted the new faith.[22]

But who, actually, were the Nagas? Who was a Naga and why? No one is even certain of the meaning of the word 'Naga'. J.H. Hutton, an early British authority on the Nagas, originally thought it was a corruption of the Assamese word 'noga', probably meaning 'mountaineer' and derived from the Sanskrit 'naga', mountain or inaccessible place. Later, Hutton recanted this opinion and concluded that it came from the Sanskrit word 'nagna', or 'nangta' in Bengali, which means naked. That the Nagas were scantily clad was true, but why would they alone be singled out for their nakedness when the same degree of nudity existed among many other tribes in the area in ancient times?

Some scholars are of the opinion that the name comes from 'naga', snake in Sanskrit. But the Nagas never worshipped snakes. So, Verrier Elwin, another old-time British Naga expert, suggested that 'the name was more probably given to them originally as being best expressive of their character, for of all wild tribes they are held to be the most subtle and treacherous.'[23] Yet other writers subscribe to the theory that 'Naga' is a corruption of 'nog', which simply means people in some of the eastern Naga dialects. The people of Cachar in Assam, on their part, assert that the hill dwellers are 'nanngra', or fierce warriors. The Assamese pronounce that word 'nawga', which the British, according to this version of history, corrupted to Naga. The Burmese believe that the name comes from 'naka', or people with pierced ears, as both Naga men and women do wear big earrings.

All that can be stated with certainty is that the name must be of foreign origin, as the Nagas at the time of the arrival of the British colonial power and the American missionaries did not have a common name for themselves in any of their many own languages. Even tribal designations such as Angami, Ao, Sema, Rengma, Lotha, Konyak and Tangkhul came with the introduction of Christianity in the late nineteenth and early twentieth century. As people in one village cluster would speak a language very distinct from that in another village cluster, even if it were only a few kilometres away, the task of translating the Bible became a formidable task. It could not be translated into hundreds of different languages; so the missionaries chose the dialect from the main village in a particular area, and put it into Roman script.

As a result of the activities of the missionaries, a more limited number of local lingua francas emerged, and village clusters were united into what eventually became tribes. The missionaries in the Naga Hills were as remarkably successful in converting the newly created Naga tribes into Christianity as they had been among Burma's tribal communities. By the beginning of the twentieth century, more than a thousand Nagas had adopted the new religion introduced by the Americans. Headhunting passed into history, and, as Verrier Elwin noted in his brief history of Nagaland: 'There was a little trouble among the Semas and there was a serious inter-village feud in the Ao area, but from 1892 onwards, it was only found necessary to dispatch one regular punitive expedition in the course of fifteen years . . . inter-village raids came to an end and the Nagas settled down to a peaceful life of cultivation and trade.'[24]

From the humble beginning of dedicated missionaries like the Thomases and the Barkers and the Assamese evangelist Godhula, grew one of the most vibrant and robust Christian congregations in South Asia. In 1913–14, the Baptist Mission was running fourteen schools, which increased to nearly a hundred in the early 1930s. Thousands of Nagas had been converted, and not only Bibles but also hymn books, dictionaries, grammars and primers appeared in the tribals' own languages and a national consciousness emerged as a result of this unique cultural and tribal awakening. With a different language and script, and a new awareness of their own identity, the gap between the people in the hills and in the plains also widened. This process was accelerated by the undeniable fact that long-standing frictions existed between the previously isolated tribals and the more sophisticated cultures in the plains. Some interaction existed, though, as shown by the fact that a kind of pidgin Assamese emerged as the lingua franca among the Naga tribes that otherwise could not communicate with each other. Called Nagamese, its very existence shows that the Nagas did have trading relations with the people of the plains. Since Assamese is an Indo-European language like Bengali and Hindi, Nagamese would fall into that category as well. Ironically, the various Naga tribes, whose many languages and dialects were of Tibeto-Burman origin and thus very different from those spoken in the plains, ended up having an Indian language, albeit in a broken form, as their main common tongue.

The hill peoples no doubt depended on the plains for essentials such as salt, cloth, gunpowder and tools other than their own *dao*s (or daggers in the Kachin language; transliterated as *dah*s in English). But no plains people settled in the hills, and very few Nagas stayed in the plains longer than it took to buy or barter goods they could not get in the hills. The tribals became even more separated from the plains people through a number of administrative reforms that were implemented when India was under British rule. In 1881, decisive British conquests had led to the formation of a Naga Hills district which, under the 1919 Government of India Act, continued to be part of the province of Assam that had been carved out of East Bengal in 1912.

In 1921, the Naga Hills district was designated a 'Backward Tract', placing it under the direct rule of the governor of Assam. Following an order issued as early as in 1873, plains people were also required to obtain 'Inner Line Permits' before entering the Naga Hills. According to Elwin: 'It was . . . a twofold attempt to protect both the tribal people and the settlers in the plains. On the one hand it prevented encroachment on tribal land; on the other, by checking irritations that might incite the tribesmen to rebellion and raids, it protected the tea planters and their labour [in Assam].'[25] More importantly perhaps, this arrangement suited the British colonial power as it facilitated their control over Assam as well as its Naga Hills district.

But the term 'Backward Tract' was seen as derogatory, especially since parts of the Naga Hills were developing quite rapidly. The Simon Commission, named after its chairman, Sir John Simon, and consisting of seven British MPs who were designated to study constitutional reform in India, even found it 'nauseating'.[26] So under the new Government of India Act of 1935, the term was changed to 'Excluded Area'. These semantics were to cause a lot of misunderstanding among the Nagas and other tribals. I have met numerous Nagas who have told me that the Naga Hills were not part of India because these were an 'Excluded Area'. I have heard the same argument from some Mizos, because their homeland, called the Lushai Hills during the British time, was then also an 'Excluded Area'. But 'excluded' simply meant that they were, as Elwin put it, 'excluded from the competence of the Provincial and Federal Legislatures' – not that they were no longer part of India.[27] It was just a new name, not a change of status. The 'excluded areas' were ruled directly by the governor of Assam, which, in turn, has led some to believe that the hill areas constituted some kind of British 'Crown Colony' – again, supposedly, separate from India.

Those myths have been perpetuated by tribal nationalists for decades, but there is no doubt that the Naga Hills as well as the Lushai Hills – and other areas such as the Chittagong Hill Tracts in today's Bangladesh, and the non-Burman, ethnic parts of Burma, which were also 'Excluded Areas' – belonged to Britain's Indian Empire. The only separation occurred in 1937, when Burma became a colony in its own right – with its 'Excluded Areas' still intact. 'Excluded Areas' in Assam at the time included the Balipara Frontier Tract, the Sadiya Frontier Tract, the Cachar subdivision of the Cachar district, and then three 'Partially Excluded Areas': the Khasi and Jaintia Hills and the Garo Hills in today's Meghalaya, and the Mikir Hills adjoining the northern corner of the Khasi and Jaintia Hills.[28]

During its heyday in the 1920s and 1930s, Britain's mighty colonial creation in South Asia stretched from the Khyber Pass on the Afghan frontier to the Three Pagodas Pass on the border with the independent kingdom of Siam, now Thailand. British India was a patchwork of directly administered colonies, princely states,

Assigned Tracts, Excluded Areas, Partially Excluded Areas, and territories that were even designated as 'unadministered', such as the eastern Naga Hills, the Triangle area in the Kachin Hills and the Wa Hills, all in northern and north-eastern Burma. The Naga Hills consisted of an 'administered area' in the south with Kohima as its headquarters, and there was also an 'unadministered area' around Tuensang to the north, over which the British claimed sovereignty, but where colonial influence was more limited.

The wild days of the 'unadministered' Tuensang area – which also included the present Mon district of Nagaland – were immortalized by the Anglo-Austrian anthropologist Christoph von Fürer-Haimendorf who, in 1936–37, spent a year among the Naga tribes on the Burmese border. Headhunting was still widespread in the Pangsha area, and the title of von Fürer-Haimendorf's classic *The Naked Nagas*, first published in London in 1939, later became a catchword to describe all Nagas.[29] That was rather unfortunate because the Nagas in the area he visited may have been almost naked, but in other parts of the Naga Hills, Christianity had helped put clothes on the tribals and caused them to adopt what the Westerner would consider stricter moral values.

By the 1920s, Impur, north of Mokokchung in the Ao Naga area, became the centre for both elementary schooling and the preaching of the gospel. The Impur dispensary was the first relatively modern clinic in the hills. Teams of converted Nagas toured the Sangtam, Konyak, Chang and Phom tribal areas to spread the new faith and to provide medical treatment in villages, which until then had had to rely on only traditional shamans and sorcerers whenever someone fell ill. Gradually, Naga preachers began to take over all aspects of missionary work from the foreigners, which made it even easier to convert still 'naked Nagas' to Christianity.

But the missionaries in the hills also encountered many serious problems. The first was to convince the Nagas to accept Christian ethics, because, as church historian P.T. Philip rather prudishly puts it, 'Animistic religion did not inspire moral behaviour whereas Christian ethics demanded certain moral standards from the people.'[30] Drinking and opium smoking had to be given up, along with sexual freedoms for the young and polygamy among older people. From time to time, the Christians also suffered persecution, intimidation and harassment from village headmen, sorcerers and others whose positions were threatened by the new teachings. Verrier Elwin was critical of the missionaries and wrote that, 'the activities of the Baptist mission among the Nagas have demoralised the people, destroyed tribal solidarity and forbidden the joys and feastings, the decorations and romance of communal life.'[31]

The relationship between the missionaries and the British colonial authorities was also not always smooth. Narola Rivenburg, the daughter of Sidney Rivenburg, a rustic farm boy from the United States who spread Christianity among the Angamis in Kohima, complains in a publication from 1941 entitled *The Star of the Naga Hills* that most of the high-ranking officers in India were the younger sons of British nobility who 'often lived with native women'.[32] This, Narola Rivenburg wrote, 'was one of the greatest obstacles which the missionary had to deal with' – presumably meaning that many British officers resented the moralistic teachings of the missionaries and therefore made life difficult for them.

The British were also more interested in using the warlike tribals as soldiers in their military forces. In 1916 and 1917, 4,000 (some say 5,000) Nagas were recruited for the Labour Corps in France. It was compulsory for every village to provide 'coolies' for the war effort in Europe, and they came from all over the Naga Hills. In the trenches on the Western Front during World War I, they discovered not only that there was a wider world beyond their hills, but also a new awareness of what it meant to be Naga. Nagas from villages and communities were grouped together, and developed a camaraderie that transcended traditional divisions along tribal and khel lines.[33]

On their return to their hills, some of the Naga war veterans decided to form an association that became known as the Naga Club. It had two branches – one in Kohima and another in Mokokchung – and consisted mainly of local government officials, *dobashi*s, or interpreters for the local administration, and some prominent chiefs from villages surrounding those towns. Social and administrative issues were discussed, and the Club also ran a cooperative store in Mokokchung and had its own football team. It was not opposed to British rule, and had in the beginning no stated political aims. But it was in the Naga Club that a new Naga nationalism was forged.[34]

The Simon Commission, whose members apart from John Simon included Clement Attlee – later a labour prime minister – and E. Cadogan, visited Kohima in 1929, and the Naga Club seized the opportunity to submit a memorandum, expressing concern over political developments in India at the time. What would happen if the British gave in to the demands of the Indian nationalist movement, which wanted independence for India?

The Naga Club stated clearly that its members were not interested in any change in the status quo as a hills district that was part of Assam, but was administered directly by the British governor. The Club also expressed fear for a possible future under the rule of the people of the plains: 'Before the British Government conquered our country in 1879-1880 we were living in a state of intermittent warfare with the Assamese of the Assam valley to the North and West of our country and Manipuris to the South. They never conquered us, nor were we subjected to their rule. On the other hand, we were always a terror to these people.' The memorandum went on to stress the fact that the Nagas belonged to several different tribes, 'quite different from one another with quite different languages which cannot be understood by each other . . . We have no unity among us and it is only the British Government that is holding us together now.'[35]

The Club urged 'that the British Government will continue to safeguard our rights against all encroachments from other people who are more advanced than us by withdrawing from the Reformed Scheme and placing it directly under its own protection. If the British Government, however, wants to throw us away, we pray that we should not be thrust to the mercy of the people who could never subjugate us, but to leave us alone to determine for ourselves as in ancient times.'[36] The letter was signed by twenty Naga elders, among them Niser, one of the first Angamis who had been converted to Christianity by Sidney Rivenburg. Others represented the Sema, the Lotha, the Rengma and even the non-Naga Kuki tribe.

The Nagas realized that they had to be better organized to meet the future. Apart from the Naga Club, the Lothas had as far back as in 1923 founded their own tribal council. An Ao Tribal Council was formed in 1928, dissolved in 1930, and reorganized in 1939. And churches continued to grow.

But not all Nagas were prepared to accept the new faith which, after all, was foreign. In the mid-1920s, a millenarian cult emerged among the Rongmei tribe, now a subgroup of the Zeliangrong in northern Manipur. (The term 'Zeliangrong' refers to the Zeme, Lingmai and Rongmei tribes combined – Naga tribes are often formed in this manner.) Its leader, Jadonang, had enlisted as an ordinary soldier and fought with the British in Mesopotamia during the War, and after his return began to preach about a god called Tengwa. His kingdom would last for a thousand years, and Jadonang himself claimed supernatural powers. If people only followed him – and obeyed *genna*, or taboo days, on the full moon of every month – sickness would vanish and there would be an abundance of food and drinks. His followers were called *khampai* and their belief *haraka*, although the exact meaning of these words is not known.[37]

Jadonang declared himself king of the Nagas, and soon thousands of tribesmen flocked around him. He kept two pet pythons in his house and performed magical tricks such as drawing water from the handle of his sword. He ordered his followers to drink the sacred water and to sacrifice mithuns to Tengwa. Jadonang's cousin, a sixteen-year-old girl called Gaidinliu became his personal priestess, and she helped spread the movement to the North Cachar Hills in Assam. But what had begun as a curious but seemingly innocent cult became far more sinister when in 1930 Jadonang had a dream in which Tengwa asked him for human sacrifice. Some of his followers ambushed four Manipuri betel-nut vendors who were on their way to the Assamese town of Silchar, cut their heads off, smashed their skulls, and distributed the bone fragments among the believers. But it would be unfair and misleading to describe the haraka cult as a purely millenarian tribal movement. It was also a genuine, spontaneous uprising against the injustices of British colonialism. Foreign occupiers had imposed restrictions on cutting bamboo, which the tribals had done for centuries, and forcibly recruited villagers for corvée labour to build roads and houses for the new masters.

The British retaliated immediately, and troops were sent to capture Jadonang and his khampais. They managed to locate and overpower Jadonang, who was sentenced to death and hanged in Imphal, Manipur's capital, on 29 August 1931. His 'temple' was dismantled and the pythons were shot – but that was not the end of the movement. Gaidinliu became its new leader, and took to the hills with a large band of followers. She told them that she did not fear the British, and that any bullet that was fired in her direction would turn into water. She managed to elude the colonial authorities for two years, until she was also captured. In 1933 she was sentenced to life imprisonment for 'insurrection against the British Government' and thus became the first Naga to be recognized by the Indian nationalist movement as a freedom fighter. Jawaharlal Nehru began to refer to her as 'Rani', lady or queen, and honoured her in one of his writings: 'What torment and suppression of spirit they have brought to her, who in the pride of her youth dared to challenge an empire! She can roam no more in the hill country through the forest glades, or sing in the fresh crisp air of the mountains. This wild young thing sits cabined in the darkness, with a few yards, maybe, of space in the daytime, eating her fiery heart in desolation and confinement. And India does not even know of this brave child of her hills, with the free spirit of the mountains in her . . . [but] a day will come when India will . . . remember and cherish her and bring her out of her prison cell.'[38] Gaidinliu was eventually released in 1946 and returned home, where she was greeted as a national hero.

But far from being part of an overall Indian struggle for independence, the haraka cult should be seen as the first serious clash between the new social and religious order in the Naga Hills and old beliefs. More turmoil and confusion were to follow after the Japanese attacked Pearl Harbour in December 1941 and World War II spread to Asia. By May 1942, Japan had occupied large parts of China, French Indochina, Malaya, Singapore, the Dutch East Indies and Burma. The Japanese were on the borders of Britain's Indian Empire, but British forces, aided by local Kachin tribesmen, were resisting the Japanese in the hills of northernmost Burma. Supplies were flown in from airbases in Assam, and over 'the Hump' – as the Naga and Kachin Hills became known – on to Chiang Kai-shek's nationalist forces in China. American troops were also concentrated at Ledo in eastern Assam, from where the Allies began the construction of a more than 1,000-kilometre-long road across northern Burma to China.

The road was the brainchild of the American commander, Gen. Joseph W. Stilwell, an abrasive general who earned the nickname 'Vinegar Joe' for his short temper. His road-building effort was one of the most ambitious projects ever undertaken in the region, adding new influences to the already bewildering scene in the Indo-Burmese border mountains. The road had to cross the wild Naga

Hills, into almost unexplored territory on the Burmese side. The labour force also was one of the most mixed in the history of road construction anywhere in the world. Lieutenant Colonel Frank Owen, a British officer in one of these teams, described the labourers:

> Chinese, Chins, Kachins, Indians, Nepalese, Nagas, Garos slashed, hauled and piled. Negroes drove machines. Black, brown, yellow and white men toiled shoulder-deep in the streams, belt-deep in red mud. In one camp, 2,000 labourers spoke 200 different dialects.[39]

It was the British Empire, with American support, that struck back against the Japanese – but they had also their plan to cut this supply route from India to Burma and China. Also in Burma then was the firebrand Indian nationalist Subhas Chandra Bose, a Bengali by birth who had escaped to Germany in 1941 to seek help for his struggle to liberate India from the British. He was not a supporter of Gandhian civil disobedience and non-violence; Bose's slogan was: 'Give me blood and I promise you freedom.'[40] With help from the Axis, he formed in July 1943 the Indian National Army, INA, which had drawn its recruits mostly from ethnic Indian soldiers from the British Army, who had been taken prisoners of war in Malaya and Singapore.

In early 1944, the commander of the Japanese Army in Burma, Lieutenant General Masakazu Kawabe, held a welcome party for Bose and his staff officers. Bose concluded his speech in his usual melodramatic and militant manner: 'My only prayer to the Almighty at this moment is that we may be given the earliest opportunity to pay for our freedom with our blood!'[41] In March, three Japanese divisions, supported by thousands of INA troops, crossed the Chindwin River in north-western Burma and attacked the Naga Hills and Manipur. Lieutenant General Renya Mutaguchi, the commander of the campaign, assembled Japanese war correspondents at his headquarters in the hill station of Maymyo in northern Burma, and declared enthusiastically:

I am firmly convinced that my three divisions will reduce Imphal in one month. In order that they can march fast, they carry the lightest possible equipment and food enough for three weeks. Ah, they will get everything from British supplies and dumps. Boys! See you again in Imphal at the celebration of the Emperor's Birthday on April 29.[42]

The Japanese–INA offensive took the British by complete surprise, but fierce resistance was organized with the help of local tribesmen. Imphal was under siege, but the Japanese failed to capture it. British war planes bombed Japanese positions, and Naga tribesmen, often armed only with their traditional weapons, ambushed the invaders. The Japanese issued a communiqué on 8 April 1944, claiming that 'Japanese troops, fighting side by side with the Indian National Army, captured Kohima early on 6 April.'[43] But Kohima had not fallen; a sixty-four-day battle was fought in and around the town, and the front line went right across its tennis court. It was there that the Japanese advance into India was halted. On 4 July, the Japanese decided to suspend the 'Imphal Operation', as it was called. The retreating troops were bombed by the Allies, and ambushed once again by the tribesmen. Of 80,000 Japanese soldiers who had taken part in the campaign, only 30,000 made it back to Burma.

The British side lost 2,484 soldiers and, when the War was over, the tennis court was turned into a war cemetery. The names of the soldiers who could be identified are engraved on bronze plates and in the front of the cemetery stands a tall stone with the moving inscription: 'When you go home tell them of us and say for your tomorrow we gave our today.' British historian C.E. Lucas Phillips did not exaggerate when he wrote: 'Kohima was to Burma what Stalingrad was to Russia and Alamein to the Desert.'[44]

The battle of Kohima proved to be not only a major turning point of the War – but also for the Nagas as a people. They had remained loyal to the British throughout the fighting, providing them with valuable intelligence. They also carried war material for the British, escorted and guided patrols, helped in the evacuation of the wounded, and harassed the Japanese in every way they could. J.H. Hutton, one-time commissioner of the Naga Hills who has written extensively about the area, wrote when the War was over:

> A Naga Government interpreter located a Japanese ammunition party of nine men and organised a band of villagers who surrounded and captured them. This is typical of the sort of assistance given. Another interpreter, hearing of an advanced Japanese patrol of 15 men, guided a British patrol to ambush and capture or destroy the party, which he assisted in doing himself. One Naga undertook a night trip behind the Japanese lines in Kohima village and its outskirts and came back with detailed information, which enabled troops to push into Kohima village and turn the whole Japanese position. Another brought back information so accurate that targets on the Japanese supply line could be pin-pointed and destroyed from the air with the greatest precision.[45]

Sir William Slim (Viscount Slim), the commander of Britain's 14th Army that eventually drove the Japanese out of Burma as well, also acknowledged the assistance rendered by the Nagas in his book *Defeat into Victory*, in which he spoke of 'the gallant Nagas whose loyalty, even in the most depressing times of the invasion, never faltered. Despite floggings, torture, execution, and the burning of their villages, they refused to aid the Japanese in any way or to betray our troops. Their active help to us was beyond value or praise ... Many a British and Indian soldier owes his life to the naked, headhunting Naga, and no soldier of the 14th Army who met them will ever think of them but with admiration and affection.'[46]

It is also evident that the Nagas themselves were proud of their achievements, and expected some recognition for their efforts during the War. Nor had they – or the British – forgotten that Bose's INA had fought on the side of the Japanese. Many amongst the Nagas and the British felt they had a common bond against the plains people, for whom both the hill peoples, and those who administered them, felt dislike. Those feelings grew even stronger after the War, when India's struggle for independence regained momentum. In April 1945, even before the war was over, the then deputy commissioner of the Naga Hills, C.R. Pawsey, had established an institution, which he called 'the Naga Hills District Tribal Council'. In February 1946, it changed its name to the Naga National Council, which emerged as the only political organization of any relevance in the hills. The actual council was composed of twenty-nine members who represented the tribes on the principle of proportional representation. But every Naga was supposed to be a member of the NNC, and every family donated money to it, ranging from a rupee to a hundred depending on how wealthy they were. The NNC also published a monthly newspaper, the *Naga Nation*, which was printed and distributed locally.

Initially, the NNC's policy was to safeguard Naga interests after India's independence, which now seemed inevitable – not separate independence for the Naga Hills, which later became its stated goal. When the British Cabinet Mission visited India in June 1946 to prepare for India's independence, the NNC submitted a four-point memorandum:

1) This Naga National Council stands for the solidarity of all Naga tribes, including those in the unadministered areas;
2) This Council strongly protests against the grouping of Assam with Bengal;
3) The Naga Hills should be constitutionally included in an autonomous Assam, in a free India, with local autonomy and due safeguards for the interests of the Nagas.
4) The Naga tribes should have a separate electorate.[47]

The second point was due to fear that Assam could be grouped together with East Bengal, which was to become the eastern part of the new nation of Pakistan, that was going to be created for India's Muslims at independence. The Nagas, obviously, had even less in common with Muslim Bengalis than with the predominantly Hindu Assamese of the plains just below the Naga Hills.

The memorandum was signed by Theyiechüthie Sakhrie, affectionally known as 'Theyieu', as the secretary of the NNC. At the same time, some British officers were actually toying with the idea of establishing some kind of 'trust territory', and even a new 'crown colony', encompassing the tribal area of India's eastern frontier and perhaps also ethnic minority areas in Burma. But this idea had few supporters among the Nagas, was opposed by the Indian National Congress and was never the official British policy. Independent India was going to comprise all former British territories in the subcontinent, except those with a Muslim majority, which would make up the new country of Pakistan.

Before long, however, the NNC was becoming increasingly radicalized, and moderates such as Sakhrie began to meet with opposition from a more militant faction led by a forty-one-year-old Naga firebrand called Angami Zapu Phizo. He was born in 1904 in Khonoma, the Angami village that had famously resisted the British in the mid- and late nineteenth century, but had left for Burma in 1933 where he ran a small insurance business. Ten years later, he and his younger brother Kevi Yalley, unlike most other Nagas who were pro-British, joined Bose's INA and served with it until the end of the War, hoping that the Naga Hills would also become independent if the British were forced to give up India. Phizo was arrested by the British when Rangoon was recaptured in May 1945 and jailed for seven months. When he was released, he found that a tribal people in Burma, the Karen, were organizing a mass movement for independence for themselves, outside any proposed Union of Burma. Led by a bearded, charismatic lawyer called Saw Ba U Gyi, the Karen were holding meetings and passing resolutions. Like the Nagas, many Karen were also Baptists.[48]

On his return to the Naga Hills, Phizo began propagating an independent 'Nagaland'. At first, he joined the NNC but later withdrew from the Council to form his own People's Independence League. A powerful organizer, he also set up the Naga Youth Movement and the Naga Women's Society. But his ideas were gaining support even within the hitherto moderate NNC. On 21 May 1947, the NNC issued a statement saying that the Nagas were determined 'not to allow themselves to be involved in a divided and chaotic India', and that they were prepared to declare their own independence, and could only consider 'entering into a 10-year treaty with an independent Assam.'[49]

But Assam was not going to be independent, and in June, Sir Akbar Hydari, a Muslim who was the first Indian governor of Assam, was sent to Kohima to negotiate with the NNC. He was received by Sakhrie, who read out a welcome address. Even the moderate NNC secretary had changed his tune: 'A constitution drawn by people who have no knowledge of Nagaland and the its people will be quite unsuitable and unacceptable to the Naga people ... We know that Your Excellency will concede that the Naga people have as much right for self-determination as any other people.'[50]

The outcome of the discussions was a nine-point agreement, which struck a balance between demands for separation and constitutional safeguards for the Nagas within the Indian Union. A ten-year 'trial period' was agreed upon, after which 'the Naga National Council would be asked whether they require the above agreement to be extended for a further period or a new agreement regarding the future of the Naga people arrived at.'[51] In the meantime, Naga courts would be recognized, the NNC would be given an almost free hand to administer the Naga Hills once the British had left, and no land or resources in the Naga Hills would be given to a non-Naga without the consent of the NNC.

The issue seemed to have been settled, but differences soon arose within the NNC on how to interpret what would happen after the ten-year trial period expired. Some thought it meant that the Nagas could then declare independence, while others saw it as an evolutionary step towards some kind of self-rule. The tension between the various factions within the NNC – and between the NNC and the plains people in general – escalated as India's independence day was approaching. In July, an eleven-man Naga delegation, including Phizo, went to Delhi to meet Mahatma Gandhi, who received them in his simple house in the Bhangi colony, a settlement in the capital populated by the lowest of India's so-called untouchables.

When they expressed fear that the Indian government would send in troops to quell any Naga uprising, Gandhi reportedly replied: 'I will come to Kohima and I will be the first to be shot before any Naga is killed.' Gandhi's commitment to non-violence is undisputed, but Phizo claimed, and many Nagas even today firmly believe, that the Mahatma also told the delegates that 'the Nagas have every right to be independent. We did not want to live under the domination of the British and they are now leaving us.'[52] Indian historians have denied that any such promises were given by Gandhi, and that none of his aides who were present during the meeting recall him saying that the Nagas had 'every right to be independent' in a separate nation which would not be part of India, which is how many Nagas have interpreted the Mahamta's message to Phizo and the other Naga delegates.

Parts of the original transcript of the meeting in the Bhangi colony are reproduced in Nirmal Nibedon's detailed account of the Naga struggle, *The Night of the Guerrillas,* and show that Gandhi's response to Phizo was far more philosophical than was later claimed by the Naga nationalists: 'Independence, yes. But if you say you will be independent of the whole world, you can't do it. I am independent in my own home. If I become independent of Delhi I will be crushed to atoms. I have not stored food. I have to get it from Delhi. I have not stored water here. Vegetables I have to get . . . [but] from where do you get your cloth? . . . I will teach you the art of spinning and weaving. You grow cotton and yet you import cloth. Learn all the handicrafts. That is the way to peaceful independence. If you use rifles and guns and tanks it is a foolish thing.'[53]

But regardless of what Gandhi did or did not say to Phizo when they met in the Bhangi colony, on 14 August 1947, the NNC declared an independent Nagaland, a day ahead of India's independence and on the same day that Pakistan became a separate dominion within the British Commonwealth. A separate homeland for India's Muslims, Pakistan, was bad enough for Mahatma Gandhi and other Indian nationalists. The Nagas became the first to challenge the idea of India that remained after Partition: a secular state where neither religion nor ethnicity would determine the character of the new nation. The Nagas wanted their own Christian republic, but it was, from the very beginning, absolutely imperative to keep the Naga Hills within the Indian Union.

The Naga Hills were remote, underdeveloped and of no economic value to India as a whole. But if independent India's leaders had allowed the Nagas to secede, a dangerous precedent would have been created that the new nation could ill afford, fragile as it was immediately after the decision to create Pakistan. If the Naga Hills were granted independence, what about Kashmir, the Tamil areas in the south, Punjab and other parts of the country with non-Hindi-speaking nationalities? For India to survive as a unified entity, even the poor and distant Naga Hills had to remain part of the new nation.

On 15 August, the Indian government tried to hoist the flag of independent India in Kohima and other population centres in the Naga Hills, but these were almost immediately taken down by angry local people. Phizo's influence over the Nagas grew, and in July 1948 he was jailed for sedition. But he was set free in December on compassionate grounds because his wife and children had suffered a bad traffic accident. One of his sons was killed, and his wife was seriously injured. Soon after his release, he assumed de facto leadership of the NNC and the entire organization began to press demands for secession from India.

In April 1950, Phizo went back to Delhi, this time to meet Nehru, independent India's first prime minister. Nehru listened sympathetically to what Phizo had to say, but could not understand why he wanted the Nagas to break away from India:

> I consider freedom very precious. I am sure that the Nagas are as free as I am, in fact more free in a number of ways. For while I am bound down by all sorts of laws the Nagas are not to the same extent bound down by such laws and are governed by their own customary laws and usages. But the independence the Nagas are after is something quite different from individual or group freedom. In the present context of affairs both in India and the world, it is impossible to consider, even for a moment, such an absurd demand for independence for the Nagas. It is doubtful whether the Nagas realise the consequences of what they are asking for. For their present demand would lead them to ruin.[54]

Phizo's response was to turn to the people in the Naga Hills to ask them to vote on the issue of independence. In December 1950, he was unanimously elected president of the NNC, and on 16 May 1951, he organized what many Nagas still refer to as 'the plebiscite', which resembled more a tribal oath-taking ceremony than a traditional referendum. Seven thousand tribesmen were said to have put their thumbprints on a long list of names on sheets of paper. Phizo claimed that 99.99 per cent voted in favour of an independent Nagaland, while the Indian authorities dismissed the exercise as 'a political hoax' without any legal validity. But even today, many Nagas consider the 1951 plebiscite a tribal oath that cannot be broken.[55]

The situation became even tenser after the plebiscite. In 1952, the Nagas boycotted independent India's first general elections. At the same time, the NNC launched its own Gandhian-style civil disobedience campaign – against India. People refused to pay house tax, government offices and schools were boycotted, and the NNC began to set up its own schools. The NNC was subsequently banned and arrest warrants were issued against its leaders, prompting many of them to go into hiding. At the same time, an assistant judge of the Angami Tribal Council was shot dead during a public demonstration in Kohima.

The Naga Hills were on the brink of civil war. In an attempt to defuse the situation, Nehru himself travelled up to the Naga Hills in March 1953. A big reception was organized for him at the Kohima football ground, but the Naga elders walked out because they were prevented by the authorities from making a representation to the prime minister just as he began his speech to the crowd. Nehru was furious and blamed Bishnuram Medhi, the then chief minister of Assam, who in turn fired the deputy commissioner. The meeting ended in disaster, and there seemed to be no more room left for a compromise, or even talks between the Indian government and the Naga leaders.

Many Indians began to suspect that the missionaries were behind the agitation. Medhi stated in December 1953: 'I cannot think of any demand for an independent, sovereign Naga state raised by a handful of leaders, mostly Christians. And probably this demand was raised by interested foreign missionaries to keep them isolated from the rest of India. During the pre-independence days, the British administrators also were greatly responsible for giving the idea of independence among a handful of Naga leaders under the influence of foreign missionaries.'[56] NNC posters with slogans like 'Nagaland for Christ' strengthened that suspicion, and the missionaries were told to leave. The Houstons in Wokha left in April 1953, and the Andersens, who had first come to Kohima in 1929 to work among the Angamis, went home in February 1954. The last of the American missionaries, the DeLanos in Aizuto, packed up in March 1955.

In early 1955, Mokokchung was declared a 'disturbed area' and a joint force of armed police and the paramilitary Assam Rifles moved into the hills, but that only exacerbated the already tense situation. Exactly a year later, in January 1956, the Indian government declared the entire Naga Hills a disturbed area, and responsibility for restoring Indian authority was handed over to the regular army. The NNC began to prepare for armed resistance against Indian rule, and several of the old moderates were purged. John Bosco Jasokie, a prominent Naga Catholic who disagreed with Phizo's militant stand, had been expelled from the NNC along with another prominent moderate, 'Theyieu' Sakhrie, in late 1955. In January 1956, Sakhrie's house was surrounded by a crowd of armed men. The erstwhile secretary of the NNC was taken out and led away into the forest, where he was hacked to death by his former comrades. Sakhrie became the first victim of the often bloody internal feuds, some tribal, some political, that have chastised the Naga independence movement since its inception.[57]

In March 1956, the NNC hoisted the Naga national flag – a white Star of David and a red, yellow and green rainbow against a blue background – in the Rengma area and proclaimed the formation of 'the Federal Government of Nagaland', uniting the Naga Hills district with the previously 'unadministered areas' of Tuensang and Mon, which after India's independence had become the Naga Tribal Area under the North-East Frontier Agency, or NEFA (today's Arunachal Pradesh).

The Naga 'government', in effect headed by Phizo, drew up its own constitution and formed a parliament of 100 *tatar*s (elders) and a cabinet of fifteen *kilonser*s ('ministers'). Governors, magistrates, deputy commissioners and other 'government officials' were appointed. The Naga Home Guards, formed by the NNC, began to use badges of ranks and uniforms. By 1956, the NNC's guerrilla army consisted of 5,000 men, equipped with traditional spears and daos as well as weapons left over from World War II. The Naga War had begun.

The first two years of the war was the most brutal in modern Naga history. Rishang Keishing, a Tangkhul Naga member of the

Indian parliament from Ukhrul in Manipur, accused the Indian Army of indulging in an orgy of rape, pillage and murder. He claimed that hundreds of villages had been burnt down, and thousands made homeless. The number of dead was in the thousands, and more than 500 Nagas had been thrown in Indian jails. British journalist Neville Maxwell, who visited the Naga Hills in 1960, was given 'sheaves of carefully typed and itemised lists of atrocities allegedly perpetrated on one particular village in the period 1956–58'.[58]

The lists contained the names of the victims, the nature of ill treatment – beating, rape and other sexual acts, torture by water or electricity, desecration of churches, and killings. Maxwell added that it was impossible to say categorically that the reports were true, 'but the Nagas have been so meticulous in presenting these charges, and there have been enough outside allegations to the same effect, for it to be concluded that the onus of proof that the charges are *not* true now rests squarely on the Indian government.'[59]

Bhola Nath Mullik, former chief of India's IB and security adviser to Prime Minister Jawaharlal Nehru in the 1950s and early 1960s, wrote in his memoirs *My Years With Nehru* that 'there were many ugly incidents; serious casualties were inflicted on both the sides; no quarter was given or asked for. The security forces exerted the maximum of pressure, but this was not enough to force the rebel Nagas to surrender.'[60] The resistance against the Indian Army was solid, and Lt Col. Vijay Kumar Anand, an Indian counter-insurgency specialist who saw action in the Naga Hills, concedes that 'in 1956, when reports of sudden and widespread violence in the Naga Hills reached New Delhi, it was not a demonstration, riot or insurrection but hot-blooded insurgency for independence involving the entire tribal community.'[61] The massiveness of the military action, Anand wrote, 'was beyond the imagination of the Nagas'. But rather than quelling the rebellion, the actions by the Indian Army were counterproductive: antagonism against the Indian state grew stronger as villages were burned, granaries destroyed and people killed. Even more Nagas, young and old, took to the hills to join the resistance forces.

The tactics then changed, according to Mullik, and the aim became to break the supply and intelligence system of Angami Zapu Phizo's 'Federal Government of Nagaland', which depended for its survival on food, information and shelter provided by local villagers. Inspiration came from Malaya, where the British at that time were conducting a campaign against communist insurgents, who had been effectively isolated from the local population by a method of grouping small villages together into huge, closely guarded settlements. The Indians thought the same would work in the war against the Naga rebels. But what had succeeded in Malaya turned into a disaster in India's remote and isolated north-east.

In Malaya, everyone above the age of twelve was issued with an identity card containing the bearer's name, fingerprints and a photograph. One week's rations were issued at a time to prevent any surplus from reaching the rebels. But, according to Lt Col. Anand, in the Naga Hills no similar procedure was possible: issuing ID cards with photographs would only 'stupefy an outside soldier, to whom all the names and faces of the Nagas sounded and looked alike.' There was also the problem of issuing ID cards to 'a people, who neither kept any boxes nor wallets on their naked bodies.'[62]

But the resettlement programme nevertheless went ahead, and it was given the code-name 'RGV' (Regrouped Villages) in Indian Army parlance. The RGVs were separated from their surroundings by three-metre-high double walls made of thick logs with pointed tops. The gap between the walls were littered with *punji*s, or sharpened bamboo spikes. There were only one or two gates to control the exit and entry of people, and checks were carried out by heavy-handed Indian soldiers who almost never spoke any local language. In the Sema area, a stronghold of the independence movement, the entire population was herded into such new villages.

Local production of food almost ceased, and the army was made responsible for feeding tens of thousands of people – in an area where there were no airfields and hardly any all-weather roads.

People starved and many managed to escape to the hills, where the war raged on. According to Mullik, there was nearly one Indian soldier 'for every adult Naga male in the Naga Hills–Tuensang Area, [but] there was never a time when it could be claimed that the Naga guerrillas had been broken into submission.'[63] Mullik decided to shift tracks, arguing that 'the ultimate solution of partisan guerrilla warfare invariably lies in a political settlement.' But what kind of settlement would be acceptable to the Nagas, who had declared their hills an independent republic? And how could the Nagas – a Mongol, largely Christian people speaking numerous Tibeto-Burman dialects – be convinced that they were also Indians?

Mullik's master plan was quite simple. First the Naga Hills would have to be separated from Assam and the plains people, who were seen as representing 'India' by the tribals. Once a separate entity, and not a tiny district overwhelmed by a larger administrative unit, Naga identity could also be more easily emphasized, and safeguarded under the special provisions of the Indian constitution for scheduled and backward tribes and castes. If that worked, the Naga Hills could even become a state within the Indian Union with its own elected assembly, ministers, high court and representatives in the parliament in New Delhi.

But 'the request for the separation should formally come from a representative Naga convention and the Government of India should generously accept it as a token of their good faith towards the Nagas,' Mullik wrote in his memoirs. Together with S.M. Dutt, deputy director of IB in the then Assam capital of Shillong – and, according to Mullik, one of the 'most intrepid and far-sighted' officers in the Indian intelligence apparatus with a 'good knowledge of Assam and of the tribals' and their history and culture – Mullik set out to look for Nagas who could be sympathetic to his plan.[64] It was not easy. Most Nagas remained hostile to India, and those who thought that the only way to end the bloodshed and the terror in the hills was some kind of accommodation with New Delhi were afraid of being accused of betraying the Naga cause. And the Naga rebels were not known for their leniency towards 'traitors', as the fate of moderate leader Sakhrie had shown.

There was also resistance from Assam, where several state officials dubbed Dutt and Mullik as traitors. The Naga Hills belonged to Assam. The very idea of statehood for the Naga Hills was absurd. No more than a few hundred thousand people lived in the hills – roughly the same number as in any middle-sized railway junction town elsewhere in India. But Dutt and Mullik argued that, at the very least, a convention of Naga elders would have to be held to nullify the outcome of the 1951 plebiscite for independence. They went ahead with their plans, which no doubt were supported by Nehru. The revered statesman was greatly troubled by the violence in the Naga Hills, and the effect reports of atrocities had on India's international reputation as a country of Gandhian non-violence, democracy and, despite its poverty, respect for human dignity.

Convening such a convention was not without serious risks and difficulties. Were there any guarantees that the Naga elders, when they met, would not just hold their stand six years before and ask for independence? Moreover, as Mullik noted, 'it was difficult to send out invitations, as the countryside was dominated by the hostiles and the emissaries sent out from Kohima were often intercepted and detained.'[65] Ultimately, a meeting of representatives of over twenty tribes was held in Kohima at the end of June 1957. It was decided to call a convention of all the tribes to discuss the future of the Naga Hills. Dutt, who attended the meeting, stressed in a speech that it lay in the interest of the Nagas to stay with India and not pursue 'a policy of fighting the Government'.[66]

The outcome surpassed even Dutt's and Mullik's wildest expectations. Four thousand delegates showed up on 22 August

1957, also in Kohima. The discussions, which lasted for four days, were open, and the representatives were free to express their demands and grievances. They voiced the view that they were 'deeply grieved by the killings and widespread sufferings caused by burning of houses and granaries, the destruction of crops, grouping of villages, restriction of freedom of movement and speech, forced labour without payment, the resultant diseases and hunger.'[67] Meanwhile, Dutt, operating in the background with some 'moderate' Nagas, had prepared a resolution, which he hoped would be adopted by the convention without casting any ballots. According to Mullik: 'There is no question of any majority decision in a convention of this type, and the decision is always unanimous and thereby binding on all the tribes till a convention similarly called rescinds the decision.'[68]

The convention elected two respected Naga community leaders as office bearers. Imkongliba, an Ao from Aonokpu village in Mokokchung, became president of what was called the Naga People's Convention, NPC, and John Bosco Jasokie, the moderate Angami member of the NNC who had the distinction of also having served as a guide and scout for the Allied Forces during World War II, was elected secretary. Jasokie had been the first important Naga figure to become a Catholic – and to openly break with Phizo. Since the 1940s, when he was expelled from the NNC, he had argued that Naga independence was an unrealistic option for a small tribal people living in a largely barren hill country without any significant natural resources.

It all seemed to be working according to plan, when a government official, who did not fully understand what was happening behind the scenes, arrived in Kohima and criticized the resolution of the convention for not specifically mentioning that the Naga Hills would remain within the Indian Union. This, he claimed, was the unequivocal condition of the governor of Assam, if any demand for separation from Assam were to be considered. Dutt and Mullik realized that it would have been impossible to reach the necessary unanimous decision if the resolution had included such a pledge. The integration of the Naga Hills with India would have to be gradual, and done in a roundabout way by first creating a separate homeland for the Nagas.

In the end, the resolution said that the only answer to the Naga question was a 'satisfactory political settlement'. As an interim measure, the old Naga Hills district and Tuensang were constituted into a single administrative unit called the Naga Hills–Tuensang Area, or NHTA for short. The next step would be to turn NHTA into a proper Union territory awaiting full statehood. But the area would not become a fully fledged state until 'the hostiles came to agreement with the conventionists.'[69] The 'hostiles' were, of course, Phizo's NNC, and the 'conventionists' were those who supported the NPC. Mullik's and Dutt's plan had worked. The Naga movement had split into two factions and, for the first time, there was an organization that supported integration with India, but as a separate, Naga-administered area with full ethnic and democratic rights, and without domination from the Assamese of the plains.

Phizo was not in the Naga Hills to oppose this, for him, unwelcome development. Following the murder of Sakhrie, a warrant for his arrest had been issued. It became dangerous for Phizo to stay in the area, and he also felt that he had to internationalize the Naga cause. Escorted by a platoon of Naga soldiers led by Thungti Chang, the illiterate commander of the Naga Home Guards, he slipped out of the country and made it to East Pakistan, where he arrived on 6 December 1956, half a year before the convention was held.[70]

What was then the eastern part of Pakistan was not far from the Naga Hills – only a relatively short trek over the Cachar Hills of Assam – and in colonial times many Nagas trekked along this route down to Chittagong on the sea to acquire salt and cowrie shells, which they use to decorate their costumes. It is possible that Phizo had expected that the Pakistanis would be eager to accept any enemy of their enemy, India, even if he was a Christian tribesman. But at this stage they showed little interest in his movement, and so Phizo left for Europe.

In 1959, Phizo managed to reach Zurich in Switzerland, where he was met by his nephew Chalie Iralu, also an Angami from the historic village of Khonoma near Kohima. Iralu, a biochemist studying science in the United States, had a year before written to Michael Scott, a British reverend who had worked at the United Nations on behalf of the Indians in South Africa and the Hereros of South West Africa (now Namibia). In his letter, Iralu had stated that he had heard from an American anthropologist about Scott's work for oppressed people and he claimed that the plight of the Nagas was just as bad as that of the tribals of South West Africa.[71]

Scott did not pay much attention to the letter, but when Iralu wrote to him again saying that his 'uncle', a senior Naga leader, needed help and was in Zurich, Scott found that Mr. Phizo was without any papers. He had a very 'irregular passport', as Scott put it in a pamphlet he later wrote about his involvement with the Nagas. Exactly what he meant is not clear, but Phizo 'didn't dare to go out of the hotel room because he had a suspicion that people were following him. He was completely by himself.' Scott, who then knew a little about Phizo's background, was clearly apprehensive: 'I said, "You know what the Indians feel about you. There's a reward offered for your capture and I can't promise that if you come to England you won't be extradited. If there's any substance in this charge against you, you had better think very carefully before you take this step and come to England. If you want to go to Austria, no doubt you could get behind the Iron Curtain. But if you want to make your appeal to the British then I will help, but I can't guarantee that when you reveal your name you won't be extradited.'[72]

Phizo agreed to come to Britain with Scott and pass through immigration, not on his phony passport, but as 'A.Z. Phizo, President of the Naga National Council'. Scott recalls that 'this took a little time at London Immigration office during the small hours of the morning; it was not made any easier when, at the height of a strenuous discussion, Mr. Phizo insisted that Nagaland was not part of India.'[73] Scott argued that Phizo was born in the British Commonwealth, and an understanding immigration official gave them three days to prove his identity, which later they did. Phizo could stay in Britain.

On 26 July 1960 – six weeks after his arrival in Britain – Phizo held an informal press conference in London, where he outlined the Naga cause and presented a pamphlet entitled, 'The Fate of the Naga People'. From a new office in Denison House on Vauxhall Bridge Road, he re-established contact with his followers in the Naga Hills, and began his crusade to make the international community aware of the Naga struggle for independence. The British government remained cool, almost suspicious of his activities. London could not jeopardize relations with India because of the Nagas and, besides, Phizo had been a collaborator with Subhas Chandra Bose and the Japanese during the War. But some Church people and journalists showed sympathy for his cause. Gavin Young, a young reporter with *The Observer*, was one of them and Phizo arranged a trip for him to the rebel-held areas of the Naga Hills.[74]

Young set out for Rangoon, Burma, from where he travelled up north and along the Chindwin River in the north-west. His Naga contacts escorted him across the border to the Naga Hills where he remained from February to March 1961. He was the first foreign journalist to visit rebel-held areas in the Naga Hills, and in articles from his clandestine journey, created quite a sensation at the time – especially since he was able to meet the crew of an Indian Air Force DC3, which had been shot down by the Nagas in August 1960. Four crew members were still held in a Naga rebel camp, where Young interviewed them.

For more than seven months, the Indian Army had been searching for the men, but in vain. Thirty-one-year-old flight lieutenant Anand Singh told Young that he did not know what to expect when he climbed out of the wreckage of the aircraft. 'I believed we might be eaten,' Singh said. 'My impression was that the rebels were a handful of guerrillas or dacoits. I knew that some of them at least were Christians. But I found that difficult to reconcile with my belief, and that of the rest of my crew, that Nagas were headhunters and even cannibals.'[75] But Singh and his comrades had been well treated, and they seemed to be getting on well with their captors, according to Young.

Young also found that, far from dying out, Christianity was flourishing among the Nagas and that the number of converts was growing. The Nagas had their own pastors, he noted, and many of them were constantly on the move, visiting villages, distributing Bibles in the Naga dialects, and dispensing religious instruction. The forced departure of the American missionaries – whom the Indian authorities suspected of involvement in the early Naga national movement – did not seem to have hampered the spread of the gospel in the Naga Hills. On the other hand, Christianity had become a unifying factor among the Nagas and a symbol of their resistance against what they perceived as Indian domination. According to Young:

> From discussions with senior Naga officers and officials, it was evident that the conviction of their 'apartness' from the Indians is based partly on their religion. But not to the extent ascribed to it by some Indians, who have thrown the blame for the Naga tragedy on to alleged para-political activities of the American missions – for which, incidentally, there seems to have been no evidence at all – and past British imperialist policies which, they say, have deliberately denied Nagas mind-broadening political access to the plainsmen. But the Nagas' spirit of independence – and their readiness to fight for it – is far older than their recently acquired Christianity.[76]

Young visited the Naga rebels when they were at the peak of their strength and influence, and commanded a well-disciplined, popular movement. He found the Naga rebels 'surprisingly free from poverty and rags. All were correctly uniformed, well fed and well armed. Morale and discipline were obviously high. Privates and orderlies stamped and saluted as smartly as in most British Army camps.'[77] They seemed to have few financial worries: an income tax of 5 per cent of each wage earner's salary was augmented with a house tax of two rupees a year per house, plus a NNC and Naga Home Guard subscription each of one rupee a year.

Although Phizo was living in exile in London, there were many other competent leaders among the rebels in the hills. Imkongmeren, a respected Ao elder from Mokokchung, became the de facto leader of the movement after Phizo's departure for East Pakistan in 1956. Scato Swu, a Sema educated in a missionary school, served as 'president' of the 'Federal Government of Nagaland' and his thirty-seven-year-old brother-in-law, Jimoni Kughato Sukhai, was the 'prime minister'. Kughato's younger brother, Jimoni Kaito, held the position of commander-in-chief of the rebel army, the Naga Home Guards. The 'foreign secretary' was a twenty-nine-year-old Sema, Scato's younger clansman, Isak Chishi Swu. A graduate from St Anthony's College in Shillong, Isak would have preferred to continue his studies at a Baptist seminary in the United States, but, as he told Young, 'I could no longer tolerate seeing the Nagas treated like beasts by Indian officials and army officers. I tried my best to explain the position of my people in an attempt to minimize their maltreatment, but my efforts were in vain. After the burning of six villages, including my own, in the Sema area round Chishi, I found that I had no reasonable alternative but to come away and work for the national movement.'[78]

The Nagas were motivated and well organized, and as part of the national drive, the NNC had even invented its own 'nationalist vocabulary'. Words were borrowed from many different Naga dialects to designate the movement's institutions, officers and officials. The Naga 'parliament', which consisted of respected, and some elected, representatives of the various tribes, became the 'Tatar Hoho' after the Sema, Lotha and Ao word for 'village elder' (tatar) and the Lotha and Sema word for assembly (*hoho*). The 'president' of the Federal Government of Nagaland was titled 'kedahge' after the Rengma word for king or supreme head. His ministers were called 'kilonsers', which is village councillor in the Yimchunger dialect. To specify what duty the respective kilonsers had, various words from different Naga dialects were added: ato kilonser (prime minister; ato = Sema for 'prime'); keyya kilonser (defence minister; keyya = Angami for 'shield' or 'fighting'); alee kilonser (foreign minister; alee = 'foreign' or 'outside' in several Naga dialects); chaplee kilonser (finance minister; chaplee = Ao for an old iron rod which was used in ancient times as a form of currency); lota kilonser (agriculture minister; lota = Khezha for 'cultivation' or to 'dig in the earth'); and rali-wali kilonser (information minister; rali-wali = Ao for 'listen and talk', village tales and gossip). A local 'governor' of a specific area under the control of the rebels was called Ahng after the Konyak word for a powerful headman.

The Naga Federal Government resided in a place called Oking, which was never a permanent location as the kilonsers had to be on the move most of the time. Oking, which means 'the place where the supreme head resides' in Lotha, became an almost mystical concept with a very special resonance to it. To many young people, it was the abode of freedom, where the Nagas ruled themselves. To others, who feared the movement, Oking had a much more sinister ring; the Naga movement could be extremely autocratic, and when an Azha ('order', from law or decision in Sema) was issued, it could mean life or death for anyone. Azhas, and any other proclamation from the rebel authorities, were always signed off 'Kuknalim!', a hybrid word which meant 'Victory for Nagaland!' (*kuk* = 'victory' in Khezha; *lim* = 'land' in Ao).[79]

But another Naga nation was also emerging as a result of Mullik's and Dutt's endeavours. In July 1960, a Naga delegation led by NPC president Ao Imkongliba met Nehru in New Delhi, and it was formally announced that a new state called 'Nagaland' would be established 'within the Indian Union and comprising the territory of the existing Naga Hills and Tuensang Area.'[80] The Nagas who preferred to live within the Indian Union had got what they asked for – except the integration of the contiguous Naga-inhabited areas of Assam and Manipur with the new state. The issue has continued to be a bone of contention between many Nagas and the Central government ever since. Ukhrul district of Manipur, for instance, is dominated by a socially and politically advanced tribe that has contributed, proportionally, a very high number of politicians, diplomats and officials to the Indian administration. The first Naga MP in New Delhi was Rungsung Suisa, a Tangkhul from Somdal village in Ukhrul, who sat in the Lok Sabha from 1957 to 1962. He had changed his mind about independence in favour of advocating a solution to the Naga issue within the framework of the Indian constitution, and joined the ruling Congress party.

Another prominent Tangkhul, Robert Kathing, had served with the Assam Regiment and as a political officer of Tuensang before joining the integration process more actively, even aggressively. He suggested that the unpopular RGVs should be disbanded and people allowed to return to their homes. But, for that, the government would have to form local village defence units to fight the rebels. The Central authorities disagreed, but Kathing went ahead with his own training programme, which finally gave birth to the Village Guards, the Flying Squads and the Village Volunteer Force, which were locally raised Naga counter-insurgency forces under the direct command of the Indian Army.

The rebels responded to these moves with even more hostility – now directed against their own people. Jasokie and Hokishe Sema, a St Anthony's graduate and one of the best-educated Nagas at the time, were branded 'puppets' of the Indians. On 22 August 1961, Imkongliba was assassinated at his home town of Mokokchung.[81] More killings were to follow, but these could not prevent the inauguration of the state of Nagaland on 1 December 1963. Shilu Ao, an Ao community leader, became its first chief minister, and his installation ceremony was presided over by Dr S. Radhakrishnan, the president of India. Hokishe Sema, who attended the event, was euphoric:

> Over 10,000 Nagas in their colourful costumes, shining shields, glittering spears, flowing hornbill feathers and bright-shash, had lined the 3-mile route from the high school helipad to the Raj Bhavan [government house] . . . the Nagas did not use the conventional form of clapping hands to express their approval, they did it with full-throated shouts and long-piercing cries of joy . . . the wonderful December weather of Kohima in the form of beauteous natural surroundings, lent its grace to the scene.[82]

The rebel movement had been following this process with utmost apprehension, especially as Phizo in London seemed unable to drum up any Western support for an independent Nagaland. But events in the region turned out to be working to the advantage of the remaining rebels in the Naga Hills. India's relations with Pakistan were becoming increasingly strained as the conflict over Kashmir had run into a stalemate, with Pakistan controlling the northern and western third of the state, and India the larger and more populous eastern parts. And, in the late 1950s, after the Tibetan uprising, relations with China had begun to deteriorate to a point that an open conflict between Asia's two giants seemed inevitable.

This turn of events led to the Nagas, a tiny people living on the edges of the vast Indian subcontinent, becoming embroiled in a regional power play, of which they presumably were never fully aware. At the same time, the failure of Phizo to get support from the West – the emergence of Naga factions that were willing to collaborate with the Indian state, even accept the statehood of Nagaland – probably convinced the rebels that they would have to accept assistance from whoever was willing to help them, even if they were Muslims or communists. The spying game had begun, and the Naga struggle was no longer just an internal Indian affair.

Phizo did not receive any help from the Pakistanis when he escaped through the eastern half of their country in 1957. But his flight paved the way for a close relationship between the Naga rebels and Pakistan's security services. Between 1962 and 1968, at least eleven groups of Naga rebels crossed over into East Pakistan. Camps were set up to train them near Rangamati, Alikadam and other towns in the Chittagong Hill Tracts. The Nagas were supplied with rifles, Sten guns, light and medium machine guns, mortars, rocket launchers, high explosives, uniforms and money.[83]

The first major contingent of 150 Naga rebel troops arrived in East Pakistan in April 1962 after a daring trek across the plains north of the Cachar Hills. It was led by Kaito, the young commander of the Naga Home Guards and one of the Nagas Gavin Young had interviewed a year before. The Nagas established their first 'Alee Command' (troops in a foreign country) which were to be followed later by similar bases outside India.

Phizo was brought over from London, and arrived in Karachi in West Pakistan in May 1962. When he returned to London in June, he travelled together with Kaito and three other rebel officers, who had been flown over from East Pakistan to Karachi. Among them was Mowu Gwizan, the thirty-one-year-old fighter from Phizo's home village Khonoma who later led missions to China. Phizo was by then a British citizen, but all four Nagas from the hills travelled to Europe on documents issued by the Pakistan government. Apart from gaining generous supplies of weapons and training facilities, the Naga rebels also managed to establish through Pakistan a direct link between the Naga Hills and Phizo's international information office in London.[84]

Another group of more than 400 Naga rebels made it to East Pakistan in October 1963. Led by Dusoi Salhü, a Chakhesang, they took a different route: through the Chin Hills of Burma. Intensified Indian Army operations on the western side of the border had forced many Naga rebels to look for sanctuaries and lines of communication through the remote and sparsely populated hills of north-western Burma, over which the government in Rangoon exercised only limited control and influence. Besides, there were also Naga tribesmen on the Burmese side of the border who, sometimes, were willing to help their cousins from north-eastern India.

Military and financial support from Pakistan gave the Naga conflict an entirely new dimension. In 1963, the Naga Home Guards were reorganized into the Naga Army, a more tightly organized force. And, according to American counter-insurgency specialist and former US Army intelligence officer Lawrence E. Cline: 'The NNC guerrillas received significant support from neighbouring countries. Some 2,500 were trained in East Pakistan by 1971. Training camps were also established in [West] Pakistan.'[85]

The Indian authorities had to act fast to prevent the war from flaring up again. The situation was further exacerbated by the fact that India had withdrawn two divisions of Indian troops from the Naga Hills in the wake of the 1962 war with China and sent them to fortify the defences along the McMahon Line. As the new state of Nagaland was being established, the Indians also stepped up their attempts to bring the Naga rebellion to an end by peaceful means as well as covert subversion of the NNC and its army rather than open confrontation.

The 1964 peace mission by Chaliha, Jayaprakash Narayan, and the Rev. Michael Scott was part of that effort. They managed to negotiate a ceasefire agreement between the Indian Army and the NNC on 24 May 1964 – three days before Nehru died. There were two issues that Nehru had wanted to settle in his lifetime: his painful conflict with Sheikh Abdullah over the status of the state of

Jammu and Kashmir, and the Naga problem. Neither was to happen, and although the cessation of hostilities began at midnight of 5 September with bonfires, singing and dancing in the villages and worship in the churches, the peace mission ended in failure.[86]

Narayan resigned from the mission on the grounds that the rebels had no confidence in him. Scott, who was seen as too close to the rebels, was deported and left India in May 1966. Chaliha grew disillusioned when the Nagas continued to send men for training to East Pakistan despite the ceasefire agreement. A spate of sabotage bombings on the railways in Assam, apparently carried out with explosives supplied by Pakistan, was the final straw. On 24 July 1968, India's new prime minister, Nehru's daughter Indira Gandhi, told the Lok Sabha that her government had no intention of resuming the peace negotiations 'because of repeated violations of the ceasefire agreement by the underground Nagas.'[87]

By then, India's second strategy – to subvert the Naga movement from inside – had also paid off. The Indian security services' first 'secret weapon' against the Naga Army was Rani Gaidinliu, the priestess of the Zeliangrong-dominated haraka cult, which had practised human sacrifice in the 1930s. After her sixteen years in jail, and having been proclaimed a hero of the anti-colonial struggle, she lived in relative obscurity in Manipur until 1960 – when she went 'underground' again and her armed followers apprehended some of the Naga rebels and handed them over to the Indian authorities. Nine Naga Federal Government personnel were also ritually murdered and some Christian villages were put to the torch. The clashes that followed between her forces and the Naga rebels posed a considerable challenge to the leadership of the Naga Federal Government. The Rani finally 'surrendered' in 1966, and received a state pension as a 'freedom fighter'.[88]

A split within the mainstream Naga movement itself caused an even deeper rift between the different tribes of Nagaland. It began as a tribal dispute over land in the Dimapur area, which was claimed by both the Semas and the Angamis. Many Angamis, who saw themselves as the founders of the Naga national movement, also resented being pushed aside by a group of Semas, who seemed to dominate both the Federal Government and the Naga Army. As soon as Kughato Sukhai, the Naga Ato Kilonser, returned from peace talks in New Delhi in 1967, he was accused of not having done enough to press Naga demands for independence. His younger brother Kaito had already in 1964 been replaced as commander-in-chief of the Naga Army by an Angami, Mowu Gwizan. By 1967, the veteran fighter Kaito was also ousted from the Tatar Hoho, and in October of that year, Kughato resigned from the position of prime minister.

In the following year, both Kughato and Kaito had in effect surrendered to the Indian authorities, but that was not the end of the tribal rivalry within the movement. On 3 August, Kaito was assassinated in Kohima while he was shopping with his elder brother. On 2 November, the breakaway Sema faction, led by former Federal Government president Scato Swu, set up a new organization called the 'Revolutionary Government of Nagaland'. The Federal Government and the NNC denounced the formation of a rival entity and branded its leaders 'traitors', 'renegades' and 'quislings'. The 'Revolutionary Government' finally 'surrendered' in 1973 and Kughato settled in Kohima.[89]

His brother-in-law Scato subsequently became a member of the Rajya Sabha (Upper House of the Indian parliament) and Kaito's close associate Zuheto Swu also gave up the struggle. Zuheto and Kaito had been friends since both of them attended the Atukuzu Middle English School in the 1940s. They joined the underground at about the same time – in the mid-1950s – and both of them had received training in East Pakistan. The assassination of Kaito in 1968 convinced Zuheto that the Semas had been betrayed, and he did not hesitate to take up arms against the now Angami-dominated underground. Zuheto was appointed commander of the local Border

Security Force by the Indian authorities, and given both arms and men to carry out his task.

The Naga movement was in total disarray, but the underground had one more card to play, which was going to prove far more dangerous for India's unity than the support they had been given by the Pakistanis: China. The Naga war flared up again, but there was little the Indians could do to stem the flow of weapons from China. An uprising in East Pakistan provided the first opportunity for the Indians to destroy some of the foreign support bases for the Naga rebels. The Bengalis of East Pakistan demanded independence from West Pakistan, and the conflict led to an Indian intervention in December 1971 and the creation of a new, independent state: East Pakistan became Bangladesh, which, at least in the beginning, was ruled by people loyal and grateful to the Indians for the help they had rendered during their freedom struggle.

When the Indian Army marched into Dhaka, they encircled a building which they knew was used by Naga rebels. They managed to arrest Thinoselie – who had trekked to China with Muivah in 1967 and, in 1969, had been made new commander-in-chief of the Naga Army – and Brig. Neidelie. Both Naga commanders were sent back to India to face stiff jail sentences, and the Naga camps in the Chittagong Hill Tracts were closed down by the new government of independent Bangladesh.[90]

A severe blow had been dealt against the Naga rebel movement, and, despite the aid from China, the Sema–Angami split had further eroded the former strength of the Naga Army. On 31 August 1972, the NNC, its Naga Army and the Federal Government were declared 'unlawful associations'. Fighting broke out all over Nagaland, but even so, American evangelist Billy Graham was able to visit Kohima on one of his 'crusades' in November to celebrate the 100th anniversary of the arrival of Christianity in the Naga Hills. The Rev. Edward Winter Clark and his Assamese assistant Godhula Rufus Brown were remembered at a grand ceremony which attracted nearly 80,000 people. The Naga rebels took advantage of the situation and fired their guns in the surrounding hills to remind people that the war was not over.

But sustained military pressure on the Naga rebels soon led to the surrender of many of the movement's staunchest fighters and, on 11 November 1975, an agreement was signed in Shillong between the Government of India and some representatives of the outlawed 'Federal Government' who 'accepted the Constitution of India of their own volition'. One of the signatories was Phizo's younger brother Kevi Yallay.[91]

Both Muivah and Isak were in Tengchong in Yunnan, when the 'Shillong Accord' – as it became known – was signed. They were furious at the 'treachery'. Even the Chinese were taken aback by the event, and ordered Muivah, Isak and their men to return home. Successive Indian Army operations, and the signing of the Shillong Accord, had deprived the Naga rebels of all their permanent and semi-permanent camps on the Indian side of the frontier. But in the course of the treks to China, a relationship had been established with a Burmese Naga leader called Shangwang Shangyung Khaplang and new bases had been established across the border in Burma.

Out of reach of the Indian Army, and angered by the turn of events in Nagaland, Isak and Muivah decided to purge the Naga movement. Nearly four extremely bloody years were to follow, with coups and counter-coups, and the execution of dozens of 'traitors'. Among them were Kilamsungba Mayanger, a well-known former Naga youth leader who had been a kilonser in the 'Federal Government'; Veenyiyi Rhakhu, a Chakhesang member of the Tatar Hoho; N. Lorho, a Mao who had served as the speaker of the Tatar Hoho; Thepuse Venuh, a Chakhesang leader from Thevipisumi village; four pastors from the Khiemngan area where the NNC was strong; Col. Supong Jamir; Lt Col. Vesazo Khamo; and scores of others. Some were shot but most of them were bludgeoned to death. It was a virtual bloodbath as Isak and Muivah purged the old movement of their enemies.[92]

The events of the turbulent 1970s gave rise to an entirely new Naga rebel movement – the NSCN – which, in its dedication to a Maoist-inspired revolutionary ideology, and penchant for violence and extreme brutality, is very different from the bands of Christian tribesmen who resorted to armed struggle in the mid-1950s to – as they saw it – defend their homes from the onslaught of the Indian Army. Assassinations of Naga and non-Naga opponents, bank robberies and kidnappings for ransom became commonplace. Peace, it seemed, was still a distant reality in Nagaland.

CHAPTER THREE

THE MIZOS: FROM FAMINE TO STATEHOOD

The road to Aizawl follows a green and fertile but sparsely populated valley with a river that flows through it. Then, in the distance, some steep hills rise towards the sky. The heights are covered in multi-storey buildings, making the peak appear almost like a huge, concrete porcupine in the otherwise tranquil, rural setting. More than a quarter of Mizoram's 900,000 people live there, at an altitude of 1,132 metres above sea level. And it is not only because the Mizos are highlanders they have settled on those hills rather than in the valley below, which plains people would perceive as much more hospitable. Aizawl, now the capital of the state of Mizoram, was originally a small village, but the lofty hills on which it is located proved ideal for a military post when the British colonial power extended its writ eastwards in the nineteenth century. The village had a commanding view over the surrounding terrains, and the British established a fort here when, in 1890, they moved up from the plains of Assam to 'pacify' the hills, as conquest was referred to in colonial parlance.

Stockades were built around 'Fort Aijal', as it was called, and those were necessary as the outpost in the hills came under frequent attacks from the native population, who evidently did not appreciate the presence of armed outsiders in their midst. Aizawl became the main base of the 1st Assam Rifles, which quelled several tribal uprisings in the area. A year later, the Mizo Hills – then called the Lushai Hills and divided into a northern and a southern district – were annexed to British India and, in 1898, placed under more direct colonial administration. The village grew into a small town and became the headquarters of the unified Lushai Hills, complete with a parade ground which, to quote historians C.G. Verghese and R.L. Thanzawna, 'gave ample space for ceremonial drills and amusements such as football and hockey. Polo was also played on it by officers in the station and any Gurkha jawans who could ride the mounts, being chiefly mules, of which a number were kept at Aijal for transport purposes.'[1]

More than a century later, Aizawl has become a booming town like no other in India's remote, north-eastern region. The traffic is horrendous in its narrow streets, which wind their way up and down the hills, and the main thoroughfare is lined with shops selling Reebok and Adidas sport shoes, Levi's jeans, clothes from the United Colours of Benetton and other multinational high street brands. Schoolchildren in trim uniforms loiter in the street corners; Mizoram's literary rate, 90 per cent, is highest of any state in India after Kerala. Despite the state's population, tiny by Indian standards, there is a disproportionately high number of Mizos in the civil service across India. And there is peace in the state. The military presence is minimal, and there are no rebels collecting 'revolutionary taxes' from individuals and local businesses, as is the case in Manipur and Nagaland. Mizoram is an oasis of peace in what otherwise is one of the most troubled corners of the Indian subcontinent.

Nearly all Mizos are Christians, and an abundance of churches tower over Aizawl's commercial houses and private homes. On Sundays, shops and offices and other workplaces in the entire town close down, and the sound of church bells and Christian hymns can be heard over the hills. The Mizos speak a language closely related to those of the Chins across the border in Burma. They are a Mongol people and are often mistaken for Thai or even Japanese tourists when they visit Delhi, Mumbai and other big cities elsewhere in India. 'It's hard for me to say that I'm an Indian, or to explain to people I meet abroad why I, as an Indian citizen, look like I do,' an older Mizo told me during my first visit to Aizawl in September 2010. 'But I'm perfectly happy to say that I am a Mizo, a people of India.'

But only a few decades ago, Mizoram was no different from other strife-ridden areas in the north-east. In fact, one of the fiercest ethnic uprisings raged here for twenty years, from 1966 to 1986. Almost the entire population was uprooted from their villages and herded into 'strategic hamlets' under the watchful eye of the Indian military. Armed rebels roamed the hills, staged ambushes against government convoys and attacked administrative centres. And, like the Nagas, the Mizo rebels also trekked through Burma to China, where they received military training and supplies. They had bases in East Pakistan until the Indian Army marched into Dhaka in December 1971 and, for a while, even in independent Bangladesh.

What is the key to the success of the Mizos? 'If you can't beat them, join them,' Sapzova, a veteran of the Mizo struggle, told me when we met in Thailand shortly after my visit to Mizoram in September 2010. In June 1986, Laldenga, the rebel leader, signed a peace accord with the Indian government. In February the following year, the erstwhile Lushai Hills District within Assam, which later were renamed the Mizo Hills, and in 1972, were designated as the Union territory of Mizoram became a state within the Indian Union. The Mizos did not get what they wanted when they rose up in arms in 1966 – an independent country – but they have made the best of what they have. And what kind of prosperity would a landlocked country with a population of less than a million have been able to achieve anyway? That is not to say that all Mizos are entirely happy with the present dispensation. Many want an official apology from the Indian state for what they had to endure during the counter-insurgency campaigns of the 1960s and 1970s, especially what is euphemistically called 'grouping of villages', i.e., how their traditional villages were destroyed and replaced by 'strategic hamlets', a practice that was universally detested and caused much grief and suffering.

The flexibility of the Mizos – and their ability to act in a unified manner – could be explained partly by their history, which differs considerably from that of the Nagas. While the Nagas speak innumerable languages and dialects, and have only Nagamese, a non-Naga language in common, the Mizos are much more cohesive as a nation. The Mizo language, like those of the Nagas, belongs to the Tibeto-Burman family, and – also like the Nagas – the original clans once had their distinct dialects. But among those, Lushai, or Lusei as the Mizos call it, was the most common and became the lingua franca of all tribes and clans due to its extensive and exclusive use by the Christian missionaries – and the power of the Sailo chiefs.

The 'pacification' – or, more correctly, subjugation – of the Lushai Hills was prompted by frequent raids by the highlanders into the adjacent British-ruled territories of Cachar, Sylhet and the Chittagong Hill Tracts. The tribal chiefs were especially upset because the colonial power had cleared their traditional, lowland hunting grounds to establish tea gardens for commercial purposes. Apart from the Lushais, there were actually ten other clans, the Aso, Chho, Halam, Hmar, Lai or Pawi, Mara, Miu-Khumi, Paite, Ralte and Thado. The clans, in turn, were divided into sub-clans like the Sailo, the Kawlni, the Thiak and others. Among them – and the Lushais – each village was in effect a separate state, ruled by its own *lal* or chief.[2] And of all the chiefs, those of the Sailo sub-clan became the most prominent – and they led many of the raids down to the Assam plains.

All Sailo chiefs claim descent from a man called Thangura, who sometimes is said to have been the offspring of a Burman man and a Paite woman.[3] Whatever his origin, the Sailo chief Lalulla had by the 1840s established his sway over what today is northern Mizoram.[4] He was reputed to be wise and benevolent, and many people moved to the area over which he reigned. Others were conquered and subdued by Lalulla. There are no written records of where he was born and where and when he died, but it is believed that he was succeeded by his four sons, who ruled over different parts of his fiefdom. According to Indian scholar Suhas Chatterjee, Lalulla and his family 'were very aggressive and enforced their customs and language over the vanquished people.'[5] The Lushai language, also called Dulien, was 'forcibly introduced by him', Chatterjee states. There are no written records of Lalulla's rule, and exactly when he lived and died, but his four sons Lalpuilena, Laliye Vunga, Mungpira and Vuta expanded their father's chiefdom to the north and the east. Other descendants also gradually increased their strength: 'They were prolific in number and each chief had many wives and concubines. They also married the local Mizos and absorbed them into the Lushai fold.'[6]

The subjects of the Sailo chiefs had no choice but to accept their language. Thus, the Dulien dialect became the lingua franca of the hills, which was quite remarkable considering that interaction between the villages was hampered by long distances over rough terrain. Then came the missionaries, who needed one main language into which they could translate the Bible. By their arrival in the late nineteenth century, the Sailo chiefs, with their Dulien language, had become by far the most powerful in the hills. The choice was obvious. Minor languages and dialects all but disappeared.

Initially, the British left the Sailos and other chiefs alone as there was nothing of any economic value that could be extracted from their mountainous country. But as the colonial power was beginning to extract timber from the Cachar lowlands around Silchar below the Lushai Hills, and tea was beginning to be cultivated on a large scale in Assam, those areas had to be secured – which meant putting an end to raids by the tribals. 'Pacification', however, was often brutal and 'punitive expeditions' into the hills often amounted to indiscriminate, collective punishment. In an 1893 *Military Report on The Chin-Lushai Country*, Col. E.B. Elly, a British colonial officer, describes how action was taken after a Lushai chief had raided a village in Cachar, 'killing several of the inhabitants, and carrying off others as slaves':

> Orders were issued to Colonel Lyster, Political Agent, Khasia and Jyntia Hills [sic] and Commandant, Sylhet Light Infantry, to go against them. Colonel Lyster's arrangement were quickly made, and on the 4th January 1850 he started from Cachar and marched nearly 100 miles due south without coming across any habitation, and at daybreak on the 15th reached the village of Mora or Mulla, and burnt it. The village consisted of 800 to 1,000 houses regularly built, and filled with grain, cotton cloths, &c. He estimated the strength of the enemy to from 5,000 to 7,000 fighting men. He only halted there one night and returned to Cachar.[7]

Many more 'punitive expeditions' followed – until the British, in the 1890s, decided to establish a permanent presence in the Lushai Hills and built their fort at Aizawl. Several chiefs who refused to surrender to the new overlords were captured and transported to other parts of India. Some of them died while in detention in the notorious Hazaribagh prison in today's Jharkhand, where many leaders of the Indian freedom movement were also incarcerated. A few were sent to faraway Andaman Islands, where the British established a penal colony for political prisoners after the first Indian war of independence in 1857.

The missionaries arrived shortly after the British had taken over the Lushai Hills. The first was Rev. William Williams of the Welsh Calvinistic Church, which was also known as the Presbyterian Church of Wales. Having had no success in converting the Hindus, the Muslims and the Buddhists, they had had remarkable progress in the Khasi and Jaintia Hills, now in Meghalaya, and then turned first to the remote eastern hills on the Burmese frontier. Williams was followed by Herbert Lorrain of the Arthington Aborigines Mission, and Fred Savidge, who were to remain his co-workers for many years in the hills. Lorrain and Savidge learnt the Dulien dialect, and romanized it. After four years of missionary work at 'Fort Aijal', they produced, in 1898, *A Grammar and Dictionary of the Lushai Language (Duhlien)*, the first book in any local tongue. As was the case with the Nagas, Christianity spread rapidly in the Lushai Hills as well.

While the Presbyterians were active in the north, Baptist missionaries preached the Christian gospel in the more sparsely populated south. According to Chin historian Vumson, 'the British administration completely ignored education for their subjects, so that educating the people was wholly in the hands of the missionaries.'[8] The missionaries also introduced modern medicine, and people soon discovered that it was more effective than traditional sacrifices when treating sick people. Accepting the new faith also became easy because of a traditional belief in a supreme being, or *pathian*, and life after death in a village known as Mitthikhua, beyond which was a paradisiacal abode of bliss called *Pialral*. These old myths and legends that may well have been modified by the missionaries to make Christianity seem less distant and alien, or, as Lt Col. J. Shakespear, an early British administrator, put it, the incorporation of the teachings of the missionaries with indigenous beliefs made is possible for a tribesman to 'admit the truth of Christianity . . . without abandoning the faith of his forefathers'.[9]

The Lushai Hills continued to be a part of Assam, but administered directly by its chief commissioner and, in 1912, the governor, when it was given the status of a self-contained province responsible directly to the viceroy of India. Like the Naga Hills and other tribal areas of Assam and Burma, the Lushai Hills was designated an Excluded Area under the Government of India Act, 1935. But here as elsewhere in Britain's Indian Empire, it simply meant that the district was outside the direct control of the provincial legislature in Assam, not that it became, or ever was, excluded from India, or proclaimed a separate 'crown colony', as many local people still believe. As the Presbyterian and Baptist churches continued to grow, so did a new national consciousness among the tribesmen. And some of the first social organizations among them came as a result of the activities of the missionaries, albeit somewhat inadvertently. A central institution in most villages in the Lushai Hills, as indeed among the Nagas and other hill peoples in the region, was the so-called bachelor's dormitory. When boys reached puberty, they moved to a special building in the village, called *zawlbuk*, where they learnt everything a young man needed to know. Shakespear put it rather prudishly that unmarried men gathered there 'in the evenings to sing songs, tell stories, and make jokes till it is time to visit their sweethearts, after which they return there for the rest of the night'.[10]

More plainly speaking, the youths enjoyed remarkable sexual freedom. The missionaries abhorred this, at the same time as they recognized the need for traditional culture and values to be preserved. This caused a dilemma and, as church historian Frederick S. Downs put it in his essay 'Christianity and Social Change': 'The missionaries and early Christians were almost all opposed to the observance of traditional festivals . . . because the songs and dances were perceived to be either sexually suggestive or celebrations of war and headhunting . . . because of their association with old religion . . . excessive dancing and drinking [were] involved.'[11] Gradually, however, the missionaries changed their attitudes, and drums and dance, which they previously had found shocking, were 'sanitised' of sexual and violent themes, and became an important part of Mizo Christianity. The indigenization of the new creed made it more readily acceptable, and today traditional Mizo dance and music are the highlights of any community gathering, in churches as well as local festivals.

To further uplift – or, as some people would say, Christianize – the morals of local youths, in June 1935, Rev. David Edwards oversaw the formation of the Young Lushai Association, which later became known as the Young Mizo Association, or YMA. As Verghese and Thanzawna noted, the YLA/YMA developed into 'the most potent non-political, non-official organisation of youths having branches all over Mizoram.'[12] It was involved in social work, adult education, construction of houses for the rural poor, and the running of public libraries. But despite its stated 'non-political' goals, it was inevitable that an organization engaged in such activities also became political in nature, as Suhas Chatterjee notes: 'The Young Lushai Association was the pioneer body to rouse the political consciousness among educated Mizos. The YLA reminds us of the Indian Association in Calcutta which was the precursor of the Indian National Congress. The YLA was opposed to the dominance of the Sailo chiefs and considered chiefdom as an impediment towards the democratisation of Lushai society.'[13]

The missionaries had brought with them new social values and, as in the Naga Hills, their desire to promote the teachings of the Christian God and 'His Kingdom in some Asiatic field' gave many poor and backward Lushais a new life. Despite the belief in a pathian, spirit worship was strong and Christianity presented the tribes a common creed instead of scattered beliefs in the power of those spirits. It also gave them a written language and their own literature. With this came self-esteem and ethnic pride, which the missionaries and the colonial authorities could handle. The real legacy of the missionaries was the challenge this posed in multiracial countries such as India – and neighbouring Burma – after independence.

Not surprisingly, considering its standing in Lushai society, the YLA was the first body to begin advocating autonomy. After the fall of Rangoon to the Japanese in March 1942, the future of the Lushai Hills – indeed of British rule over India as well – became uncertain. At about the same time, US president Franklin Roosevelt issued a declaration on the right to self-determination. This,

Chatterjee argues, encouraged the YLA to pass a resolution demanding the right of self-determination of the Lushais. This was the first time such a demand was raised, and even if the central committee of the YLA disapproved of the resolution on the grounds that it was not a political organization, 'there is no denying the fact that the above resolution contained the seeds of Mizo aspiration for autonomy which was to take concrete shape in future.'[14]

As soon as World War II was over, Lushais – or Mizos – who had benefited from Christian education banded together to form the Lushai (later Mizo) Union, a political party. Formally established on 6 April 1946, and then as the Lushai Common People's Union, it did not support the plan of some British colonial officers to turn the tribal areas in the north-east into a 'crown colony' once India became independent; instead, the Lushai Union became an associate of the Indian National Congress. But elements within the Union broke away and, in 1947, formed the Lushai Union Council, which later became the United Mizo Freedom Organization, UMFO, which was close to the chiefs and more separatist in character.

The policies of the Lushai Union paid off, and the Sixth Schedule of the Constitution of India, which granted limited autonomy to the tribal areas on the periphery of the Assam plains, was implemented in the Lushai Hills. The transition from British rule to independence was relatively smooth and, unlike the Nagas who boycotted elections, the Lushais, except for the chiefs, took part in the 1952 elections for three seats in the Assam Legislative Assembly as well as the newly established Lushai Hills District Council. The Lushai Union swept the polls everywhere, and it was more interested in social reform than independence. And reform meant curtailing the power of the traditional chiefs, who supported UMFO. It was a situation entirely different from that in the Naga Hills, where local politicians as well as tribal leaders rallied behind the pro-independence Naga National Council.

One notable exception was UMFO leader Lalmawia, a former leader of the Lushai Students' Association who had served as an officer in the Burmese Army during World War II. He had contacts with Burma's Anti-Fascist People's Freedom League, the main nationalist party in neighbouring Burma, and supported by some of the chiefs, he wanted the Lushai Hills to become part of Burma after its independence. Some, even within the Lushai Union, had advocated a 'middle way' by which the Lushai Hills district would remain part of India for a ten-year trial period and then decide its future status. A memorandum to that effect was submitted to the authorities in Assam, but did not receive much attention from the provincial or Central governments.[15] Secession in 1947 or later, or joining a neighbouring country, was not an option; British India was going to be partitioned into Muslim Pakistan and the secular but predominantly Hindu Indian Union. There was no third alternative.

The 1952 District Council election and, more importantly, the grandly named 1954 'Assam Lushai Hills District (Acquisition of Chiefs' Rights) Act', effectively abolished the power of the chiefs. Originally, there had been sixty chiefs altogether, but by the time of independence the number had swelled to 259 Lushai chiefs and fifty from the Pawi-Lakher, a related tribe. Under the new act, the rights they had enjoyed were now transferred to the elected government and the administration of their land handed over to the District Council.[16] In 1954, another piece of legislation was enacted, changing the name of the Lushai Hills district to the Mizo Hills district. The term Mizo, it was argued, covered all the tribes in the district, not only the Lushais but also the Raite, the Hmar, the Paite, the Mara – or Lakher – and the Pawi.[17] But the Lushai, or Lusei-Dulien, language remained the undisputed lingua franca among all the tribes and clans.

And the churches continued to grow, even in remote parts of the district. A primary school project was launched by them, and by 1952, every Mizo village with more than a hundred houses was provided with its own school. Here is one account of these unique developments in an otherwise undeveloped part of India:

It was the enthusiasm of the villagers that made the system work. Everywhere they took responsibility for erecting buildings and making the bulk of the school furniture. The Church, with Mission help, provided teachers' salaries and some of the equipment, including the brass gong suspended at the entrance to every school. The dedication and ability of the teachers was remarkable and the vast upsurge in literacy is down to them ... In 1959 an American literacy expert, working for the National Christian Council of India, visited Aizawl and the surrounding villages. It was with considerable difficulty that a few Mizo illiterates were found for him on that occasion. It was obviously a new experience for him. The literacy rate is 95 per cent.[18]

It seemed to be going mostly well in the Mizo Hills – until disaster struck in the late 1950s. Every few decades or so, an invasion by rats attracted by the abundance of protein-rich bamboo seeds after the bamboo flowers. But the rats also eat anything in their way, devastating crops and food storages. The Mizos call it *mautam*, 'bamboo death', which is said to occur every forty-eight years, and it hits their hills especially badly as most of them are covered by thick bamboo forests. If a bamboo variety called *thing* is affected, the crisis is called *thingtam*, but since that kind of bamboo grows only in certain parts of the hills, it becomes more localized and not as long-lasting.

But thingtams can also be severe, as in 1881 when a famine killed 15,000 people. In 1911 the bamboo flowered again, this time as a mautam, and for more than a year people in the Lushai Hills as well as the Chittagong Hill Tracts and the Chin Hills of Burma were severely affected. Wise from their experiences of previous crises, the government and the missionaries were better prepared when the bamboo started flowering in the mid-1920s. By the time a thingtam famine hit the hills in 1929, people had saved food, and the missionaries secured aid from their churches in Britain and the United States. As a result, the number of Christians almost doubled as local churches distributed supplies, and people sought solace in the Bible.

The first signs of a mautam after India's independence could be seen in late 1958 – as expected, forty-eight years after the 1911 mautam. On 29 October, the Mizo Hills District Council, sensing the impending doom, issued a statement:

> With the flowering of bamboos in the Mizo District, the rat population has phenomenally increased and it is feared that in the next year the whole district would be affected. As a precautionary measure against the imminence of famine, following the flowering of bamboos, the District Council feels that the Government be moved to sanction to the Mizo District Council a sum of Rs. Fifteen lakhs, to be expended on a test relief measure for the whole of Mizo district including the Pawi-Lakher region.[19]

The government of Assam, however, at first did not take the report seriously. Bimala Prasad Chaliha, the then chief minister of the state of which the Mizo Hills formed a part, and his colleagues, 'even ridiculed the connection between bamboo flowering, increase in rodents and the consequent famine as tribal beliefs,' to quote Indian researcher M. Bhattacharjee.[20] As Sajal Nag, a historian at the Assam Central University in Silchar, also points out, by the time famine hit the Mizo Hills – and this time it was a severe mautam – 'neither the "paternalistic" British nor the powerful chiefs were there. A great number of foreign missionaries had also left the hills. The affairs of the Mizos were theoretically in their own hands, but they still had to depend on the government of Assam for almost everything as the district council had no money of its own.'[21]

Further aggravating the crisis was the fact that the 1947 partition of British India had meant that the Mizo Hills had been cut off from what used to be the nearest port and main railhead, Chittagong, which now was in East Pakistan. This had already caused economic hardships among the Mizos since Chittagong had also been the main outlet for products from the hills, and no alternative market had yet been found. The only lifeline of the Mizo Hills was a narrow, winding road built in 1942 from Silchar in the plains immediately north of the hills down to Aizawl – and that was far from adequate for the needs which arose when hunger swept across the eastern mountains in the late 1950s. This time, the Mizo Hills were much more isolated than during the 1929–30 thingtam famine.

Local people moved into action, and the Mizo Cultural Society, a social club, was converted into a non-governmental famine relief organization called the Mizo National Famine Front, MNFF.[22] And one person emerged as the saviour of the Mizo people in these dire times of a severe mautam: a thirty-two-year-old fiery orator and former soldier in the British Indian Army called Laldenga. Born in Pukpui village, 8 kilometres north of Aizawl, he was educated in missionary schools and, as a very young man, joined the army during World War II and became a havildar clerk. After independence, he served as an accountant for the Mizo District Council and never tried to hide his disdain for people from the Indian plains. He believed in an independent country for the Mizos, and the famine catapulted him to the fore of the hitherto simmering separatist movement.[23]

The MNFF recruited young Mizos and sent them to remote villages to distribute relief supplies – and to propagate a new slogan: 'Mizoram for the Mizos!' 'Ram' means land or country in the local language, and Laldenga wanted nothing less than an independent nation for his people, who he said were neglected by the Indian authorities. Although it was the initially sceptical Assam government that, in the end, sponsored the MNFF with relief supplies, Laldenga was able to take political advantage of the situation. Whatever the Assam government eventually did, it was perceived to be too little, too late. An estimated 10,000 people perished in the aftermath of the 1958–59 mautam.

In October 1961, the MNFF dropped 'famine' from its name and became the MNF, the Mizo National Front, with Laldenga as its president.[24] It was proclaimed as a full-fledged political party with the aim of achieving 'the highest sovereignty' and to unite all the Mizos to live under one political boundary, to uplift the Mizos socially, and to 'preserve and safeguard Christianity'.[25] The same ideas were also disseminated through the newspaper *Zalenna*, 'Freedom', which was edited by a prominent Mizo national activist, R. Vanlawma.[26]

Preparations were also underway to organize an armed force to fight for that 'highest sovereignty', a euphemism for independence and separation from India. But in order to build a viable fighting force, Laldenga and his men needed weapons, training and careful preparations for the attacks they intended to launch on the Assam Rifles, the main unit of the security forces responsible for the defence of the hill district.

Laldenga knew that the Nagas, who had already been fighting for several years, were receiving substantial support from Pakistan. In 1963, the first teams of MNF volunteers slipped across the border to the Chittagong Hill Tracts in East Pakistan, where the authorities were delighted to find out that another hill people in India's north-east were willing to rise up in arms. As with the Nagas, Pakistan's Muslim army commanders and intelligence operatives had no qualms about supporting a band of Christian rebels as long as they could destabilize India, and perhaps pull troops away from the border with West Pakistan and the Line of Control in Kashmir. Pakistan had not given up hope of capturing the whole of Jammu and Kashmir, which they had failed to do during the conflict of 1947–48. Muslim Kashmir stood for the 'K' in Pakistan; without it, the dream of a Muslim state carved out of British India would be incomplete.[27]

The initial contact with Pakistan's intelligence services was made through the office of the Pakistan High Commission then maintained at Shillong. At that time, Shillong was the capital of Assam, and the proximity to East Pakistan warranted a diplomatic mission there. But it was hardly surprising that it was also a den of spies, right in the centre of India's volatile north-eastern region. It was closed only after the 1965 India–Pakistan war. The Pakistanis gave the green light, and Laldenga himself, along with MNF vice-president Lalnunmawia and Sainghaka, a third Mizo nationalist who worked for the Accountant General's office in Shillong, crossed over into East Pakistan.[28] They were given a warm welcome in Dhaka and promised generous supplies of weapons.

There was a minor setback when Laldenga and his close aide, MNF vice-president Lalnunmawia, were arrested in the Mizo Hills in December 1963. They had just returned from East Pakistan, a mission that they could not keep secret. The two Mizo leaders were incarcerated in Silchar jail, but somehow Laldenga managed to convince his captors that he had gone to East Pakistan only to visit fellow Mizos in the Chittagong Hill Tracts. Miraculously, he was believed, and he and Lalnunmawia were set free on 17 February 1964. They returned to a heroes' welcome in Aizawl.[29]

Their release was immediately followed by more future guerrilla fighters crossing the border into East Pakistan. At the end of 1964, Lt Col. Vivek Chadha writes, 'a group of 22 MNF volunteers crossed into . . . East Pakistan . . . and camped near Dhaka where they were given training in the use of arms and explosives. The group was given arms and explosives as much as they could carry.'[30] This group was followed in 1965 by 200 Mizo volunteers led by Sapzova, a British-trained former radar operator in the Indian Navy who also had also worked as a customs officer in Champhai on the Burmese border. In February 1966, another 160 young Mizos were sent to East Pakistan.

The Nagas had begun their revolt armed with crossbows, antiquated hunting rifles and weapons of World War II vintage and only later received modern arms from Pakistan and, eventually,

China. The Mizos received Sten guns, Bren guns, .303 rifles, explosives and hand grenades from Pakistan. Sapzova, who now lives in the northern Thai city of Chiang Mai, laughingly told me in January 2011: 'In East Pakistan we were introduced to several army officers, among them Lt Gen. Tikka Khan. They gave us all the weapons we needed. And as a former customs officer, I knew how to smuggle things across borders! Not a single bullet was lost.'[31]

And there was no shortage of people who could, or wanted to, use those guns. A group called Mizo National Volunteers, MNV, had grown out of the famine relief effort and, on 2 June 1961, soldiers from the 2nd Assam Regiment had mutinied at Srinagar airfield in Kashmir. Many of them were Mizos, and led by Havildar Biakvela, they were court-martialled and dismissed from service. Back home in the Mizo Hills, these experienced soldiers swelled the ranks of disgruntled Mizos who were ready to fight.

The Mizo rebels were well armed and well prepared when they, in the beginning of 1966, decided to launch simultaneous attacks on all urban centres in the Mizo Hills. It was code-named 'Operation Jericho', the same as for an Allied bombing raid on a prison in German-occupied France in February 1944. As recounted in the Book of Joshua, the sixth book of the Hebrew Bible, the walls surrounding Jericho miraculously fell after a seven-day siege by the Israelites who had been walking around the city shouting and blowing horns. It led to the conquest of the Promised Land of Canaan by Joshua, the leader of the Israelite tribes after the death of Moses.

Such Biblical allegories aside, the timing of the attacks was perfect from a strictly military point of view. The 1962 war with China had prompted India's security services to concentrate their attention on the Himalayas and the Chinese frontier. At the same time, the situation seemed to be improving in Nagaland, which in December 1963 had become a state, and where a ceasefire agreement was agreed upon in September the following year. Despite the mautam, the thousands of deaths it had caused and louder calls for autonomy and even separation from India, no one thought of the Mizo Hills as a potential flashpoint.

In October 1965, the MNF had indeed submitted a memorandum to the prime minister of India to 'represent the case of the Mizo people for freedom and independence' and stating that, 'The Mizos from time immemorial lived in complete independence from foreign interference . . . however . . . border disputes and frontier clashes with their neighbouring people . . . ultimately brought the British Government to the scene in 1844. The Mizo country was subsequently under the British political control in 1895 when a little more than half the country was arbitrarily carved out and named Lushai Hills [Now Mizo District] and the rest of their land was parcelled out of their hands to the adjoining pool for the sole purpose of administrative convenience without their will or consent . . . [and] during fifteen years of close contact and association with India, the Mizo people had not been able to feel at home with Indians or India . . . they do not, therefore, feel Indian . . . in a nutshell, they [the Mizos] are a distinct nation, created, moulded and nurtured by God and nature . . . whether the Mizo Nation should shed her tears in joy to establish firm and lasting friendship with India in war and in peace or in sorrow and in anger is up to the Government of India to decide [sic].'[32]

But few took that 'memorandum' seriously, especially since it repeated the misconception that the Lushai Hills, because they had been an 'Excluded Area' under the British, never were part of British India. And 'Mizo independence'? There was no way any security planners in New Delhi were going to take that demand seriously. There were even fewer Mizos than Nagas in India and, on the surface, the Mizo Hills did not seem ripe for an insurrection.

That was a serious miscalculation, or, as General Sam Manekshaw, commander of the Eastern Command of the Indian Army, later confessed: 'We were caught with our pants down.'[33] And the

Indians were, when D-Day came: the night of 28 February 1966. Despite a few hitches in the planning and initial execution of the plan, Operation Jericho was a smashing success. Aizawl, Champhai, Lunglei and other towns were attacked along with smaller outposts at Marpara, Chawngte, Vaseitlang, Vaphai, Hnahlan, Tuipuibari, Tuisen, Vanbawng and Demagiri.[34] The entire Mizo Hills were up in flames as gunfire and explosions could be heard everywhere. In Aizawl, the treasury was looted and guns snatched from the Assam Rifles camp in the centre of the town. In Champhai, soldiers of the Assam Rifles were captured and wireless sets and stores were seized. The Lunglei garrison was overrun by between 500 and 1,000 Mizo rebels, and 1.8 million rupees were taken from the local treasury. The loot was carried away in a jeep, along with arms, ammunition and rations for the soldiers which were loaded onto mules and brought to rebel camps in the surrounding hills. The same pattern was repeated in town after town, village after village, where the Assam Rifles, the Border Security Force or the local police had camps and outposts.

Lalchamliana, then a sixteen-year-old 'volunteer', took part in the fighting in and around Aizawl:

> We gathered late at night at specified meeting places, in the cover of darkness on February 28 and had brought with us knives, mosquito nets, blankets and rice for three days. We also had Beretta sub-machine guns and one Tommy gun. There were some disagreements among the leaders. Some of them were reluctant to launch an all-out offensive, because they feared the consequences. But fighting broke out when a grenade went off accidentally, and then there was no stopping it. A curfew was imposed and the Assam Rifles tried to patrol the town. We ambushed them in the streets, but failed to capture their post. It was well defended. But we kept on fighting in the hills around Aizawl.[35]

Then came a declaration of independence. Signed by sixty Mizo nationalist leaders with Laldenga's name at the top of the list, the two-page document was distributed everywhere in the hills, stating that Mizoram, as they called their land, was no longer part of the Indian Union:

> Our people are despised, persecuted, tortured, manhandled, murdered without displaying justice where they preached and confessed before us and throughout the world that they have instituted for us a separate administrative set-up in conformity with the principle of democracy. To conceal their evil selfish design, religious assimilation and Hindu indoctrination, they preached to have established secularism which cannot be accepted as it leads to suppression of Christianity . . . we, therefore, the representatives of the Mizo people meeting on this day, the First of March in the year of our Lord 1966 appealing to the Supreme Judge of the world authority of the good people of this country, solemnly publish and declare that Mizoram is and out of right ought to be free and independent, that they are absolved from all allegiance to India and its Parliament . . . we appeal to all freedom-loving nations and individuals to uphold human rights and dignity and to extend help to the Mizo people for our rightful and legitimate demand for self-determination. We appeal also to all independent countries to give recognition to the independence of Mizoram.[36]

Not unexpectedly, no 'independent country' ever recognized Mizoram's independence, and no support came from any outside power except Pakistan, which continued to supply weapons to the rebels and provide them with sanctuaries in the Chittagong Hill Tracts. But China soon began to show interest in yet another tribal rebellion in India's north-east. In the months after Operation Jericho, MNF representatives met officials at the Chinese consulate in Dhaka and were given wireless transmitters, medicines and 400,000 Yuan in Chinese currency, which was converted into Indian rupees. And, in 1970, Laldenga and his secretary, Zoramthanga, flew from their new base in Dhaka to Beijing to attend the Chinese National Day celebrations in the Chinese capital.[37] The Mizo rebels too had made their contacts with the Chinese and, like the Naga National Council, they were going to be handsomely rewarded. What began as a tribal uprising soon became drawn into the geopolitics of the region.

At the same time, Operation Jericho provoked a prompt response from the Indian security authorities. The road to Silchar – still the only road connecting the Mizo Hills with the Assamese lowlands – was cut at the initial stages of Operation Jericho as Mizo rebels had blown up several bridges. The Assam Rifles camp in Aizawl remained besieged for several days and, on 4 March 1966, air strikes by the fighter jets of the Indian Air Force strafed the town. The next day, more planes flew low over Aizawl, firing machine guns in what became the only instance of the Indian military resorting to air strikes in its own territory. Apart from Aizawl, the nearby villages of Tualbung and Hnahlan were also hit. Almost the entire population of Aizawl fled and took refuge in remote villages in the surrounding hills.

Aizawl was recaptured by Indian forces on 7 March and a relentless counter-insurgency campaign was launched throughout the Mizo Hills. Due to its proximity to East Pakistan, with which it shared a long, porous border, the Mizo Hills were a potentially much more dangerous theatre of war than Nagaland. The Naga rebels could sneak across into Burma, but there was nothing on the other side apart from some impoverished villages inhabited by hilltribes. In the Chittagong Hill Tracts, the Mizo rebels had established camps where they could receive supplies and be trained by Pakistan's intelligence services.

In that precarious situation, India decided to unleash one of its most controversial counter-insurgency initiatives in the north-east: a programme which euphemistically was called 'regrouping' into 'Protected and Progressive Villages.' A similar programme had been tried to separate the Naga rebels from the civilian population, but in the Mizo Hills it was carried out much more thoroughly and systematically. According to Vijendra Singh Jafa, former chief secretary of Assam: 'The years 1967–69 saw the entire rural population of Mizoram (roughly eighty per cent of the total population) uprooted from their homes, to be relocated miles away . . . the army argued that the segregation and control of the population by this method was necessary for a successful counterinsurgency campaign. The general humiliation, less of freedom and of property, and, very often, injury and death involved in this process of so-called "grouping of villages" . . . was tantamount to annihilation of reason and sensibility and certainly not the best policy to follow against our own ethnic minorities.'[38]

Between 4 January and 23 February 1967 – the first forty-nine days of the operation – 45,107 inhabitants of 109 villages were relocated in eighteen so-called 'group centres' on the main road through the Mizo Hills, which connects Vairangte on the border with Assam proper and with Aizawl and Lunglei. And more 'regroupings' were to follow in a similar, forced manner. An Indian Army officer recounted to Jafa the heartbreaking scenes he witnessed during the campaign:

> Darzo was one of the richest villages I have ever seen in this part
> of the world. There were ample stores of paddy, fowls and pigs.
> The villagers appeared well-fed and well-clad, and most of them
> had some money in cash. We arrived in the village about ten in the
> morning. My orders were to get the villagers to collect whatever
> moveable property they could, and set their own village to fire at
> seven in the evening . . . night fell and I had to persuade the
> villagers to come out and set fire to their homes. Nobody came
> out. Then I had to order my soldiers to enter every house and
> force the people out. Every man, woman and child who could
> walk came out with as much of his or her belongings and food as
> they could. But they wouldn't set fire to their homes. Ultimately, I
> lit a torch myself and set fire to one of the houses. I knew I was

carrying out orders, and would hate to do such a thing if I had my way. My soldiers also started torching other buildings, and the whole place was soon ablaze. There was absolute confusion everywhere. Women were wailing and shouting and cursing. Children were frightened and cried. Young boys and girls held hands and looked at their burning village with a stupefied expression on their faces. But the grown up men were silent; not a whimper or a whisper from them. Pigs were running about, mithuns were bellowing, dogs were barking, and fowls setting up a racket with their fluttering and crackling. One little girl ran into her burning house and soon darted out holding a kitten in her hands.[39]

The programme was modelled on Sir Robert Thompson's regrouping of villages in Malaya during the communist insurrection there in the 1950s. The colonial authorities had then successfully resettled half a million ethnic Chinese in new villages guarded by military units and surrounded by barbed-wire fences. But that worked because the ethnic Muslim-Malay majority in Malaya had shown little sympathy for the Chinese-dominated rebellion, and the inhabitants of those 'new villages' were given ample support for their survival.

In Mizoram, the entire population was regarded as 'hostile', and as Jafa also points out: 'All tribal societies are kinship based, with strong ties to the land which has, through the proximity of the ancestral graves, a spiritual significance. The land contains their history and sense of identity. The people are part of a habitat, and the hills, rivers, paths, trees, and woodlands establish a living pattern which is passed from generation to generation and becomes the essence of tribal life, music, arts, crafts and agriculture. Better medical and educational facilities, some minimal roofing material, free food for a few months, and better employment opportunities offered in the new re-settlement centres were no substitute for the tribal life which the shifting destroyed.'[40]

Hence, it did little to quell the insurgency. The Mizo National Army, MNA, as it was called, was reorganized in 1967 with Maj.

Gen. Thangzuala as the overall commander. He could count on thousands of fighters, organized into two brigades: the Lion Brigade and the Dagger Brigade. There were four battalions under the Lion Brigade and three under the Dagger Brigade, each consisting of 500–1,000 men and all named after heroes in Mizo history. One battalion under the Lion Brigade was named after Vanapa, a nineteenth-century Mizo warrior, while Chawngbawla, also a nineteenth-century warrior and hunter, gave name to another. The Dagger Brigade's Zampuimanga battalion derived its name from another nineteenth-century hunter who was reputed to have killed thirteen tigers. The Khuangchera battalion, another unit under the Dagger Brigade, was named after a warrior who had died in battle against the British in 1890.[41] The Mizos evidently saw their uprising as apocalyptic in a Christian sense, but also as traditionally Mizo because of its cataclysmic nature.

Shortly after Operation Jericho and the attack on Aizawl, the young fighter Lalchamliana and his companions went to East Pakistan to get more arms and ammunition. They linked up with Laldenga in the forest east of the Kapitai dam in the Chittagong Hill Tracts. By April 1966, they were back, fighting in Mizoram, with Lalchamliana as a member of the MNA's special forces. And they were going to spread the war across the border into the Chin Hills of Burma. The Chins, who are closely related to the Mizos, gave them shelter. Tialkhala, a local Chin leader, was sympathetic to the Mizo cause and helped them launch a spectacular raid on the town of Tiddim and Falam, and a police post at Tuibual near the Indian border. In the early hours of 1 June 1968, Mizo rebels, led by Lalchamliana, overran the Burmese Army post at Falam and captured three light machine guns, sixteen Sten guns, a few carbines, .303 rifles numbering 122, and nineteen .38 pistols – along with twelve million Kyats in Burmese currency. As planned, attacks were also carried out on Tiddim and Tuibual, which were also briefly overrun.[42]

The Burmese Army's response was swift and without mercy. The Mizos fled, with their loot, back to the Indian border where they set up a base near the Tiau River south of Champhai. The river forms the international frontier, and the camp was going to be used for another, much more ambitious scheme the MNF had been planning for quite some time: to send armed units across Burma to China. Through their contacts with the Chinese consulate in Dhaka, they knew that they would get support once they reached Yunnan. But being Christian and, actually, not communist, the Mizos also wanted to reach out to the West.

In February 1968, before the attack on Falam, two men from the Karen National Union, KNU, an ethnic group fighting the Burmese government, had come to an MNF camp in the Mizo Hills. Like the MNF, the KNU was also led by Christians, and they agreed to form a coordinated movement against Burma's military government – which could have been one of the reasons why the Mizo rebels decided to attack targets in the Burmese side of the border. The Karen, they believed, had contacts with the CIA. Two men were selected for the missions: the MNF's intelligence chief, Vanlalngaia, was told to get to China while Sapzova, the former naval and customs officer, left for Karen rebel-held areas on Burma's border with Thailand.

Sapzova was for long periods based in Dhaka, where he, apart from handling arms supplies across the border to the Mizo Hills, helped several contingents of Naga rebels reach East Pakistan. They as well as the wounded Mizo rebels received medical treatment in a hospital near Chittagong. Sapzova was well travelled and well connected, but the only Burmese he knew was 'I have a toothache!' which was convenient to slur if asked about his identity by police or immigration on his way through Burma to Thailand.

In April 1968, he managed to travel undetected by steamboat on the Irrawaddy River to Mandalay and continued by train south to Toungoo, where he hid in the town's Karen Baptist Church. A pastor helped him on to the Thai border, where he was met by eight

Karen rebels who escorted him to their camp. The fact that Mizo rebels had attacked targets in Burma – Falam and Tiddim – helped establish his rapport with the anti-Rangoon ethnic rebels. When in Thailand, he met William Young, a former CIA officer who was sympathetic to ethnic causes.

From Chiang Mai in northern Thailand, he was also able to contact his comrades in East Pakistan, which was done through a Western missionary at the Baptist church in Dhaka. The Indian authorities have frequently accused the missionaries of 'being behind' the ethnic rebellions in the north-east. While that is a clear exaggeration, many missionaries were sympathetic to the Mizos, the Nagas, the Karen, the Kachin and other Christian hill tribes fighting what they perceived as oppressive regimes. Even the former CIA agent Young was the son and grandson of Christian missionaries in Burma.[43] But Sapzova did not manage to get any material support for the Mizo rebellion, and eventually settled in Chiang Mai, where he became an English teacher at a local school.

Vanlalngaia, the other Mizo emissary to go abroad, had probably the most colourful background of all the Mizo rebel leaders. Born in a small village near the Burmese border in Champhai in 1936, he was as a child sent to Burma to study. Although a Christian, he stayed in a Buddhist monastery for five months before he could travel on to Rangoon, where he attended a proper school. Vanlalngaia was a bright and outstanding student and, in 1956, he was selected to go to Britain for training with the Royal Air Force. He spent three years with a technical squadron at Halton Air Force Base near Wendover in Buckinghamshire, where Lord Kitchener's fabled armies had trained during World War I.

He returned to Burma in 1960 to serve under Air Commodore Tommy Clift, the Anglo-Shan chief of the Burmese Air Force. When the military under General Ne Win took over in a coup d'etat in March 1962, Clift was first included in the Revolutionary Council that seized power. But Clift soon fell out with the power-hungry general, and escaped to Thailand where he joined the resistance led by ousted prime minister U Nu and his close associate Edward Law Yone, a former newspaper editor.

Vanlalngaia returned to his old homeland, the Mizo Hills, where he, in June 1966, joined the MNF. He stayed with Laldenga in Dhaka and took part in military operations in the Mizo Hills, until he set out for China. Because he was fluent in Burmese, Vanlalngaia had no difficulty travelling through the country disguised as an ordinary person. He reached Lashio in northern Shan state, where he managed to contact the Kachin Independence Army, another predominantly Christian rebel movement. With the help of the KIA, he crossed the border into China in June 1968 and spent five months with the People's Liberation Army. He did not speak any Chinese, but the PLA had English as well as Burmese interpreters. Through them, a PLA officer told Vanlalngaia: 'Seven-hundred million Chinese support the Mizo cause.' But, even so, he returned to the Mizo Hills empty-handed. The KIA had also promised him weapons, but, in the end, decided that its own soldiers needed them more than the Mizos. Then, Laldenga sent him to try to negotiate peace with the Indian government, 'not because we were desperate', as Vanlalngaia told me, '. . . we had bases in East Pakistan and supplies from there as well. But we wanted to find out what the Indian position was.'[44] However, Vanlalngaia was promptly arrested and sent to Silchar jail.

The Chinese connection did not come into fruition until after a major setback for the Mizo rebels: the 1971 Bangladesh war for independence. Until then, Laldenga had been spending most of his time in Dhaka, and the Mizo rebels by then had established permanent camps and training facilities in East Pakistan. But, in 1971, the Bengalis there had had enough of their union with Pakistan, with which they had little in common apart from the Muslim religion. A bitter liberation war was fought, and the Pakistani officer who had received Sapzova in 1966, Lt Gen. Tikka Khan, gained notoriety as 'the Butcher of Dhaka' for his role in the attempts to suppress the Bengali rebellion. He later became the commander-in-chief of the Pakistan armed forces as defence minister under Zulfikar Ali Bhutto.

When Indian troops, which had intervened in the war in East Pakistan, captured Dhaka in December 1971, they were also looking for rebels from the north-east. But while Thinoselie and Neidelie of the Naga National Council were caught in a safe house in Dhaka, Laldenga and several of his officers managed to flee to Burma. Travelling south along the highway to Chittagong, then to Cox's Bazar and down to the banks of the Naaf River, which formed the short border East Pakistan – now Bangladesh – shared with Burma, they escaped the onslaught of the Indian Army.

The Arakan Hills on the Burmese side of the border was a haunt of an abundance of rebel groups: nationalist Arakanese Buddhists, Muslims called Rohingya but never recognized as such by their Buddhist neighbours, a local communist party which wanted to turn Arakan into a people's republic, Red Flag communists who admired Stalin and were among the most radical in Asia at the time, and the slightly more moderate and pro-Chinese Communist Party of Burma, CPB. But it was the CPB that was the strongest among them, and communist veteran Kyaw Mya remembers the sudden influx of armed men from East Pakistan, which just had become Bangladesh:

> The Mizos arrived in 1971 after India had invaded East Pakistan. Some Pakistani soldiers came with them, too, and we got their guns. The Mizos numbered about a thousand, and we had to feed them. Laldenga was among them, and we arranged for his flight to Pakistan through the Pakistani consulate in Sittwe. But most Mizos stayed with us for about a year, after which they moved to remote corners of the Chittagong Hill Tracts where there are a people called Bon who are related to the Mizos. Others stayed on in upper Arakan, on the banks of the Kaladan river.[45]

At that time, there was a Pakistani consulate in Sittwe which is also called Akyab, the capital of Arakan, and the CPB sent Lalsangliana, one of Laldenga's closest confidantes, there to negotiate. He managed to convince Burmese officials in the town that his parents were tribal refuges loyal to Pakistan. The ruse worked and Lalsangliana went to the consulate to prepare for Laldenga's flight out of the country. He arrived at Sittwe with his wife, both disguised as tribals from the Chittagong Hill Tracts. In March 1972, they were issued with Pakistani passports – Laldenga's was in the name of 'Mr Zolkeps' – and then boarded a KLM flight in Rangoon, bound for Karachi.[46]

The loss of the sanctuaries in erstwhile East Pakistan was a serious blow to the MNF. In the same year, 1972, the Mizo rebels sent their first batch of armed men to China to get support and training. Thirty-eight guerrillas led by Maj. Damkhosiaka trekked through the sparsely populated Chin Hills up to Kachin State, where they linked up with the KIA. They crossed into China at Pangwa Pass in early 1973, as Muivah and Thinoselie had done in January 1967, and were well received by the Chinese. They received training at Kotong post on the Chinese side of Pangwa, and then returned to the Mizo Hills. The good news from China encouraged the MNF to send a second batch, which left their hideouts in the Arakan Hills on 14 November 1974. Rama, a Mizo guerrilla, was among them:

> From Arakan we went back to Mizoram to collect more recruits. We marched off on January 20, 1975 and reached China in August, having followed a zigzag route through the Chin Hills and Manipur, Burma's Sagaing Division and then Kachin State. Our group consisted of 108 men led by Biakvela, and we were trained at Meng Hai. Six of us were left in Kachin State with the KIA, while the others went back to Mizoram.[47]

Meng Hai, a small town in a Shan- or Dai-inhabited area of southern Yunnan called Sipsongpanna, which the Chinese corrupt to Xishuangbanna, was an odd choice for a training camp for insurgents from north-eastern India. It meant that the 108 Mizos had to travel hundreds of kilometres through Chinese territory from Pangwa. Whatever the reason for sending the Mizos to Meng Hai, they were trucked back to the Kachin border in the north in January 1976 and returned home loaded with Chinese weapons. By then, however, fundamental changes had taken place in the Mizo Hills. A jungle warfare training facility for the Indian Army had been set up in Vairangte near the border with Assam proper in May 1970. It was clear that a new, more professional approach was needed after the negative experiences with the 'Protected and Progressive Villages' scheme.

Known officially as the Counter-insurgency and Jungle Warfare School, CIJWS, it was the first of its kind in India. Rather than providing courses for only officers and special operatives, entire battalions were trained at Vairangte, whose campus sprawls over eighty acres in and around the village. The site was chosen because, being close to Assam's Cachar district, insurgency was not too endemic in the area, but the foothills provided ideal training terrain for the troops. By the time CIJWS was established, the Naga insurgency had been raging for fourteen years and the Mizo revolt for four. According to Maj. Gen. Ardeshir Gustadji Minwalla, commandant of the facility in the early 1980s: 'The thrust of counter-insurgency was wrong in the '60s. Troops were inducted on an ad hoc basis; the soldiers weren't physically or mentally prepared to fight insurgency. Many of them suffered from fear of the unknown, and battles were unsatisfying ding-dong affairs. What was needed was the evolution of techniques, doctrines and concepts to fight insurgency.'[48]

Part of the new strategy was a political approach to the problem. As Laldenga and his men were fleeing Bangladesh, the Mizo Hills were well under way to become a Union territory, separate from Assam. In May 1971, representatives of the Mizo Hills District

Council held talks with Prime Minister Indira Gandhi in New Delhi, asking for statehood for the Mizo Hills. As a first step, on 21 January 1972, the Mizo Hills became the Union territory of Mizoram with a thirty-three-member Legislative Assembly and a representative in the Lok Sabha in New Delhi. An amnesty for rebel fighters was also announced, and among those released from custody was the MNF's intelligence chief, Vanlalngaia, the movement's first emissary to China. Rather incongruously for a former rebel from India's tribal north-eastern region, he joined the Congress party and became active in the movement to promote khadi, the homespun cloth once made popular by Mahatma Gandhi when he, during the struggle for independence, launched a boycott of foreign-made clothes.[49] And people who had been dislocated during the unpopular Protected and Progressive Villages, or PPV, programme were allowed to return home and rebuild their old villages. Peace, at last, seemed to be a real possibility in Mizoram.

Local, above-ground politicians also began to emerge. One of the most prominent of them was Thenpunga Sailo, a World War II veteran in the British Indian Army and, after independence, the first Mizo to become an officer in the Indian Army. He was made a brigadier in 1966 and became famous as a sub-area commander in Bihar and Orissa, where he provided relief to flood victims and was awarded an AVSM, Ati Vishisht Seva Medal, for his efforts, which is given to recognize 'distinguished service of an exceptional order'. But in 1966, his sons joined the insurgency and were drafted into the special force that protected Laldenga in East Pakistan. One of them was Lalsangliana, who had helped Laldenga escape to Burma and arranged for him to get a passport from the Pakistani consulate in Sittwe.

On retirement from the army in 1974, Sailo formed a group called the Human Rights Committee to protect local people from harassments by the security forces. His movement was converted into a political party, the People's Conference, and Sailo served as chief minister of Mizoram from June to November 1978, and again from May 1979 to May 1984. According to one assessment, Sailo's emergence as a political leader was largely due to his stance against abuses committed by the security forces, rampant corruption within the local administration, his opposition to the PPV programme and, more controversially, his support for an old dream among many Mizos: the integration of all Mizo-inhabited areas into one political entity.[50] Such a scheme would include amalgamating Churachandpur district in Manipur, areas of the Chittagong Hill Tracts in Bangladesh, where there are Mizo-related tribes, as well as the Chin Hills of Burma, with an extended Mizoram, which presumably would still be part of India. It is hardly likely that either of India's neighbours would even contemplate giving up parts of their respective territories to such a 'Greater Mizoram'.

But many Nagas have the same dream: to unite Nagaland with the Naga-inhabited areas of Arunachal Pradesh, Assam, Manipur and Burma. The Naga as well as the Mizo argument is that the British 'divided' their 'homelands' by creating 'artificial boundaries'. But the truth, of course, is that there were never any Naga or Mizo–Chin 'homelands' in the past, just areas where the people were ethnically related but constantly at war with each other, sometimes from village to village. But say that to a Naga or a Mizo, and he or she will be infuriated. These are sensitive issues that have become part and parcel of local politics.

Although sporadic fighting continued throughout the 1970s, the insurgency was by and large over. In June 1975, Zoramthanga, Laldenga's secretary, met representatives of the Indian government in the Thai capital Bangkok, paving the way for a meeting between the Mizo rebel leader and 'Singhal', an Indian intelligence officer whose real name was Hassanwalia, in Geneva, Switzerland in August.[51] It took considerable effort and master trickery to lure Laldenga out of Islamabad, where he was staying, and travel to Switzerland. But it worked.[52]

At a subsequent meeting of Mizo rebel leaders in exile in Cologne, Germany, Laldenga told his men to accept a settlement within the Constitution of India and that the talks had to continue.[53] The armed struggle was not going anywhere and it was becoming clear to many Mizos that their quest for independence was not going to be supported by any foreign power. In the 1960s, the MNF approached the US consulate in Dhaka, but were given the cold shoulder. The response was the same at the British, Japanese and French diplomatic missions in Dhaka. Even Indonesia was approached, but its representative in Dhaka made it clear that his country was not going to supply the Mizos with any arms or other assistance.[54]

The demise of East Pakistan and the emergence of Bangladesh as an independent nation had made Pakistan a much more distant force to appeal to the Mizo rebels. And China's foreign policy was changing rapidly as well after the death of Mao Zedong in September 1976. The new leadership under Deng Xiaoping were 'capitalist roaders'; trade, not support for revolutionary movements, now became China's way of expanding its influence in the region. And despite what the Chinese had told Vanlalngaia in 1968, 'seven hundred million Chinese' did not support the Mizo cause; China's only interest in the Mizo rebellion was that it needed a fifth column in India. It was part of the Great Game that was being played out in north-eastern India's borderlands, nothing more.

After several rounds of talks between the MNF and the Indian government, an agreement was finally reached on 30 June 1986. Like Nagaland, Mizoram was going to become a state within the Indian Union. Known as the Mizo Peace Accord, it was signed by Laldenga on behalf of the MNF, Lalkhama, the chief secretary of the Mizoram government, and R.D. Pradhan, India's home secretary. Apart from granting statehood to Mizoram, the accord also stated that the MNF would undertake not to extend any support to other insurgents in the region such as 'the Tripura/Tribal National

Volunteers, TNV, the People's Liberation Army of Manipur, PLA, and any other such groups, by way of training, supply of arms or providing protection or in any other manner'.[55]

On 21 September 1986, former rebel supremo Laldenga was installed as head of the interim government of the new state-to-be. In the 1987 elections, he was elected to the Legislative Assembly and, in February, he became the first chief minister of the state of Mizoram. India's policy of accommodating former insurgents had paid off again. But, unlike Nagaland, peace had come to stay in Mizoram. The MNF became a legitimate political party and, when Laldenga died of cancer on 7 July 1990 at London's Heathrow airport on his way home from New York, his body was flown back to Mizoram where he was accorded a state funeral. 'If you can't beat them, join them,' Sapzova told me in Chiang Mai in January 2011.

But, as far as the Mizos were concerned, one unresolved issue remained, which was going to have repercussions beyond India's borders: the dream of a Greater Mizoram. While Mizoram was developing socially and economically, the Chin Hills across the border in Burma were officially constituted as a 'Chin State', but hopelessly neglected and underdeveloped. Despite this, the Chin were the only major ethnic minority in Burma that had never raised their own rebel army. Like the Mizos, the Chin were animists until the arrival of Christian missionaries in the late nineteenth century. They put the Chin dialects into written form as well, using the Roman alphabet. But the difference was that whereas Dulien became the lingua franca of the Mizos, the Chin remained divided by at least forty-four different, mutually unintelligible dialects.

Politically, the northern Chin tribes were ruled by hereditary chiefs and an aristocracy, while many of the southern Chin had a democratic type of social organization.[56] In the south, each village was governed by a council that was elected to represent the main families or residential sections of the village. Contributing to the diversity and lack of ethnic cohesion in the Chin Hills was the fact that each village was usually autonomous. And there was no single clan, such as the one led by the Sailo chiefs in the Lushai Hills, that was able to dominate the others.

In 1961, an attempt to form a Chin rebel army was made and supported by the Kachin Independence Army, which had just taken up arms against the government in Rangoon. Modelled after the KIA, it was called the Chin Independence Army – with the unfortunate acronym CIA. But it failed to ignite an uprising in the Chin Hills, where many poor peasant boys actually had little or no chance of social advancement outside the regular armed forces. During the British time, the Chin – as well as the Kachin and the Karen – made up the backbone of the colonial army. After Burma's independence in 1948, many Chin chose to serve with the Burmese Army. Like the Gurkhas of Nepal, they saw military employment as the best way to support their families back home in the hills. Consequently, the CIA never became more than a local irritant for the Central government. It ceased to exist in the late 1960s.

But, in the mid- and late 1980s, dissatisfaction with the lack of development in Chin state led to the formation of new local movements. In 1985, a small group of Chin met to set up the Chin National Front, CNF. It was officially constituted on 20 March 1988 and, on 14 November the same year, it established an armed wing called the Chin National Army, CNA. Several hundred recruits were trained by the KIA, and the CNA set up bases near the Indian border opposite Champhai. Through contacts in Mizoram, they were able to buy supplies from the Indian side, but it was also clear that India's intelligence services were playing their own games. A loyal armed force on the Burmese side of the border could prove useful for policing the other side, to make sure there were no remnants of the MNA that wanted to continue to struggle for an independent Mizoram, and to collect intelligence about, and if possible curtail, the activities of Manipuri and other rebels who were launching raids into India from sanctuaries in Burma.[57] Needless to say, India was not interested in the CNF/CNA cause as such, so whatever support the Chin received, it was limited and the Indians made sure it never posed a real threat to Burma's central military authorities.

A far more serious threat to neighbourly relations was posed by another, more broad-based and better organized movement: the Zomi Reunification Organization, or ZORO. The Chin of Burma call themselves Zomi, which is the same as Mizo, but with the syllables in a different order. Many Mizos felt they had a moral obligation to help their less fortunate brethren on the Burmese side, and they responded with nationalist gusto and bravado. On 18 November 1988 – shortly after a nationwide uprising for democracy had swept across Burma and been brutally suppressed – two hitherto unknown organizations called Burma Zomi Liberation Front and Burma Zomi Students Union issued a joint proclamation assuring the outside world that 'we are no longer citizens of Burma and forsake Burma Union citizenship. We pledge solidarity to keep the integrity of Zoland [Zogam]. Our decision to join the Indian Union none can undo.'[58]

A few months prior to that, on 1 September 1988, the CNF had sent a letter to the prime minister of India stating that it was 'fervently seeking merger of the part of the land inhabited by Chins with the Indian Union', and 'desiring a political reunification of the Chins with their ethnic brethren living in India.'[59] Much to the embarrassment of the Indian government, supporters of the movement hoisted the Indian flag in several towns in Chin state. On the Mizoram side, Brig. T. Sailo supported the movement and thousands of Mizos staged marches up to the Burmese border to welcome their 'Chin brethren' with flags, dance and music. It is reasonable to assume that the declaration of Mizoram as a state within the Indian Union had encouraged the Chin in Burma to look westwards for inspiration and political leadership. Why stay with

Burma, where the ruling military only oppressed the people, when the Mizos in India were enjoying democracy and a large degree of autonomy? They could even organize their own human rights organizations.

Lacking support, or even the slightest sympathy from New Delhi, the once very active and locally entrenched ZORO movement eventually fizzled out. But it made alarm bells go off in Rangoon. In the 1990s, the long-neglected Chin state, which previously had not been a security concern for the Burmese authorities, saw a massive build-up of government forces. With it came severe repression as Burma's security forces went looking for rebels. As in other ethnic minority areas of Burma, this meant rampaging through villages, taking goods at will and even raping young women, some barely in their teens.[60]

Then, in 2006, it was forty-eight years since the *mau* bamboo had flowered in the then Lushai Hills. A new mautam could be expected, with the usual explosion in the rat population and ensuing famine. In November 2007, Mizoram's bamboo groves burst into flower.

Ironically, the then chief minister of Mizoram was Zoramthanga, once a close associate of Laldenga and his right-hand man during both the famine as well as in the armed struggle waged by the MNF. He was criticized for being slow to react to the impending crisis.[61] There were severe food shortages, but this time the Mizos were well prepared for such a disaster; it never developed into a famine on the scale of the one in the late 1950s.

It was quite another story on the much less developed Burmese side. Project Maje, a US-based charity, reported in August 2008:

> In contrast to the bordering regions of India, there had been little to no government response to the impending *mautam* by Burma's military regime . . . 'Critical Point' (a July 2008 report by the Chin Human Rights organization) cites other factors contributing to 'food insecurity' in the Chin State even before the *mautam*, particularly the regime's forced conversion of food crop land to

tea and jatropha plantations (*jatropha* is an introduced crop intended for biofuel use). 'Critical Point' also cited pressures on farmers from corruption and excessive taxation such as the regime's 2,000 kyats per family 'farming permit' plus confiscation of 240 kilograms of harvested rice. [62]

The Mizoram-based Chin Famine Emergency Relief Committee said that 'although famine has been reported, the [Burmese military] has done nothing about it' while local press reports stated that the military 'has continued to demand forced labour, collect excessive taxes and fees, and enforce restrictions against traditional cultivation methods without providing training in alternative farming methods in affected areas . . . there is no food to eat in Chin State.'[63]

The militarization of Chin state in the 1990s had already crated a new, more repressive climate there. The 2007–08 mautam turned discontent into disaster, and the outcome was a flood of Chin refugees into Mizoram. In January 2009, Human Rights Watch, HRW, released a 104-page report titled 'We Are Like Forgotten People: The Chin People of Burma, Unsafe in Burma, Unwanted in India', according to which 'the Chin population in Mizoram is estimated to be as high as 100,000, about 20 per cent of the total Chin population in [Burma's] Chin State.'[64] Or, one might add, slightly more than 10 per cent of the population of Mizoram.

Once settled in India, the Chin remain stateless and, according to HRW, 'the Chin face discrimination and threats of forced return by Mizo voluntary associations in collusion with the Mizoram authorities.' Only about 1,800 Chin have made it to New Delhi, where the United Nations High Commissioner for Refugees, UNHCR, has an office, which makes it possible for them to have their refugee claims decided and be considered for resettlement in third countries.

A few are comparatively well educated and find qualified jobs in Mizoram. But the vast majority of the Chin refugees end up eking out a living as house servants, or working on construction sites, or as drivers, woodcutters, handloom weavers, hawkers and farm hands. Many do the lowest types of jobs with the poorest income, often below what an ordinary person can survive on. And, as a local human rights activist points out: 'Faced with the prospect of starvation, they engage in illegal activities [wine production, drug peddling] which causes conflicts and hatred between the Chins and Mizos.'[65]

While there has always been a trickle of the Chin coming into Mizoram, the massive influx, which began in the late 1990s and escalated into a flood after the 2007–08 mautam, developed into a local crisis and nurtured widespread resentment against the 'outsiders'. There were simply too many of them, and they soon were accused of being behind all kinds of crime in the state and became targets of 'anti-foreigner' campaigns. The influential and powerful Young Mizo Association, YMA, was at the fore of several of those campaigns, issuing orders for the Chin to leave Mizoram before certain deadlines.[66] HRW highlighted this and other abuses and maltreatment of Chin refugees in Mizoram in its 2009 report, which provoked a strong response from the YMA.

On 3 March 2009, the YMA held a meeting with at least twenty-three Mizo groups and accused Chin leaders of misinforming HRW and asked them to refute the report. The YMA claimed that the report was not true and tainted the image of the Mizos 'who have provided support to the Chin people in their state and allowed them to stay'. Meenakshi Ganguly, HRW's South Asia researcher, retorted that, 'it is a fact that Chin people receive help from the Mizo people as they flee their home country, but HRW, as a human rights group, had documented the lack of protection by state agencies for any form of violation against the Chin people.' According to Ganguly: 'No Chin had ever complained to us about the Mizos . . . Mizo people certainly help Chin people. That's why so many Chin people are living in Mizoram. Chin people also praised the Mizos for having helped them.' But Ganguly also urged both Mizoram and the Indian government to shelter and provide assistance to Chin refugees, who have no official status or documentations in India.[67] However, no one criticized, or questioned, the testimonies of the Chin refugees who were interviewed for the HRW report.

The Mizos, like the Nagas, are a proud people and do not take lightly to people criticizing their way of life, or anything 'Mizo' for that matter. In fact, many of them – also like the Nagas – believe they are God's chosen people. There is even a strong belief in Mizoram that they actually are one of the lost tribes of Israel. Their traditional belief in pathian points to monotheism, although it is possible that the first Christian missionaries exaggerated this belief in order to facilitate conversion to the new faith.[68] According to another legend, the original Mizos, and the Chin, were driven away from an ancient homeland called Sinlung, Chin Lung or Chhinlung. Yet another legend says that Chin Lung was a man, and not just any man but the son of Shih Huang-ti, or Qin Shi Huang in Pinyin, who in 221 BC became the first emperor of a unified China. Chin Lung later, this legend claims, gave name to a mountain range called Chin Lung Shan (Shan being mountain in Chinese).[69]

Whatever the origin of Chin Lung, or the Mizo people, or the Chin, in 1951 a Pentecostalist called Chalianthanga, or Mela Chala – no one seems to know for sure – dreamt that God told him to tell his people to revert to their pre-Christian religion. And that, God said, was Judaism. He also instructed them to 'return' to their original 'homeland', Israel, which had been resurrected as an independent state only three years before. His followers called themselves Bnei Menashe, which is sometimes spelt Bene Menasseh, and means 'the Children of Menashe/Menasseh', the son of Joseph in the Old Testament and Jewish scriptures. The numbers of believers increased steadily among the Mizos, the Chin and the related Kukis in Manipur.

According to Shalva Weil at the Hebrew University of Jerusalem, 'it is difficult to assess with certainty whether [this] millenarianism was indigenous to pre-Christian religion, or whether it was a reaction the type of Christianity introduced in the region.'[70] But in 1979, Amishav, an Israeli organization dedicated to locating the 'lost tribes' heard about the movement founded by Chalianthanga and travelled to Mizoram. He was followed by Hillel Halkin, a US-born Israeli journalist and author who wrote a book titled *Across the Sabbath River: In Search of the Lost Tribe of Israel*.[71] The Bnei Menashe rejected the faith in Jesus and made direct contact with Israel. During 1994–2003, altogether 800 'lost Israelites' emigrated to Israel, where most of them were resettled in the occupied Gaza strip, which they were forced to evacuate in 2005 as part of the plan to disengage Gaza from Israel. But by then the Israeli chief Rabbi, Shlomo Amar, had announced that the Bnei Menashe were indeed one of the ten lost tribes of Israel.[72] Therefore, they could emigrate to Israel, but only after a complete conversion to Judaism because they, according to this belief, had been separated from their 'original religion' for millennia.

But not everyone was convinced. Halkin, who is actually a believer in the tale, initiated a collection of genetic samples from more than 300 Mizos and Kukis, which were tested at the Israel Institute of Technology at Haifa. No evidence was found to indicate a Middle Eastern origin for the Mizos and their related tribes. They were unmistakeably Tibeto-Burman in origin.[73] It was either a fantasy or a hoax, but migration from India's north-eastern borderlands helped populate certain parts of Israel, or Israeli-occupied territories, so immigration continued for several years. Money was also collected among Jewish communities abroad and sent to Mizoram as well as Chin state. And after being forced to leave Gaza, they settled mostly in the West Bank to boost the Israeli population in areas claimed by the Palestinians.

Critics accused Israel of taking advantage of the Bnei Menashe for obvious political reasons while others, among them L. Thanggur, a pastor in Churachandpur in Manipur, said: 'They are simply economic migrants. If they had better employment opportunities here, they would never have imagined going to Israel or wanted this conversion.'[74] Another church leader, Dr P.C. Biaksiama of the Aizawl Christian Research Centre, was equally critical of the movement, but from another, more serious viewpoint: 'The mass conversion by foreign priests will pose a threat not only to social stability in the region, but also to national security. A large number of people will forsake loyalty to the Union of India, as they all will become eligible for a foreign citizenship.'[75]

Nevertheless, a stroll around Aizawl reveals sites like Zion Street, Israel Point, Nazareth and Bethlehem. The belief in the 'lost tribe' legend is still strong, but it is still the Christian churches that dominate social and even political life in Mizoram. Apart from Nagaland, there is no place in India where the influence of the church is stronger, and its teachings more evangelically fundamentalist. These days there are also more denominations than the old Presbyterian and Baptist churches. One of the main relatively new Christian congregations in Mizoram is the Salvation Army – and, fortunately for the Mizos, with peace established in their hills, it is actually the only army that is much in evidence there today.

CHAPTER FOUR

MANIPUR: THE ETERNAL
IMBROGLIO

Irom Sharmila is no ordinary patient. Outsiders need special permission to visit her secluded ward at Jawaharlal Nehru Hospital in Imphal, the capital of Manipur. And she is being force-fed through a tube in her nose. She is on a hunger strike. That is not illegal, or unusual, in Mahatma Gandhi's India. Sharmila is kept in 'judicial custody' to prevent her from 'committing suicide,' which is what the law allows for. But she can be held in such custody for only a year at a time, so she is released once a year, goes on a public hunger strike in an open tent near the hospital and is led back into detention in her closely guarded room. Sharmila began her fast in November 2000. When I met her in May 2010 and again in September 2011, she had been refusing to eat for more than a decade – longer than anyone in recorded history.

As I was allowed past the female security guards outside the ward where she is kept I was expecting to meet a highly spiritual, saint-like person, not unlike the Mahatma himself. But I found a very ordinary young woman, likeable and full of human warmth and even humour despite her long, lonely struggle against what she perceives as gross injustice against the people of Manipur. She smiled and joked about how the tube in her nose had 'become part of her body', and even talked about her plans for the future. She also showed me stacks of religious literature, poetry and novels she kept in a cupboard in her room, and read out loud some of her own poems, which she had written neatly with a pen in school-type notebooks. And she was duly humble and modest about the awards and recognitions she has received from India and abroad. It was impossible not to take a strong liking to Sharmila, a truly courageous woman.

It all began on 2 November 2000. Early that Thursday morning, an Assam Rifles unit was attacked in the vicinity of Malom in Imphal West district. One of Manipur's many insurgent groups – and there are almost thirty of them in the state – was most probably behind it. This infuriated some jawans from the Assam Rifles, but they could not determine which band of rebels had carried out the attack. So they opened fire on a group of people at a bus stop on the main road from Malom to downtown Imphal. Ten people were gunned down, among them Sana Devi, a sixty-year-old woman and three teenage boys. It was indiscriminate revenge; none of the victims were known to have any contacts with the state's rebels. One of the boys had even been honoured for bravery by former prime minister Rajiv Gandhi.

On the same day, major civil society organizations in Manipur demanded an official inquiry into the incident. But that was dismissed. The military invoked the Armed Forces (Special Powers) Act 1958, AFSPA, which gives the army the right to open fire 'against any person who is acting in contravention of any law or order for the time being in force in the disturbed area prohibiting the assembly of five or more persons.' Under this draconian law, army personnel are also absolved of any responsibility for their actions in those 'disturbed areas'.[1]

Modelled on the Armed Forces (Special Powers) Ordinance, which was promulgated by the British colonial power in August 1942 to suppress Mahatma Gandhi's Quit India movement for independence, the AFSPA was enacted by the Indian Parliament on 11 September 1958. It was designed to tackle insurgency in 'disturbed areas' of the north-east, which at that time meant the Naga rebellion. The law was supposed to be in force for only a year, but the Naga struggle continued, and then came the 1962 border war with China, the Mizo rebellion and the unrest in Manipur and other areas in the north-east. The law was never revoked and now applies to any 'disturbed area' in Arunachal Pradesh, Assam, Manipur, Meghalaya, Mizoram, Nagaland and Tripura. And the whole of Manipur was declared a 'disturbed area' in 1980. It has been lifted only in certain parts of Imphal municipality.

On hearing of the Malom massacre, Sharmila, then twenty-eight, took a decision that was going to change her life forever – and force many Indians, even far away from Manipur, to question the validity of the army's special privileges under the law. She went on a fast 'unto death' to have the AFSPA revoked. The law remains in force, but, in 2007, Sharmila was awarded the prestigious South Korean Gwangju Prize for Human Rights and, in September 2010, the Rabindranath Tagore Peace Prize.[2] The youngest of nine children born into an ordinary Manipuri family, Sharmila, whose only social activism before she went on this hunger strike was a brief internship with a local human rights organization, has become a beacon of hope in one of India's most troubled areas.

Imphal could have been one of the prettiest towns in India. Located in a green, fertile valley with an abundance of water and rich farmland, it has been populated for centuries and once was the capital of an independent kingdom. In the town's centre are the ruins of the Palace of Kangla, surrounded by a moat and the remnants of an old wall, which were built over the centuries to protect the seat of the Manipuri rulers from Chinese and Burmese invasions. Imphal also boasts the oldest polo ground in the world, for it was here the British discovered and popularized the sport that is played on horseback and now has spread as far as Europe,

Canada, the United States, Latin America and Australia. The subtle, gentle Manipuri dance is one of India's eight 'classical' dances.

But decades of civil strife have torn not only Imphal but the entire state apart. The majority, or 57 per cent, of the population of Manipur is predominantly Hindu Meitei and dominates the central lowlands, while various Naga tribes in the surrounding hills make up 13–14 per cent, and the Kukis, another hill tribe, 12–13 per cent. There are also a number of smaller ethnic groups in the state such as Mizo/Chin and Paite-related tribes in Churachandpur; Muslim Meitei Pangal in the Imphal Valley, Bishnupur, Thoubal and Chandel; Komrem in Senapati; and even a sizable population of Nepalese and 'mainstream' Indians mostly in Imphal and the Burmese border town of Moreh. The Meiteis as well as the Nagas, the Kukis and other tribals all speak tongues that belong to the Tibeto-Burman family of languages.

Most of the rebel groups, which claim to represent one ethnic group or another, collect 'taxes' from businesses and individuals. Even hospitals and medical institutions are required to pay heavy 'taxes' to the rebels. In September 2007, pharmacists in Imphal shut their drug stores because an insurgent faction demanded a million Indian rupees from each of them. According to sources in the state, the rebels will approach local businesses as well as government departments with demands for 'taxes'. If those demands are not met, threatening phone calls will follow. If still no payments are forthcoming, bullets will be sent to the homes of businessmen and officials, or, in some cases, grenades will be lobbed into their compounds.

Frequent strikes and blockades disrupt daily life in the state, and goods, including medicines, cannot be brought in. The rebels also recruit young people, including children, into their ranks.[3] Narcotics from across the Burmese border – heroin as well as methamphetamines – are easily available in the state, and civil society groups accuse both the authorities and the rebels of turning a blind eye to the traffic, perhaps even benefiting from it. One in sixty inhabitants is infected with HIV, four times the national average in India – but those are official figures and the actual number could be much higher. According to the Manipur State AIDS Control Society, Manipur with barely 0.2 per cent of India's population contributes nearly 8 per cent of India's total HIV positive cases.[4]

Armed police and paramilitary units patrol Imphal, which is nearly deserted after sunset. Streets are empty and businesses closed. The security forces act with impunity, while extortion by the rebels – and corruption within the local administration – hinders any serious development efforts. The main highway from Kohima to Imphal is in bad shape after the Nagaland–Manipur border because no private contractor wants to repair it for fear of being forced to pay the rebels. Money sent by the Central government for such projects tends to disappear into the pockets of local officials. Manipur provides an extreme example of how a civilian population can be squeezed between ruthless security forces and an array of often equally ruthless rebels.

As a result, many young Meiteis are leaving the state and have settled in Assam, Delhi and other parts of India. They complain about harassment by the security forces as well as the rebels in Manipur – and racial discrimination elsewhere in India because of their different looks and habits. 'Sometimes we don't even feel we are Indians,' is a typical comment by young Meiteis, indicating that they want to be Indians, but are treated differently. The US consul general in Kolkata reported in a cable on 1 November 2006 that was made public by WikiLeaks in 2011:

> In the Consul General's many interactions, even with some government officials, a recurring comment was that Manipur was less a state and more a colony of India. The general use of the AFSPA meant that the Manipuris did not have the same rights of other citizens of India and restrictions of travel to the state added

to a sense of isolation and separation from the rest of India 'proper.' The overwhelming presence of military, paramilitary and police officers contributed to the impression that Imphal was under military occupation. Several Manipuris argued that they had greater rights under the British Raj than under the present federation.[5]

But the US consul general, who was reporting from a visit to the state, was equally critical of the rebels:

Insurgent groups that may have initially intended to advocate for various community rights have developed into criminal gangs and have splintered as individual members seek their own financial benefit.[6]

The outcome of all this is the present sad state of affairs in Manipur, which is far worse off than any of the other north-eastern states. And this has prompted ordinary citizens like Sharmila to take matters into their own hands because the government – and the rebels – seem insensitive to the plight of the people. Romesh Bhattacharji, a former commissioner of customs in Assam, wrote in 2002: 'You can smell fear, and feel the wariness. The Kukis and the Nagas are fighting each other. The Meiteis, the Nagas and the Kukis are all against authority . . . here yesterday's headlines will be repeated tomorrow. They tell the same story. Ambush, massacre, abduction, extortion, raid and retaliatory raid, and rape. The most unthinkable is commonplace here. Army raiding a High Court Judge's house in Imphal, Kukis firing on Naga huts in Tamenglong, Nagas killing Kuki passengers on National Highway 39. The list is endless.'[7]

Other Indian writers said that the state, whose name means 'jewelled land', has now become 'a piece of rusting iron . . . Manipur's saga is . . . a reflection of what is perhaps the world's most complex and longest-running web of ethnic insurgencies.'[8] In no other part of India have I seen that many children play with toy guns, and the game is often 'insurgents and the security forces'.

Some may argue that Manipur's suffering is nothing new. It is a 'frontier country' where the Indian subcontinent meets South-east Asia and, as such, always exposed to cross-border raids, pillage, rape and smuggling. And, at times, even foreign invasions. Unlike Mizoram and Nagaland, where the sharp escarpments of steep, almost impenetrable mountains separate those states from Burma, the access to and from Manipur is relatively easy. This is where the Japanese tried to launch their invasion of India during World War II and, long before them, the Chinese and the Burmese.

Sir James Johnstone, a colonial administrator during the British era, wrote in his 1896 book *My Experiences in Manipur and the Naga Hills* that, 'the early history of Manipur is lost in obscurity but there can be no doubt that it has existed as an independent kingdom from a very early period.'[9] But much is recorded in the *Chaithariol Kumbaba*, Manipur's Royal Chronicles; so we know that the Chinese armies invaded this ancient kingdom in the thirteenth century. Chinese prisoners of war are believed to have introduced brick making and silk weaving, for which Manipur is famous.[10] In the seventeenth century, the Chinese tried once again to invade Manipur, but failed, and the defeated soldiers were resettled at a locality that became known as Khagempali. Some sources claim that the name of the place is derived from the Manipuri words for China, *khagi*, and victory, *ngamba*.[11] Others say Khagempali refers to the damming of rivers. But whatever the actual meaning, it shows that the Chinese left a strong impression on the Manipuris.

But the Manipuri kings were also conquerors. During the long reign (1709–48) of Maharaja Pamheiba, who was also called Garibnawaz, the Manipuri kingdom extended up to Mandalay in Burma.[12] During this period, Hinduism spread eastwards from Assam to Manipur, and Garibnawaz, who is actually believed to have been a Naga adopted by the previous ruler of Manipur, became an ardent believer in the new faith. From then on, lowland Manipuris, or Meiteis, embraced Hinduism – although it continues, even to this day, to coexist with the animistic, ancestor-worshipping, shaman-led *sanamahi* tradition, which honours the creator aspect of Sidaba Mapu, the pre-Hindu trinity god of the Meiteis. Followers of sanamahi also worship forces of nature like fire, water and mountains, and their best-known place of worship in Manipur today is at Andro, 25 kilometres east of Imphal town.

But even if Garibnawaz was a Naga adopted and converted as a Meitei, his own tribal brethren did not become Hindus. Like the Nagas in Nagaland, they were converted into Christianity by Western missionaries. And here, as in today's Nagaland to the north, the missionaries selected one predominant dialect and turned it into the lingua franca of one specific area. One of these dialects was Hunphun in the Ukhrul area of north-eastern Manipur, which became the Tangkhul language and the name of a tribe as well, even though perhaps as many as a hundred different dialects are still spoken among them. A Baptist missionary called William Pettigrew translated the Bible into Tangkhul, using the Roman script. Other groups of Nagas who became tribes in a similar manner – where missionaries grouped smaller ethnic groups to form 'tribes' to avoid having to translate the Bible into hundreds of languages – include the Mao and Maram in Senapati, the Kabui in Senapati, Bishnupur, Imphal and Churachandpur, and the Kacha in Tamenglong. But there are also many other tribes which consider themselves Nagas. Among the non-Naga tribes, most Kukis also became Christians, as did the Mizos and the Chins.

But long before the arrival of Christianity, Manipur was at war again. The eighteenth century saw numerous battles between the armies of Manipur and the Burmese kings, and the royal centre at Kangla was fortified with wider moats and stronger walls. Then, in the early nineteenth century, the Burmese sent a stronger force than usual, led by their legendary general Maha Bandula. Manipur was subjugated along with Assam, and one king after another had to flee to Cachar. The period from 1819 to 1826 is known in Manipuri history as *Chahi Taret Khuntakpa*, or the Seven Years of Devastation, and still evokes bitter memories. The Burmese looted every house in sight and killed men, women and children. Thousands of others were marched off to Burma as slaves, and were resettled in villages, where many of their descendants still remain. They brought with them certain types of silk weaving that were considered the most exquisite in Burma. In Manipur, the Burmese only kept as many local people as they needed to grow rice and produce food for their garrison. But the Manipuris did not just stoically accept Burmese rule. Marjit's nephew, Hirachandra, led bands of armed men who, as the nineteenth-century British captain R.B. Pemberton put it, 'continued to . . . annoy the Burmah garrison left in Manipur, who in vain attempted to capture him; he was secretly supported by his countrymen, who admired his gallantry, and by keeping him acquainted with the movement of the enemy, enabled him to cut off many of their small detachments.'[13]

According to a contemporary Meitei writer, 'Today Hirachandra is regarded as the father of guerrilla warfare in Manipur, especially by the younger generation who take pride in the fact that the Manipuris do not have to look up to the Cubans or the Vietnamese for this kind of warfare. The present day movement activists as well as supporters trace back the origin of current guerrilla activities to Hirachandra.'[14]

The Burmese were eventually driven out by a force led by a former ruler, Gambhir Singh, who, supported by the British, had raised a 500-strong army called the Manipur Levy. British forces also participated directly in the campaign and managed to kill the Burmese commander Maha Bandula. The Burmese were defeated and had to retreat. On 26 February 1826, a treaty was signed between the British and the Burmese at a place called Yandabo near Ava, then the site of the kings of Burma. Assam became British and Manipur regained its independence. But, as a token of goodwill, the British, after vacillating for several years, let the Burmese keep the Kabaw Valley. Thus, this fertile, teak-wooded area opposite Moreh has been Burmese since 1833, but the ownership of the area remains an important issue for many Meitei nationalists even today.

The king of Manipur, and many – but not all – of his subjects could return to Manipur, but the British reserved the right to station a so-called political agent in Imphal. He was like an ambassador, but frequently interfered with palace affairs. This led to the Anglo-Manipuri war of 1891, after which Manipur came under British rule as a princely state. With the advent of British overlordship came the introduction of the Bengali script, which was forced upon the people of the kingdom. Until then, the Meitei language, or Meiteilon, had its own script, Meitei-mayek, which dates back to the eleventh and twelfth centuries. Centuries of war in the region seemed to be over and *Pax Britannica* was reinforced by the final British conquest of Burma in the late nineteenth century.

But with colonial rule, even if it was indirect, came a cultural and national reawakening, which, as elsewhere in India, was partly fuelled by the introduction of Western-style education and communications. The most central figure in the first Meitei nationalist movement in modern times was Hijam Irabot, whose name purists prefer to spell Irawat. Born into a poor family in 1896 and orphaned at an early age, he attended Johnstone Higher Secondary School in Imphal till Class 7 and later Pugoj High School in Dhaka. But poverty forced Irabot to discontinue his studies in 1915 and he went to Tripura, where he, for the first time, read books and articles about the 1871 Paris Commune, labour strikes in the United States, the exploitation of blacks in Africa and the Russian Revolution.[15]

Back in Manipur, Irabot became acquainted with the royal family and married King Churachand Singh's elder brother's daughter Khomdonsana. Irabot also joined the Nikhil Manipuri Mahasabha, which was headed by the king. Originally a Hindu nationalist organization called Nikhil Manipuri Hindu Mahasabha, Irabot, as its vice-president, dropped 'Hindu' from its name, and much to the displeasure of the king turned it into a political party, the first of its kind in Manipur.

The first to rise against the king – and his British political agent, Mr Gimson – were the women of Manipur who, in 1904, launched a *Nupi Lan*, or 'women's war', an agitation against what they perceived as oppressive economic and administrative policies by the court and the colonial power. One of the participants in a Second Nupi Lan in 1939 was a woman called Tonsija Devi – Irom Sharmila's grandmother. As a child, Sharmila was captivated by the stories she heard from her grandmother, and these probably inspired her to fight for justice and social change.[16]

Irabot himself was not in Manipur when the women launched their struggles, but returned in January 1940, when he began to agitate for the formation of a proper Legislative Assembly. He was promptly arrested and charged with sedition. Incarcerated in Sylhet in what is now Bangladesh, he became acquainted with two prominent communist leaders, Brihesh Misra and Jyotirmoy Nanda, who had also been jailed for their political activities. Sylhet Jail, Manipuri academic Rajendra Kshetri points out, 'proved to be a revolutionary training centre for Irawat [Irabot]'.[17] He came out of jail in 1943 as a dedicated Marxist.

Manipur had seen some of the fiercest battles during World War II in Asia, when the British Empire fought to repel the advance of another empire, the Japanese. The Japanese were defeated, but the end of the war also meant that the British would have to give up their empire. The dawn of a new era was rising over Asia, which began with India's independence on 15 August 1947. But the king, or maharaja, of Manipur, Bodhachandra Singh, the son of Churachand, continued to rule with the help of an 'interim council' for almost two years. To stay in power, Bodhachandra tried to introduce a constitutional monarchy. But there was no way Manipur would become independent. India's home minister, Sardar Patel, who oversaw the integration of the princely states, moved into action and summoned the maharaja to Shillong, then capital of Assam. The maharaja was told that his state was to become part of the Indian Union. He wanted to discuss the matter with the 'legislative assembly' he had formed in 1947, but was warned in no uncertain terms that there was no choice. On 21 September 1949, Bodhachandra signed an agreement merging Manipur with India.[18] A few weeks later, on 15 October, a chief commissioner was posted in Manipur to take over the administration of the state. The ancient kingdom of Manipur was no more. In 1956, Manipur was made a Union territory and, in 1972, a state within the Indian Union.

However, it was not the old royals who came to oppose integration with India – the idea was not popular with large segments of the population. Irabot had gone underground to organize revolutionary cells with the aim to establish an 'Independent Peasant Republic' in Manipur. In March 1950, he and his fellow revolutionaries formed the Red Guards, an organization armed with whatever weapons they could lay their hands on to resist the Indian state.[19] Unable to establish 'liberated zones' inside Manipur, they crossed the border into Burma, where they linked up with the powerful – and insurgent – Communist Party of Burma, which had been waging war against their government since Burma's independence from Britain in 1949. Irabot managed to secure support from the Burmese communists for the return of the Kabaw Valley to Manipur once their respective revolutionary movements had succeeded. But that was not to be. The CPB was pushed back to strongholds in the Pegu Yoma mountains north of Rangoon – and Irabot died of typhoid at his headquarters in the Kabaw Valley on 26 September 1951.

The first Meitei revolutionary movement died with Irabot. It was not until the mid-1960s that Manipur experienced another upsurge in violent, anti-government activities. On 24 November 1964, the first resistance group was formed since the 'unfinished revolution of 1948', as the Meitei militants call it.[20] Called the United National Liberation Front, UNLF, it was headed by Arambam Samarendra Singh and stated as its aim not only an independent, socialist republic in Manipur but also that it had a 'historic mission' to liberate Manipur 'from Indian colonial occupation in the larger context of liberating the entire Indo-Burma region, for a common future'.[21]

Exactly what that meant is unclear, but, from the very beginning, the Meitei revolutionaries were factionalized and badly divided among themselves. In December 1968, a breakaway faction led by UNLF foreign secretary Oinam Sudhir Kumar broke away and established the Revolutionary Government of Manipur, RGM, in Sylhet, East Pakistan. Being already involved with the insurgencies in Nagaland and Mizoram, Pakistan's intelligence services now lent a helping hand to the Manipuri revolutionaries. The Manipuris were inspired by Marxism, while the Nagas and the Mizos adhered to Christian fundamentalist beliefs. But that mattered little to the Pakistanis as long as they were all fighting the Indian government. The Manipuris underwent military training in East Pakistan and some of them even supported the Pakistani Army during the 1971 Bangladesh liberation war.[22]

Freedom for Bangladesh meant an end to the Naga and Mizo presence there, and a number of Manipuri militants were apprehended when the Indian Army marched into Dhaka in December 1971. About 150 rebels were arrested while they tried to return to India's north-east after the defeat of the Pakistani Army.[23] The Manipuri militants had lost their bases in what had been East Pakistan. But there was another option, China. Before the 1968 split, UNLF leader Arambam Samarendra Singh, was reported to have contacted the Chinese consulate in Dhaka, but what came out of it is uncertain other than that they were given copies of Mao Zedong's Little Red Book.[24] It was not until after Manipur had been declared a state in 1972, and a general amnesty for former rebels was announced, that contacts with China were re-established. An erstwhile RGM member, Nameirakpam Bisheswar Singh, who was one of those who had been arrested on the Indian side of the border on his way back from what was now Bangladesh, had ended up in jail in Tripura where he met Indian Maoist revolutionaries, so-called Naxalites, and through them had been introduced to radical communist thought.

Back in Imphal, Bisheswar organized some of his old comrades to prepare for a daring journey. While the Nagas and the Mizos had trekked for months over the mountains and through the jungles of Burma, Bisheswar and his comrades decided to take an entirely different route. In early 1976, they travelled to Nepal and into Chinese-occupied Tibet. The Manipuris did not travel as one group – that would have been too suspicious – but split up into small groups which crossed the Nepalese border at different points, like Kakarbhitta, Raxaul and Gorakhpur. Once on the Nepalese side, they did not encounter any difficulties. On the contrary, the authorities there let them travel freely, and without papers, across the border into Tibet where they were all reunited. One of them was Soibam Temba Singh, a RGM veteran, and this is what he told me about the trip when I met him at a rebel camp in northern Burma, ten years after the secret mission to Lhasa:

> There were sixteen of us when we set out from Manipur in April 1976. Another three comrades followed a few months later. We stayed in Tibet for two years. The Chinese were quite strict during the first six months, but after a while we could move about more freely by bicycle and sometimes by car. We received political as well as military training, and the Chinese offered us weapons. But Bisheswar declined the offer. He gave me six rupees and fifty paise, saying: 'This is the price of a big dagger. You must use that and capture arms from the Indians.'[25]

The Chinese minders were very accommodating and communicated with the Manipuris in English and Hindi. According to Temba, one of the Chinese instructors was fluent in Hindi. He sent Temba back to Manipur twice during the time the Manipuris were being trained near Lhasa, to send messages and collect intelligence. When he and his comrades returned for good in March 1978, they became known as the *oja*s, or 'teachers' or 'masters' in the Meitei language, and immediately set out to establish a new revolutionary group. On 25 September 1978, they formed the People's Liberation Army, PLA. Truly revolutionary Marxist in character, it even borrowed its name from the armed forces of the People's Republic of China. And its message was clearly Maoist:

> We openly oppose the Communist Party of India, which betrayed the revolution of the working class . . . the most urgent issue for the people of India at the present stage is a real Marxist party, guided by Marxism-Leninism and Mao Tsetung [Zedong] thought, a party which by mobilising the whole masses, can lead the people to an armed revolution . . . our leader [Bisheswar] has explained quoting Chairman Mao Tse-tung's analysis of war . . . that war is the highest form of struggle for resolving contradictions.[26]

In the late 1970s, China and the Soviet Union were still bitter rivals in the world communist movement, so the Manipuri revolutionaries declared:

> The Soviet Union is the chief betrayer of the world revolution. Today, it represents global expansionism, endangering the security of the people [of the world] and threatening a Third World War.[27]

Not surprisingly, the Manipuri PLA also expressed its support for the Chinese occupation of Tibet – and accused India of expansionism in the Himalayan region:

> If they [the Chinese] are eager to [occupy] territory, why did they not occupy Indian territory in 1962, though Nehru's orders [were] to launch an aggressive war to occupy Tibet to form a greater Indian Empire. It is China that defends the national security of the Himalayan kingdom Nepal against the expansionism of India which is still busy plotting underhand activities to turn Nepal into another Sikkim.[28]

After the Vietnamese had driven out Pol Pot's murderous – and China-supported – Khmer Rouge from Cambodia in January 1979, the PLA declared:

> We are quite sure that the Kampuchean people under the leadership
> of premier Pol Pot with the vast majority of the people of the
> world will defeat the Vietnamese invaders and certainly
> shatter underhand plots of any kind of new expansionism by
> Moscow [sic].[29]

China could not possibly have gained a more loyal ally, and even if
the PLA's rhetoric was bombastic and not always entirely clear, it
was much more ideologically pure as far as the Chinese were
concerned than the Marxist–Christian mumbo-jumbo – mixing
Maoist concepts such as the dictatorship of the people with praise
for 'the Eternal God of the Universe' – that the National Socialist
Council of Nagaland espoused in its January 1980 manifesto. Besides,
the Chinese were becoming wary of their support for the Nagas.
According to Kachin rebel officers I interviewed in the mid-1980s,
the Chinese had become increasingly annoyed with the Nagas
because they prayed and sang hymns all the time while in China,
and surrendered, along with their Chinese-supplied weapons, when
they returned to Nagaland.[30]

In the late 1970s, the PLA unleashed a reign of terror in the
Imphal Valley, killing Indian security personnel as well as suspected
'traitors' to its cause, among them several RGM veterans such as
Sudhir Kumar, who was assassinated in his home at Singjamei in
Imphal in January 1979. Banks were looted and weapons snatched
from police stations and other outposts. To establish its revolutionary
credentials, the PLA formed a political wing called the
Revolutionary People's Front, RPF, on 25 February 1979. Bisheswar
was its first chairman.

The Manipuri revolutionaries were certainly a safer bet for the
Chinese to support than the Naga and the Mizo rebels and, in the
end, even the staunchly Maoist Naxalites of the Communist Party
of India (Marxist-Leninist). But that the Maoists elsewhere in India,
outside Manipur, would be unreliable was not what the Chinese
had expected when a peasant rebellion broke out in a small village

called Naxalbari near the border between northern West Bengal and Nepal in March 1967. In January, the first Naga batch, led by Thinoselie and Muivah, had reached China after their long trek through northern Burma and, by March, more than 100 Naga guerrillas were undergoing military training in Yunnan. Then the news came from India about the uprising in Naxalbari. The Chinese were ecstatic. A revolution similar to their own in the 1930s and 1940s seemed to be brewing in rural India – and not only among a Christian hill tribe in a north-eastern corner of the country.

Naxalbari was quite remote as well, but different from the north-eastern borderlands. Located on the foothills below the hill station of Darjeeling, it was an important tea-growing area and populated to a large extent by scheduled castes and tribes who had come there to seek employment. Suniti Kumar Ghosh, one of the many intellectuals from Kolkata who later joined the Naxalite movement saw it in more Marxist terms: 'Innocent tribal men and women were duped by the planters' recruiting agents with false hopes. Santals, Oraons and other tribal people, who worked in the tea gardens, were treated virtually as slaves and subjected to brutal treatment by the planters. It was a story of deceit and oppression.'[31] Moreover, the local peasants were poor and the area had a very active communist cell led by a forty-nine-year-old firebrand called Charu Mazumdar. He was actually born into a family of zamindars, or wealthy landowners in the nearby town of Siliguri, but had become an ardent revolutionary even as a teenager. As early as in 1949, he began to organize the tea garden workers in the Darjeeling area and became president of their local trade union.

Mazumdar, or Charu Babu as he became affectionately known by his inner circle of trusted comrades, had joined the undivided Communist Party of India, CPI, in 1938, when it was outlawed. After independence, he belonged to its far-left faction and openly sided with China during the 1962 war. India was the aggressor, he said, and issued an open statement saying exactly that. After the first split in the CPI in 1964, he joined the more radical Communist Party of India (Marxist), but even that was not revolutionary enough for him. He studied Mao Zedong and was enthralled by his war cry: 'Political power grows out of the barrel of a gun.'[32]

West Bengal, at the time of the Naxalbari uprising, was ruled by a United Front government, a coalition of mainly leftist parties – including the CPI and the CPI (M) – but also a breakaway faction of the Indian National Congress as well as others. Charu Babu, however, did not believe in its parliamentary way to socialism. He began preparing the tea garden workers and poor peasants in Naxalbari for armed revolution. The spark came when a sharecropper, Bigul Kishan, was evicted by a landlord without any legal basis. When he protested, he was attacked and badly beaten by the landlord's goons. In response, thousands of villagers armed with bows, arrows and spears took over landholdings and food storages, basically running the area as a 'liberated' commune. People's courts were established and judgements passed. And, as a pro-Naxalite website put it, 'Any resistance by the landlords and their gangs was smashed and a few killed.'[33]

Between 15,000 and 20,000 people participated in the movement. By the end of May 1967, it reached the level of armed uprising. Jyoti Basu, the CPI(M) leader who was then home minister of West Bengal and ten years later became its chief minister, sent in the police and violent clashes followed. The peasants snatched firearms and ammunition from the landowners and fought back. Nine women and children were killed when the police opened fire. Then, on 19 July, paramilitary forces were deployed in the area. Activists were beaten or arrested, or both, while some like Charu Mazumdar escaped and went underground.

The revolt lasted only a few months, but, as Sumanta Banerjee wrote in his classic *In the Wake of Naxalbari*, it 'left a far-reaching impact on the entire agrarian scene throughout India. It was like the premeditated throw of a pebble bringing forth a series of ripples in the water. It was also a watershed in the Indian Communist movement. It helped expose the political failure of the parliamentary Leftists in power, and unrolled a process of rethinking among the Communist ranks.'[34]

The Chinese were quick to express their support for the uprising. On 5 July 1967, the *People's Daily*, organ of the Central Committee of the Communist Party of China, ran an editorial titled 'Spring Thunder Over India':

> A peal of spring thunder has crashed over the land of India. Revolutionary peasants in the Darjeeling area have risen in rebellion. Under the leadership of a revolutionary group of the Indian Communist Party, a red area of rural revolutionary armed struggle has been established in India . . . [they] have thrown off the shackles of modern revisionism and smashed the trammels that bound them . . . . but no matter how well the imperialists, Indian reactionaries and the modern revisionists cooperate in their sabotage and suppression, the torch of armed struggle lighted by the revolutionaries in the Indian Communist Party and the revolutionary peasants in Darjeeling will not be put out. 'A single spark can start a prairie fire.' The spark in Darjeeling will certainly set the vast expanses of India ablaze.[35]

Those 'revolutionaries' in the 'Indian Communist Party' were the group within the CPI (M) led by Charu Mazumdar. In September, only a few months after the momentous events in Naxalbari, a group of twelve Indian communists, among them Kanu Sanyal, one of the most prominent leaders of the uprising, managed to get to China. In the country of their dreams, they underwent military and political training – and, to their great delight, also met their hero, Mao Zedong. But, according to Banerjee, direct Chinese aid . . . did not extend beyond this initial military training and moral support through Chinese communist journals and Radio Beijing.[36]

In November, Mazumdar and his militant group of Maoists who had either rebelled against the leadership of the CPI (M), or already been expelled, met in Kolkata to map out a new strategy. Banerjee states that the participants recalled Mao Zedong's call for 'bombarding the headquarters during the Cultural Revolution to draw a parallel with their then fight against the CPI (M) bureaucracy'.[37] They decided to form a new organisation, the All India Coordination Committee of Communist Revolutionaries, AICCCR, which sought contact with likeminded militants elsewhere in India.

Throughout 1968, smaller, Naxalbari-type struggles erupted in different parts of India, especially in Srikakulam in north-eastern Andhra Pradesh, an old revolutionary stronghold. On 22 April 1969 – the 100th anniversary of the birth of Vladimir Lenin – the AICCCR set up a new party, the Communist Party of India (Marxist-Leninist). The party's formation was announced by Kanu Sanyal at a massive May Day rally in the Kolkata Maidan – the big open area along the Chowringhee thoroughfare in the heart of the city. Charu Mazumdar became its first general secretary. It is believed that a few months before the AICCCR decided to transform itself into a genuine party, a young Maoist student from Kolkata had gone to London, from where contacts with Chinese communist leaders was made.[38]

According to Suniti Kumar Ghosh, China gave 'lavish support' to their struggle over Radio Beijing, which beamed out revolutionary bulletins from India and extracts from articles written by Mazumdar. Then, by the spring of 1970, Chinese broadcasts suddenly ceased all mention of the 'revolutionary struggle' in India. 'Our leaders were feeling anxious,' Ghosh writes, and 'on further enquiry' – he doesn't say how – 'we were advised to send our representatives to Beijing for discussion with the Chinese leaders.'[39] Ghosh and two other CPI (ML) leaders, Saroj Datta and Souren Bose, were selected for the mission. But Datta and Ghosh were not able to go, so Bose travelled alone via London and the Albanian capital Tirana to Beijing in August 1970. On 29 October, he met Chinese premier

Zhou Enlai and Kang Sheng, security and intelligence chief and the official who usually received representatives of foreign fraternal parties. It became clear why the Chinese were not pleased with the CPI (ML) and its policies. Out of extreme admiration for Mao Zedong, the Indian party had declared that 'China's Chairman is our Chairman, China's path is our path!' Zhou told Bose that, 'we don't deny that Chairman [Mao] is [an] international authority . . . [but] to regard leader of one country as the leader of another party is against the sentiment of the nation; it is difficult for the working class to accept it.'[40]

Kang Sheng told Bose that he could not understand the real meaning of the CPI (ML)'s 'annihilation policy', which he likened to the methods used by 'left adventurists' after the Chinese communists had been defeated in Shanghai in 1927. During its heyday in 1969–70, the CPI (ML) had attracted a motley crew of supporters, ranging from Bengali intellectuals who liked to discuss literature, art and movies over tea and coffee at the Paradise Cafe in Kolkata, to rural activists and outright goons and thugs drawn from the city's lumpenproletariat. Hundreds of 'class enemies' had been 'annihilated' by the Naxalites, which in plain English meant that they had been either shot or beaten to death. The victims of the CPI (ML)'s 'Red Terror' included landlords, moneylenders, policemen and government officials whom the Naxalites considered corrupt, or just politicians and others who were opposed to their movement.

Bose returned to London and flew from there back to Kolkata, bringing with him the depressing news from Beijing. It was clear that they were not going to get any more support, moral, material or otherwise, from China. At a meeting in Kolkata on 8 December 1970, CPI (ML) leaders were told not to disclose to anybody that the Chinese were critical of their party's actions and policies.[41] But the problems could not be hidden from ordinary members, and many of them began to challenge Mazumdar's leadership, and especially his brutal policy of 'annihilation of class enemies'. On 16 July 1972, a broken Mazumdar was tracked down and arrested by the police. He died twelve days later of what was described as a heart attack while in custody at Lal Bazar's police station in Kolkata. The Naxalite movement did not die with him, but split into a multitude of factions and smaller groups, which were of little or no political or strategic interest to the Chinese.

It was in many ways easier for ordinary people to understand and relate to the Manipuri revolutionaries in their turf than the Naxalites in their areas of operation. The UNLF and the PLA fought not only for what they believed was 'social justice' in the shape of socialism, but also for 'their country'. Nationalism, even it if is separatism, is often a stronger force than pure ideology and the belief in complex political theories. Many Manipuris felt that their maharaja had been tricked and forced to join India in 1949. Because of their distinct ethnic identity, they continued to feel that they should not belong to India either. Independence, and socialism, would deliver them from the evils of the oppressive Indian state and restore their national pride. At least, that was what many Manipuris thought, and some still think.

But the Manipuri underground also suffered from factionalism and infighting, which was worse, and bloodier, than in Nagaland and Mizoram. Among the Meiteis, yet another Marxist revolutionary outfit was formed in 1977, the People's Revolutionary Party of Kangleipak, or PREPAK, which, in turn, split into several different factions. Kangleipak was the name they gave the independent socialist republic they were fighting for. There is also the Kangleipak Communist Party, KCP, which traces its self-proclaimed origin to Irabot's movement but did not raise its first armed units until the 1970s. Parts of Manipur had been declared disturbed areas after the adoption of the AFSPA in 1958, and on 8 September 1980, the entire state was brought under the act.

Military pressure on the insurgents and ideological disputes among themselves led to splits within the PLA as well as the UNLF, and some cadres chose to surrender while others were apprehended in the swoops that the security forces carried out all over Manipur. Among the latter was rebel supremo Bisheswar who was arrested in an encounter with security forces at Thekcham in Thoubal district in August 1981. While languishing in Imphal Central Jail, he contested local elections in January 1985 – and won in his constituency, Thongju in the Imphal Valley. He was released and became a state politician. But that was enough for his old comrades to brand him a traitor. In the early morning of 11 August 1994, his bullet-ridden body was found at his home in Imphal.

The PLA had by then split into different factions, the strongest headed by Temba, one of the few returnees from China who had not been arrested, killed, or surrendered. And he wanted badly to re-establish contacts with the Chinese.[42] He made his first attempt as early as in 1979. With the help of Naga guerrillas on the Burmese side of the border, he reached areas controlled by the Kachin Independence Army, KIA, on 20 December. There, Temba decided to learn the Kachin language, or rather Jingphaw, the main dialect which is also the lingua franca of the seven Kachin tribes.

The KIA escorted him to the Chinese border and, in February 1981, he made it to Ruili in Yunnan. From there he crossed back into Burma, to areas controlled by the Communist Party of Burma, CPB. Temba joined one of their armed units and fought together with them in a battle with Burmese government forces. But neither the CPB nor the Chinese were willing to give him any arms to carry back to Manipur. By then, Mao Zedong was dead, and the new leader Deng Xiaoping's trade-oriented policies were having an adverse impact on revolutionary groups all over the region – the Nagas, the Mizos, also the Manipuris. Even the CPB, a long-time Chinese ally in the region, now had difficulty getting supplies from across the border in Yunnan.

But Temba had found a new ally in the KIA. For reasons that are not entirely clear, they decided to support him. On 14 September

1981, he set out for home, reaching Manipur on 21 May 1982. He met old friends and even the UNLF to prepare them for a renewed armed revolt in Manipur. Some arms were snatched from Indian security personnel and money obtained through assorted robberies. By November, Temba and his group had thirty guns, and he set off for Kachin state again, this time with seventy-six other men and ten women, all of them young and new recruits as nearly all of his old comrades were dead or in jail. Three of the young men died in a Naga ambush on their way eastwards and one was left as a liaison officer at the NSCN's headquarters in the Patkai Hills near the Indian border. Eighty-three Manipuri militants, including Temba, reached Kachin state, where three died from malaria and other diseases. The Manipuris, mostly city kids, were not used to the tough life in the jungles of northern Burma. And two young men were executed for disobeying Temba's orders. The leader of the Manipuri revolutionaries was no democrat who would tolerate opposition in the ranks.

But the survivors underwent rigorous military training in KIA camps and did well, according to their Kachin instructors. In return, the Manipuris volunteered to teach in the KIA's schools and did other jobs that they were better at than the Kachins. They had their own camp adjacent to the Kachins' own headquarters at Pa Jau, which was located only a few hours' march from the Chinese border. Supplies, but not necessarily weapons, could be obtained quite easily from Chinese sources. Pa Jau was a huge base, or rather a small town, with its own schools, clinic, church, a marketplace where all sorts of goods were sold, and even jade shops that generated a comfortable income for the KIA, as well as a video parlour where mostly American movies were shown. Diesel-operated generators provided electricity for this rather unique rebel settlement on the Chinese frontier.

In early 1986, most of them returned to Manipur, in new uniforms provided by the KIA and brandishing Chinese-made automatic rifles and other weapons.[43] But Temba was no longer the leader. He had made the mistake of being married to two women at the same time – a sin according to his puritanical comrades, who deposed him at a meeting at Pa Jau. The Kachins were upset: Temba was their oldest and best friend among the Manipuris. And then a group of about a dozen PLA guerrillas slipped out of Pa Jau one night, crossed the border and travelled through China down to an area inside Burma which was controlled by the CPB.

The PLA's brief alliance with the KIA remains somewhat of a mystery. It could hardly have been in the interest of the KIA to antagonize the Indians by supporting an extreme left-wing guerrilla group in the north-east. And the Kachins' priority was to arm and equip their own young recruits the best they could. There was no reason, therefore, for them to share their stocks with a sizeable contingent of Manipuri guerrillas who were not fighting the KIA's enemy, the Burmese government.

One theory is that the KIA did it for money. The PLA paid them handsomely for weapons, uniforms and training. But there is nothing to suggest that Temba arrived at Pa Jau with more than pocket money for himself and his soldiers. A distinct possibility – although KIA leaders deny it – is that the Chinese were behind it. The KIA was just acting as a convenient proxy for the China's military intelligence. The Chinese had lost interest in the Mizos and the Nagas as strategic partners. The Manipuris, it seemed – at least before they started fighting among themselves – were more reliable. But at this stage in modern China's development, it was not to fight the Indian government, but to collect useful intelligence in the Sino-Indian border areas.

During my stay at Pa Jau from April to October 1986, I had almost unhindered access to the Kachins' files and records because I was compiling a history of their struggle, and working on articles for my magazine, the *Far Eastern Economic Review*. In one of those files containing records about the PLA, I found a curious document:

a list of towns in Arunachal Pradesh and hotels and guest houses, some in rather remote places in this sensitive territory. The Kachin rebel leader, Brang Seng, was not pleased when I asked him what that was all about. Manipuris could travel freely in areas such as Arunachal, but of what interest would it be for them in a state that borders China, quite far from their own home turf? Were the Chinese using the Kachins as a proxy to train Manipuris as intelligence assets in India's north-east? Whatever the reason, Brang Seng took his secrets with him to the grave when he died on 8 August 1994. He had received medical treatment in a Kunming hospital and passed away in a car while he was being driven through Yunnan back to his headquarters in northern Burma.

Manipuris continued to be trained by the Kachin rebels until they, to the surprise of many, began negotiating peace with Burma's military government in the early 1990s. By April 1993, they entered into a ceasefire agreement with Rangoon, which was finalized and signed in September the following year. As a result all 'foreign forces' – which also included militants from the United Liberation Front of Asom, ULFA – were told to leave KIA-controlled areas. But both PLA and ULFA were able to open unofficial liaison offices in Ruili across the border in Yunnan, where they were able to buy Chinese-made guns and smuggle them across Burma to north-eastern India.

The PLA units that had returned earlier had already made their presence felt in Manipur. Apart from ambushing the Indian security forces, they also took up so-called 'public-friendly issues': no alcohol, no drugs, no rape. They also copied the populist tactics of the South Vietnamese guerrillas during the Vietnam War, and called on the general public to inform them of any 'wrongdoings' by government civil servants and other individuals so that 'necessary punishments' could me meted out.[44] Even drug addicts were apprehended and put on public display in bamboo cages.

The insurgents' campaign for new moral order was soon taken over by the UNLF, which in the early 1990s went from being a mainly social organization to a formidable military force. In 1991, an armed wing called the Manipur People's Army, MPA, was set up and guns were procured from sources in Pakistan and South-east Asia, and smuggled through Burma and Bangladesh to its hideouts on both sides of the Indo-Burmese border. One of the MPA's first actions was an ambush against Indian security forces in the Loktak hyderoclectric project area, 30 kilometres from Imphal in December that year. Five Central Reserve Police Force, CRPF, personnel were killed by MPA militants, who from then on became the main armed group in Manipur. On 31 August 1995, in a daring midnight raid on a paramilitary Manipur Rifles outpost guarding a telecommunications station on Kangchup Hill, west of Imphal, the MPA looted a large quantity of arms and ammunition without firing a single shot.[45] Bloodier ambushes took place in Churachandpur, Thoubal and various places in the Imphal Valley.

The UNLF also undertook a 'social reformation campaign' similar to the PLA's against alcoholism, gambling, drug peddling and drug abuse in Manipur. The group even helped in solving private and petty disputes, and meted out its own version of justice. It claims to have shot dead more than fifty rapists in the 1990s.[46] But the security forces were also accused of heavy-handed methods in their work. Human Rights Watch, an internationally respected organization, reported in August 2008:

> Human rights violations by security forces engaged in counterinsurgency operations in Manipur have occurred with depressing regularity over the last five decades. Torture, which includes beatings, electric shocks, and simulated drowning, is common. Arbitrary arrests and extrajudicial executions continue. New 'disappearances' stopped after the Manipur government introduced a system of providing 'arrest memos' but at least 17 remain missing since they 'disappeared' in the 1980s and 1990s.[47]

The violence in Manipur was spiralling out of control and, on 10 June 2000, the UNLF's founder, Arambam Samarendra, was shot by unidentified gunmen. He had become a public figure after his release from jail in the early 1970s. A leading playwright and social activist, he had many followers among the Meiteis and the anniversary of his death is celebrated annually in Manipur. But who killed him? No one ever took responsibility for the gruesome murder of one of Manipur's best-known literary personalities. In the midst of the chaotic situation that prevailed there, it could have been anyone: the security forces, a rival nationalist group, or a lone assassin who wanted to settle personal scores. Manipur was sliding into a state of lawlessness and anarchy.

In the 1980s, the leadership of the UNLF had been taken over by Rajkumar Meghen who also uses the name Sana Yaima. A remote descendant of the old kings of Manipur and a law graduate from Jadavpur University in Kolkata, he had joined the UNLF in 1969. After being elected its general secretary in January 1984, he crossed the border into Burma to contact other revolutionary organizations fighting the Indian as well as the Burmese governments. Sana Yaima, the mastermind behind the transformation of the UNLF's social and political struggle into an armed insurrection, teamed up with the then undivided NSCN. A UNLF representative, Yumnam Shinnaba, was stationed along with five other Manipuri militants at the Naga headquarters in the rugged mountains across the border from Nagaland's northernmost Mon district.[48]

Sana Yaima seemed to get on well with the NSCN's general secretary, Thuingaleng Muivah. They shared similar leftist views on life and society, and escorted by Naga guerrillas, Sana Yaima and ten other UNLF militants trekked through northern Burma to the headquarters of the Kachin rebels in early 1985. They met Temba and his PLA militants at Pa Jau, but the two groups failed to unite. Sana Yaima also tried to contact the Chinese, but without much success: 'We were not allowed to cross the border into China,' Sana Yaima told me when I met him in northern Kachin state in March 1986. 'The immediate concern of the Chinese was Cambodia and

Afghanistan. But if we Manipuris were united again, they could not afford to ignore us.'

Sana Yaima wanted to form a united front with NSCN and ULFA, and reached out to the Mizos and the tribal guerrillas in Tripura as well. But nothing came of it. The driving forces behind their respective insurgencies were entirely different. ULFA, like the PLA, was a leftist organization motivated by ideology. The Nagas and the Mizos fought to 'protect' their 'tribal homelands', and both laid claims to land in Manipur and elsewhere. Sana Yaima fell out with Muivah in 1990 and the two became bitter enemies.

Although Marxist, with a supposedly internationalist outlook, the UNLF's main demand was for a 'plebiscite' in Manipur under the auspices of the United Nations, where people could opt for independence from India. But India would not meet that demand unless the Manipuri resistance was strong enough. So more weapons were acquired mainly from the black market for arms in South-east Asia. The UNLF, like dozens of other armed groups in Manipur, began collecting 'taxes' from local companies, shops and individuals.

Such extortion runs into tens of millions of rupees. In December 2002, Sana Yaima was arrested near the town of Tamu across the border from Moreh by Burmese authorities with a large consignment of guns and ammunition. UNLF activists then demanded at least thirty million Indian rupees, or approximately US$650,000, in 'taxes' and 'donations' from government departments in Manipur to have their leader released. It is uncertain exactly how much was collected in the end, but Sana Yaima was released, and the 'campaign' set the scene for even more massive 'tax collections' in the state.

The reason why Sana Yaima was arrested in Burma is equally typical of the lawless situation in north-eastern India and northern Burma. The weapons had been bought from the United Wa State Army, UWSA, an ethnic army in north-eastern Burma. But UWSA was no 'ordinary' rebel force in that strife-torn country. In March–April 1989, the rank-and-file members of the CPB belonging to the hill tribe had risen in mutiny against the party's leadership, which consisted of ageing, orthodox Maoist Burmans. Tired of fighting for a cause they understood little of, the tribesmen had driven the CPB leaders into exile in China, and the communist 'Burmese People's Army' subsequently split up into four regional forces based on ethnic lines, of which the UWSA was by far the most powerful – and best connected. There was a smaller ex-CPB army in Kachin state, another in Kokang, a district on the Chinese border in north-eastern Burma which is populated by ethnic Chinese, and one in the multi-ethnic hill country north of Kengtung in easternmost Burma, bordering both China and Laos.[49]

The CPB mutiny occurred in the wake of a massive, pro-democracy uprising in Rangoon and other cities and towns in central Burma. In August and September 1988, millions of people from virtually every town and major village across Burma had taken to the streets to demand an end to twenty-six years of stifling military rule and the restoration of democracy, which existed before the army's coup d'etat in 1962. The protests shook Burma's military establishment, which responded fiercely. Thousands of people were gunned down as the army moved in to shore up a regime overwhelmed by popular protest. The crushing of the 1988 uprising was more dramatic and much bloodier than the better publicized events in Beijing's Tiananmen Square a year later.

In the wake of the massacres in Rangoon and elsewhere in the country, more than 8,000 pro-democracy activists fled the urban centres for the border areas near Thailand, where a multitude of ethnic insurgencies were active. The Burmese military now feared a renewed, potentially dangerous insurgency along its frontiers: a possible alliance between the ethnic rebels and the pro-democracy activists from Rangoon and other towns and cities. But these groups based along the Thai border – Karen, Mon, Karenni and Pa-O – were unable to provide the urban dissidents with more than a handful of weapons. None of the ethnic armies could match the strength of the CPB, which then had 10,000 to 15,000 troops and controlled a 20,000-square kilometre territory along the Sino-Burmese border in the north-east. Unlike the ethnic insurgents, the CPB had vast quantities of arms and ammunition, which were supplied by China from 1968 to 1978 when it was Beijing's policy to support communist insurrections in South-east Asia. Although the aid had almost ceased by 1980, the CPB had enough munitions to last through at least ten years of guerrilla warfare against the Central government in Rangoon.

Despite the Burmese government claims of a 'communist conspiracy' behind the 1988 uprising, there was no linkage between the anti-totalitarian, pro-democracy movement in central Burma, and the orthodox, Marxist-Leninist leadership of the CPB. However, given the strong desire for revenge for the bloody events of 1988, it is plausible to assume that the urban dissidents would have accepted arms from any source. Thus, it became imperative for the new junta that had seized power on 18 September 1988 – the State Law and Order Restoration Council, SLORC – to neutralize as many of the border insurgencies as possible, especially the CPB.

Then came the CPB mutiny. Suddenly, there was no longer any communist insurgency in Burma, only ethnic rebels, and the SLORC worried about potential collaboration between these four new, well-armed forces in the north-east and the ethnic minority groups along the Thai border, as well as the urban dissidents who had taken refuge there. The ethnic rebels sent a delegation from the Thai border to negotiate with the CPB mutineers soon after the break-up of the old party, but the authorities in Rangoon reacted faster, with more determination, and with much more to offer than what the ethnic rebels could do. Within weeks of the CPB mutiny, the chief of Burma's military intelligence, Maj. Gen. Khin Nyunt, helicoptered up to the country's north-eastern border areas to meet personally with the leaders of the mutiny.

Step by step, alliances of convenience were forged between Burma's military authorities and various groups of mutineers. In exchange for promises not to attack government forces and to sever ties with other ethnic rebel groups in the country, the CPB mutineers were granted unofficial permission to engage in any kind of business to sustain themselves.

The threat from the border areas was thwarted, Burma's military regime was safe. But the consequences for the country, and the outside world, were disastrous. 'Any kind of business' in the hills along the Sino-Burmese frontier inevitably meant opium, the main cash crop of the area. The Burmese sector of South-east Asia's Golden Triangle has always produced the bulk of its opium, with smaller quantities grown and harvested in northern Thailand and Laos. And opium can be refined in laboratories into heroin, a much more expensive product with enormous export potential. Today, opium is smoked only locally in tribal villages in the hills – and, in northern Thailand, by foreign tourists – while there are multimillion-dollar markets for heroin in China, India, Australia and the West.

In 1987, a year before the CPB mutiny, 836 tons of raw opium was harvested in the Burma; by 1995, production had increased to 2,340 tons. Satellite imagery showed that the area under poppy cultivation increased from 92,300 hectares in 1987 to 142,700 ha in 1989, and 154,000 ha in 1995.[50] The potential heroin output soared from 54 tons in 1987 to 166 tons in 1995, making narcotics the country's then only growth industry. In June 1996, the US embassy in Rangoon released a report charging that the 'export of opiates (i.e., the derivative heroin) alone appears to be worth as much as all legal exports.'[51]

Within a year of the CPB mutiny, intelligence sources in Thailand were able to locate at least twenty-five new heroin refineries in the former communist base area along the Yunnan frontier. The ceasefire agreements with Burma's military government enabled the UWSA and other former CPB forces not only to rapidly increase poppy production, but also to bring in chemicals, mainly acetic anhydride – which is needed to convert opium into heroin –

by truck from China as well as through Manipur in the west. The heroin trade took off with a speed that caught almost every observer of the South-east Asian drug scene by surprise. And, paradoxically, at a time when almost the entire population of Burma had turned against the regime, thousands of former insurgents rallied behind the ruling military, lured by lucrative business opportunities and unofficial permission to run drugs with impunity.

While drugs went to China and South-east Asia – and beyond – new heroin refineries were also established along the Chindwin River, close to the Indian border: north of Singkaling Hkamti, near Tamanthi, Homailin, Tamu, Kalemyo, Tiddim and Paletwa on the western edge of Chin and Arakan states. For the first time, refineries were established in traditionally 'white', or insurgent-free, areas, close to major Burmese Army installations.[52]

Given the fact that the only main road between India and Burma crosses the border from Moreh in Manipur to Tamu on the opposite side, the state soon found itself awash in drug from the Golden Triangle. Manipur had about 600 addicts in 1988. A couple of years later, there were at least 15,000 and by 1997 the estimate had climbed to 30,000–40,000 regular or casual users – many of whom were HIV positive.[53] The Indian daily *Telegraph* reported in its 5 March 1999 issue that drug traffickers had 'opened up new routes for both raw opium and heroin from Shan State to the plains around Mandalay, through Chin State and Sagaing Division to the Indian border states of Manipur, Mizoram and Nagaland'. Opium production had also spread to the Indian border areas, the newspaper reported:

A former policeman from Tiddim [in Burma's Chin State], whose former duty was to monitor the local drug eradication programme, said opium poppies were planted in about 15 acres of land in almost very village in Tiddim and Falam [another town in Chin State] areas. Each opium grower paid an annual flat fee of 10,000 [Burmese] Kyats to the [Burmese] State Drug Control authorities and 5,000 Kyats to the local police, regardless of the acres they cultivated.

The ceasefire agreements made all this possible and, in January 2000, the Hong Kong weekly *Far Eastern Economic Review* reported that 200 members of the UWSA had arrived at Tamu, opposite Moreh in Manipur where they set up an unofficial 'trade office'. The weekly concluded that the move from the Wa Hills adjacent to China to a town on the Indian border 'could not have happened without logistical support from the central authorities in Rangoon'.[54]

The Golden Triangle drug lords became richer than ever, and more diversified. Burma's opium production declined after 2000, but there were alternatives: synthetic drugs – and guns. As early as in February 1999, Indian frontier police at Moreh confiscated nearly 1,000 methamphetamine pills from two men who had brought them in from Burma. The pills were stamped 'WY', a brand produced at Ho Tao, a UWSA-operated refining centre near the Chinese border. The drugs had been transported across northern Burma, and were the first seizure of Burmese-produced speed pills in India. The year before, Indian customs officials had seized nearly a ton of ephedrine – which is used to manufacture methamphetamines – from couriers who tried to carry the chemicals across the border to Burma. Interrogations revealed that they had been hired to transport the chemicals from Kolkata and other cities to the north-east. If they made it into Burma, they had to travel on to Monywa and Mandalay, where they were told to deliver the goods to middlemen. These middlemen then hired local couriers for the rest of the journey to the Chinese border, or used the trucks supplied by the Burmese government to the UWSA under its ceasefire agreement.[55]

When I first visited Manipur in December 2009, heroin as well as methamphetamines, pills stamped 'WY', were readily available everywhere. The situation was bad also in Mizoram and Nagaland, partly because Christian social organizations had managed to make those states 'dry'. No alcohol, so young people turned to drugs, which, in any case, were often cheaper than beer or hard liquor.

North-eastern India also became a main market for all kinds of weapons – hardly surprising given the abundance of rebel groups in the area, which also, as a result of decades of insurgency, had developed local 'gun cultures'; even ordinary people were armed, either for self-protection or because they were simple kidnappers, extortionists and other criminals. The UWSA was able to sell off some of its old Chinese-made weapons as it acquired new and more modern weaponry from the so-called 'black market' in China, which actually is more grey than black.

Even after the CPB mutiny, the UWSA remained well connected with former Chinese Army officers who had become 'private businessmen', but maintained their links to China's military and its thriving arms industry. It was no longer China's official policy to support the insurgents in India's north-east, but they were welcome to buy weapons so long as they could pay for them. Such 'businessmen' were known to have sold off munition stockpiles without Beijing's approval – but neither did the authorities try to stop it. These activities intensified in the 1990s in the wake of Beijing's ambitious modernization campaign for its armed forces. While various army units were reshaped and re-equipped, many others, particularly in far-flung Yunnan, were reluctant to hand in officially retired arms because of their black-market value in neighbouring Burma and elsewhere. After years of whittling down those retired stocks, and with still strong demand for Chinese armaments from many regional insurgent groups, there was strong market incentive for Yunnan's underworld arms dealers to create a new supply of weapons.

But it had to be done semi-clandestinely. Then, in about 2005, the UWSA decided to establish its own production lines for assault rifles and light machine guns inside the area under its control, which has become a de facto buffer state between China and

Burma. The area was technically part of Burmese territory, but autonomous; so the Burmese authorities could say that they have no jurisdiction over it. But it is not China either, so the Chinese can make the same claim. It is a convenient arrangement for plausible deniability, which suited both countries – and, of course, the UWSA.

With technical assistance from Chinese weapons experts, the factory became operational in September 2006, and occupied a structure inside UWSA chairman Bao Youxiang's heavily guarded seventeen-building compound in his home town of Kunma, 125 kilometres north of the group's main headquarters at Panghsang right on the Chinese border. The plant was able to manufacture replicas of the Chinese-designed M-22 assault rifle – a knock-off of Russia's AK-47 – and the Chinese M-23 light machine gun, as well as 7.62mm ammunition that is used by both weapons.[56]

But it became a major embarrassment for the Chinese authorities and, in 2010, they ordered the UWSA to dismantle the Kunma factory. Nothing of it remains today, but Chinese-made guns continue to flow across Burma to north-eastern India, or, at least until recently, were shipped to Bangladesh and then smuggled across the border into Assam, Nagaland and Manipur.

So, if both Chinese and Burmese authorities are turning a blind eye to the traffic, why was Sana Yaima's consignment seized, and he arrested, in December 2002? According to sources I have in the area, the weapons had been bought from the UWSA, but they included not only Chinese-made assault rifles and machine guns, but also some arms that the Was had obtained from the Burmese government's army. It would have been too embarrassing, and difficult to explain, for the Burmese if weapons made in their own defence industries showed up on battlefields in north-eastern India.

But Sana Yaima was released after the Burmese officials had been paid off and he could return to his men in camps along the border, some located in the Kabaw Valley, which many Manipuris still consider rightfully theirs. The UNLF grew from strength to strength, mainly through its superior organization, effective propaganda work, and extensive 'tax collection' in Manipur. The cross-border trade at Moreh has been booming for several years, and markets all over the north-east are flooded with goods that originate in China and have been transported through Burma. Any visitor to Imphal cannot miss the so-called Paona International Market, which is popularly referred to as 'the Moreh market'. Named after Paona Brajabashi, a hero of the 1891 war against the British, it is full of Chinese-made electronics, clothes, bags, household utensils and other consumer goods.

The UNLF and other groups collect 'taxes' on this trade. While the UNLF as well as the PLA and other rebel groups claim that they are not engaged in the drug trade – they routinely punish drug traffickers, even kill them – not everyone is convinced. Several people I have met during my visits to Imphal (and I am not talking about government officials) assert that these groups collect money from drug traffickers as well. In May 2011, a top commander of the Kangleipak Communist Party, KCP, was arrested from as far away as New Delhi for selling drugs. Earlier in April, a young Manipuri connected to the KCP was apprehended in the Indian capital with 200 kg of ephedrine worth twenty million rupees.[57]

It is not known exactly how much Manipur's 'revolutionaries' collect in 'taxes' and other types of extortion, but the best research into the matter has been done by Rakhee Bhattacharya, a fellow with the Maulana Azad Institute of Asian Studies. In her 2011 study *Development Disparities in Northeast India*, she argues convincingly that economic development in resource-rich north-eastern India has been arrested due to many complex issues, including the illegal economy of insurgency.[58]

That in itself may not be news to anyone familiar with the insurgency-infested north-east. But Bhattacharya goes further to explain how the region's many ethnic insurgents raise funds by taxing local enterprises and individuals, even government officials, as well as by kidnapping for ransom, looting banks, siphoning off government development funds and smuggling arms and narcotics from across the border with Burma.

Ordinary citizens and government employees are pressured to pay a 'revolutionary tax' on a monthly basis in Nagaland. The money goes straight to one of several factions of the Naga rebel movement, or into the pockets of someone claiming to represent one faction or another. In Assam, ULFA has over the years collected vast amounts of money from tea gardens, one of the state's main industries. In Manipur, shopkeepers are required to pay off not one but several insurgent groups, as are truck and bus drivers whose vehicles ply the state's remote roads and main highways. To show how well organized these practices are, Bhattacharya reproduces a printed and numbered receipt from the 'Revenue and Tax department' of the 'Government of Twipra Kingdom,' the insurgents' name for the former princely state of Tripura that borders Bangladesh.[59]

The income from all these activities is used to pay for arms and other necessities for the rebel armies. Bhattacharya goes on to say, 'The political ideology of such groups in the initial years, is a long forgotten dream today. The illegal accumulation of huge money has been contributing to the lavish and luxurious lifestyles of the insurgents.'[60] An insurgent leader who had been arrested was found to have spent around 60,000 rupees per month (out of the tens of millions his outfit extorted from various companies and individuals in the north-east) on 'his cosmetics, body massages and facials, besides splurging on women.'[61]

Many rebel leaders from India's north-east are known to travel frequently to South-east Asia, China and even Europe and North America. In 1988, the NSCN split and the main faction, led by Muivah and Isak Chishi Swu, moved their main area of operation to the Indian side of the border. Now known as 'the National

Socialist Council of Nagalim (Isak-Muivah), or NSCN (IM), it collected 630 million rupees, or US$14.6 million, in 'taxes' and other 'revenues' in 2007–08, according to Bhattacharya's research.[62] At the same time, between 2001 and 2006, more than 2,500 civilians were killed in crossfire between the rebels and government forces, or murdered because they failed to pay their rebel taxes.

Considering the extent of extortion, it is hardly surprising that Manipur and other states remain highly underdeveloped. Bhattacharya argues compellingly that India's recent spectacular economic growth remains elusive in its north-eastern region because of 'rampant corruption, dismal failure of governance and an insurgent economy that drives a sinister parallel economy within the region ... terrorism, drugs and arms trafficking, corruption, money laundering, cross border migration and ethnic conflicts ... devastated its political, economic and social fabric.'[63] Unchecked money laundering is one of the region's most serious problems, which Bhattacharya argues has eroded the integrity of the financial institutions in the north-east and helps to sustain its huge illegal economy: 'The indigenous people of the northeast are otherwise exempt from paying taxes to the government, but a major share of their income goes to the militants, helping them run a parallel terror economy.'[64]

While insurgents collect 'taxes' all over the north-east, the multitude of rebel groups in Manipur has made the situation there much worse than elsewhere in the region. On top of the NSCN (IM)'s agenda is the creation of 'Nagalim', or the 'integration' of all Naga-inhabited areas into one political entity. Maps produced by the rebel outfit show nearly all of Manipur as part of their 'Nagalim', the only exception being the valley around Imphal and some parts of southern Manipur, although Nagas make up only 13–14 per cent of the state's population. The rationale behind this is that Naga tribes live in most parts of Manipur, but it does not take into account that those areas are sparsely populated, and, in any case, never inhabited by one single ethnic group only. Manipur without the hills would not be a viable entity, and the hills are totally dependent on the lowlands for food and virtually all other necessities.

Naturally, the Meiteis, who make up the majority of Manipur's population, are staunchly opposed to the idea of their state being dismembered in such a fashion, as are the Kukis and other ethnic groups in the state who have long been embroiled in conflicts with the Naga rebels. On 12 June 2002, the Manipur Legislative Assembly passed a resolution 'unanimously reiterating the earlier resolutions to maintain the Territorial Integrity of the State of Manipur, resolves to urge upon the Government of India to make suitable amendments of Article 3 of the Constitution of India or to insert appropriate provisions in the constitution of India for protecting the Territorial Integrity of the State of Manipur and pending the aforesaid amendments and incorporation, the Government of India be urged upon to assure the People of Manipur on the floor of the Parliament that the Territorial Integrity of Manipur will not be disturbed at any cost.'[65] On 6 February 2007, Congress president Sonia Gandhi stated that her party – the main party in the present coalition government in New Delhi – 'was committed to protecting the territorial integrity of Manipur at all costs.'[66]

When I visited Ukhrul, Muivah's native district, in May 2010, the NSCN (IM) seemed to run the place. Since August 1997 the NSCN (IM) has actually had a ceasefire agreement with the Government of India, but it is confined to Nagaland and, therefore, does not extend to Manipur. But when I drove in to Ukhrul, a small town perched on a hilltop in the north-eastern corner of Manipur, there were posters with pictures of Muivah everywhere, and with slogans demanding the 'integration' of all Naga areas. Rather curiously, there were also pictures of Mahatma Gandhi. The belief that he once promised the Nagas that they could be independent if they so wished is strong here and elsewhere in Manipur and Nagaland.

I met several local community leaders in Ukhrul, and they insisted that a 'Nagalim' had to be created. When I asked them how that should be done, one of them said: 'First we have to integrate all the Naga-inhabited areas of Manipur, Assam and Arunachal Pradesh with Nagaland, and then we'll talk to the Burmese.' Presumably, the idea was to convince the authorities in Burma to give up their Naga Hills, so that the Nagas then could join 'Nagalim'. It was meaningless to try to argue that international boundaries cannot be broken up in that manner, and that Burma would never let their Naga Hills join some other entity. All I could get myself to ask was whether he thought it was a good idea for a landlocked place like Nagaland, or Nagalim, to have territorial claims on *all* its neighbours and thus turn them into enemies. There was no answer, and when I asked if he thought the Kukis, about a tenth of the population even in Ukhrul, would be happy with their solution to the Naga issue, he and others claimed that was not a problem.

I left Ukhrul, thoroughly depressed at the lack of realism among the community leaders I met there. It was not only their dream of persuading Manipur, Assam, Arunachal – and Burma – to give up large portions of their territories. They also did not want to be reminded of the fact that, in the 1990s, bloody turf wars were fought between NSCN (IM) and various rebel outfits from Manipur's Kuki population resulting in hundreds of mainly civilian deaths.[67] A book produced by the Kukis contains gruesome pictures of men, women and even small children, who had been bludgeoned or shot to death by NSCN (IM) fanatics. It was an extreme case of ethnic cleansing, not unlike what happened in former Yugoslavia in the 1990s.[68]

The carnage began when, in 1992, the United Naga Council, an overground Naga entity, told the Kukis to leave 'Naga areas'. The Nagas considered the hills of Manipur 'their' territory, and the Kukis were only 'tenants' who had settled there, encroaching upon Naga areas. The Kukis, on their part, assert they are natives of the areas they inhabit today and see no reason to move elsewhere. But many Kukis were resettled into what could be considered traditional

Naga areas following a war between the Kukis and the British during 1917–19. During World War II, many Kukis joined the Japanese-supported Indian National Army and fought the British. Many Nagas, on the other hand, remained loyal to the British, acting as guides for their forces in the mountains along the border between India and Japanese-occupied Burma. It is perhaps not surprising that the Nagas and the Kukis do not get along.

However, in more recent years, the Naga–Kuki conflict – understandably, considering the vast amount of money it involves – appears to be a fight for control, and therefore lucrative taxation, of trade routes from Burma to India. While the NSCN (IM) were fighting the Kuki National Organization, KNO, a Kuki rebel outfit, for control over strategically and economically important roads to and from the India–Burma border crossing at Moreh–Tamu, the KNO established links with the NSCN (K), the Naga faction that Muivah and Isak had broken away from in 1988 after yet another bloody fighting among the Naga rebels. 'K' stands for Khaplang, actually the most prominent leader of the Burmese Nagas.

In an email to me dated 12 February 2010, KNO chairman P. Soyang Haokip described his organization's relationship with the NSCN (K) as 'good' and insisted that it 'helps to maintain stability among our respective peoples.' He also pointed out that there had been no clashes between the KNO and the NSCN (IM) for 'quite a while', which could indicate a 'balance of terror' between the two groups, perhaps due to the alliance with the NSCN (K).

The stated aim of the KNO is a separate state for the Kukis comprising the Kuki-dominated districts of Chandel and Churachandpur, and what the Kukis refer to as 'the Sadar Hills' in southern Manipur.[69] 'It is not seeking secession from India,' Haokip said. The NSCN (IM), on its part, has accused the KNO of being a creation of India's security services to fight a 'proxy war' against it in Manipur. While this is impossible to prove, it seems beyond doubt that India's security services did little to prevent the clashes between the two groups from taking place. A weakened NSCN (IM) would also suit India's strategies in the area.

Both Naga and Kuki groups reportedly maintain links with state authorities and local politicians. The Meitei groups are said to be even more influential in local politics. According to Manipuri sources, 'underground' cadres often hide in houses belonging to members of Manipur's Legislative Assembly and are driven around in their cars. Some are even protected by state ministers. This would hold true for rebels from all three major ethnic groups in Manipur: the Meiteis, the Nagas and the Kukis. State politicians depend on critical support from – and intimidation by – 'underground' activists during local elections, while the latter need the former to move around the state, hide and collect 'taxes'. There is in Manipur a solid, symbiotic relationship between state politicians and authorities on one side, and the state's various rebel groups on the other. Nothing is clear-cut in Manipur, where guns and money rule, and where no one knows who is on whose side.

The Naga–Kuki conflict is just one of many ethnic issues that has torn the state apart. The divide between the Nagas and the Meiteis deteriorated to the point of open confrontation when Muivah, in early 2010, decided that he wanted to visit his home village of Somdal in Ukhrul. But rather than flying there by helicopter, which the Indian authorities could arrange because of the ceasefire agreement with the NSCN (IM), he decided he wanted to go by car from Nagaland. The drive would take him through nearly all the hill districts of Manipur, where he also intended to address public rallies. This was perceived by non-Naga communities as an attempt to stake out the NSCN (IM)'s claim to areas which it wants included in its proposed 'Nagalim'.

The state government of Manipur would have nothing of it and sent paramilitary forces to prevent him from entering Manipur. A fight broke out and two Naga students were killed. This led to a sixty-nine-day blockade by Naga civic groups of National Highway

39, the main road to Imphal, which enters Manipur from Nagaland. The blockade caused shortages in Manipur of essential goods, including food and medicines, and also resulted in an even deeper divide between Naga and Meitei communities in the state. I was in Manipur at the time and witnessed endless queues of cars outside petrol stations, where fuel was sold at inflated prices.

This polarized the various communities in Manipur to the extent that Meitei civil society groups decided to penalize the state's hill districts and, in retaliation, prevented food and other supplies from being taken from the valley to the hills. Activist groups and politically minded intellectuals in other parts of India became involved as well, mainly in support of the Naga cause.

According to the *Telegraph* of 9 May 2010, 'The London-based Amnesty International has asked the Centre and the Manipur government to pave the way for the safe visit of the NSCN (IM) general secretary Thuingaleng Muivah to his village Somdal in Ukhrul District.'[70] The paper quoted Jaya Vindhyala, a member of Amnesty International and vice-president of the People's Union for Civil Liberties, as condemning the Manipur government's decision not to allow Muivah to visit Somdal. However, when queried about those statements, Amnesty International's secretariat in London denied that Vindhyala had spoken on behalf of the international human rights organization. It is not Amnesty International's policy to support people representing insurgent movements that are or have been involved in violent activities. But Amnesty International never issued a statement distancing itself from Vindhyala and the news report; the denial came in a private email I received on 6 July from Madhu Malhotra, its London-based South Asia director.

The blockade was eventually lifted, but Muivah never made it to Somdal. And Manipur's many problems remain unresolved and more serious than ever. Meanwhile, there are civil society groups which are doing their utmost to strive for peace. Among the main groups are the Meira Paibis, or 'women torch-bearers', who started out as a force against alcohol abuse and drug addiction, but soon became a potent force in dealing with security personnel. According to one writer for the website *Manipur Online*:

> They make a human wall in cases where innocent local youths are forcibly being taken away by the Armed Forces in the name of insurgents. They are the only ones who can dare to warn and scold the people in under-ground movement for their excesses. Everybody is cautious of them. They dare to get *lathi* charged, to sit for hunger strikes and even go to jail for a right cause. Manipuri women's groups are the Watchdogs of their society. They are the Mothers. Like any other mother they can go to any extent to safeguard the lives and interests of their children – their society. Nowhere else, will one find such vast network of organisations of women.[71]

The Meira Paibis became famous when a group of them demonstrated in the nude outside the Imphal headquarters of the Assam Rifles at the ancient Kangla Fort in July 2004. The immediate provocation was the gunning down of thirty-two-year-old Thangjam Manorama by troops of the 17th Assam Rifles after she was picked up from her Imphal East residence in the early hours of 11 July. She had been accused of being a PLA 'explosive device expert'. The Meira Paibis charged that Manorama was raped before she was killed. 'Indian Army, come and rape us all,' the twelve naked women shouted at the Kangla gate. The charge of rape was vehemently denied by military authorities. They maintained that the woman was killed when she tried to escape from their custody.[72]

However, the Manipuris I have met also assert that the Meira Paibis are divided into four or five different factions, and that they are not as independent as they claim. According to these people, they stage protests only against excesses committed by the security forces, and rightly so, but never when the rebels commit atrocities, which they often do. Allegedly, the various Meira Paibi factions have their links with different underground groups. When a Meira Paibi, Menaka Devi, was killed by the PLA in June 2006, some women's groups protested, but there was a lukewarm response to Menaka's murder in the state capital, Imphal. Most civil society groups in Imphal were divided in protesting the incident. 'There are still people who believe the PLA's version of things. They think Menaka Devi misused her social influence for personal gain,' comments an Imphal-based journalist on condition of anonymity. While women in Manipur enjoy a traditional liberty, they have had to watch out for – as recent events show – more than 30 underground outfits with agendas of their own. This, in spite of the fact that they have, in effect, been shielding insurgents. Meira Paibis have taken to the streets many a time to demonstrate against the all-powerful Armed Forces Special Powers Act (AFSPA). Even as they protest against the actions of security personnel, they create a slipway for insurgents to get through arrest or detention. Compounding the problem is the undeniable fact that most Meiteis harbour an anti-New Delhi sentiment, if in varying degrees.[73]

There is also another, darker and more sinister side to the celebrated Meira Paibis. Like the insurgents, they like to play 'moral police' and punish 'wrongdoers' – whatever and whoever they are. The way to the airport in Imphal is lined with huts and ramshackle houses with signboards outside saying 'Fast Food'. They look – and are – seedy, but that is not why the Meira Paibis find them repulsive. While it is possible to buy a snack and a soft drink there, the main purpose of these 'eateries' is for young lovers to meet in private. Because it is dangerous to venture out in Imphal after dark, there are no discotheques, bars, cafes and similar establishments. So teenagers go to these 'fast food' shacks, which are open in the daytime, to spend some time together. Immoral, the Meira Paibis growl. It has happened that they have raided these places, dragged young couples out and paraded them through the streets, sometimes with shaven heads and shoes slung around their necks to humiliate them.

I have always found it strange that of all degenerate colonial concepts that independent India inherited from the British, Victorian

Puritanism seems to be the most cherished. And that in the country that has produced the Kama Sutra and Khajuraho. It is not easy to be young in Manipur. Violence, a deep-rooted gun culture, drugs, lack of development, unemployment, the draconian AFSPA – and then the Meira Paibis. Not surprisingly, many young Manipuris prefer to stay in Delhi, where they feel free and, to a large degree because of their 'exotic' looks, quite easily find work in hotel receptions and as waiters and waitresses in restaurants – and at 'real' fast-food outlets such as Kentucky Fried Chicken and McDonald's.

Manipur may be India's 'Gateway to South-east Asia', but it is a passage that needs serious mending before it can see some real economic and social development. But, somewhat ironically, East Asia has found its way to Manipur in a curious, unexpected and totally unintended manner. In order to promote Manipur-specific cultural and historical heritage, underground groups have put pressure on everyone to start using the traditional Manipuri script rather than the one based on Bengali. Some rebels are even attempting to revive and promote sanamahi, the ancient religion of the Meiteis, which is undergoing a modest revival. Then, in 2000, the rebels ordered a ban on Hindi movies in cinemas and satellite TV channels to 'protect Manipuri culture'. Until that happened, entertainment for young and not-so-young Manipuris was largely supplied by Bollywood. The new ban was enforced by threats to bomb recalcitrant cinemas and cable operators, so no one dared to show Hindi movies any longer.

But people in the direst of situations tend to be ingenious and there was a way out: the twenty-four-hour English-language Arirang network, which is based in South Korea, replaced Bollywood. Today, there is a craze for all things Korean in Manipur: dramas, soaps, music, fashion, even food. Even the service in the only 'Korean' restaurant in Imphal differs from those in other eateries in that patrons have to sit on the floor. And according to the French

Press agency AFP: 'Hairdressing saloons are covered with head shots of Korean celebrities and offer a wide range of spiky, "Korean-style" cuts which are hugely popular with young Manipuris of both sexes.'[74] At the very least, there is some joy in this beautiful but truly depressing corner of India.

CHAPTER FIVE

ASSAM AND BANGLADESH: FOREIGNERS? WHAT FOREIGNERS?

Paresh Barua seemed pleased when he received the news over his satellite phone on 29 April 1996. One of his comrades told him that Devendra Tyagi, an Indian Army lieutenant colonel, had been assassinated the day before while paying a visit to the sacred Kamakhya temple atop Nilachal Hill outside Guwahati in Assam. Another officer, Lieutenant Colonel A.K. Ghosh, was wounded when what the press described as 'unidentified gunmen' opened fire at the temple.[1] But they were not unknown to Barua, the commander-in-chief of the United Liberation Front of Asom. And he was not alone when he received the news. He was in a safe house in Dhaka, flanked by two officers from the Directorate General of Forces Intelligence, DGFI. I was there, too, and it was obvious that Barua's minders from Bangladesh's main intelligence agency were not pleased to see a foreign journalist in what was supposed to be a top secret safe house. Officially, of course, Bangladesh did not provide sanctuary to militants from India's north-east. That was done only during the days of the erstwhile East Pakistan.

I had gone to Bangladesh on a reporting assignment for the *Far Eastern Economic Review*, and in Dhaka contacted Anup Chetia,

ULFA's secretary general. We had previously met in Bangkok and I knew him quite well, so he did not hesitate to take me to the safe house to meet other ULFA members. The solid, two-storey concrete building with a basement was located in an open field, at the end of a dirt road and, unusually in overcrowded Dhaka, with no other houses in the immediate vicinity.

In June, just over a month later, elections were held in Bangladesh and the Awami League, which is considered more sympathetic to India than other political parties, was back in power as leader of a 'government of national unity'. The Bangladesh Nationalist Party, BNP, whose leader Khaleda Zia had formed the previous government, was forced into Opposition. Almost the entire ULFA leadership, including its chairman, Arabinda Rajkhowa, boarded a plane to Bangkok shortly afterwards. I met them at the Foreign Correspondents Club of Thailand's clubhouse in the Thai capital, and they made it clear that it was no longer safe for them in Bangladesh under the new government.

The only top leader who remained in Bangladesh was Barua, still protected by his powerful DGFI connections. Not even the new prime minister, Sheikh Hasina Wajed, was ever able to fully control the country's many wily intelligence operatives. He was never arrested, but Chetia, who had returned from Bangkok to move ULFA money out of Bangladesh, was picked up in Dhaka in December 1997. He was charged with illegally carrying foreign currencies and a satellite phone, and was sentenced to seven years' imprisonment by a Bangladeshi court.

But then, in October 2001, new elections were held. The BNP won and Khaleda Zia became prime minister for a second time. All the ULFA leaders and other militants from north-eastern India could return to their old safe houses and other sanctuaries in Bangladesh. In March 2002, I was back in Bangladesh and had made arrangements to meet Sashadhar Choudhury, ULFA's foreign secretary, in Chittagong. I waited in my hotel, sent him emails through an approved contact. But no one showed up. Later I learnt that the DGFI had warned Choudhury and other ULFA leaders not to meet me. I was 'an Indian spy', the DGFI claimed – a remarkable allegation, given that, for years, I had been on the immigration blacklist in India for my illegal escapades in Nagaland in 1985. In reality, I am convinced that the DGFI, after my visit to the Dhaka safe house in April 1996, did not want any foreign journalists snooping around ULFA's hideouts in Bangladesh.

But even if I did not meet any Assamese militants at that time, I was able to establish that the ULFA had a solid presence in Chittagong, a port city where arms shipments could be received from abroad. The full extent of ULFA's regional arms procurement network – and China's role in it – was exposed when, in April 2004, a huge consignment of military material was seized in Chittagong. It was so massive that, had it been successful, it could have had a devastating impact on the situation in the entire Indian north-east. It included automatic and semi-automatic weapons, Kalashnikov-type assault rifles, rocket-propelled grenade launchers, hand grenades and a large quantity of all kinds of ammunition.[2] The total value of the shipment was estimated at between 4.5 and 7 million US dollars.[3]

The shipment originated in Hong Kong and, at that point, only involved new Chinese weaponry. From Hong Kong, the ship carrying the goods continued to Singapore, where more weapons of Israeli and US manufacture were added. According to the well-respected defence journal *Jane's Intelligence Review*: 'The shipment was then transported north through the Strait of Malacca to be trans-shipped in the Bay of Bengal to two trawlers, the *Kazaddan* and *Amanat*, which ferried the weaponry to a jetty on the Karnapuli [sic] river, Chittagong.'[4] It has never been made clear why the shipment was intercepted, but *Jane's* speculated that, 'following a tip-off – understood to have probably come from Indian intelligence sources – the off-loading of the weapons was interrupted in the early hours of April 2 by the Chittagong Port Police and Bangladesh Rifles. Nine truckloads of munitions were seized, although it is believed that one loaded truck had left the jetty before the arrival of the port police.'[5]

There was no question as to where the guns were destined. Barua, using the pseudonym 'Asif Zaman', had checked in at Hotel Golden Inn in Chittagong's Station Road shortly before the two trawlers arrived at the jetty on the Karnaphuli. He was even supervising the unloading of the weapons when the police arrived, accompanied by Anthony Shimray, the chief arms procurement officer of the NSCN (IM).[6] Shimray, who was based in the Philippine capital Manila, had flown into Bangladesh via Bangkok just before the shipment was expected to arrive in Chittagong.[7]

Somehow, both of them got away after the incident. It was clear that the guns were seized more or less by accident, much to the displeasure of Barua, Shimray – and the DFGI. The loss of the weapons in Chittagong was a devastating blow for ULFA. It was meant to replenish ULFA's arsenal after it had been forced out of Bhutan in December 2003. Assamese militants and other insurgents from the north-east had had a presence in the Himalayan kingdom since the early 1990s. Taking advantage of the difficult terrain – and the weakness of the tiny Royal Bhutanese Army – ULFA had established at least seventeen camps across the border in Samdrup Jongkhar in south-eastern Bhutan. The National Democratic Front of Bodoland, representing tribals from the Assamese plains, and the Kamtapur Liberation Organization, KLO, also had camps in Bhutan. The KLO's aim was to carve out a separate 'Kamtapur' state comprising parts of West Bengal and western Assam, which would include the narrow and strategically sensitive 'Siliguri Neck' that connects north-eastern India with the rest of the country.

In December 2003, the Bhutanese Army, with full support from India, eventually moved against the unwelcome intruders and they were flushed out in an operation code-named 'All Clear'. Large quantities of weapons were seized, which ULFA had to replace. Hence the anger over the loss of weaponry in Chittagong in April 2004. But, as Indian author and researcher Subir Bhaumik points out, 'While the Chittagong arms haul, the biggest seizure of illegal weapons in South Asia, was successfully foiled, many similar consignments have reached the ULFA through Bangladesh.'[8]

South-east Bangladesh especially – with its fluid population of migrants from Burma and elsewhere and lack of any effective law enforcement – has long been a haven for smugglers, gunrunners, pirates and assorted ethnic insurgents. Throughout the 1990s and early 2000s, the region saw a massive influx of weapons, especially small arms, not only through Chittagong but also the fishing port of Cox's Bazar.[9] Guns were brought in across the Andaman Sea from South-east Asia, but the actual origin and manufacture of the weapons were more often than not Chinese.

The new, commercially oriented China may not be interested in exporting communist revolution to the rest of the world, but the arms trade is lucrative business, and as long as there are buyers Chinese 'private arms dealers' are willing to sell. While the weapons actually come from arms manufacturers such as the state-owned China North Industries Corporation, or NORINCO, deals can be made through front companies in China or, more conveniently, Hong Kong with its freewheeling economy and well-established financial institutions.

Based on interrogations of surrendered ULFA cadres, the Indian media in about 2000 began reporting about a 'mysterious organization' in China known as 'Black House' which delivered arms, often after erasing all original Chinese markings.[10] But 'Black House' is just a direct translation of the Chinese *hei she-hui*, a generic term which refers to the black market in general. Most of the weapons seized in Chittagong in April 2004 were destined for ULFA, but the NSCN (IM) had better contacts in the arms trade through its master smuggler, Anthony Shimray. Payment for the original shipment on behalf of both organizations was made by the NSCN (IM) to an unnamed agent in Hong Kong.[11]

But where did the money to buy the weapons come from? Some details came to light after Sheikh Hasina and the Awami League once again returned to power after the December 2008 election. In May 2009, the Bangladesh press reported that a former National Security Intelligence chief, Brig. Gen. Abdur Rahim, admitted publicly that he had visited Dubai, and there had been several meetings with a business group called ARY in connection with bringing in the arms that were seized in Chittagong.[12] ARY, which runs an immensely lucrative gold business in Dubai and a popular digital television company, was publicly accused of acting as a conduit for funds from Pakistan's notorious spy agency, the Inter-Services Intelligence, ISI. *The Star Weekend Magazine* of the Bengali newspaper *Daily Star* reported on 22 May 2009:

> The ARY Group's Abdul Razzak Yaqoob (whose initials form the acronym) has been linked with the Pakistani establishment. He has offered the Pakistan government cash to bail it out. Pakistan, on the other hand, has strategic interests in funding the ULFA and other such Indian insurgent groups, as the country wants to wage a proxy war against its archrival India. Every country can have its own idea of safeguarding itself; Pakistan may have its own too. But making Bangladesh a battleground for its dummy war against India can never be justified.[13]

Bangladesh had broken away from Pakistan and emerged as an independent nation with the help of India. But the country had undergone some fundamental changes since the 1971 liberation war. And Pakistani influence was soon restored, waning and waxing depending on who was in power in Dhaka: the India-friendly Awami League or the BNP, which has always been closer to Pakistan.

Bangladesh actually emerged from a strong opposition in East Pakistan to the notion that all Muslim areas of former British India should unite in one state. The Awami League, which led the struggle for independence, grew out of the Bangla language movement, and was based on Bengali nationalism, not religion. At the same time, independent, secular Bangladesh became the only country in the subcontinent with one dominant language group and very few ethnic and religious minorities.

It is also important to remember that a Muslim element has always been present; otherwise, what was East Pakistan could easily have merged with the predominantly Hindu Indian state of West Bengal, where the same language is spoken. The importance of Islam grew as the Awami League fell out with the country's powerful military, which began to use religion as a counterweight to the League's secular, vaguely socialist policies. At the same time, many hard-line socialists were opposed to the idea of a separate Bengali state in Bangladesh, which they branded as 'bourgeois nationalism'.

The late Bangladeshi scholar Muhammad Ghulam Kabir argued that Maj. Gen. Zia ur-Rahman, who seized power in the mid-1970s, 'successfully changed the image of Bangladesh from a liberal Muslim country to an Islamic country.' Kabir also points out that 'secularism' is a hazy and often misunderstood concept in Bangladesh. The Bengali term for it is *dharma nirapekshata*, which literally translates to 'religious neutrality'. Thus the word 'secularism' in a Bangladeshi context has a subtle difference in meaning from its use in the West.[14]

In 1977, Zia dropped secularism as one of the four cornerstones of Bangladesh's constitution – the other three being democracy, nationalism and socialism, although no socialist economic system was ever introduced – and made the recitation of verses from the Koran a regular practice at meetings with his own political organization, the BNP, which soon became the second biggest party in the country after the Awami League. The marriage of convenience between the military – which needed popular appeal and an ideological platform to justify its opposition to the Awami League – and the country's Islamic forces survived Zia's assassination in 1981.

In some respects, it grew even stronger under the rule of Lt Gen. Hossain Muhammad Ershad in the 1980s. In 1988, Ershad made Islam the state religion of Bangladesh, thus institutionalizing the new brand of nationalism with an Islamic flavour that Zia had introduced. Ershad also changed the weekly holiday from Sunday to Friday and revived the Jamaat-e-Islami to counter the secular Opposition. The Jamaat had supported Pakistan against the Bengali nationalists during the liberation war and most of its leaders had fled to (West) Pakistan after 1971. Under Zia, they came back and brought with them new, fundamentalist ideas. Under Ershad, Islam became a political factor to be reckoned with.

Ershad was deposed in December 1990 following anti-government protests, and was later convicted of a number of offences and jailed for several years. But this did not lead to a return to old secular practices. Zia's widow and the new leader of the BNP, Khaleda Zia, became prime minister after a general election in February 1991. The BNP rode on a wave of dissatisfaction with the Awami League, which many perceived as corrupt. Expectations of the first BNP government were high, and many hoped it would be 'cleaner' than the previous one.

But very little changed in that regard. Further, violence gradually became widespread and much of it appears to have been religiously and politically motivated. Non-Muslim tribal people in the Chittagong Hill Tracts as well as Hindus came under attack. Hindu places of worship were ransacked, villages destroyed, people were driven from their homes and scores of Hindu women were reported to have been raped.

While the Jamaat may not have been directly behind these attacks, its renewed acceptance as a political force has meant that more radical groups feel they now enjoy protection from the authorities and can act with impunity. By the early 2000s, the most militant group, the Harkat-ul-Jihad-al-Islami, HuJI, or the Movement of Islamic Holy War, was reported to have 15,000 members.

Bangladeshi Hindus and moderate Muslims hold them responsible for many of the attacks against religious minorities, secular intellectuals and journalists.

In a statement released by the US State Department on 21 May 2002, HuJI was described as a terrorist organization with ties to Islamic militants in Pakistan.[15] While Bangladesh was far from becoming another Pakistan, Islamic forces were no doubt on the rise, and extremist influence was growing, especially in the countryside. Or as one foreign diplomat in Dhaka told me during one of my visits there in the 1990s: 'In the 1960s and 1970s, it was the leftists who were seen as incorruptible purists. Today, the role model for many young men in rural areas is the dedicated Islamic cleric with his skull cap, flowing robes and beard.' Grinding poverty and constant political crises gave rise to militants for whom religious fanaticism equalled national pride, and a way out of misrule, disorder and corrupt worldly politics.

Furthermore, the emergence of Islam as a potent political force, and the rise of the BNP and its Jamaat ally, meant that the ISI was back in a country that once had been part of its turf. And it was not only ULFA that was allowed to have safe houses in Dhaka and Chittagong, and training facilities mainly around Sylhet in north-eastern Bangladesh. Other ethnic rebels from India's north-east, who were driven out in 1971, could also return. Mizo insurgents maintained a presence in the Chittagong Hill Tracts up to the 1986 peace accord with New Delhi. Naga rebel leaders began travelling abroad on Bangladeshi passports and smaller bands of militants from Tripura frequently sneaked across the border into Bangladesh. After 1990, the DGFI – and the ISI, with which it had an on-and-off relationship – also developed close links with Manipuri groups such as the PLA and the UNLF.[16]

The reason why the ISI supported ULFA was explained to me by the latter's commander-in-chief himself. When I met Barua in a Bangkok coffee shop in March 1992, he made no secret of the fact that Pakistan supported ULFA and encouraged him and his comrades to step up their activities in Assam.[17] The 8th Mountain Division of the Indian Army had been withdrawn from the northeast and sent to Kashmir. If serious trouble erupted in Assam, this division, and possibly even other units, would have to be pulled out of Kashmir, which would suit Pakistan's interests. Nothing had obviously changed since Pakistan began to support the Naga rebels in the 1950s, and the Mizos and others in the 1960s. Barua had just arrived in Bangkok from Singapore, where he had bought radio equipment and walkie-talkies. He was in Thailand to try to procure arms. I am not sure that he managed to order any weaponry during that visit, as I did not see him again until we met in Dhaka four years later.

The first time I met Barua was actually at the then undivided NSCN's headquarters in north-western Burma in 1985. The ULFA chairman, Rajkhowa, was there as well as its vice chairman, Pradeep Gogoi. While I was there with my wife and newborn daughter, the camp was attacked by the Burmese Army. The assault began with heavy gunfire early in the morning of 20 December. Fortunately for us, a platoon of battle-hardened guerrillas from the Kachin Independence Army had just arrived to escort us to Kachin state. While most of the Naga guerrillas ran for their lives, the KIA fought back – together with Barua and some of the Assamese. The former footballer from Dibrugarh, who had become an underground rebel commander, displayed bravery as well as fighting skills, and the Kachin were impressed as well. Three KIA guerrillas, some Nagas and at least a hundred Burmese government soldiers died in the battle which lasted for several days. But we escaped unscathed, and so did Barua and his comrades.

Shortly after our trek though northern Burma, ULFA sent more than 300 men to the KIA's base area near the Chinese border, where they underwent rigorous military training. They remained there until 1991, and it is possible that ULFA at that time made its first contacts with Chinese arms dealers. ULFA was not allowed to use Chinese territory for any training or other obvious military activity. But the group maintained a discreet liaison office in the western Yunnanese town of Ruili until 2007, and managed to buy weapons from Chinese dealers as well as some former rebel groups like the United Wa State Army, which by then had made peace with the government in Rangoon.[18]

It may be understandable, although not excusable, for Pakistan to support ULFA, and China has its strategic and commercial interests in maintaining some links with the militants in north-eastern India. But the role of Bangladesh is more complex and cannot be explained only because Pakistan and the ISI had managed to re-establish influence in this bastion of Bengali nationalism.

India had played a crucial role in the liberation of Bangladesh, it is true, but serious problems in bilateral relations erupted soon after independence. In April 1975, India finished building the barrage across the Ganga, roughly 16 kilometres before the river flows into Bangladesh. Water could now be diverted from the Ganga into the Hooghly River to help alleviate the problem of silt in Kolkata port. In 1996, India and Bangladesh signed a thirty-year agreement on sharing of Ganga water, but little came of it. The two countries have still not found an arrangement that would suit both parties. On the Bangladeshi side, people complain about dry river beds and severe water shortages because of the barrage, even resulting in the desertification of certain areas. India, they say, is behaving like a big bully towards its weaker neighbours.

Then there is the issue of Bangladesh's Hindu minority. Being the only South Asian country that can claim to be a genuine nation state – one people, one language and one main religion – its ethnic minorities feel they are discriminated against. Many of the tribals in the Chittagong Hill Tracts are Buddhists or Christians, and have even resorted to armed struggle against attempts to resettle Muslims from the lowlands in the highlands which are sparsely populated by Bangladesh standards. Many Hindus have simply left. According to the 1941 Census of India, Hindus made up 11.88 million, or 28.3 per cent of the population of the then East Bengal. Twenty years later, when East Pakistan was well established, the number had decreased to 18.5 per cent. By 1974, only 13.5 per cent of the population of independent Bangladesh was Hindu. According to the 2001 census, the figure was down to 9.2 per cent, and many Hindus are still leaving Bangladesh. In a decade or so, there may be no more Hindus at all in Bangladesh.

The first main exodus took place when the former British India was partitioned into India and Pakistan in 1947. Severe communal riots took place in Bengal, which was divided into an eastern part with an overwhelming Muslim majority – which bizarrely, many would argue, became part of Pakistan although it was separated from the rest of this new country by hundreds of miles of Indian territory – and West Bengal, which had a Hindu majority and became a state within the Indian Union. Millions of Bengali Hindus emigrated or fled to West Bengal and Tripura, and by 1951 the Hindu proportion of the population of East Pakistan had dropped to 22 per cent.

The controversy began already at this time. In the old, undivided Bengal many Hindus had been wealthy zamindars and shopkeepers. Through a series of acts and ordinances, they were prevented from taking with them more than a negligible portion of their movable assets. Land and other immovable assets were administered under the East Bengal Evacuees (Administration of Immovable Property) Act of 1951. In effect, the land they left behind was taken over by the state, which, through its Evacuee Property Management Committee, leased it to others.[19]

The inclusion of East Bengal in the new Muslim state of Pakistan actually turned out to be a disaster for both communities. According to Bangladeshi journalist and writer Saleem Samad, the Bengali Muslims were discriminated against by the West Pakistanis, and the minorities in East Pakistan were doubly discriminated against.[20] The wealthy Hindus lost their land and much of their assets when they left for India, while the poor and middle-class Hindus who remained in East Pakistan became targets of discrimination by the federal authorities in West Pakistan through a string of new laws. In 1965, when war broke out between Pakistan and India, a law called 'the Defence of Pakistan Ordinance' was promulgated to 'ensure the security, the public safety, interest and the defence of the state.'[21] This was followed by an even more draconian regulation termed 'the Enemy (Custody and Registration) Order II of 1965'. India was declared an enemy, and the law allowed 'enemy' – in practice Hindu – lands to be expropriated by the state.

The next big exodus took place during and after the long and bitter liberation war of 1971. When the rebellion first broke out, and the Pakistan Army tried to quell it, the Hindus especially were targeted, as they were seen as a 'fifth column' for India, which openly supported the independence movement. In a statement dated 1 November 1971, US Senator Edward Kennedy wrote: 'Field reports to the US Government, countless eyewitnesses, journalistic accounts, reports of International agencies such as the World Bank and additional information available to the subcommittee document the reign of terror which grips East Bengal (East Pakistan). Hardest hit have been members of the Hindu community who have been robbed of their lands and shops, systematically slaughtered, and in some cases, painted with yellow patches marked "H". All of this has been officially sanctioned, ordered and implemented under martial law from Islamabad.'[22]

By the end of 1971, nearly ten million people had fled to West Bengal, where they were sheltered in makeshift refugee camps. Eighty per cent of them were Hindus, 15 per cent Muslims, and 5 per cent Christians and Buddhists. When the war was over, and Bangladesh created, very few of the non-Muslims returned to their homes. Therefore, by 1975, only 13.5 per cent of the population was Hindu, and those who remained were no longer landowners and shopkeepers. Most were poor and low-caste farmers and fishermen; the new elite that had emerged was almost exclusively Muslim.

A third campaign against the Hindu minority began in 2001 as Islamic fundamentalists went on a rampage through non-Muslim communities. Thousands of people fled to India, and many more were internally displaced. Many Hindus moved together because they felt safer if they were surrounded by more members of their own community, but this has created severe pressure on land in a country that already is overpopulated.

While India has been forced to receive and accommodate millions of Hindu refugees from East Bengal/East Pakistan/Bangladesh, Bangladeshi nationalists have continued to blame India for many of its internal problems. Even after independence, the Hindus were branded Indian stooges and therefore untrustworthy citizens who stood in the way of the fulfilment of the dream of a Bengali Muslim nation state. Moreover, India was accused of supporting ethnic rebels in the Chittagong Hill Tracts. India the liberator thus became the perceived enemy for certain quarters in Bangladesh.

It is also an ironic twist of history, to say the least, that nearly all ULFA leaders came to use Bangladesh as a base for their activities. Their movement grew out of a vicious agitation in Assam in the 1970s and 1980s against the influx of 'foreigners' – mainly Muslim illegal migrants from Bangladesh. And then they ended up in Bangladesh, dependent on the DGFI for protection and using Muslim names in their Bangladeshi passports and other documents to conceal their actual identities. I posed that question to ULFA Secretary General Anup Chetia when we discussed his group's policies in a Dhaka coffee shop in 1996. He just smiled and shrugged his shoulders: 'That's the way it turned out. Nothing we can do about it.'

While it is impossible to distinguish an Assamese from any other 'mainstream' Indian today, they do have a separate ethnic and cultural heritage rooted in South-east Asia, which is one of the reasons for the rise of a separatist movement among them. Many Assamese nationalists insist that they, like the Nagas, the Mizos and the Manipuris, are also a Mongol people and related to the Thais. Far-fetched as it may seem, as Assamese not only look like other Indians, but also speak an Indo-Aryan language related to Bengali, Maithili and Oriya, this is not totally without foundation.

The Brahmaputra basin has been inhabited for thousands of years, and ancient Assam, known as Kamarupa, was ruled by several powerful dynasties. But then, in the early thirteenth century, a Tai people from the east entered the scene. Led by a ruler the Assamese today call Sukapha, they mounted a military expedition across the Patkai range into the Brahmaputra Valley, where they established a new kingdom. Sukapha, however, is just a corruption of Seu Ka Hpa, or 'the Tiger from Heaven' in the language of the Tais, who are better known by the name the Burmese gave then: Shan.[23] According to ancient chronicles, Seu Ka Hpa came from Mong Mao, the area around today's Namkham in the northern Shan state of Burma, and Ruili across the border in Yunnan. His title was *saohpa*, which is Tai, or Shan, for 'Lord of the Sky', or more formally *saohpalong*, 'Great Lord of the Sky'. The equivalent in Thai, the related language spoken in Thailand, is *chaofa*, still a royal title.

Nearly eight centuries later, ULFA set up its unofficial liaison office at precisely that town in Yunnan. Paresh Barua and his comrades must have been aware of Ruili's historical significance to the Assamese. But convenience and expediency, not historical pride, was the reason why ULFA chose Ruili. Located right on the Burmese border, it is China's gateway to South-east Asia and beyond, an important trading town which has attracted legitimate merchants as well as shady wheeler-dealers from the entire region. All kinds of smugglers and black marketeers – including arms dealers – flocked to Ruili when China reverted to capitalism and the Burmese border opened for trade in the late 1980s.

Seu Ka Hpa's people became known as Ahom and his descendants ruled the Brahmaputra Valley from 1228 to 1826, when the British conquered the area after a two-year war to drive out the Burmese who had invaded Assam and Manipur. Over the centuries, the original Ahom language, which is clearly Tai and had its own script, died out and was replaced by Assamese. Today it is used only for liturgical purposes and studied by scholars, although ULFA and other ultranationalist groups have tried to revive it.

There is, however, still a Tai language spoken in India's north-east: Tai Khamti. But the Tai Khamtis migrated from upper Burma in the late eighteenth century and are not descendants of the Ahoms. Today, they live in the Lohit Valley in Arunachal Pradesh and in some villages in North Lakhimpur, Assam. The Tai Khamtis chose to settle in the same kind of green lowlands they had been forced to leave behind in northern Burma following several rebellions against British expansion east of the Patkai range. By then Assam was British too, but the rebellions left the Tai Khamtis scattered in pockets on both sides of the mountain divide. Unlike the Ahoms who became Hindus and in the seventeenth century adopted Assamese as their court language, the Tai Khamtis have kept their native tongue and Buddhist religion.[24]

After the British conquest, Assam was made part of the Bengal Presidency, which was headquartered in Kolkata and then covered most of northern India. In 1906 Assam became part of the newly created 'East Bengal and Assam Province', and was made a completely separate administrative entity only in 1912. Partition in 1947 saw Assam's Sylhet district, a rich tea-growing area, joining East Pakistan, while Indian Assam at that time encompassed the entire north-east except the princely states of Tripura and Manipur.

Assam was reduced in size even further after independence. The Naga Hills became Nagaland in 1961 and was given full statehood in 1963. With the implementation of the North-Eastern Reorganization Act of 1972, Mizoram and Arunachal became separate Union territories. In 1970, the Jaintia, Garo and Khasi Hills of Assam had become the autonomous state of Meghalaya – 'the Abode of Clouds' in Sanskrit – and a fully fledged state in 1972. When Meghalaya was carved out of Assam, the latter lost its former capital Shillong as well. All that remained of Assam in the 1970s was the Brahmaputra Valley, a few other plain areas, the Mikir Hill District, which was renamed Karbi Anglong in 1976, and the North Cachar Hills. A new administrative centre was established at Dispur in Guwahati.

But shrunken Assam still held some of the most fertile agricultural lands in India, and therefore attracted hordes of migrants from poorer parts of the subcontinent – especially Bangladesh. To them, Assam remained a land of opportunity and an estimated five million Muslim Bengalis fled to Assam in the wake of the liberation war. Assam already had a population density of 245 per square kilometre. So there was really no abundance of land, and jobs were not necessarily easy to come by. A group of militant students began a campaign to expel the state's millions of 'foreigners', claiming that they had stolen jobs in paper, tea and oil industries. Worse, they argued, was the political threat to the Assamese. Local politicians, eager to build up pools of loyal voters for elections, had helped the 'foreigners' get ration cards and other documents which made it possible for them to register as voters. The student radicals claimed that illegal immigrants from Bangladesh, and some from Nepal as well, formed nearly 45 per cent of the electorate. Many Assamese feared that they would lose political control of their native land.[25]

In early 1983, state elections were going to be held in Assam, but the All-Assam Students Union, AASU, and other militant groups called for a statewide boycott of the polls. More than a hundred people were killed in clashes with security forces, and native Assamese militants turned to violence to halt the voting. It was not only a question of mainstream Assamese against the 'foreigners'; tribal people of the plains and hills of Assam, Bodos and others, seized the opportunity to rise up against the majority Assamese. *Asiaweek*, a Hong Kong-based newsweekly, in its 4 March 1983 issue ran a graphic eyewitness account of what happened:

> As the days passed ... political lines became blurred and an atavistic bloodlust seemed to envelop certain parts of the state. Screaming tribal warriors from the hills wielding spears, bows and arrows, and homemade bombs descended on rural villages, slaughtering women and children indiscriminately. Festering religious and communal animosities erupted, with many groups seizing the opportunity to settle old scores ... The tribals are killing Bangladeshi Muslims and local Assamese, the Muslims are killing the Assamese, including Assamese Muslims, and all of them are killing the tea plantation workers, who are mostly Biharis ... nobody knows who is against whom in Assam.[26]

The worst violence occurred near the town of Nellie in Nowgong district, 100 kilometres east of Guwahati. *Asiaweek's* Delhi correspondent P.P. Balachandran arrived at the scene shortly after the carnage:

> We were proceeding toward the area when we noticed a thick pall of smoke in the distance. When we arrived we found an entire village in flames. Hundreds of people were running towards a nearby stream. Close on their heels was a mob of tribals, perhaps 2,000 in number, armed with spears, bows and arrows, and swords. The Muslims made a desperate attempt to cross the 8-metre-wide waterway, but another crowd of tribals was waiting on the other side. In the ensuing melée, babies and women were hacked to death ... after the slaughter the tribals returned to the burned-out thatched huts in the village to scavenge for valuables like gold and jewellery ... as we watched, a few tribals approached and asked who we were, threatening to kill us if we wrote anything against them. When we asked why they were killing innocent children, one replied: 'We are avenging our children's killings by Muslims.' It took almost an hour for the police to reach the spot. By then the

dance of death was over and the tribals had fled, leaving a rivulet of blood flowing into the waters of the stream.[27]

At least 500 people were killed at Nellie, and the official death toll throughout Assam was well over a thousand. Seventy thousand paramilitary forces were deployed to restore order, but the situation was already out of control. Assam was up in flames, and even the arrival of units from the regular Indian Army at the request of the Assam state authorities did little to improve the situation.

ULFA grew out of the agitation against the influx of 'foreigners' in Assam, but most of its founders and leaders were Assamese intellectuals rather than sword-wielding tribal warriors. According to its own version of history, the group – using the supposedly more indigenous 'Asom' rather than 'Assam' in its name – was founded on 7 April 1979 at Rang Ghar, the ruins of an old Ahom palace in today's Sibsagar. ULFA leaders told me in 1985 that the founder and first chairman of their movement was a history professor from Sibsagar called Byas Gogoi.[28] It is not clear who this mysterious character was; most other sources attribute the founding of ULFA to Bhadreswar Gohain, who had played an active part in the anti-foreigner agitation, along with Bhimkanta Buragohain, a painter and a sculptor who was the chief ideologue of the movement.

Whatever the case, Arabinda Rajkhowa, a radical student leader whose real name is Rajiv Rajkonwar, assumed the chairmanship of ULFA in the early 1980s; Pradeep, or Samiran, Gogoi, a former worker of the Assam State Electricity Board from Sibsagar became the vice-chairman, and Anup Chetia – who was born Sunil Barua – its general secretary. Paresh Barua, who had played football with the Assam Junior National Team and three times represented Dibrugarh University as captain in matches in Kolkata, was appointed commander-in-chief of ULFA's armed forces.

It was a closely knit group of idealistic young intellectuals who decided to launch a war for an independent Assam. ULFA wanted to restore the glory of the old Ahom kingdom, free from Bengali

Muslims and other 'foreigners' – but in the context of the politics of the modern age. The independent nation that ULFA envisioned would have to be a socialist people's republic. The young Assamese nationalists were also dedicated Marxist-Leninist revolutionaries.[29]

From modest beginnings, ULFA eventually grew to become the most formidable anti-government fighting force in the north-east with thousands of men, and some women as well, in arms. Weapons were snatched from Indian security forces and procured from abroad. Money was not a problem; the militants robbed banks and collected vast amounts of 'revolutionary tax' from tea gardens and other industries in Assam. And ULFA did not hesitate to kill real and imagined enemies of their cause. Among its first victims in the early 1980s were Bimal Roy, a communist member of the Assam Legislative Assembly – but he was a Bengali – and Robin Mitra, another Bengali and a well-known geologist. Mitra was punished for having shown the authorities a place where some ULFA activists were in hiding, resulting in the death of five of them. Scores of people were killed in bomb blasts at Guwahati railway station and a cinema hall in the city.

One of the best known of ULFA's victims, and fortunately one of the last, was Sanjoy Ghose, a well-respected rural development activist who had made significant contributions to community health among poor people on the river island of Majuli in the Brahmaputra. ULFA accused him of being an 'Indian spy', and he was abducted and killed in July 1997.[30] In another attack on innocent civilians, a bomb planted by ULFA killed ten schoolchildren and three women as they were celebrating India's Independence Day on the grounds of a college at Dhemaji in north-eastern Assam in August 2004.

Violent agitation in the Brahmaputra Valley continued until an accord was signed on 15 August 1985 between the Government of India and some of the leaders of the Assamese student movement. The accord led to elections and a new state government was installed, led by Prafulla Mahanta, one of the leaders of the radical students; but this did little to restore peace. ULFA condemned AASU and the All-Assam Gana Sangram Parishad, AAGSP, a leading force in the agitation, as 'traitors and capitulationists'.[31]

Even before the agreement was signed, thirty-two ULFA militants had crossed the border into Burma, where they were undergoing military training at the NSCN's headquarters at Kesan Chanlam, opposite Nagaland's Mon district. ULFA also linked up with the United National Liberation Front and other Manipuri militant rebel groups, and a new phase in the armed struggle began. Until then, ULFA had operated primarily through the student movement and other mass organizations. Now it became a guerrilla force that launched raids into India from sanctuaries in north-western Burma not controlled by the Central government in Rangoon. Additional sanctuaries in Bhutan served the same purpose in the 1990s. And then came the new bases and safe houses in Bangladesh – the ultimate irony, considering the background of their struggle.

In the end, as we have seen, the demise of East Pakistan did not deprive India's north-eastern militants of access to the Chittagong Hill Tracts, Sylhet and Dhaka. Apart from the Assamese, the Mizos, the Nagas, the Manipuris and militant groups from Tripura also took refuge in Bangladesh. According to Subir Bhaumik, two groups from Tripura, the National Liberation Front of Tripura, NLFT, and the All-Tripura Tiger Force, ATTF, had no less than forty-eight bases in Bangladesh until the Awami League, once again, returned to power in January 2009.[32]

Tripura, the smallest of the seven northeastern states and the third smallest in India after Sikkim and Goa, was ruled by a succession of 186 princes for hundreds of years till 15 October 1949, when it merged with the Indian Union. In 1941, Tripura had a total population of only some 650,000 people. Today, with 3.7 million inhabitants, it is, despite its size, the second most populous state in the north-east after Assam. Tripura saw a massive influx of Hindu Bengalis after partition in 1947, in addition to ethnic Bengalis who had fled Burma after the Japanese occupation of that country in the early 1940s. Today, Bengalis make up 70 per cent of Tripura's population, and native tribal peoples the rest.

Unrest broke out in Tripura in the late 1970s, when the Tribal National Volunteers, TNV, an offshoot of the Tripura Upajati Juba Samity, TUJS, a tribal political party, resorted to armed struggle, driven by hatred for the Bengali settlers. According to Bhaumik, the TNV attacked Bengali settlers to scare them away from the state, while the NLFT and the ATTF resorted to kidnappings. Between 1995 and 2005, nearly 3,500 such abductions were reported to the police. The kidnappings served a double purpose: to spread fear among the Bengalis and to collect huge sums of money, which were used to buy weapons and other necessities for the rebels.[33]

Local rebel forces also emerged in Meghalaya to scare away settlers from elsewhere in India from that state. The Hynniewtrep National Liberation Council was set up in 1992 to fight for Meghalaya as a state exclusively for the Khasi tribe and free it from 'domination' by the Garos, another tribe. The Garos, on their part, formed the Achik National Volunteer Council in December 1995 to establish a homeland called 'Achikland' in the areas of the Garo Hills of Meghalaya. When it entered into a ceasefire agreement with the Indian government in July 2004, a new, more militant outfit called the Garo National Liberation Army was formed. But none of these groups, or other smaller outfits in Meghalaya and the nearby 'Kamtapur' in Assam ever became really powerful. The Garo and Kampatur 'liberation armies' served mainly as conduits for ULFA militants crossing back and forth between Bhutan and Bangladesh. On the other hand, the plain tribals of Assam set up several militant groups that carried out bombings and assassinations all over Assam. The most prominent of these were the National Democratic Front of Bodoland and the Bodo Liberation Tiger Force.[34]

It was enough chaos and mayhem in all the north-eastern states for any government official in New Delhi to throw up his hands in despair. But the Central authorities also decided to tackle the matter in a more systematic manner, especially because nearly all of the north-eastern rebels also had foreign connections, in Bangladesh, Pakistan, Burma and China. B.N. Mullik and his Intelligence Bureau had with remarkable efficiency managed to split the Naga movement and neutralize several of its factions. But the failure to anticipate a war with China in 1962 as well as not having a clear understanding of Pakistan's infiltration of Kashmir prior to the 1965 Indo-Pakistan war prompted India to reorganize its special services. Foreign intelligence capabilities especially were seen as weak and hugely inadequate for India's security requirements. And there was almost no capacity to conduct covert operations abroad, something that India felt it needed at a time when ethnic insurgents from the north-east had links with Pakistan as well as China.

The answer came in 1968 when Indira Gandhi's government set up a new spy agency called the Research and Analysis Wing, R&AW to its operatives and simply RAW to the public and the press. At a meeting on the afternoon of 21 September, Rameshwar Nath Kao, who had served under B.N. Mullik in the Intelligence Bureau, was assigned a new designation, secretary (research) in the Cabinet secretariat of the prime minister. He was India's new spymaster and K. Sankaran Nair, another IB veteran, was made his deputy. To begin with, this new, highly secretive organization had 250 employees and a budget of twenty million rupees, or US$444,000 at the exchange rate of the time. R.N. Kao built up RAW from scratch and remained its chief until he resigned after Indira Gandhi's defeat in the 1977 elections. But he left behind an intelligence agency which today is one of the world's largest with stations in all major capitals. The number of operatives, analysts and technicians is a tightly guarded secret and estimates of its annual budget vary between 31 and 150 million US dollars.

Many books have been written about the inner workings of the United States' CIA, Britain's MI-6, Israeli Mossad, China's intelligence agencies and the erstwhile Soviet Union's KGB, but RAW has by and large been spared such public exposures by authors and investigative journalists. One of few exceptions is *Inside RAW: The Story of India's Secret Service*, a slim 120-page volume written by Asoka Raina and first published in 1981. A more recent work, B. Raman's *The Kaoboys of R&AW: Down Memory Lane*, is more a memoir than an account of how RAW operates, as are similar books about Indian intelligence. 'Kaoboys', of course, is a wordplay on the name of the first RAW director.

RAW may be younger than most of its foreign equivalents but its modus operandi is deeply rooted in Indian history. Raina traces India's culture of intelligence back to ancient Indian scriptures, the Vedas, where there are references to *sapasah*, or spies, with 'a thousand eyes'. The Laws of Manu, compiled around 1500 BC, stipulates that 'the King must explore by means of spies both within the state of his own kingdom and his foe's,' and then goes on to describe five classes of spies in various disguises.[35] But the main work about Indian statecraft, including espionage, was written more than 2,000 years ago by the Indian philosopher Kautilya who also used the name Vishnugupta and may have been a man called Chanakya, a scholar and later prime minister of the Maurya Empire.

Known as *The Arthashastra*, it deals with every issue that a society and its ruler would have to deal with, from how to conduct wars and deal with famines to sexual relations and different kinds of marriage, how taxes should be collected, disputes settled and wrongdoers punished. And how to rely on spies to detect discontent among the king's subjects and demoralize enemy troops in times of wars. Kautilya was also one of the first thinkers in history who understood the importance of psychological warfare by 'declaring the successes of their own preparations and failure of the enemies'.[36]

In Kautilya's view, 'the creation of a secret service, with spies, secret agents and specialists such as assassins' was a task of highest priority for the king who should also initiate 'battles of intrigues' and 'secret wars' to demoralize the enemy.[37] Secret agents, Kautilya wrote, could pretend to be itinerant monks, impoverished farmers and merchants; and he speaks of 'spies who are residing as traders in the enemy's forts, and those living as cowherds or ascetics in the district borders of the enemies' country'.[38] The art of conducting espionage, counter-espionage, covert operations and surveillance of potentially unruly subjects is nothing new in India. Kautilya wrote about it when people in Europe were still living in caves.

In modern times, as Subir Bhaumik points out, 'India has been able to control, if not end . . . insurgencies by a complex mix of force, political reconciliation, economic incentives and by splitting the insurgents.'[39] Those tactics are straight out of *The Arthashastra*: 'Kautilya's four principles of *sham* (political reconciliation), *dam*[40] [sic] (monetary inducement), *danda* (force) and *bhed* (split) has been amply applied in dealing with the insurgents in the North East – more than anywhere else in postcolonial India.'[41] In a modern context, Bhaumik argues, the Indian state has offered political negotiations and some concessions – but nothing that would jeopardize the integrity of the state – which is sham; liberal doses of development funds from the centre in New Delhi, or dan; military campaigns whenever needed, or danda; and RAW and other secret agencies have been masters at creating splits within the rebel movements, or bhed, which have led to factional infighting and surrenders.

Failure to understand these concepts have led well-meaning Western NGOs and foreign 'conflict-resolution' outfits to believe that they somehow can 'mediate' in India's many ethnic conflicts. The Reverand Michael Scott's peace mission to Nagaland in the 1960s was the first and last time India even considered seriously involving a third party to settle an internal problem that posed a threat to national security. Kautilya prescribed much more effective ways of dealing with such issues than any outsider ever could suggest. And that was two millennia ago.

More recently, but still well before the ethnic conflicts in the
north-east and the formation of RAW, India has also shown that it
is no stranger to undercover, cloak-and-dagger work outside its
own boundaries. During the first Great Game in the nineteenth
century, the British employed local surveyors who were sent to
explore the strategically important areas on India's north-western
frontier and beyond the Himalayas. They became known as pundits
after the Sanskrit word *pandita*, 'a learned man' and, disguised as
traders or holy men, were able to go where no white man could.
The pundits were trained at the clandestine department of the
Survey of India at Dehra Dun run by British Captain George
Montgomerie. One of the most celebrated of the pundits was the
legendary Nain Singh Rawat. Here is an account of the type of
training in survey these pundits used to get:

> First they were trained by endless practice to take a pace which,
> whether they walked uphill, downhill or on the level, always
> remained the same – thirty-three inches in the case of Nain Singh.
> Next they learned how to keep an exact count of the number of
> such paces they took in a day, or between any two landmarks. This
> was done with the aid of a Buddhist rosary, which as we have
> noted normally comprises one hundred and eight beads. Eight of
> these were removed, leaving a mathematically convenient one
> hundred, but not a sufficient reduction to be noticeable. At every
> hundredth pace a bead was slipped. Each complete circuit of the
> rosary, therefore, represented ten thousand paces – five miles in
> the case of Nain Singh, who covered a mile in two thousand paces.
> Because the Buddhist rosary has attached to it two short secondary
> strings, each of ten smaller beads, these were used for recording
> every completed circuit of the rosary.[42]

A number of other tricks were developed as well to disguise what
the pundits were actually doing:

> Not only was the Buddhist rosary ingeniously adapted to
> Montgomerie's purpose, but so were prayer-wheels. These were

fitted with a secret catch which enabled the pundit to open the copper cylinder and insert or remove the scrolls of paper bearing his route notes and other intelligence. Later the workshops at Dehra Dun were to conceal compasses inside the wheels, so that a pundit could take bearings while pretending to be at prayer. Larger instruments like sextants were concealed in specially built false bottoms in the travelling chests which native travellers carried, while secret pockets were added to their clothing. Thermometers, for measuring altitude, were concealed in hollowed out staves, and mercury – necessary for setting an artificial horizon when taking sextant readings – was hidden in a sealed cowrie shell and poured into a pilgrim's bowl whenever needed.[43]

Each time someone Nain Singh did not want to talk to came too close, he would start whirling the prayer wheel around and thus pretend to be in deep religious contemplation. Usually, this would be enough to stop others from addressing him. Another way of remembering their observation was to turn them into a poem, and recite it over and over again during their travels. Rudyard Kipling borrowed at least two of his characters from Captain Montgomerie's twilight world of spies disguised as holy men for his novel *Kim*, which was written nearly forty years after Nain Singh and his colleagues graduated from the Dehra Dun spy school.[44]

A main weakness of modern Western intelligence is its lack of effective human intelligence. Montgomerie sent his pundits into areas he wanted to survey, but the colonial era is gone and to assign a Westerner to similar duties in Asia would be impossible. But Indian intelligence can do precisely that. Its human intelligence capabilities are unsurpassed by any international secret service, with the possible exception of China's, which may deploy similar methods. Combined with Kautilya's maxims on statecraft, this makes RAW a formidable force.

RAW's first great success was the creation of Bangladesh. *The Sunday Times* of London reported in its 12 December 1971 issue: 'It took only 12 days for the Indian Army to smash through on its way to Dacca [Dhaka], an achievement reminiscent of the German *blitzkrieg* across France in 1940. The strategy was the same – speed, ferocity, and flexibility.'45 And this Bangladesh operation also helped locate and apprehend insurgents from North-east India who were based in Dhaka, one might add. This was made possible only because RAW operatives and their contacts among the Mukti Bahini freedom fighters had provided accurate intelligence from behind Pakistani lines.

Later, when Bangladesh turned from friend to foe, RAW found a willing partner in tribal guerrillas fighting for autonomy for the Chittagong Hill Tracts. The problems in the Hill Tracts predates the formation of Bangladesh, but political organization among the tribals began in earnest only in 1972, when the Parbatya Chattagram Jana Sanghati Samiti, PCJSS, or the United People's Party of the Chittagong Hill Tracts, was formed to safeguard the interests of the tribals. Before it was set up, co-founder Manabendra Larma had belonged to the short-lived Rangamati Communist Party, which opposed 'Bengali irredentism, Indian expansionism, Soviet neo-colonialism, US imperialism and Pakistani Islamic fundamentalism.'46 Manabendra's brother, Jyotirindra Larma, known as Shantu, was but in charge of the PCJSS's armed wing, the Shanti Bahini, literally 'peace force' in 1973.

It may seem incongruous that India would support a force that sprung from a group that opposed, among all its other proclaimed enemies, 'Indian expansionism'. But the answer lies in the background to the problems in the Chittagong Hill Tracts – and India's need to get a 'fifth column' inside the area that could provide information about the north-eastern rebels who had bases and other sanctuaries there.

Bangladesh has fewer ethnic minorities than any other country in the subcontinent and nearly all of them live in the Chittagong Hill Tracts. Anthropologists believe that these non-Bengali hill peoples migrated from areas now in Burma between the sixteenth and mid-nineteenth centuries. They can be divided into two broad categories: those who live in the valleys within the hills – the Chakma, the Marma and the Tippera – and those who live in the actual hills – the Bawm, the Mru, the Khumi and several smaller tribes. The predominantly Buddhist Chakmas are the largest group with some 400,000 people today.[47]

During the colonial era, the Chittagong Hill Tracts, like the Naga, Lushai and other hill districts, enjoyed the status of an Excluded Area, which meant that people from the plains were barred from settling there, as they were in the Naga and Lushai Hills and some other hill areas in British India. It may seem strange that the area was given to Pakistan, a country which was built on the idea of uniting all the Muslim areas in India into one state. Islam was non-existent in the Chittagong Hill Tracts, but it was traded off for the predominantly Sikh areas of Ferozepur and Zira in Punjab, which were given to India.[48]

During the early years of Pakistan's independence, the special status of the Chittagong Hill Tracts was retained. But in 1955, the then East Pakistan cabinet decided to bring the district under the administrative system of the rest of the country. After the military takeover in Pakistan in 1958, the 'opening up' of Chittagong Hill Tracts was accelerated, and the construction of a massive hydroelectric power station and dam at Kaptai in 1963 caused the first batch of refugees from the area to flee into India. About 40,000 tribals were resettled mostly in the foothills of what today is Arunachal Pradesh, where they still remain. However, though allowed to stay, most of them are still stateless.

After 1964, migration from the plains into Chittagong Hill Tracts was no longer illegal, and a steady flow of poor Bengali settlers entered the district. German anthropologist Wolfgang Mey believes this attempt to 'Bengalise' the district served the double purpose of somewhat easing the land scarcity in the plains and of strengthening the position of the government in the hills by increasing the proportion of 'loyal', i.e., Bengali Muslim, inhabitants.[49]

Then came the liberation war and the king of the Chakmas, Raja Tridib Roy, made the mistake of siding with Pakistan, a move that was prompted by fear of being overwhelmed by Bengali nationalists. Many Chakmas suffered as a result and, after independence, the Government of Bangladesh became even more repressive in its treatment of the hill people than the Pakistani authorities had been.

The mass resettlement of plains people in the hills caused not only tens of thousands of hill people to flee to India, but it also ignited an armed struggle against the government and the settlers from the plains. For years, the Shanti Bahini staged hit-and-run attacks on the Bangladeshi Army and police posts as well as settler villages. The army responded fiercely, and one of the bloodiest incidents took place on 25 March 1980. Upendra Lal Chakma and two Opposition members of parliament reported from the area:

> After visiting the place of occurrence, we found the evidence of the killings and atrocities committed by one unit of the Army at Khaukhali Bazaar of Kalampati Union ... The newly arrived settlers also took part in the act of killing and looting of the tribal people. Even after one month of the incident a reign of terror is prevailing in the entire area.[50]

Buddhist temples and religious images had been destroyed, the MPs reported. A survivor showed them a mass grave, where fifty to sixty people had been buried. According to one estimate, 300 hill people had been butchered.[51]

In 1997 a peace accord was eventually signed between leaders of the resistance and the Bangladesh government, which should have brought twenty-five years of struggle to an end. By the time the peace accord was signed, the Bengalis had reached 50 per cent of the total population of CHT, up from 3 per cent in 1947.[52] No government of Bangladesh would risk antagonizing those settlers –

and their relatives in the plains – by giving in to demands from the ethnic minorities, such as forcing the settlers to leave.

Prior to the 1997 accord, there were 65,000 Chakmas and other tribals from the Chittagong Hill Tracts in refugee camps in Tripura. Fifty thousand of them did return after the accord, and the Shanti Bahini formally laid down their arms. The PCJSS entered mainstream politics, and the former commander of the Shanti Bahini, Jyotirindra Larma, became chairman of the Chittagong Hill Tracts Regional Council.

During its heyday in the 1980s, Shanti Bahini consisted of 5,000–7,000 men with about 1,000–1,200 weapons, and the leaders could move relatively freely around Tripura, including the state capital Agartala.[53] At that time, they were RAW's eyes and ears in the Chittagong Hill Tracts, and the Larma brothers soon forgot their initial anti-Indian stance. They had to be pragmatic when India provided them with protection and some material support. In Dhaka and other towns, it is plausible to assume that RAW had other trusted sources, and it is not inconceivable that ULFA and other organizations were infiltrated by Indian intelligence.

India's need to keep an eye on Bangladesh became even more important when Islamic fundamentalists became active there in the 1990s. The most extreme of the groups, the HuJI, was set up in 1992 reportedly with funds from Osama bin Laden.[54] The existence of firm links between the new Bangladeshi militants and the Al Qaeda were first proven when Fazlur Rahman, leader of the 'Jihad Movement in Bangladesh' – to which HuJI belonged – signed the official declaration of 'holy war' against the United States on 23 February 1998. Other signatories included bin Laden himself; Ayman al-Zawahiri, chief of the Jihad Group in Egypt; Rifa'i Ahmad Taha, who is also known as Abu-Yasir, of the Egyptian Islamic Group; and Sheikh Mir Hamzah, secretary of the Jamiat-ul-Ulema-e-Pakistan.[55]

HuJI was headed by Shawkat Osman alias Sheikh Farid in Chittagong and, according to a 2001 US State Department report, then had 'at least six camps' in Bangladesh.[56] According to an eyewitness I contacted at about that time in Ukhia, a small town south of Cox's Bazar, hundreds of armed men were staying in one of these camps near the Burmese border. While some of them spoke Bengali, the vast majority appeared to be Arabs and others of Central and West Asian origin. The militants warned villagers in the area that they would be killed if they informed the media or raised the issue with the authorities.[57]

Bangladesh's Islamist radicals first gained international attention in 1993, when author Taslima Nasreen was forced to flee the country after receiving death threats. The fundamentalists objected to her critical writings about what she termed outdated religious beliefs. Extremist groups offered a reward of US$5,000 for her death. She now lives in exile in Europe.

While Nasreen's outspoken feminist writings caused controversy even among moderate Bangladeshi Muslims, the entire state was shocked when, in early 1999, three men attempted to kill Shamsur Rahman, a well-known poet and a symbol of Bangladesh's secular nationhood. During the ensuing arrests, the police said they seized a list of several intellectuals and writers, including Nasreen, whom Bangladeshi religious extremists branded 'enemies of Islam'.[58]

Bangladeshi human rights organizations openly accused HuJI of being behind both the death threats against Nasreen and the attempt to kill Rahman. The US State Department noted that HuJI had been accused of stabbing a senior Bangladeshi journalist in November 2000 for making a documentary on the plight of Hindus in Bangladesh and a July 2000 assassination attempt on the prime minister at that time, the Awami League's Sheikh Hasina.[59]

As with the Jamaat-e-Islami and its militant youth organization, the Islami Chhatra Shibir, HuJI's main stronghold is in the lawless south-east, which includes the border with Burma and, therefore has easy access to weapons and other contraband. Typically, the winner in the 2001 election in one of the constituencies in Cox's

Bazar, BNP candidate Shahjahan Chowdhury, was said to be supported by 'the man allegedly leading smuggling operations in [the border town of] Teknaf.'[60] Instead of the regular army, the paramilitary Bangladesh Rifles was deployed in this constituency to help the police in their electoral peacekeeping. This was, according to the Society for Environment and Human Development, SEHD, a Bangladeshi NGO, 'criticised by the local people who alleged that the Bangladesh Rifles were well connected with the smuggling activities and thus could take partisan roles.'[61]

In one of the most recent high-profile attacks in the area, Gopal Krishna Muhuri, the sixty-year-old principal of Nazirhat College in Chittagong and a leading secular humanist, was killed in November 2001 in his home by four hired assassins, who belonged to a gang patronized by the Jamaat.[62] India, which was viewing the growth of Bangladesh's Islamist movements with deep concern, linked HuJI to the attack on the American Center in Kolkata in January 2002, and a series of bomb blasts in Assam in mid-1999.[63]

In early May 2002, nine Islamic fundamentalist groups, including HuJI, met at a camp near Ukhia and formed the Bangladesh Islamic Manch, or Association. This new umbrella organization also included one outfit purporting to represent the Rohingyas, a Muslim minority in Burma, and the Muslim United Liberation Tigers of Assam, MULTA, a small group operating in India's north-east. By June, Bangladeshi veterans of the anti-Soviet war in Afghanistan in the 1980s were reported to be training members of the new alliance in at least two camps in southern Bangladesh.[64] Therefore, it was plausible to assume that Pakistan's ISI was also present in the Bangladesh–Burma border areas.

The links to Assam were of special concern to India. On 30 October 2008, a bomb blast in the state killed eighty-five people and injured nearly 500. Ryan Clarke, a US researcher wrote in a March 2010 paper for the US Army War College:

Sophisticated weaponry and unknown smuggling networks were used to carry out these attacks as opposed to the relatively crude locally assembled explosives used elsewhere in India such as New Delhi, Mumbai, Hyderabad, and Varanasi. The bombs used in Assam have raised concerns over the region's porous borders as well as links between local separatist militant groups, especially from Bangladesh and Myanmar (Burma). Security experts say that the car and motorcycle bombs used were often laden with over 80 kilograms of RDX, well beyond the capability of domestic separatist outfits such as the United Liberation Front of Assam (ULFA) or the National Democratic Front of Bodoland (NDFB).[65]

Prior to the bombings, there had been brutal riots against Bengali Muslims in Assam and communal tensions were high. According to Clarke:

India's Home Ministry believes that HUJI-B [HuJI-Bangladesh] was involved in the Assam bombings and that the group maintains close ties with IM [Indian Mujahideen]. In Assam, HUJI-B is believed to utilize its close connections with illegal immigrants from Bangladesh for new recruits, safe houses, and logistical support, and reports suggest that the Indian government has identified 46 points along the border with Bangladesh that are being used as exit and entry points by HUJI-B.[66]

There were even some reports suggesting that Islamic fundamentalists had linked up with elements within the local Muslim community in Manipur, the Meitei Pangals. In 1993, a group called the People's United Liberation Front, PULF, was formed by some Meitei Pangals following communal clashes between them and Hindu Meiteis. PULF is a tiny group, but if it is true that it has links with HuJI and groups such as Lashkar-e-Taiba, it could also be because Islamic militants are interested in Manipur's proximity to the Burmese border, a haven for gun smugglers. In December 2006, three Manipuri members of Lashkar-e-Taiba were arrested in Delhi with 2 kg of RDX explosives.[67]

In April 2002, I wrote a cover story for the *Far Eastern Economic Review* which had the relatively provocative title 'Beware of Bangladesh'.[68] But it was more precisely an account of the changing face of Bangladesh's national identity and the rise of Islamic fundamentalism in a country that was actually formed on Bengali nationalism. There was actually nothing in the story which had not been published before in Bangladeshi newspapers and magazines. But the fact that it appeared in a regional publication caused an uproar among some Bangladeshis, most of whom, judging from their inane comments, had never read the story. The *Review*'s head office in Hong Kong was inundated with hundreds of angry emails, a mob burnt copies of the magazine in the street outside, and I received more than one death threat. I had tarnished the international reputation of Bangladesh and had to be punished.

Some claimed that I was a tool in the hands of the Awami League and had been chauffeured around Dhaka in a car belonging to Sheikh Hasina, then in the Opposition, against the BNP and Jamaat government. In reality, I travelled around the city exclusively in motorized rickshaws, a cheap and convenient mode of transportation which I had to pay for like everybody else. In a desperate attempt to discredit the story, some Bangladeshis tried to sue the magazine for defamation, claiming that the angry demonstrator in the picture on the cover had nothing to do with Islamic fundamentalism. The picture, they claimed, was of a 'Bangladeshi freedom fighter' taking part in a protest against attacks by Hindus on Muslims in the Indian state of Gujarat. It was not my picture, but taken by a local photographer working for an international agency, and there were other pictures of the same event and the same person – under a banner saying 'Stop Attacks on Afghanistan' – which did not seem to have much to do with the plight of the Muslims in Gujarat.[69] The picture was taken during a pro-Taliban demonstration in Dhaka shortly after the US-led action against Afghanistan began in October 2001.

It had never been my intention to 'defame' Bangladesh as a nation, just to highlight some important, and disturbing, developments there. And in August 2005, as some Bangladeshis were continuing to claim that there were no Islamic terrorists in their country, more than 300 explosions took place simultaneously in fifty cities and towns across the country, including the capital Dhaka. More than thirty people were killed and scores injured. Victims included lawyers, judges, police officials and journalists. An outlawed Islamic group, Jamaat-ul-Mujahideen Bangladesh, said it carried out the attacks.[70] And more bombings followed in December.

The Bangladeshi authorities and others were forced to take the warning signals more seriously. In the end, seven Islamic militants were sentenced to death for the attacks. Then, in December 2008, the Awami League won the election and Sheikh Hasina was back in power. A year later, Bangladesh detained several ULFA activists and handed them over to the Indian authorities. Among them were Chairman Arabinda Rajkhowa, Deputy Commander Raju Barua, and Foreign Secretary Sashadhar Choudhury, whom I tried but failed to meet in Chittagong in 2002.[71]

Their Islamist and Pakistani link also suffered when, on 27 January 2010, Bangladesh executed five former army officers convicted of the 1975 murder of the country's independence leader and Sheikh Hasina's father, Sheikh Mujibur Rahman. Among those executed was Lt Col. Syed Faruque Rahman, who, in 1988, first met ULFA's then foreign affairs chief Munim Nobis. That marked the beginning of ULFA's clandestine presence in Bangladesh. In that year, Nobis travelled from Dhaka to Pakistan where his Bangladeshi contacts introduced him to ISI.[72]

Faruque and his accomplices fled the country after the murder of president Mujibur Rahman but returned in the 1980s from their self-imposed exile and formed the Islamic and right-wing Freedom Party, which, according to an official 2002 compilation from the Immigration and Refugee Board of Canada, has alleged ties with 'ultra right-wing groups such as the Harkatul Jihad' – HuJI – which is also linked to the ISI.[73]

It is unclear why ULFA had to close its Ruili office in 2007, but as the organization's leaders were being rounded up in Bangladesh and deported to India in late 2009, Commander-in-Chief Paresh Barua was spotted in the border town of Yingjiang opposite Burma's Kachin state.[74] Thus, Barua was the only top ULFA leader who was not affected by the arrests in Bangladesh. In line with Kautilya's principle of sham, the arrested leaders were later released on bail and negotiations were initiated between Rajkhowa and representatives of the Indian government. Or why not a dose of dan? There might even be a bhed, if Rajkhowa joins mainstream politics – like ULFA founder Bhadreswar Gohain has done – and Barua remains defiant and determined to carry on the armed struggle.

With the loss of their old bases in Bhutan and now in Bangladesh, the militants are cornered. Their only remaining outlet to the rest of the world is through Burma. And Burma provides links with China. Burma is also the corridor between India's north-eastern frontier states and South-east Asia, and therefore plays an important role in the strategic thinking of government agents, merchants, rebels and smugglers alike.

CHAPTER SIX

BURMA: A STATE OF REVOLT

Panghsang is a booming town like no other. Located in a horseshoe bend of the Nam Hka River – which forms Burma's border with China – it has the best of both worlds. The economic prosperity of China is reflected in new, concrete buildings, luxury cars, paved roads and shops stocked with the latest consumer goods. Only Chinese currency is accepted here; no one wants the almost worthless Burmese kyats. But, then again, this is not China. And on this side of the border no one has to worry about rigid law enforcement and government restrictions on certain types of trade and commerce – because Panghsang and the surrounding areas are not controlled by the Burmese authorities either. Panghsang with a population of more than 20,000 people is the unofficial 'capital' of the more than 15,000 square kilometre area in north-eastern Burma controlled by the United Wa State Army, the strongest of the four ethnic armies that once made up the fighting force of the Communist Party of Burma, CPB. Panghsang lies in the heart of the area where the UWSA has been running its own affairs – and armed forces – since the 1989 ceasefire agreement with the Burmese government.

Before the 1989 CPB mutiny, Panghsang's only concrete structures were a cluster of small houses where the party leaders resided, and a Chinese-built broadcasting station where important meetings were also held. The rest of Panghsang consisted of huts made of wood and bamboo, and the only commercial activity was an old-fashioned marketplace where locals sold vegetables, pork, chickens and opium – the last readily available and taxed by the party.[1] Occasionally, traders from China came across to sell clothes, toys and trinkets, or ice cream from boxes they carried on the backs of bicycles.

On a hill overlooking Panghsang, adjacent to what used to be a memorial to fallen CPB comrades, now stands the Golden Baby Disco, a two-storey, fancy-looking building. The upper level is a nightclub with a glass wall offering a view of the lights of Panghsang by night. The lower level has karaoke lounges with private party rooms where VIPs can entertain their guests and, for an extra fee, buy the company of young hostesses in skimpy miniskirts. Not far from the Golden Baby Disco is a large casino, operated by the UWSA's Ying Yuang Entertainment Corporation. Across the street is a wooded rest area where several moon bears and a monkey are kept in cages. They are given beer and lit cigarettes by onlookers, and look quite miserable.

Commercial sex is available not only in the karaoke lounges. Panghsang's many hair salons double as venues to employ prostitutes at night under pink neon lights. For a fee, the women can be taken to nearby hotels. No doubt the old CPB chairman Thakin Ba Thein Tin and his comrades would turn in their graves if they saw what has become of the headquarters from where they tried to launch a proletarian revolution in Burma.

Today, Panghsang even has its own bank, the Wa Pang Bank, or Wa State Bank, which is located on the main road. Cars parked outside include luxury sedans and SUVs with number plates issued by the local Wa authorities. There is a cinema, a day market, a bumper car arena and a roller skating rink, where skates can be rented by the hour. One of the UWSA commanders even had a bowling alley built for him and his close associates. It was open to the public, but with a private lane reserved for the Wa leaders.

Neatly uniformed UWSA troops in formation can be seen drilling in town as Wa police vehicles patrol the streets. Signs tell visitors not to step on the flower beds that separate the lanes of the main roads in Panghsang. Offenders are charged a hefty fine of Renminbi 300, or US$44.

Under the ceasefire agreement with the government, the Burmese military maintains a liaison office in Panghsang, staffed by about ten officers. But they rarely leave the compound where they are staying, and the only Burmese flag in Panghsang flies over a government-run clinic. All other official buildings fly the UWSA flag alongside the Wa state flag – a blue-and-red banner with a star, a sun and a crossed dagger and spear. 'The Wa state', which does not appear on any official maps, has for all intents and purposes become a semi-independent, but unrecognized, buffer state between Burma and China, with its own rules and local administration.

The new prosperity of Panghsang and other towns in the former CPB-controlled area also shows quite clearly that profits from the drug trade have been enormous. One factor was that the string of new heroin refineries was conveniently located near the main growing areas in northern Burma, cutting out several middlemen. Equally important, they were close to the rapidly growing Chinese drug market and the seemingly easier routes through Yunnan to the outside world rather than the old ones down to the Thai border, where laboratories had been converting raw opium into heroin since the early 1970s. In the early 1990s, the same laboratories in northern Burma also began, for the first time, to produce methamphetamines. And the gun factory that the UWSA managed from 2006 to 2010 provided additional income from sales to Assamese and Manipuri rebels. Thanks to the ceasefire agreement with the Burmese government, the guns could quite easily be transported across the country to north-eastern India.

With the collapse of Burma's communist insurgency in 1989, several smaller ethnic armies that had depended on the CPB for arms and ammunition also gave in. The 2,000-strong Shan State Army, SSA, which for decades had waged a war for autonomy for Shan state, made peace with Rangoon on 24 September 1989, and was granted timber concessions in the Hsipaw area in northern Shan state. They were followed by smaller groups of Pa-O and Palaung rebels who also operated in Shan state. By 1997, more than a dozen ethnic rebel armies had made peace with Rangoon.[2]

With the CPB out of the way, China and Burma, for the first time in decades, could establish cross-border trade – directly in the areas that the Burmese government controlled, or indirectly in areas held by the ceasefire groups. The first steps had already been taken when, on 6 August 1988, the two countries signed a bilateral agreement on border trade. By then the days of Mao Zedong's support to communist movements in the region were well and truly over, and Deng Xiaoping's pragmatism was guiding Chinese foreign policy. This agreement was the first of its kind that the hitherto isolated Burma had entered into with a neighbour. It was especially significant because it was signed at a time when Burma was in turmoil. Two days later, a pro-democracy uprising broke out in all major cities and towns across the country.

But the Chinese, renowned for their ability to plan far ahead, had expressed their intentions, almost unnoticed, in an article in the official weekly *Beijing Review* as early as on 2 September 1985. Titled 'Opening to the Southwest: An Expert Opinion', the article, which was written by the former vice minister of communications, Pan Qi, outlined the possibilities of finding an outlet for trade from China's landlocked provinces of Yunnan, Sichuan and Guizhou, through Burma, to the Indian Ocean. It mentioned the Burmese railheads of Myitkyina and Lashio in the north and north-east, and the Irrawaddy River as possible conduits for the export of goods from those provinces, but omitted to say that all relevant border areas, at that time, were not under Burmese Central government control.

All that changed, of course, after the CPB mutiny of March–
April 1989. By late 1991, Chinese experts were assisting in a series
of infrastructure projects to spruce up Burma's poorly maintained
roads and railways. Border trade was booming, and China emerged
as Burma's most important source of military hardware. Additional
military equipment was provided by Pakistan – which also helped
Burma modernize its defence industries – and by Singapore and
later even by North Korea. The total value of Chinese arms deliveries
to Burma to date is not known, but intelligence sources estimate it
to be about US$1.4 billion. Deliveries include fighter, ground attack
and transport aircraft, tanks and armoured personnel carriers, naval
vessels, a variety of towed and self-propelled artillery, surface-to-air
missiles, trucks and infantry equipment.

With the open border also came heroin. Before the 1949
communist takeover, China had vast poppy fields and millions of
opium smokers, and addiction was considered the country's most
serious social problem. The communists effectively put an end to
both poppy cultivation and the sale of narcotics. The methods were
brutal, but they worked. Scores of petty gangsters, opium dealers
and even addicts were rounded up and shot after summary trials.
Other addicts were sent to rehabilitation centres and the vast
poppy fields in the Chinese interior were destroyed.

Then, in the early 1990s, drugs were back again – and this time
mainly from the new refineries across the Burmese border. By the
early 2000s, China had at least 900,000 known drug addicts, and
probably several million others who had not been registered by the
authorities. Some unofficial estimates put the figure as high as
twelve million. In 2001, 83.7 per cent of the registered addicts were
male and 73.9 per cent were under the age of 35.[3]

Given the involvement of the UWSA and other ex-CPB forces in
the narcotics trade, it may seem incongruous that these forces are
not only tolerated but are getting Chinese help too. Officially,
several of the former CPB commanders were barred from entering

China because of their known involvement in the drug trade. But the fact that all of them had been operating for years along the Sino-Burmese border meant that they had long-standing working relationships with Chinese security authorities in Yunnan and perhaps even elsewhere.

A well-placed source from north-eastern Burma insisted in an interview in early 1991 – just as drugs were beginning to flow across the border into China – that this personal friendship enabled them to visit China regularly and own property across the border, including hotels and private houses. 'Sometimes they are even escorted by Chinese security officials and driven around in their cars,' the source told me.[4]

For reasons of border security, China needs to have at least a working relationship with the new and mighty UWSA, which controlled a long stretch of the common, Sino-Burmese frontier. Somewhat paradoxically, the UWSA soon became stronger and better equipped than the CPB had ever been – and the new weaponry came from China: Kalashnikov-style assault rifles, light, medium and heavy machine guns, rocket launchers, mortars and even a small arsenal of HN-5N Chinese-made man-portable air defence systems.[5]

China, obviously, is playing several games in Burma, and although it no longer seeks to export communist revolution, it wants to expand its economic influence down the South-east Asian peninsula. And given the uncertain future of Burma's military regime, relations with a group like the UWSA secure a foothold for China inside the country.

A clear sign of Chinese approval of the UWSA presence across the border also came when, in November 2007, a new, concrete bridge across the Nam Hka River to Panghsang was completed. It replaced the old, rickety steel and wooden bridge that had been there since the CPB days. The border crossing now resembles similar crossings anywhere in Asia, and there is a steady traffic across the bridge with Chinese officials on one side and Wa on the other.

But the Wa leaders also had to deal with anger from the Chinese side. During the 1990s, UWSA leader Bao Youxiang, an ethnic Wa with a Chinese name, was summoned several times to Kunming and read the riot act: no drugs into China. The Chinese were growing increasingly frustrated as vast quantities of heroin were flowing across the border. In the early 1980s, heroin was almost unheard of in China, but in 1995, the authorities seized 2.376 tonnes of the drug. This jumped to 4.347 tonnes in 1996, 5.477 tonnes in 1997, 6.281 tonnes in 2000 and a record 13.2 tonnes in 2001. While smaller quantities of heroin enter China from the so-called Golden Crescent in Central Asia – Afghanistan, Pakistan and Tajikistan – nearly all of it comes from Burma. In 1991, there were 8,080 drug-related arrests in China. A decade later, the number of arrests had increased to 40,602.[6]

How many of those arrested were sentenced to death is not clear, but China regularly executes most prisoners convicted of serious drug offences. When China celebrated Anti-Drugs Day on 26 June 1996, as declared by the United Nations, it did so in its own way: by sentencing 769 drug offenders to death.[7] Many were taken immediately from the courtroom to the execution ground to be shot, and most executions were carried out in Kunming.

The answer from the UWSA leadership was to switch to the production of drugs other than opium and its derivative heroin: methamphetamines, a synthetic drug that does not require laborious cultivation of unpredictable crops such as opium, which run the risk of being destroyed by bad weather.

Synthetic drugs do have a market in China as well – but there, they are locally produced in the country and, therefore, considered an internal problem. The market for methamphetamines produced in areas controlled by the UWSA and other former CPB forces is in Thailand, increasingly also Laos and Cambodia, and north-eastern India.

Despite efforts by the Chinese to stem the flow of narcotics, atleast into their own country, drugs are an issue of secondary concern. Strategic considerations, whether it is spreading revolution or economic expansion, are much more important for whoever has been in power in Beijing since the communist takeover in 1949. And China's involvement with Burma's many insurgents – ethnic, communist and post-communist – is even older and more solid than its connections with Naga, Mizo, Manipuri and Assamese rebels. For historical and political reasons, China's contacts with the CPB and its latter-day offshoots have been especially close and cordial.

The communist revolution in Burma that went so awfully wrong began on 15 August 1939, when a group of young Burmese intellectuals met in a small flat in Barr Street, Rangoon. Among them were several student leaders from the *Dohbama Asiayone*, or 'Our Burma Association', the most militant nationalist group in Burma before World War II. The most famous of them, the twenty-four-year-old Aung San, was elected general secretary while the party's main theoretician was a Burma-born Bengali, Hemendranath Ghoshal, who was also known as *yebaw*, or comrade, Ba Tin. Aung San later left the party and was destined to become independent Burma's first prime minister – but then he was assassinated in Rangoon by a rival politician on 19 July 1947. His daughter, Aung San Suu Kyi, only two years old when he was shot, now is the country's main pro-democracy icon.

In official party history, the unpretentious meeting in Barr Street in 1939 is called the CPB's First Congress. Burma had then just been separated from British India and been a colony in its own right for only two years. But Indian influence was still strong. In fact, 45 per cent of the population of Rangoon was Indian before World War II – Bengali, Tamil, Gujarati, Punjabi – and the urban working class, coolies, dock workers and other manual labourers, almost exclusively Indian.[8] Apart from H.N. Ghoshal, another

Bengali, known as 'Dr Nag' and, in Burmese, Yebaw Tun Maung, was one of the founders of the party. A qualified medical doctor, he later educated the CPB's first medics.

Quite independently from the emergence of an Indian- and British-inspired radical student movement among Burmese intellectuals, communist ideas had also penetrated Rangoon's Chinese community in the pre-World War II era. 'Chinese communism' was first introduced into Burma by Wu Wei Sai alias Wu Ching Sin and his wife who arrived in Rangoon in May 1929 from Shanghai. Wu became editor-in-chief of a Chinese-language daily newspaper called *Burma News*, while his wife became a teacher at a Chinese-medium school in Rangoon. They distributed communist leaflets among the Chinese in Rangoon and built up a small circle of followers. Their activities were discovered when the Special Branch of the British police intercepted a letter Wu had written in invisible ink to the South Seas Communist Party in Singapore.[9] His message appears to have been that there was no fertile ground for a communist revolution among the largely business-oriented Chinese community in Burma. Wu left Burma and was never heard of again. And there were many years before the two trends – Burmese and Chinese – were to merge under the common banner of the CPB.

But even if they had no links with Wu's Chinese communist cell, the young Burmese did also look to China for inspiration. In China, Burma's northern neighbour, Mao Zedong's revolutionaries were on the march, and had a formidable 'people's army' of its own. In 1940, the CPB decided to send Aung San and his close comrade, fellow student leader Hla Myaing – later known as Bo Yan Aung – to China to contact the Communist Party of China. They stowed away on a Chinese ship in Rangoon, hoping to reach China. They did, but reached Amoy, or Xiamen, which was then occupied by the Japanese. The two young Burmese radicals were tracked down by Japanese intelligence and instead of ending up with Mao's partisans in the mountains of China, they were taken to Tokyo.

The Japanese promised them help to 'liberate' Burma from the British, and Aung San returned to Burma to pick up his friends, while Hla Myaing remained behind in Bangkok. Eventually, twenty-nine young Burmese were smuggled out of Rangoon on Japanese freighters. In Tokyo, they were joined by a Burmese drama student, and the group became known as 'the Thirty Comrades'. In modern Burmese history they are celebrated as the heroes who led the fight for independence.[10]

But they did not end up in Japan only because Aung San and Hla Myaing had got on the wrong ship in Rangoon. Among the Thirty Comrades were several right-wing nationalists who had had contacts with the Japanese already before they went to Tokyo. Among these was Ne Win, who later became the military ruler of Burma.

After training on the Japanese-held islands of Taiwan and Hainan, the Burmese nationalists went to Bangkok where they formed the Burma Independence Army, BIA. In early 1942, they followed the Japanese into Burma accompanied by, among others, fighters from Subhas Chandra Bose's Indian National Army. But the 'independence' the Japanese had promised the BIA turned out to be a sham and, the Burmese nationalists sent two prominent communists, Thakin Thein Pe and Thakin Tin Shwe, to Kolkata to contact the British.[11] On 27 March 1945, they switched sides, broke with the Japanese and joined the British- and US-led campaign to drive the Japanese out of Burma.

But by then, thousands of Karens and Kachins had been waging guerrilla war against the Japanese for several years. They remembered atrocities against the minorities carried out by the BIA. As a result, the gulf between the majority Burmans and the country's ethnic minorities widened, and to create a common nation of the ethnic jigsaw in Burma has been the most important task for any government in the country since it eventually gained independence from Britain on 4 January 1948.

This problem is reflected in the still ongoing dispute over the name of the country. Should it be Burma or Myanmar? Today's

Burmese rulers claim that Burma, or *bama*, is a colonial name while Myanmar is more indigenous and encompasses all the many nationalities of the country. But it was not the British who 'named Myanmar Burma'. The once British colony has always been called Burma in English and bama or *myanma* in Burmese. The best explanation of the difference between the two names is found in the old Hobson-Jobson Dictionary of 'Colloquial Anglo-Indian Words and Phrases', which despite its rather unorthodox name remains a very useful source of information: 'The name [Burma] is taken from Mran-ma, the national name of the Burmese people, which they themselves generally pronounce Bam-ma, unless speaking formally and empathically.'[12] Both names have been used interchangeably throughout history, with Burma being the more colloquial name and Myanmar a more formal designation.

If Burma meant only the central plains and Myanmar the Burmans and all the other nationalities, how could there be, according the Myanmar Language Commission, a 'Myanmar language'? Its official *Myanmar-English Dictionary* also mentions a 'Myanmar alphabet'.[13] Clearly, Burma and Myanmar, and Burmese and Myanmar, mean exactly the same thing, and it cannot be argued that the term 'Myanmar' includes any more people within the present Union than the name 'Burma' does.

But the confusion is an old one and when the Burmese independence movement was established in the 1930s, there was a debate among the young nationalists as to what name should be used for the country: bama or myanma. The nationalists decided to call their movement the Dohbama Asiayone instead of the *Dohmyanma Asiayone*. The reason, they said, was that:

> since the *dohbama* was set up, the nationalists always paid attention to the unity of all the nationalities of the country ... and the *thakins* [Burmese nationalists] noted that *myanma* meant only the part of the country where the *myanma* people lived. This was the name given by the Burmese kings to their country. *Bama naing-ngan*

is not the country where only the *myanma* people live. Many different nationalities live in this country, such as the Kachins, Karens, Kayahs, Chins, P-Os, Palaungs, Mons, Myanmars, Rakhines and Shans. Therefore, the nationalists did not use the term myanma naing-ngan but bama naing-ngan. That would be the correct term
. . . all nationalities who live in *bama naing-ngan* are called *bama*.[14]

Thus, the movement became the Dohbama Asiayone and not the Dohmyanma Asiayone. The Burmese edition of *The Guardian* monthly, another official publication, also concluded in February 1971: 'The word *myanma* signifies only the *myanmars* whereas *bama* embraces all indigenous nationalities.'

In May 1989, however, the present government decided that the opposite was true and changed the name in English to Myanmar – although it had been myanma naing-ngan, 'the State of Burma', in formal Burmese since independence in 1948. The bitter truth is that there is no term in Burmese or in any other language that covers both the bama/myanma and the ethnic minorities since no such entity existed before the arrival of the British. Burma with its present boundaries is a colonial creation, and successive governments of independent Burma have inherited a chaotic entity which is still struggling to find a common identity. But 'changing' the name of the country to what it has always been called in formal Burmese is unlikely to make any difference. Burma has been in a state of revolt since independence in 1948, with no lasting solution to its ethnic and political problems in sight.

Rangoon or Yangon is another reflection of the same kind of misunderstanding. Rangoon begins with the consonant 'ra gaut', or 'r', not 'ya palait' or 'y'. In English texts, Rangoon is therefore an etymologically more correct spelling. The problem is that the old 'r' sound has died out in most modern Burmese dialects and softened to a 'y' – but not in Arakanese and Tavoyan, which both have a very distinct 'r' sound. Further, there is another dimension to the recent 'name changes' in Burma. It was not only the names of the country and the capital which were 'changed'; in the minority areas new names were also introduced as well, and here it was a real change. A few examples from Shan state: Hsipaw became Thibaw, Hsenwi became Theinli or Thinli, Kengtung became Kyaingtong, Mong Hsu became Maing Shu, Lai-Hka became Laycha, Pangtara became Pindaya and so on.

The problem here is that all the original names have a meaning in the Shan language; the 'new' names are just Burmanized versions of the same names, with no meaning in any language. This undermines the argument that the changes were done in order to make them 'more indigenous' and not only reflecting the majority Burmans. This has prompted Gustaaf Houtman, a Dutch Burma scholar, to coin the term 'Myanmafication' to refer to the top-down programme of replacing 'unity in diversity' – which had been Aung San's vision of an independent Burma – with a more ethnically streamlined nation state.[15] Others would claim it is just a concerted drive to Burmanize the whole country and wipe out the separate identities of the ethnic minorities.

After Aung San's assassination in July 1947, another Burmese nationalist, U Nu, took over and served as the country's first prime minister for most of the time from independence on 4 January 1948 to Ne Win's military takeover on 2 March 1962. U Nu was a devout Buddhist and an outstanding intellectual, but hardly the strong leader Burma needed during its first, difficult decade of independence. The Karen minority was the first to rise up in arms, followed by the Mons and, in 1958, the Shans. In 1961, the predominantly Christian Kachin set up their independence army. Smaller groups of Karenni, Pa-O, Palaung, Padaung, Arakanese Buddhists and Rohingya Muslims also resorted to armed struggle for autonomy or, in many cases, full independence for their respective areas.

But it was the CPB that posed the most serious threat to the survival of U Nu's beleaguered government in Rangoon immediately after independence. The CPB had played an important role in the struggle against the Japanese during the war and, in the post-war era, it was one of the country's most powerful parties after the ruling front organization, the Anti-Fascist People's Freedom League, AFPFL, of which it initially was a member. The CPB went underground in March 1948, only two months after independence, to fight for a socialist republic.

According to a version of events often repeated by Western scholars, the outbreak of communist rebellions almost simultaneously in Burma, Malaya, Indochina and the Philippines were a direct result of two major events in the late 1940s. At Wiliza Gora in Poland on 22 September 1947, a prominent Soviet theoretician, Andrei Zhdanov, had given a speech on the occasion of the founding of a new organization that united revolutionary groups from all over the world, the Cominform. He had advocated a much more confrontational line than the global communist movement had followed since World War II, arguing that the world had become divided into 'two camps': the US, Britain, France and other 'imperialist' powers on the one hand and the Soviet Union and the newly established 'people's democracies' in eastern Europe on the other. 'Progressive' nations and movements had to support this second camp if they were to have Soviet support and sympathy. Many Western observers saw the Cominform as a reincarnation of the powerful Communist International, Comintern, of the 1930s.[16]

The other crucial event, according to Western scholars, took place in Kolkata in February 1948. Communists and leftists from all over the world gathered in the city to discuss the situation in a world that was changing rapidly in the wake of World War II. The Soviet Union had not only emerged as one of the winners of the War, but it had also proclaimed itself as champion of the peoples of Asia, Africa and Latin America who were fighting against colonialism in various forms. Détente with Britain and the US, which in any case had been little more than a marriage of convenience against Hitler's Germany, Italy and Japan, was irrevocably over.

This new militant tendency permeated the meeting of 'the Southeast Asian Youth Conference' in Kolkata, which had been called under the auspices of the Soviet-controlled World Federation of Democratic Youth and the International Union of Students. On 19 February, an impressive gathering of representatives from India, Pakistan, Ceylon, Nepal, Burma, Indonesia, Vietnam, the Philippines and Malaya congregated in a building facing the old Wellington Square in Kolkata – now Raja Subhodh Mallick Square – in the city's crowded Bow Bazar area. The meeting hall had been provided by Mallick, a prominent Bengali nationalist in whose honour the square was later renamed.

Observers and guests had come from Korea, Mongolia, the Soviet Union, Australia, Yugoslavia, France, Canada and Czechoslovakia. Six representatives of the communist student movement in China unexpectedly showed up as well; they had not been invited, but their request to be included among the delegates was immediately granted, reflecting growing admiration for Mao's rapid advances in China at the time.[17] The revolutionary bloc was further strengthened by the presence of Australia's firebrand communist leader, Lawrence Sharkey.

Not all delegates were communists, however. There were also other Asian nationalists with no particular sympathy for the Soviet Union. Messages of greetings were read out from a wide range of dignitaries such as Burma's U Nu, the Vietnamese partisan Ho Chi Minh, the Czech communist leader Klement Gottwald, the late US president Franklin Roosevelt's widow Eleanor and even Jawaharlal Nehru.[18]

Zhdanov's speech at Wiliza Gora is said to have been the impetus and the Kolkata youth conference the vehicle for 'starting unrest in Asia'.[19] But there is absolutely no evidence to support these conspiracy theories. Some young communists argued that the leaders of their respective countries had achieved a 'sham independence' by collaborating with 'the imperialists', which prompted the Burmese delegates from the AFPFL and the Indian National Congress to walk out in protest. Some other delegates, notably the Filipinos, even returned home, denouncing the meeting as 'Soviet-dominated'.[20] The whole affair was in fact so messy that some of the Indian delegates found it necessary to carry firearms to the meeting hall at Wellington Square.[21] No uprisings anywhere were initiated at that meeting.

A group of Burmese communists were in Kolkata at that time, and a few days after the ill-fated youth conference, six of them – including CPB chairman Thakin Than Tun and his close comrade and later party chairman Thakin Ba Thein Tin – attended the second congress of the Communist Party of India, which was also held in Kolkata. The six CPB delegates, Australia's Sharkey, two Yugoslavs and a young Russian woman identified only as 'Comrade Olga' were the only foreign observers at the congress. The Yugoslav delegates went back to Belgrade after the congress; they did not, as claimed by some historians, go to Burma and stir the peasants there to rise up in rebellion against the government in Rangoon.[22]

But a clear radicalization of the communist movements in Asia was no doubt taking place at this time, but this seems to have been inspired more by internal developments in the countries in the region than by Zhdanov's speech in Poland, or the chaotic Kolkata youth conference. In India, for instance, a rural rebellion had broken out in Telengana in what was then Hyderabad state and was still continuing when the Kolkata meetings were held. The slogan at the time was: 'Telengana today means communists, and communists mean Telengana.'[23] The idea of a revolution centred on the peasants had also taken firm root in China, from where it was spreading to South-east Asia. And in several South-east Asian countries, communist guerrillas had fought valiantly against the Japanese during World War II and emerged as heroes. They had also retained their guns. This was the case in Burma, Malaya, the Philippines and Indochina – precisely the countries where communist rebellions broke out in the 1940s.

Than Tun returned home by plane after the CPI congress, while Ba Thein Tin remained in the city for a few days before boarding an ocean liner bound for Rangoon. At the time of his departure, the new militant CPI general secretary, Bhalchandra Trimbak Ranadive, accompanied him to the jetty. In parting, Ba Thein Tin said: 'You have helped our party a lot. But now we have learned that we have to rely on ourselves. But it's up to us to accept your criticism, and we won't blame you if we take the wrong steps.'[24] Ranadive bid his Burmese comrade farewell and the two men parted, never to meet again. The CPB decided to follow the 'Chinese' path and resorted to armed struggle in March 1948, while the CPI in the end deposed the revolutionary Ranadive and decided to continue working within India's democratic framework, despite the seeds of revolution that had been sown in Telengana.

Apart for misperceptions about the nature of the 1948 meetings in Kolkata, the other myth about the communist rebellion in Burma is that Ghoshal, the CPB's main theoretician, authored a 'thesis' outlining the strategy for a peasant rebellion in Burma. Some Western scholars even claim that he attended the Kolkata meetings and brought the 'thesis' with him back to Burma.[25] But Ghoshal attended neither the youth conference nor the CPI's congress; he visited Kolkata in late 1947 and did not write anything. He gave only an interview to the CPI's daily *People's Age*, in which he advocated a more militant line for the CPB. But Ghoshal was no advocate of peasant rebellions. As an ethnic Bengali, his main constituency was among the Indian working class in Rangoon, and he was trying to organize labour strikes in the urban areas at the time the CPB decided to move from their offices in Rangoon to rural villages in central Burma.

Nevertheless, a 'thesis' titled *On the Present Political Situation in Burma and Our Tasks* is attributed to him. But no CPB leader I interviewed in Panghsang during 1986–87 had ever heard of this 'thesis'. To my surprise, therefore, Martin Smith writes in his *Burma: Insurgency and the Politics of Ethnicity*, that 'Bertil Lintner has speculated that the absence of copies of Ba Tin's [Ghoshal's] thesis on the CPB side has meant the document is not authentic . . . Ba Thein Tin does not support this view.'[26] Smith goes on to refer to correspondence he said he had with Ba Thein Tin during 1988–90, and writes extensively about the alleged importance of the 'thesis' for the CPB's armed struggle.

But Smith never met Ba Thein Tin. After the mutiny, I gave Smith the contact details for the deposed CPB chairman in China, and his personal assistant exchanged letters with Smith. I do not know what that personal assistant wrote, but it is inconceivable that Ba Thein Tin himself would have commented on the so-called 'Ghoshal thesis' in such terms. In fact, Ba Thein Tin was one of the CPB leaders who had told me that he had never heard of it. Back in Thailand, I sent a copy of the thesis to the CPB leaders then in exile in Kunming, and its general secretary Khin Maung Gyi wrote back to me, saying: 'Many thanks for this document. As for us, this is the first time that we have got the opportunity to read the so-called "Ghoshal thesis", which was non-existent inside our party and is merely a fabrication.'[27]

It remains, however, unclear who wrote the so-called 'Ghoshal thesis' and why. Khin Maung Gyi suggests that it was an attempt to blame the civil war on the CPB and, indirectly, outside instigators. But there was, in fact, no outside involvement, material or otherwise, with the CPB's struggle inside Burma until the 1960s – when China decided to lend all-out support to the Burmese communists.

This could be perceived as little more than academic pedantry, but by focusing on the Kolkata meetings in 1948 and the fictitious Ghoshal thesis – which not only Smith but most other Western scholars do as well – serious research into Burma's internal problems is led in the completely wrong direction: west towards India and

Europe, rather than east to China, by far the most important player in Burma's internal conflicts. For China, Burma has always been of utmost strategic importance. It is China's gateway not only to South-east Asia, but South Asia as well.

Burma could well have fallen to the communists and myriads of other rebel groups in the years immediately after independence when even ordinary people were talking about the 'Rangoon government' because it did not control much more than the then capital. U Nu's fledgling parliamentary democracy would most probably have fallen, had it not been for massive support from Nehru in India.[28] At the height of the civil war in 1950, both India and Britain provided Burma with 10,000 small arms each and arranged with other Commonwealth countries, including Australia, Ceylon — now Sri Lanka — and Pakistan to provide a loan of six million pounds sterling to tide over the state's treasury until the insurgent forces could be suppressed.[29]

A cordial relationship between India and Burma emerged as a result, and there were only two problems facing Indo-Burmese relations in the 1950s: the largely undemarcated border with India that independent Burma had inherited and a debt incurred during the colonial period when Burma was an Indian province. There was no urgency to solve either problem, and not until 1953 did U Nu and Nehru personally inspect a disputed area in the Naga Hills. Burma's debt to India was also smoothly solved. In 1954, the governments of the two countries signed an agreement according to which Burma sold 900,000 tons of rice to India at a special low price and agreed to make payment towards the pension fund of civil servants of Indian origin that had been incurred when Burma was a part of British India.[30]

After a few years of heavy fighting, the CPB seemed defeated and some of its leaders began advocating a 'Peace and Coalition Government', that is, the CPB would give up its armed struggle and join the AFPFL as an equal partner in Rangoon. Not everyone agreed, and some party hardliners began to leave secretly for China to ask for aid. The first batch of thirty Burmese communists trekked north in late 1951. Early the following year, Ba Thein Tin, then vice chairman of the party, set out on what was going to be a year-long, arduous journey by elephant and on foot towards Yunnan. His party crossed into China near Laiza in Kachin state – where the KIA later set up a main base – and were escorted by local Chinese border guards to the town of Baoshan, where they boarded a plane for Kunming and, later, Beijing. One more group followed, bringing the total of CPB cadres in China to 143. They were well received by the Chinese and allowed to remain in Sichuan province, where they were given political training. But no military aid was forthcoming at this stage. China was not willing to sacrifice the friendly relations that it actually had with the U Nu government for the sake of the CPB.

Much to their surprise, however, the newly arrived CPB members were introduced to an old comrade who had disappeared almost a decade earlier: Aye Ngwe, a Sino-Burman ex-student from Rangoon University. When it became clear that Aung San and Hla Myaing, or Bo Yan Aung, had failed to reach communist-controlled areas in China in 1941, the CPB in Rangoon had sent Aye Ngwe overland to Yunnan.

He had walked across the border bridge at Kyuhkok-Wanding, where the fabled Burma Road crosses the international frontier, in September 1941. It had taken five years for Aye Ngwe to make contacts with the Communist Party of China, CPC, by which time he had lost touch with the CPB. In 1957, he had become a member of the CPC and learned Chinese. When the CPB cadres began arriving from Burma in the early 1950s, Aye Ngwe was called in to act as interpreter.[31] And there is little doubt that he worked closely together with China's intelligence services.

The whole political landscape changed when, on 2 March 1962, General Ne Win staged his coup, arrested the leaders in the government and abolished the constitution. Military rule was combined with an apparently idealistic political programme called 'the Burmese Way to Socialism'. But Ne Win was no Marxist revolutionary. He was a notorious playboy with an extravagant lifestyle and a lust for power. Ne Win's brand of 'socialism' simply meant that everything in sight was nationalized and handed over to a number of military-run state corporations. There were many military takeovers in Asia at that time, but only in Burma did the military seize not only political but also total economic power. It was an entirely new concept in regional politics, and one that would outlast all other military dictatorships in Asia.

The actual takeover was not bloody, but there was one casualty: on the night of the coup, heavily armed soldiers entered the Rangoon residence of Burma's first president, the Shan leader Sao Shwe Thaike. His seventeen-year-old son Sai Myee was gunned down and the former president was led away into captivity, not to be seen again. All other state leaders, including Prime Minister U Nu were also arrested, but not extrajudicially executed while in custody.

For the first few months, people seemed to tolerate the military regime. But when it became clear that basic freedoms had been restricted and companies were being nationalized, the students, always at the forefront of any protest movement in Burma, began to demonstrate. The response from the new power holders was fierce: on 7 July 1962, government troops opened fire on a crowd of students at the Rangoon University campus. Officially, fourteen students were killed; unofficial estimates put the death toll in the hundreds. In the early hours of 8 July, Rangoon residents were awakened by an explosion that reverberated through the city. The army had dynamited the historic Students' Union building. The building was a symbol for Burmese nationalism: it was where the independence movement was born and grew. Now it was reduced to rubble. And the CPB's ragged forces in the Pegu Yoma region north of Rangoon were unexpectedly boosted by the arrival of scores of young intellectuals who wanted to take up arms against the new military regime.

That was not the only change for the CPB after the 1962 coup. China had long been wary of the ambitious and sometimes unpredictable Ne Win – and the leaders in Beijing decided that the time now was ripe to give all-out support to the Burmese communists. The CPB was for the first time allowed to print propaganda leaflets and other material in Beijing. Already on 1 August 1962, the Beijing- and Sichuan-based exiles published a document, titled *Some Facts about Ne Win's Military Government*, denouncing the army takeover.[32]

Then came an unexpected twist of events. Ne Win's new military government called for peace talks after about a year in power. Representatives of the CPB as well as the Karen, Mon, Shan and Kachin rebel armies attended the negotiations in Rangoon, with guarantees of free and safe passage to and from the peace parley, regardless of the outcome. The colourful Thakin Soe, leader of a breakaway radical faction of communists called 'the Red Flags' attracted the most attention when he arrived accompanied by a team of attractive young girls in khaki uniforms. He placed a portrait of Stalin in front of him on the negotiating table and then began attacking the revisionism of the new Soviet leader, Nikita Khrushchev and the opportunism of Mao Zedong's China. But twenty-nine veterans from the main CPB in China also arrived by air from Beijing, purportedly to participate in the peace talks. Back in Burma, one of them – Thakin Ba Thein Tin – seized the opportunity to visit the CPB's then headquarters in the Pegu Yoma, bringing with him radio transmitters and other aid from China.

The talks, not unexpectedly, broke down as the government was not willing to offer anything more than an amnesty for rebel fighters. There would be no political concessions, or restoration of the federal system that had existed before the 1962 coup. Thakin

Ba Thein Tin and one of his comrades returned to Beijing. But the other twenty-seven CPB cadres who had come from China joined their old comrades and retreated with them into the hills of the Pegu Yoma. The government had unwittingly helped the CPB exiles in China not only re-establish de facto leadership of the remnants of their 'People's Army' in Burma, but also set up a direct radio link between them and the leadership in Beijing.

In late 1963, shortly after the peace talks, an experienced party cadre was put in charge of a team that began surveying possible infiltration routes from Yunnan into north-eastern Burma. His name was San Thu and he was one of a handful of Burmese communists who had been educated in Moscow before the Sino-Soviet split in the communist movement. The CPB had sided with China, so San Thu and his comrades were expelled from the Soviet Union and went to Beijing. San Thu had not been long in China before he was given his special task. The plan was to build up a new CPB base area along the Chinese frontier in north-eastern Burma. Aid could then be sent across the border – and the north-eastern units would push further into Burma, and link up with old base areas such as the Pegu Yoma. If that scheme succeeded, Burma would become a communist-run Chinese client state in South-east Asia – and with a long border with India.

For that purpose, a new 'People's Army' was being assembled in China. But the 140 or so Burmese communists were mostly city-bred intellectuals with no fighting experience. The answer was to enlist another group of exiles from Burma: a band of Kachin fighters led by Naw Seng, a World War II hero who had been twice awarded the Burma Gallantry Medal by the British for his role in the anti-Japanese resistance in the Kachin Hills in the 1940s. After Burma's independence – and a decade before the KIA was formed – Naw Seng had joined the plethora of rebels who fought against the government in Rangoon. His dream, his old comrade-in-arms from World War II, Scotsman Ian Fellowes-Gordon, wrote much later, 'was an independent Kachin country, independent like Nepal, and prospering as that gallant country does by hiring out its fighting men.'[33] Like the Gurkhas, the Kachin were renowned for their fighting abilities and had served with the British Army in both World Wars.

But cornered by the Burmese government's army in extreme north-eastern Burma, Naw Seng and 300 of his men had been forced across the border into China in 1950. They were allowed to settle in the southern Chinese province of Guizhou, where they became ordinary farmers.

In early 1963, already before the peace talks in Rangoon, the Chinese had introduced Naw Seng to Thakin Ba Thein Tin and the other CPB leaders in China. Among them was Zau Mai, who had joined Naw Seng's rebel army when he was only seventeen. According to Zau Mai: 'We were told that the time had come to go back to Burma and fight. It was not a difficult choice. We were eager to leave our people's commune in Guizhou. All of us left for a training camp in Yunnan, where our military skills were rehearsed.'[34]

The trigger – or perfect excuse – for launching the planned CPB push into the north-east came when anti-Chinese riots broke out in Rangoon in 1967. The Chinese community in the Burmese capital had been influenced by the Cultural Revolution in China and many young Sino-Burmese began wearing the red Mao badges. This violated an official Burmese regulation, and the young 'Red Guards' were ordered to take off their badges. When some of them resisted, anti-Chinese riots broke out in June and July that year. Chinese shops and homes were ransacked and looted, and many Sino-Burmese were killed. A mob even attacked the Chinese embassy in Rangoon before the situation was brought under control.

The role of the Burmese authorities in this affair was a matter of dispute: the Chinatown riots in Rangoon came, hardly by coincidence, at a time when there were acute shortages of rice and basic foodstuff in the country. According to eyewitnesses, the police did not interfere with the killings and the looting until the Chinese embassy was attacked. It is widely believed that Burma's military government encouraged the riots in order to deflect attention from the country's internal problems at that time. The incident was followed by the withdrawal of ambassadors from both capitals and the expulsion of the *Xinhua*, New China News Agency, correspondent in Rangoon. Beijing also suspended its aid programme to Burma, granted under a friendship treaty signed with U Nu's government in 1960. Radio Beijing began broadcasting fierce attacks on the Ne Win regime branding it 'fascist'.[35]

In the early hours of 1 January 1968, Naw Seng and his Kachin group crossed the border into Burma. The incursion took place at Mong Ko in north-eastern Shan state – the very same place on the Sino-Burmese frontier from which Naw Seng had retreated into China eighteen years earlier. Khin Maung Gyi, later CPB general secretary and, like San Thu, a returnee from Moscow, accompanied them as political commissar. Within hours, the Burmese garrison was overrun. Fighting also broke out in surrounding areas, and for the first time in a confrontation with a rebel force, the Burmese Army found itself outgunned, and in some cases even outnumbered, as thousands of Chinese 'volunteers' streamed across the border to fight alongside the CPB.

An entirely new era in Burma's civil war had been ushered in. Within the next six years of heavy fighting with thousands of dead and wounded on both sides, the CPB managed to wrest control over nearly all areas across the border in Shan state, from the Mekong River in the east to where Burma Road crosses into China in the north, and a stretch of territory around some important border passes in Kachin state, including Pangwa, where Thuingaleng Muivah and Thinoselie Medom Keyho had crossed into China in January 1967.

The Chinese poured more aid into the CPB effort than any other communist movement in Asia outside Indochina. Unlike the old units in the Pegu Yoma, these new troops had new Chinese uniforms with red stars in their caps, and were well equipped with modern Chinese assault rifles and machine guns as well as anti-aircraft guns and mortars. Radio equipment, jeeps, trucks, petrol, and even rice, other foodstuffs, cooking oil and kitchen utensils were sent across the frontier. The Chinese also built two small hydroelectric power stations inside the CPB's new north-eastern base area. A clandestine radio station, the People's Voice of Burma, was officially inaugurated on 28 March 1971, and began transmitting from the Yunnanese side of the border in April.[36]

The CPB's only major defeat during this period was suffered at Kunlong, where a strategic bridge crosses the Salween River. A forty-two-day battle was fought from November 1971 to January 1972 at the river crossing. But the CPB failed to capture the bridge and suffered heavy casualties due to its Chinese-inspired tactics of human-wave attack against the well-entrenched government troops near Kunlong. Many of the CPB soliders who fell in this battle were actually Chinese 'volunteers'; the CPB had yet to build up a truly indigenous fighting force.[37]

And the 'new' CPB failed to push far enough inside Burma to link up with the 'old' cadres in the Pegu Yoma and elsewhere. Realizing that it was not possible to defeat the CPB in the north-east, the Burmese government turned its attention to the weaker, old base areas in the central part of the country. Its campaigns there were made a lot easier by a number of suicidal purges that the CPB had carried out in the central base areas. In the early 1960s, the 'Beijing returnees', as the cadres who had come back for peace talks were called, staged grisly mass trials in the Pegu Yoma to secure a truly Maoist leadership of the party before the planned thrust into the north-east was due to take place. Yebaw, or comrade, Htay, who had led the delegation to the peace talks, was branded 'Burma's Deng Xiaoping' and executed. The Bengali theoretician H.N. Ghoshal was denounced as 'Burma's Liao Shaoqi' and also killed. Bo Yan Aung, or Thakin Hla Myaing, who had gone with Aung San to Amoy in 1940, was also killed.

It was all modelled after the Cultural Revolution which was raging in China at the same time, when scores of leading Chinese communists, among them 'the capitalist roader' Deng and 'the revisionist' President Liu, were purged. Those two were not executed, but many other Chinese party veterans were. The CPB's leadership was further weakened when the party's official chairman, Thakin Than Tun, was assassinated in the Pegu Yoma by a government agent on 24 September 1968 – less than a year after the CPB's thrust into Mong Ko. By the early 1970s, government troops had recaptured the Pegu Yoma and driven the CPB out of almost all its former base areas in central Burma.

But the 'new' CPB was not about to give up. And it did manage to forge alliances with a number of ethnic rebel armies in the frontier areas. They were not communists, but needed weapons to fight and were prepared to get them from anyone who was willing to support them. The Karen rebels in the south could buy weapons from Thailand, but the Kachin were far away from the Thai border and could only get limited supplies from there, and the Shans somewhere in between. In 1975, the most experienced fighting commander of the powerful Shan State Army led a delegation to Panghsang and returned with new Chinese weapons. In the following year, the even stronger KIA forged an alliance with the CPB. Smaller ethnic rebel armies, such as those among the Pa-Os, the Padaungs and the Karenni, split into pro- and anti-communist factions.

The Chinese were pleased at this development, and even introduced the Indian Nagas to the CPB leaders who frequently visited China. Thuingaleng Muivah, then general secretary of the Naga National Council, told me when I interviewed him in 1985:

> We met the CPB's vice chairman, Thakin Pe Tint, in Beijing, and later, in 1975, its secretary general, Khin Maung Gyi and others. Pe Tint was the most impressive of the CPB leaders I got to know.

The Chinese told us to form a united front with them, under the leadership of the CPB. We explained that our cause was different from that of the ethnic minorities in Burma. Our struggle was against India, and the Chinese accepted that. The Chinese also recognized that we'd never been part of India. They supported fully our struggle for an independent Nagaland.[38]

The KIA's alliance with the CPB was particularly peculiar. Like the Nagas, they were ardent believers in the Christian faith, and did not compromise in this regard even when they fought together with the CPB. Moreover, the KIA had been staunchly anti-communist, at least until they forged an alliance with the communists. They had maintained a base on the Thai border, which they shared with the Nationalist Chinese Guomindang – which, in turn, had ties with Taiwanese intelligence and most probably also the CIA. Since their defeat in the Chinese civil war in the late 1940s, defeated Guomindang troops had sought refuge in Burma and northern Thailand, and well into the 1970s they had still not given up their dream of 'liberating' China from the communists.

The Kachin brought jade and opium from Kachin state down to the Thai border to finance their purchases of arms and ammunition from Thailand. The Kachin rebels even joined the Asian People's Anti-Communist League, APACL, which was sponsored by the intelligence services of Taiwan and South Korea. The APACL and some like-minded groups merged in 1966 to form the World Anti-Communist League, WACL, which was led by John Singlaub, a retired US Army colonel who had headed CIA operations in Manchuria during the communist revolution in China and later fought in the Korean War. The then KIA commander, Zau Seng, carrying his Kachin flag with a red-and-green field and two superimposed dahs, attended several APACL and WACL meetings in Saigon and Manila.

But in August 1976, Zau Seng, his brother Zau Tu, and Pungshwi Zau Seng, another prominent KIA leader, were assassinated at the camp on the Thai border. The assassin, a low-ranking KIA officer, was accused of being a 'government agent', charged with the murder and executed. But it is widely believed that the KIA leaders in the north were tired of fighting a two-front war, which they were at the time: against the government's army on one side and the CPB on the other. Zau Seng and his anti-communist colleagues on the Thai border stood in the way of an alliance of convenience against what should be the common enemy: the Burmese government. Shortly after the murders on the Thai border, the CPB sent a congratulatory message to the KIA, and Brang Seng, a former headmaster of the Baptist High School in the Kachin state capital Myitkyina, became chairman of the KIA's political wing, the Kachin Independence Organization, KIO.[39]

Within a year of the alliance with the CPB, the KIA, now strengthened with a new arsenal of Chinese weapons, was able to take over most of Kachin state. The government controlled little more of Kachin state than most major towns and the roads between them – but even when those roads were used, the Burmese Army had to move in heavily guarded convoys. It could take up to ten days or more to cover the 350-kilometre distance between Myitkyina and Sumprabum to the north. A new political headquarters for the KIO was built at Pa Jau, close to the Chinese border, and the KIA established its main military base at Na Hpaw in the same area.

The Kachin were now able to deal directly with the Chinese authorities in Yunnan, but not on the same level as the CPB. Chinese connections with the KIA were maintained through the foreign relations branch of the foreign ministry, which maintained offices not only in the Yunnanese provincial capital Kunming, but also in remote border towns near Kachin state such as Yingjiang and Tengchong. The CPB, which was recognized as a 'fraternal communist party', dealt with China's security apparatus, headed for many years by the dreaded Kang Sheng and his international liaison department of the CPC.[40]

Support to the CPB and its ethnic allies remained the main element of China's Burma policy until the late 1970s. The change towards a less militant foreign policy began when an internal power struggle broke out within the Chinese communists after Mao Zedong's death in 1976. In April that year, when China's radical Left reasserted itself and ousted Deng Xiaoping, the CPB – unlike other communist parties in the region – spoke out loudly in favour of the hardliners: 'The revisionist clique with which Deng was linked headed by Liu Shaoqi has been defeated,' the Burmese communists declaimed in a congratulatory message on the fifty-fifth anniversary of the Communist Party of China in June 1976, and went on to say: 'The movement to repulse the Right deviationist attempt at reversing correct verdicts, and the decision of the Central Committee of the CPC on measures taken against rightist chieftain Deng Xiaoping, are in full accord with Marxism-Leninism, Mao Zedong thought.'[41]

In a second message mourning the death of Mao in September 1976, the CPB stated:

Guided by Chairman Mao Zedong's proletarian revolutionary line, the Chinese people seized great victories in the socialist revolution and socialist construction in the Great Proletarian Cultural Revolution, in criticizing Liu Shaoqi's counter-revolutionary revisionist line, in criticizing Lin Biao and Confucius and in criticizing Deng Xiaoping and repulsing the Right deviationist attempt at reversing correct verdicts and consolidating the dictatorship of the proletariat, thus, consolidating the People's Republic of China – the reliable bulwark of the world proletarian revolution.[42]

The CPB had reason to re-evaluate the reliability of that bulwark the following year when Deng reassumed power in Beijing. The CPB, which once had branded its own 'revisionist' Yebaw Htay as 'Burma's Deng Xiaoping' and Ghoshal as 'Burma's Liu Shaoqi' respectively, fell silent. The *Beijing Review* and other official Chinese publications, which had previously published battle news and CPB announcements, stopped printing anything about the 'revolutionary struggle in Burma'. The CPB was mentioned for the last time in November 1976 when Thakin Ba Thein Tin and his vice-chairman Thakin Pe Tint, called on the new Chinese chairman Hua Guofeng in Beijing, who was soon to fall into disgrace.[43]

The Burmese government quickly and shrewdly exploited the rift by lending its good offices to China in Cambodia, by then the focus of Chinese interest, as concern in Beijing increased over Vietnam's designs on its Indo-Chinese neighbour. In November 1977, Burma's military ruler Ne Win became the first head of a non-communist state to visit Phnom Penh after the Khmer Rouge takeover. The Chinese were no doubt behind the unusual visit, hoping to draw the Khmer Rouge out of its diplomatic isolation. Ne Win played along, hoping that Beijing would further reduce its support for the CPB.[44] He was not disappointed. In 1978, the CPB's entire China-based central office, including the broadcasting station, the People's Voice of Burma, was forced to return to Panghsang. The Chinese 'volunteers', who had fought alongside the CPB since 1968, were also recalled.

But Chinese support did not stop entirely. After all, there was a formidable fighting force across China's strategically important south-western frontier which Beijing could not afford to ignore. It is also plausible to assume that the Chinese wanted to maintain their foothold inside Burma, which the CPB provided, but with a new leadership and a different direction.

Already in 1981, the Chinese had begun offering retirement in China to CPB leaders and high-ranking cadres. This offer included a modest government pension along with a house and a plot of land, on condition that they refrained from political activity of any kind in China. The offer was repeated in 1985 and again in 1988. Some of the younger, low-ranking CPB cadres accepted the offer, but none of the top party leadership did so.

In early 1989, the Chinese once again approached the CPB and tried to persuade the CPB leaders to give up and retire in China. Beijing's interest in Burma was now firmly motivated by trade, commercial interests and political influence through the country's government, with which it had steadily improved relations since the mid-1970s. A crisis meeting was convened on 20 February at Panghsang. For the first time in his life, CPB chairman Thakin Ba Thein Tin – then seventy-five years old – lashed out against the Chinese. In an address to the secret meeting, he referred to 'misunderstandings in our relations with a sister party. Even if there are differences between us, we have to co-exist and adhere to the principle of non-interference in each other's affairs. This is the same as in 1981, 1985 and 1988. We have no desire to become revisionists.'[45]

The minutes of the secret meeting were leaked by some of the participants, or the Chinese themselves decided that enough is enough and told the CPB's military commanders, who were tired of fighting for an ideology which seemed more and more anachronistic, to go ahead. Less than a month later, the mutiny began. The rebellious rank and file of the CPB's Army seized Panghsang on 17 April 1989, and captured the armoury and other important buildings. While they were smashing portraits of communist icons Marx, Engels, Lenin, Stalin and even Mao Zedong and destroying party literature in an outburst of anti-party feelings, the CPB's ageing, staunchly Maoist leadership fled headlong across the Nam Hka River to safety in China. Thus ended one of Asia's longest-lasting communist insurrections.

While the SSA and other groups followed the UWSA's example and entered into similar ceasefire agreements with the Burmese government shortly after the mutiny, the KIA began to look for an alternative to China and the CPB from where they would be able to secure military supplies. The choice was India. The Indians were also willing to comply. With the Kachin rebels on their side, the Indians could persuade them not only to stop training Manipuri and the Assamese insurgents, but they would also be able to make sure that the Naga rebels would be deprived of their cross-border sanctuaries in Burma as the KIA intended to establish a new base area along the Indian border.

RAW agents met Brang Seng and other Kachin leaders who had made it to Thailand, and they were also invited to visit New Delhi. The Kachin already had a toehold on the Indian border – at a small placed called Binuzu, or Pinawng Zup, just opposite the Indian Army base at Vijaynagar, Arunachal Pradesh, where a nose-shaped piece of Indian territory juts into Burma and ends at the Chaukan Pass.

The area had never been controlled by the Burmese government, and Pinawng Zup was actually founded by a family of American missionaries, the Morses, who were active among the Lisu and Rawang tribes in the Putao area of northern Kachin state in the 1950s and early 1960s. In 1965, three years after the military takeover in Burma, the Morses had been ordered to leave the country. Ne Win's government was suspicious of all foreign missionaries, but the impact the Morses had had on the situation in northern Kachin state went beyond what it was prepared to tolerate. The Morse family had turned the Putao Valley, and especially their own village near Muladi, into a model settlement, challenging the moral authority of the central government. Schools and churches had been built, and vast orchards had been cleared where the missionaries experimented with the cultivation of imported North American fruit as well as other varieties. By the early 1960s, as many as 20,000 Lisus and Rawangs had settled in more than thirty villages around Putao.

The Morses were not about to desert their tribal followers that easily. They met in the local church to contemplate the situation that had arisen after the expulsion order. They had once organized a Lisu exodus from Yunnan to Kachin state – and now they decided to lead their Lisu flock on another long march, this time to the remote mountains near the Indian border. There, they hoped, they would be beyond the reach of any Burmese government troops or immigration officials.

Between Putao and the Chaukan Pass lies more than a hundred kilometres of some of the most awesome topography on the face of the earth. The entire Morse family, including grandmothers and grandfathers, their children and grandchildren, left Muladi in the middle of the night – together with about 5,000 of their Lisu followers. Like some latter-day Children of Israel fleeing from the land of the Pharaohs, the Morses and their tribal flock walked over the mountains towards the Indian border. And they made it to a place known to Lisu hunters as the Hidden Valley. Some settled in Binuzu, where there were already some Lisus living, while others cleared the forest and built new villages. Within a year or two of their arrival, the Morses had turned the Hidden Valley into a thriving community. Soon, even fruit trees were blooming in the once inhospitable valley. Some supplies were bought from Vijaynagar across the border, but the Lisus and the Morses were basically self-sufficient, living off farming in the narrow valley and hunting in the surrounding forest.

When Isak Chishi Swu and Mowu Gwizan from the Naga Army trekked to China in early 1968, they passed through one of the villages in the Hidden Valley. When the party of 300 well-armed Nagas arrived, Isak was astonished to hear that an old white couple was there: 'I didn't believe it at first. I thought it must be some mistake and that the people were Indians,' Isak told me when I met him at the NSCN's headquarters in 1985. But it turned out to be J. Russell and Gertrude Morse. They joined in prayer for the safety of Isak's and Mowu's onward journey.

Isak, Mowu and their Naga soldiers were the only outsiders to visit the Hidden Valley – until a patrol of Burmese government soldiers suddenly arrived there in December 1971. The Morses had been found at last. On 18 March 1972, a Burmese Army helicopter landed in the Hidden Valley, along with some officers who were sent to carry out the expulsion order that had been issued seven years before. While some of the Morses were airlifted out, others were escorted by Burmese troops down to the nearest town, Namyung, close to the Indian border. Some of the younger Morses crossed over into Vijaynagar and were flown out of India via Kolkata.[46]

But many of the Lisus remained in Binuzu and the Hidden Valley, and this remote place with its highly unusual history proved ideal for a new KIA base. The main mode of communication between Vijaynagar across the border and the nearest town further to the west inside Arunachal Pradesh, to which the garrison town belongs, is by helicopter. It is a military base that attracts no outside visitors. According to Subir Bhaumik, India's foremost expert on insurgencies in India's north-east:

> A senior RAW official who set up India's links with the KIA says they were given at least two consignments of weapons between 1990 and 1992 and promised more. The estimates of Indian weapons supplied to the KIA vary between 700 and 900 assault rifles, light machine guns, carbines, grenades and assorted ammunition. For its part, the KIA agreed to deny support, bases, weapons or training to North East Indian rebel groups. Indeed, for two years, a full team of RAW agents, equipped with communication equipment, were based ... there ... a Burma-born Indian officer was in charge of this team, which quietly monitored the movement of all North East Indian rebel groups in that strategic corridor.[47]

India's security authorities were especially worried because ULFA fighters had begun arriving at KIA camps near the Chinese border in northern Burma in 1987. ULFA had actually intended to link up with the SSA because of old historical ties and emotional links between the Shans and the Ahoms. But the SSA had barely enough weapons to arm their own rebel soldiers. It was also a guerrilla army that moved over large swathes of land in Shan state. Unlike the KIA, the SSA had no area which was securely under its control, and no base camps where the training that ULFA required could take place. More than 300 ULFA guerrillas were trained by the KIA in camps near the Chinese border until the programme came to a halt under Indian pressure. By 1991, the last batch of ULFA left KIA-held areas in Kachin state – and the Indians showed their gratitude by arming the Kachins.[48]

But it all went wrong. Through their old contacts with the WACL, the Kachin sent a delegation that travelled via Pakistan to Afghanistan, where they met Gulbuddin Hekmatyar, the leader of one of the Mujahideen forces at that time fighting the Soviet Union. They believed he had Stinger missiles to sell. The Indians found out about it and stopped the deal. Then the KIA made another mistake. The Indians had told the KIA not to attack Burmese camps near the Indian border, which would jeopardize supply lines and alert the government in Rangoon. But the KIA's chief of staff, Gen. Zau Mai, disregarded the request. Eager to try out his new arsenal in the battlefield, his troops attacked and captured Pangsau, where the Ledo Road crosses the Patkai range on the Indo-Burmese border, and the nearby township centre of Namyung on 5 June 1992. Heavy casualties were inflicted on the Burmese Army, which struck back with air strikes and land assaults. Both Pangsau and Namyung were retaken from the KIA.

This was the last major battle with the Burmese Army, and even the battle-hardened Zau Mai seemed to have run out of the will to fight. That was the main reason why, in April 1993, Kachin rebel representatives came down from their mountains along the Chinese frontier to meet with Burmese government officials in Myitkyina. All hostilities came to an end when, on 24 February 1994, the official ceasefire agreement was signed by the KIO and the Burmese government. The ceasefire lasted until fierce fighting once again broke out between government forces and the Kachin in June 2011. Peace, it seems, remains as elusive as ever in the wilds of northern Burma.

But the Nagas were not faring that well either. After being driven out of India in the 1970s and having established base areas across the border in Burma, frictions were soon to arise between the Nagas from the Indian side and the Burmese Nagas. This was not surprising given the different backgrounds of the tribes on either side of the Patkai range, which separates the two countries. No foreign missionaries made it to the Burmese hills, so there were almost no schools or modern health care, and no infrastructure worth mentioning. During the British time, the Burmese Nagas were left to fend for themselves in their remote and rugged hills.

The only outsiders who ventured into the Naga Hills after Burma's independence were missionaries from the Kachin Baptist Convention. As the Kachin had been converted into Christianity at the turn of the century, and the new religion had spread rapidly among them, they decided that it was their duty to convert other tribes in the area too. They began to work through the schools that did exist in a few Naga villages along Ledo Road, where the first Kachin missionaries to the Nagas – Labwi Hting Nan, Zau Tu and Tinghkaw – arrived in the early 1950s. They based themselves at Shingbwiyang, a small town on the road which had been a major base for the Americans and other Allied forces during World War II.

Zau Tu baptized the first batch of six Naga schoolchildren in 1954, followed by another group of twelve young converts won over by Tinghkaw the following year. But the real pioneer in the field was Labwi Hting Nan, who opened a new school in Rangkhu Sumri in 1956, and another in Kalawn three years later. This was well south of Ledo Road, inside the actual Naga Hills where there were not even proper mule tracks. He remembers seeing 'plenty of skulls in the villages, especially in long houses belonging to chiefs.'[49] But even the Kachin missionaries did not dare to venture into the wildest area of them all: the mountainous country between the Namphuk River and the Indian border. That was where the Nagas from the Indian side later established their base area.

'Thieves, adulterers and prisoners of war were sacrificed to the spirits and their heads kept for ceremonial purposes,' Labwi Hting Nan told me when I met him in Kachin state in 1986. People believed there was spiritual value in a head, and the cutting of heads was the ultimate celebration of victory in war, or for a young warrior to show his manliness. Although the practices had been the same as on the Indian side of the border before 'pacification' by the British and conversion to Christianity by the missionaries, the Nagas in India had moved well beyond that stage in the early twentieth century. On the Burmese side of the border, headhunting and slavery continued in the Burmese Naga Hills well into the 1970s. The Burmese Naga Hills have also always been very sparsely populated. No one knows exactly how many tribesmen live there, but the most reliable estimates vary from 100,000 to 150,000.[50] Their hilltop villages are spread out in western Sagaing division, from the Pangsau Pass in the Patkai Range in the north to near the riverine town of Thaungdut in the south, and from the Indian border in the west to the Chindwin River in the east.

Given the extremely low literacy rate among the Burmese Nagas, and the absence of a common religion such as Christianity, no political movement emerged among them until the mid-1960s. One of the very first organizers was Shangwang Shangyung Khaplang, a young Naga from Waktham village near Pangsau. Born in 1940, he was one of the twelve Naga schoolchildren who the Kachin evangelist Tinghkaw had baptized in 1955. Four years later, the Kachin missionaries sent him to the Baptist High School in Myitkyina, where Brang Seng was then the headmaster.

Perhaps inspired by the Kachin rebels, who had taken up arms against Rangoon in 1961, Khaplang and some of his Naga friends set up a small armed unit called the Naga Defence Force in

February 1964. The KIA, however, looked upon this development with disapproval, as they did not want the Nagas to have their own armed group. The Nagas, the Kachin reasoned, were their younger cousins, and as such they should join the KIA. In April, 300 KIA troops attacked Khaplang's training camp at Konkeeto near Tagap in the Burmese Naga Hills.

The conflict with the Kachin forced Khaplang to turn to other Naga groups for support, and in 1965 he met for the first time Imkongmeren Ao and other leaders of the Naga National Council, and with some Tangkhuls from Somra in Burma, who until then had not been part of the movement on the Indian side. On 7 April 1965, they formed the Eastern Naga Revolutionary Council, ENRC, with Chouboh, a Tangkhul from Somra as president, and Khaplang as his deputy. Three years later, Khaplang was the leader. He was only twenty-eight, but reasonably well educated by local standards as he had a few more years than basic primary education.

The NNC's missions to China in the late 1960s and early 1970s led to a closer relationship between Khaplang and the Nagas from the Indian side of the border, and in 1972, the ENRC became the Eastern Naga National Council, ENNC, to emphasize the new partnership. The Indian Nagas needed help from the Burmese side; it was not uncommon that groups of soldiers from the NNC's Naga army were ambushed – and beheaded – by hostile villagers who had no idea who those strange-looking intruders with guns were.

Following the signing of the Shillong Accord between some representatives of the NNC and the Indian government in November 1975, cooperation with the Burmese Nagas became a question of survival for the Indian Naga militants who refused to honour the peace treaty. Deprived of their old bases in Nagaland, they had to establish new sanctuaries on the Burmese side, and that would not be possible without Khaplang's full cooperation.

This new base area would have to be beyond the reach of both the Indian and the Burmese armies, and the choice was obvious:

the wild hills between the Namphuk River and the Indian border, where not even the Kachin missionaries had dared to go in the 1950s. This was one of the wildest places on earth, where few outsiders had ever been. Even the maps were inaccurate showing rivers going in the wrong direction as no ground survey had been carried out at any time in history.[51]

To 'pacify' this area proved a formidable task. For the NNC hardliners Thuingaleng Muivah and Isak Chishi Swu, it was not only a matter of purging their own ranks of 'traitors', which they did with true cultural revolutionary fervour. The local people were also bound to fight against any outsider who would try to control them. The stiffest resistance came from Kayu Noknyu and its six satellite villages. Kayu Noknyu was well fortified with stockades and trenches with punji sticks, and the villagers were armed with dahs, spears, old muzzle-loaders and some .303 rifles and Sten guns left over from World War II.

In 1976, the NNC's Naga army attacked, supported by Khaplang and his men. The village was burned to the ground, more than a hundred villagers were killed, and its headman captured and later executed in public to instill fear among the local people. Two years later a similar action was taken against Chuyang Noknyu, where 500 villagers vowed to expel the intruders. Once again, the resistance was crushed and seven village leaders were executed. The superior firepower of the Indian Nagas, with their brand new Chinese weapons, had spoken.

A few years later, plague hit the area and hundreds of people died of the disease. The new masters told the villagers that it was 'God's punishment' for opposing them. There was no more resistance against the new order that Isak and Muivah were about to introduce in the Burmese Naga Hills. Oking, always the name of the Naga rebel headquarters wherever it was located, taught, on the one hand, that resistance to them could bring down divine retribution, but, on the other, that cooperation could lead to beneficial changes.

The new National Socialist Council of Nagaland, set up when Isak and Muivah broke away from the NNC in 1980, built bigger and better houses, wide footpaths, schools and churches. Some basic health care was introduced and the gospel was spread in remote villages in north-western Burma. Khaplang, whose support was crucial for maintaining NSCN's cross-border sanctuaries, was appointed vice-chairman of the new rebel outfit.

Gradually, the people of the eastern hills were beginning to leave the old pre-tribal stage. The larger area – which was controlled and governed by the NSCN – was becoming more important than the traditional village cluster. The Rangpangs and the Heimis were lumped together to become the Pangmi, a new tribe. But there was still no common language. The NSCN did its best to introduce Nagamese, but it never caught on. If the Burmese Nagas spoke any other language, it was Shan, Kachin or Burmese.

It was also uncertain how deep the conversions to Christianity – 30,000 in three years, according to the NSCN – actually were. Headhunting was common in the Naga villages on the Burmese side well into modern times. The last heads in the Kesan group of villages, for instance, were taken as late as in 1980. And the brand of Christianity that the Indian Nagas taught was very different from the down-to-earth approach of the early Kachin missionaries, who had left the area when the Naga–Kachin conflict broke out in the early 1960s. The NSCN's Maoist rhetoric was mixed with beliefs and practices which appeared almost pre-Christian. When all the foreign missionaries were ordered out of the Indian Naga Hills at the outbreak of the insurgency in the mid-1950s, the stabilizing effect these had had vanished; the old Naga animism seeped in again, perhaps revitalized by the wild environment in the Burmese Naga Hills, but expressed in the context of Christian terminology.

A document published by the 'Publicity Department of the Government of the People's Republic of Nagaland' in 1982 hails the progress that had been made in 'Eastern Nagaland', as the

NSCN calls the Burmese Naga Hills. It tells how God had sent 'some women blessed with healing power' to work miracles: 'Through the name of Our Lord Jesus Christ many people were healed of incurable diseases [from which] they had suffered for years.' A forty-five-year-old paralysed man who had been bedridden for twenty years suddenly stood up and walked again, and 'a man suffering from oozing bud [sic] in his private parts for 30 years was cured; lepers were cleansed and advanced cases of TB were successfully healed.'[52]

The 'women' in question were three oracles who the NSCN believed could communicate with God. 'God told us that he has chosen the Nagas as he had once chosen the children of Israel to be his own people. "Your war will be a peculiar one, your battles not like those fought by other armies. Just as Joshua captured Jericho by blowing trumpets to summon my help, so will your war be," God said,' Isak told me when I interviewed him in the Naga Hills of Burma in December 1985. And he seemed to mean it literally, not just figuratively as the Mizos did in 1966. Consequently, the NSCN built camps where there were no bunkers and trenches, but huge wooden crosses for protection. And endless prayers. Magical words were invented, like 'UN Seti' and 'Iphai', which had no meaning in any language, but were believed to have some divine significance.

When my family and I were staying at Kesan Chanlam, the Naga rebel headquarters in the Burmese Naga Hills, and it was attacked by the Burmese Army on 20 December 1985, there was nowhere to seek shelter. We had to run for our lives over open terrain until we reached a forested area a few kilometres away from Kesan Chanlam. A huge wooden crucifix in the middle of the camp was supposed to be enough to ward off any enemies, we had been told. Had our KIA escorts not arrived a few days before the attack occurred, none of us would have been alive today. But three young KIA soldiers had to die defending my wife, our newborn daughter and me.[53]

More onerously for the local people, however, the 'Government of the People's Republic of Nagaland' demanded forced labour from the villages it controlled across the border in Burma. People who disobeyed orders were beaten, or even executed. During my stay in the area from October to December 1985, I witnessed on several occasions young Tangkhuls from the Indian side whipping men old enough to be their grandfathers with sticks and canes. The rulers were the Indian Nagas and the ruled their poorer and more backward Burmese cousins whom they controlled with an iron fist.[54]

Eventually, the inevitable happened. On 30 April 1988, Khaplang and his men broke with Isak and Muivah and attacked their headquarters. Nearly eighty Indian Nagas, mostly from Muivah's Tangkhul faction, were slaughtered. Muivah and Isak managed to escape.[55] They fled south to Somra opposite Manipur, where the NSCN still had supporters among the local Tangkhuls. The old base area across the border from Nagaland remained in the hands of Khaplang and his Burmese Nagas – and some Konyaks and Aos from the Indian side who had decided to join his faction.

But the Naga rebellion against India was far from over. Deprived of their base areas in Burma and having lost most of their weapons, the NSCN (IM) – as Isak's and Muivah's faction became known to distinguish it from NSCN (K); K for Khaplang – sent Muivah to Thailand to purchase new arms. A few shipments got through via Bangladesh, and by 1993, the NSCN (IM) had regained some of its previous strength. It also changed the last 'N' in the name of the organization to 'Nagalim' from 'Nagaland' to underscore its territorial claims and ambitions.

But even after taking delivery of those new weapons, the NSCN (IM) was unable to carry out any successful military operations because it now lacked cross-border sanctuaries to retreat to after ambushing Indian Army patrols. Isak and Muivah then put more emphasis on political work and went on a campaign to internationalize the Naga issue. They managed to attend meetings with UN human rights bodies in Geneva and the UN Working Group on Indigenous People, and their movement became a member of the Unrepresented Nations People's Organization. Despite the acronym UNPO it is not a UN agency, or even an UN-affiliated organization, but a privately run NGO based in the Netherlands.[56]

In 1996, the Indian government began to express the need to seek a political, negotiated solution to the conflict. Indian intelligence agents made contact with Muivah, the undisputed leader of NSCN (IM). Isak, the official chairman, had begun to devote almost all his time to Bible studies. Equipped with a Bangladeshi passport, he travelled frequently between Thailand and the Philippines, often sponsored by local church groups. But meetings were arranged with Muivah and his men through go-betweens in Thailand and elsewhere resulting, on 1 August 1997, in a ceasefire agreement between the NSCN (IM) and the Indian government. Peace talks followed, in Paris in 1998 and twice in Amsterdam in 1999.[57] Later, talks were held in India, and the model was clearly the 1986 peace settlement with the Mizos, whereby their leader Laldenga returned home and was absorbed into the Indian political system. The Naga faction led by Khaplang entered into a de facto ceasefire agreement with the Indian government in 2001, but formal peace talks are yet to take place.

After decades of bitter fighting, it was not difficult to understand why the Naga rebels began looking for a peaceful solution to the conflict. Years of war had also resulted in bloody infighting among the Nagas themselves, and their long isolation from the rest of the world had created unique beliefs based on a mixture of Christianity and Maoist rhetoric – topped with what was clearly age-old tribal superstition and outright barbarism. But perhaps more exposure to the outside world would make the leaders of the Naga underground more adaptable to political realities.

While one round of peace talks after another was held between the Indian government and the NSCN (IM), in January 2003, Isak and Muivah paid homage to Mahatma Gandhi at Rajghat in New Delhi. They carried a wreath up to the memorial, still firmly believing that Gandhi had indeed promised them independence. The Indian government officials who accompanied them to Rajghat, of course, did nothing to undeceive them of this illusion. The main task was to get the Naga rebels to feel that India was also theirs. It seemed that RAW has struck yet another victory in the north-east through one of Kautilya's four cardinal principles: sham, or political reconciliation. But the problems in India's north-east are far from over, and Burma remains a cockpit of anarchy that continues to have a severe impact on India's national security. And the regional rivalry with China is actually becoming more serious – even in areas far away from the traditional conflict zones in India's north-east.

Pancharampara
Chakma
Refugee Camp,
Tripura, 1990

ARIF (Arakan Rohingya Islamic Front) camp in southeastern Bangladesh, near Teknaf (Burmese border)

Arabinda Rajkhowa, ULFA
chairman, Burma, 1985

Paresh Baruah, ULFA commander-
in-chief, Burma, 1985

Rajkhowa and Pradip Gogoi (ULFA vice chairman), Burma, 1985

Thuingaleng Muivah, NSCN general secretary, 1985

ULFA at NSCN headquarters, 1985

'Eastern
Nagaland'
(Burma), 1985,
'Nagaland for
Christ'

ULFA with NSCN training officer, 1985

ULFA and NSCN troops; from left to right: Isak Chishi Swu
(NSCN chairman), S.S. Khaplang (NSCN vice chairman), Thuingaleng
Muivah (NSCN general secretary), Arabinda Rajkhowa (ULFA chairman),
Pradip Gogoi (ULFA vice chairman)

Isak Chishi Swu (behind him, Muivah)

Isak Chishi Swu on a 'preaching tour' in the Naga Hills of Burma, Bible in hand, armed troops, and flag ('Nagaland for Christ')

A.Z. Phizo (picture taken in London)

Zekope Krome, young NSCN activist (and former editor, *Oking Times*), killed by the NSCN

Village scenes, the Naga Hills
of northwestern Burma

Oking: The NSCN's headquarters (always called 'Oking'wherever it is), near the village of Kesan Chanlam in northeast Burma (it was attacked and destroyed by the Burmese army in December 1985)

The village of Kesan Chanlam: Burnt down by the Burmese army in December 1985

WHEN YOU GO HOME
TELL THEM OF US AND SAY
FOR YOUR TOMORROW
WE GAVE OUR TODAY

Kohima Memorial stone, World War II cemetery, Kohima

The People's Liberation Army (PLA) of Manipur: Pictures taken at the KIA's headquarters near Burma's border with China, 1986

PLA soldiers and Kachin Independence
Army (KIA), Burma

The Kachin Independence Army, Burma

HSENG NOUNG LINTNER

The KIA, Burma, with Chinese-supplied anti-aircraft gun

The Communist Party of Burma, pictures taken 1986-1987: Soldiers and leaders meeting under portraits of Stalin and Mao

Chinese-supplied army truck

CHITRA AHANTHEM

Protests in Imphal, Manipur

CHITRA AHANTHEM

Sharmila Irom

CHAPTER SEVEN

THE INDIAN OCEAN:
A TALE OF TWO ISLANDS

Port Blair must be one of the prettiest towns in India. Perched on a series of green hills overlooking an azure-blue ocean, and with a population of just over 100,000, it has a laid-back feel to it. There is hardly any litter even at the bus and taxi stand near what is still called Aberdeen Market. Indigenous tribes of black people inhabit the interior of the islands, but Port Blair itself and other towns here have over the past century and a half been settled by Bengali, Tamil, Punjabi, Telugu, Malayali and other migrants from the Indian mainland – and even some Burmese – who now all live in harmony with each other.

Port Blair and towns and villages throughout the Andaman and Nicobar Islands were badly hit by the December 2004 earthquake and tsunami that devastated communities around the entire Indian Ocean. But Port Blair has been rebuilt and has recovered from the disaster. Incongruous as it may seem, this picturesque place has also been the setting for one of the most bizarre cloak-and-dagger stories in recent Asian history. And behind that remarkable tale lies a tangled web of diverse interests that could turn these islands, and the Indian Ocean which surrounds them, into the next flashpoint in the rivalry between India and China.

In February 1998, the Indian media reported that a gang of international gunrunners had been intercepted in a joint operation mounted by the army, the navy, the air force and the coastguards. More than seventy men had been apprehended on 'Longoff Island' in the Andamans and 145 guns seized. Six gunrunners were said to have been killed in a skirmish with the security forces, according to the reports. The shipment was headed for Chittagong, *The Times of India* reported, and consisted of automatic rifles, rocket launchers, machine guns, communication sets and several hundred thousand rounds of ammunition. The guns had been purchased in Cambodia, transported through Thailand, and were meant to be delivered to rebels in India's north-east.[1]

No one was really surprised, because it had been known for years that Cambodia was awash with all sorts of weapons left over from decades of civil war in that country, and that insurgents in the region were procuring guns from there. At the time, it was also common knowledge that weapons from the black market were being transported regularly across the Andaman Sea to the Tamil Tigers in Sri Lanka – or across the Bay of Bengal and onto Bangladesh, where Naga, Manipuri and Assamese rebel groups had sanctuaries and regularly took delivery of guns from South-east Asia. Gunrunners, based at the Thai resort island of Phuket, had fleets of small boats and fishing trawlers specifically for that purpose.

But there was something that did not sound just right in the press reports about this particular incident. 'There is certain information we cannot give owing to the sensitivity of diplomatic relations involved,' assistant chief of navy staff operation, Rear Admiral Madanjit Singh, rather cryptically told *The Times of India*. And no one could find 'Longoff Island' on any map of the area. The action, which was code-named 'Operation Leech', had in fact occurred on Landfall Island, the northernmost of the Andamans.

And the so-called gunrunners turned out not to be that at all. There were two Thai captains and thirty-five Thai and Cambodian crew on the fishing trawlers that had brought them there. But thirty-six of those arrested were Arakanese and Karen rebels from Burma – who had worked closely with Indian intelligence officers and provided them with information about the activities of northeastern insurgents. In 1995, they had even passed on information that helped Indian security forces capture arms being smuggled by those rebels from Cox's Bazar in Bangladesh to India in an operation code-named 'Golden Bird'.[2]

Nandita Haksar, an Indian lawyer who looked into the case, quotes in her book *Rogue Agent* one of the detained Arakanese rebels as saying that they had had meetings in Thailand with a Burmese-speaking colonel of the Indian military intelligence named Vijay Singh 'Gary' Grewal long before they set sail for the Andamans. He and other Indian intelligence officers had actually invited them to use Landfall Island, which is uninhabited, as a base for their struggle against the military regime in Rangoon.[3] Weapons could be stored there and the rebels could retreat to the island after conducting operations on the Burmese mainland. In return, the Burmese rebels would monitor the illicit arms traffic in the Andaman Sea to make sure ships carrying guns to the Nagas, the Manipuris and the Assamese could be intercepted.

More importantly, the Indians wanted them to spy on a new radar station on the Burmese Coco Islands, which is located just north of Landfall Island. The radar station, it was reported, had been built with assistance from China. And if China gained a toehold in the Indian Ocean, even indirectly through the Burmese naval base on the Coco Islands, they would be able to collect intelligence about India's movements in the region. And, as had been reported already in 1994, Indian coastguards on the Andamans had intercepted three fishing trawlers flying the Burmese flag – but with a Chinese crew and stocked with radio communication and depth-sounding equipment.[4]

The rationale for supporting certain groups among the Karen and Arakanese rebels was the same as for sending arms and ammunition to the Kachin in the far north of Burma: to prevent arms from reaching the insurgents in the north-east and, of course, to keep an eye on China. This policy was the brainchild of Bibhuti Bhusan Nandy, a veteran Indian intelligence officer who served as station chief of RAW in Bangkok in the 1980s and later became director of the agency's Special Services as well as additional secretary in New Delhi.[5]

In 1997, however, Nandy had been transferred to the post of director general of the Indo-Tibetan Border Force and eventually was appointed national security adviser to the Government of Mauritius. As Nandy was being sidelined, India's Burma policy was changing rapidly. The Kachin Independence Army had made peace with the government in Rangoon, and the Karen and Arakanese rebels were too insignificant. India now embarked on its diplomatic offensive to wean Burma's military government from its close relationship with China. And cooperation with the Burmese military, not some rebel groups, was deemed necessary to curtail the activities of the north-eastern rebels.[6]

By the time the Arakanese and Karen rebels arrived at Landfall Island, their new 'mentor', Colonel Grewal, was already well connected in Rangoon. He had simply lured them into a trap. Six of the rebels were shot on the island before the others were arrested. There was not going to be any Burmese rebel base on Landfall Island. In May 1999, the ordinary members of the crew were released and repatriated to Thailand. But the Arakanese and the Karens languished in jail, first in Port Blair and later in Kolkata. Nandy was upset that contacts he had nurtured carefully over years were ruined and signed a petition asking for their release, blaming the fiasco on 'a rogue agent'.[7] But it is plausible to assume that Grewal's actions were more in line with India's new Burma policy than Nandy's. It was not until June 2011, thirteen years after their arrest, that they were set free and flown to New Delhi. Burmese exiles received them as heroes at the airport, cheering and bedecking them with garlands.

But regardless of differences in opinion when it came to how India should deal with Burma's military government, the main concern has always been the same: what is *really* happening on the Coco Islands? Are the Chinese there, and, if so, in what capacity? Is there a signals intelligence post on the island? And is it monitoring the movements of the Indian Navy in the Indian Ocean or, even more menacing, India's test range for ballistic missiles and space launch vehicles on its eastern coast, the Indian Space Research Organization at Sriharikota in Andhra Pradesh, and the Defence Research and Development Organization at Chandipur-on-Sea in Orissa? Some Indian analysts suggested that the reported construction of a military base in Great Coco, the main island in the Burmese territory, was linked to China's long-term expansionist designs in the entire Asia-Pacific region.[8]

Others began talking about China's 'String of Pearls' – a series of planned Chinese bases, or bases which China would have access to – stretching from the Middle East to Gwadar in Pakistan, Sri Lanka, Bangladesh and Burma. The term was coined by Christopher J. Pehrson in a 2006 paper for the US Army War College: 'String of Pearls: Meeting the Challenge of China's Rising Power across the Asian Littoral'.[9] It would certainly make sense. No longer self-sufficient in fossil fuel, China now has to import oil and gas from the former Soviet Central Asia and the Middle East. China is also planning to build a pipeline through Burma to avoid the sensitive and potentially volatile Strait of Malacca to facilitate its oil imports from Middle Eastern countries. For this purpose, and to import natural gas from the fields in the sea south of Burma, China signed an agreement with Burma in March 2009 to build a natural gas pipeline and, in June 2009, a crude oil pipeline from the new deepwater port of Kyaukphyu near Sittwe in Arakan state all the way to Kunming in Yunnan.[10]

I was one of the first to report on China's new focus on the Indian Ocean in the *Far Eastern Economic Review* as far back as in

1993. Apart from the delivery of Chinese-made, Hainan-class fast-attack craft to Burma, Chinese technicians were also helping the Burmese upgrade their naval facilities near Rangoon and in the south-east, and to build new ones. I mentioned the Coco Islands, adding that, 'although China's presence in the Bay of Bengal is currently limited to instructors and technicians, the fact that the new radar equipment about to be installed in the Coco Islands is Chinese-made – and likely to be operated at least in part by Chinese technicians – will enable Beijing's intelligence agencies to monitor this sensitive maritime region.'[11]

My reports as well as those by others caused alarm bells to go off in India and elsewhere, leading to wild exaggerations and misperceptions of what was actually happening on the Coco Islands. Indian analyst and commentator on regional security, Brahma Chellaney, went so far as to say that Chinese 'security agencies already operate electronic-intelligence and maritime-reconnaissance facilities on the two Coco Islands in the Bay of Bengal. India transferred the Coco Islands to Burma in the 1950s, and Burma then leased the islands to China in 1994.'[12]

Nothing could be more incorrect. The British colonial authorities in Kolkata transferred jurisdiction of the Coco Islands, which then had little more than a lighthouse on them, from the Andaman Islands administration to British Burma, then an Indian province, in 1882. When Burma was separated from India in 1937 and became a separate Crown Colony, the Coco Islands remained Burmese territory.[13] They were formally handed over to Subhas Chandra Bose's provisional Azad Hind government when the Japanese occupied the Andamans during World War II. But in reality the Coco Islands were administered by the Japanese navy until the end of the war. In 1945, they were once again under Burma, and remained a Burmese territory after independence in 1948. In 1953, India sought to lease the lighthouse on Great Coco, but the request was denied.[14]

The Burmese government established a penal colony on Great Coco in 1959 to which it sent former rebels it had captured and thought should be 'reeducated'. But it was not until after the 1962 military takeover that the Coco Islands gained notoriety. In 1969, Indonesia had turned Buru Island into a penal colony for political prisoners who had been arrested in the wake of general Suharto's takeover a few years earlier, and a subsequent massacre of communists and other dissidents. Burma decided to model its new, enlarged penal colony after Buru Island, turning it into a hell on earth.[15]

Aung Htet, a Leftist sympathizer and later a prominent member of the Communist Party of Burma, was in the first batch of prisoners to be sent to Great Coco. He was transferred along with other political prisoners from Rangoon's central jail at Insein down to the docks:

> Prison wardens with clubs lined our way to a row of Hino buses outside the jail compound. The windows of the buses were covered with white sheets. We were herded aboard and driven to Butataung jetty where a Five Star liner, the Pyi Daw Nyunt, was waiting for us. There were searchlights everywhere, focusing on our way up to the ship. I saw lines of soldiers; their steel-helmets and bayonets glistered eerily in the searchlight. All of us, 233 political prisoners, were brought in chains to the ship's cargo room. It took two days to reach the Coco Islands. When we arrived, an army colonel, Tun Yin Law, gave a speech: 'This is the Coco Islands, which you may have heard of. Try to escape if you dare. The waters around here are full of sharks. This is also a different kind of prison. You have to work and to grow your own food. If you don't work, you'll have nothing to eat.[16]

Only three prisoners managed to escape from the island. They secretly built a boat from coconut trees and made a sail from bedspreads sewn together. They set sail at night and voyaged for fourteen days before reaching the coast near Ye in south-eastern Burma. The trio had barely managed to survive on dried biscuits, tortoise flesh and rainwater. Almost dead from starvation, they staggered ashore – and were promptly arrested. Only one of them managed to get away, but died from malaria in a Karen rebel camp a year later.[17]

It did not work out as the Burmese authorities had expected. The prisoners had been given spades, shovels and other tools to till the soil on the island, which was why those three inmates had managed to build their own boat. Other prisoners also collected scrap metal from a shipwrecked Greek ocean liner and managed to arm themselves with crude, homemade weapons with which they kept the guards at bay.

The CPB sympathizers sewed their own flags with the hammer and the sickle, and began to openly celebrate May Day and have regular meetings in the penal colony on Great Coco. The prison authorities had given them radios which were fixed on the frequency of Radio Rangoon, but the prisoners managed to manipulate them and were soon able to tune into the CPB's clandestine People's Voice of Burma, which had just begun transmitting from Yunnan.

There were several hunger strikes among the prisoners and the most serious came in May 1971 to protest against the concept of isolation on a remote island in the Bay of Bengal. The strikers committed themselves to fast unto death, and as soon as a prisoner had died, he was put in a homemade wooden coffin draped in CPB flags. The others clenched their fists and sang the Internationale as the coffins piled up outside the prison barracks.

On the fifty-third day of the hunger strike, by when eight prisoners had died, the authorities finally gave in. In December 1971, a ship was dispatched from Rangoon to pick up the deportees. They were transferred back to Insein Jail on the outskirts of the capital, and the Coco Islands were handed over to the Burmese navy, which maintained a small garrison there.

Nothing much then happened on the islands until the early 1990s, when Burma began upgrading its naval capabilities. While some reports have been grossly exaggerated, there is indeed a radar station on Great Coco, although very rudimentary, and a new airstrip. There are also some suspicious-looking structures, including a tower, on a smaller island just north of Great Coco, and strange-looking buildings in the middle of the forest on the supposedly uninhabited Little Coco. The Coco Islands have had no civilian population since the departure of the political prisoners, and everything there must be deemed to be of military significance.

And there is little doubt that India is keeping a watchful eye on the strategically located Coco Islands – an interest New Delhi seems to share with the United States. When I visited Port Blair in January 2011, a US naval ship was visiting the Andamans to conduct what was described as exercises in search and rescue operations, and on how to salvage shipwrecks and repair naval vessels. The commander of the US vessel, Derek T. Peterson, 'lauded the cooperation' of the Indian Navy and said he was impressed with its capabilities.[18]

It was far from the first US naval visit to the Andamans. In March 2010, the USS Patriot arrived in Port Blair. The news site of the commander of the US 7th Fleet reported that 'Patriot Sailors will train with the Indian Navy; special emphasis will be put on damage-control and mine countermeasures training,' and quoted Douglas Woods, one of its officers, as saying: 'In Port Blair we got a couple of things going on. First day we pull in we got a flag football game with the Indian navy and a soccer game with the Indian navy. We also have cricket lessons for all personnel that want to go out and participate in. Indian navy personnel will provide the lessons.'[19]

Indian naval officers I interviewed in Port Blair assured me that there was nothing more to the US naval visit than just some joint training exercises. But it is hard to imagine that some routine exercises were the main purpose of the visits by US naval vessels. Burma – and China – must have been watching the cooperation between Indian and US navies with some concern, to say the least. Both the Burmese and the Chinese knew that India's military had upgraded its presence on the Andaman and Nicobar Islands to meet the new challenges in the maritime region and to safeguard its interests in South-east Asia and the Malacca Strait. There were certainly more important issues of concern for India and the United States than diving for sunken ships and teaching American sailors to play cricket.

The idea of a new Indian Far Eastern Naval Command, FENC, was reportedly hatched in 1995 following a closed-door meeting in Washington between India's then prime minister, P.V. Narasimha Rao, and the US president, Bill Clinton. The plan was finalized when Clinton visited India in 2000, and as an Indian journalist reported at the time, 'FENC will have state-of-the-art naval electronic warfare systems that can extend as far as Southeast Asia.'[20]

The newly created Andaman and Nicobar Command of the Indian armed forces coordinates the activities of all three services in the Indian Ocean. This is India's first such integrated command and an Indian Navy website points out that the archipelago 'is at a distance of approximately 1,200 kilometres from India's Eastern seaboard and 450 kilometres from the Malay Peninsula. Myanmar's (Burma's) Coco Islands towards the North, are just 42 kilometres away and Aceh in Indonesia is 163 kilometres from the southern-most tip of Great Nicobar Island.'[21] Idyllic Port Blair has become as crucial to the defence of India as any major military base in the Himalayas, and it is not difficult to understand why. And, speaking at a round-table conference held on 12 April 2010 – organized by the New Delhi-based think tank, the National Maritime Foundation – Chief Admiral Gary Roughead of the US navy stated that America's leaders at the highest level have declared that the US and India would be strategic partners for the twenty-first century: 'I'm here to say that the United States navy in particular is a committed friend to India for the long term.'[22] The aim of this cooperation has never been stated officially, but is nevertheless clear: to counter the rise of China.

The Chinese, on their part, won approval in August 2011 from the Jamaica-based International Seabed Authority – which organizes and controls all mineral-related activities in the international seabed area beyond the limits of national jurisdiction – to explore a 10,000 sq. km area in the Indian Ocean for 'polymetallic sulphide ore'.[23] *The Times of India* reported at the time: 'The move is bound to draw close scrutiny from India, which is worried about China's military goals in the area.'[24]

This is not the first time that the strategic importance of the Andamans and the Nicobars has been recognized. These islands have a much stormier history than the Burmese Cocos, and tales that are even more extraordinary. While the Cocos were uninhabited when the British arrived there in the nineteenth century, indigenous tribes have populated the Andamans for more than 2,000 years. No outsiders tried to colonize the islands until the British East India Company sent Lieutenant Archibald Blair there to survey the islands. He established a small settlement, which was later named after him: Port Blair. The early colonizers encountered the aborigines in the interior of the islands and, because their skin colour was absolutely black, assumed they were descendants of African slaves the Portuguese had to abandon there when their ships ran into storms on their way to Macau or some other colony they then had in East Asia.[25]

This was, of course, nonsense. So-called 'Negrito' peoples can be found in pockets all over the region such as the Semangs of the Malay Peninsula and the Aetas of the Philippines. These aboriginal peoples are rapidly dying out – except on the Andamans, where the main tribes are the Great Andamanese, the Jarawas, the Jongils, the Onges and the Sentinese. Many of them are hunter-gatherers even today and live in protected reserves.

The most isolated are the Sentinese on North Sentinel Island in the sea to the west of South Andaman Island. They are still vigorously resisting any contact with outsiders. An Indian naval officer I met in Port Blair had once tried to land there with gifts in an attempt to establish some kind of rapport with the islanders, and was met with a barrage of arrows. Other attempts to land on North Sentinel Island have been equally unsuccessful and no one knows for certain how many people live there today. It could be as few as forty, perhaps as many as 500. The 2001 Census of India records thirty-nine individuals, twenty-one males and eighteen females. But that was based on observations from a safe distance as they could not actually meet any of the islanders.[26] Other aboriginal tribes, however, are gradually being brought into the modern world, even if it is a slow and sometimes painful process.

The Nicobars are entirely different. The native population there is not related to any of the Andaman tribes, but are a Mon-Khmer-speaking people with their own plantations and vegetable gardens. The first European power to take possession of these islands were the Danes. The Danish East India Company needed a station somewhere between Tranquebar – now called Tharangambadi – then a Danish colony on the coast of southern India, and Siam, where the Danes had strong commercial interests. The Danes named the islands Frederiksøerna – 'The Frederick Islands' – after their king, but had to abandon them time and again because of malaria and other diseases. In the late eighteenth century, Austria, believing that Denmark had given up its claims to the islands, tried to colonize them – the only colony that Austria even tried to establish outside Europe.[27] The Danes returned, however, and eventually gave up their self-proclaimed rights to the Nicobars and sold them to Britain in 1868. The only legacy of Danish rule over the islands is that most Nicobarese were converted to Christianity.[28]

The Andamans, meanwhile, had been abandoned by the British after Lieutenant Archibald Blair's initial attempt to colonize them. But after the first War of Independence in 1857, the British again took possession of the islands – to establish a penal colony.

Thousands of freedom fighters were sent there to construct prisons and harbour facilities. The British established their own secluded world on the tiny Ross Island 2 km off the coast near Port Blair. Ruins of the Victorian era still remain there, abandoned and overgrown. But once Ross Island, less than a square kilometre in area, had everything the colonials could desire: a secretariat, an officers' club, a hospital, bakery, tennis court, church, bazaar, water treatment plant, ice factory and printing press. The British probably felt safe there. No arrows fired by the aborigines could reach them on Ross Island.[29]

As India's independence movement grew, so did the prison population on the Andamans. Between 1896 and 1906, a huge, high-security prison was constructed where freedom fighters from all over India were interned. Called the Cellular Jail because of its shape, the penal colony became better known as *kalapani*, black water, denoting the vast, open sea in the Bay of Bengal between the islands and the mainland, and the horrors of the exile that awaited those who were sent there. And they came from all over India. Prisoners who tried to escape or revolted against the authorities were flogged or hanged. The few who made it outside the walls of the Cellular Jail risked being killed by aborigines who did not like any outsiders – and many were found in the surrounding forests, hacked to death or with arrows in their chests or backs.

In the 1930s, several long hunger strikes among the prisoners made the British think twice about the wisdom of deporting people to a remote island. Some would even say that the Cellular Jail had become a school for the freedom fighters; there, they met new comrades and like-minded people from parts of India other than their own. The last hunger strike, which occurred in 1937, was terminated only after intervention by some of India's most prominent personalities at the time. Mahatma Gandhi sent the prisoners a telegram on behalf of Rabindranath Tagore and the Congress Working Committee, advising them to abandon the hunger strike and assuring them that their grievances would be addressed. Later that year, the first batch of prisoners was returned to jails in the mainland, and by 1938, many more were gone from across the kalapani.[30]

Then, in March 1942, the Japanese Army attacked the islands and captured them from the British. Ross Island was strafed from the air and some of the buildings were destroyed to make place for Japanese bunkers. The convicts who remained in the Cellular Jail were released. But several of the British officers, and some Indians as well, were beheaded in public to scare the population into submission. With the Japanese came Subhas Chandra Bose and the Indian National Army. On 29 December 1943, the Indian tricolour flew for the first time over 'Free India', as Netaji renamed the Andamans Shahid Dweep and the Nicobars Swaraj Dweep.[31]

In reality, however, 'freedom' meant only that British brutality was followed by Japanese brutality. Locals accused, usually wrongly, of being 'British spies' were mercilessly caned in the nude in public. Others were executed by firing squad or tortured to death. Nearly half the population starved during the Japanese occupation and hundreds of innocent islanders were massacred for no obvious reason. Japanese-sponsored 'freedom' just meant another kind of brutal foreign rule.

The British reoccupied the islands in October 1945. The penal colony was closed down once and for all, and those who so wished could return to the mainland. The Cellular Jail is today a museum to honour all those who were interned or died there. In 1979, it was declared a national monument by the then prime minister of India, Morarji Desai.

After independence, the Andaman and Nicobar Islands were placed under the direct administration of New Delhi and, on 1 November 1956 they were declared a Union territory. Communications and the infrastructure were improved, people from the mainland were encouraged to settle there, and proper agriculture was introduced as well as a local fishing industry. The old sawmill on Chatham Island, built during colonial days, remains one of the main industries on the islands – and in recent years they have become a major destination for Indian and foreign tourists. But the main concern for New Delhi in its easternmost Union territory is security. C. Uday Bhaskar, a retired commodore of the Indian Navy, wrote in the September 2010 issue of the Kathmandu-based *Himal* magazine that 'access to and control of the Indian Ocean long remained an abiding strategic concern for the major powers.' Bhaskar goes on to quote Olaf Caroe, governor of the North-West Frontier Province before partition in 1947, who wrote a book called *Wells of Power* about the extension of the nineteenth-century Great Game into the twentieth:

> The strategic movements of the Allies in Iraq and Persia in the Second World War were made possible from the Indian base . . . the importance of the [Persian] Gulf grows greater, not less, as the need for fuel expands, the world contracts and the shadows lengthen from the north. Its stability can be assured only by the close accord between the States which surround this Muslim lake, an accord underwritten by the Great Powers whose interests are engaged.[32]

Bhaskar adds that almost seven decades after World War II, the enemy, which Caroe referred to as the 'shadow from the north' is no longer the Soviet Union, 'the Russian bear seeking in vain to access the warm-water ports of the Indian Ocean', but 'the oriental dragon', China. And the focus of attention has shifted from west to east in the Indian Ocean. In between China and the Indian Ocean lies Burma – and India and Burma share a complicated and delicate history, one marked as much by mistrust as amity.

The role Indians played as intermediaries between the colonial British and the native population gave rise to sometimes fierce anti-Indian sentiments. Throughout the 1930s and 1940s, the Burmese nationalist movement had strong undertones of communal tension.

Even today, people of South Asian origin are often looked down on in Burma, popularly referred to as *kala*, a Burmese language pejorative meaning 'foreigner' or 'Indian'. Curiously, Caucasians are still called *kala pyu*, which translates from the Burmese to 'white Indians'.

Still, Burma's relations with India were in the main cordial after independence. Burma's first prime minister, U Nu, never forgot that without India's massive military and economic aid, his government would most probably have collapsed. However, Indo-Burmese relations chilled after General Ne Win's military coup in March 1962, when the revolutionary council, after a few years in power, moved to nationalize privately owned businesses and factories, of which an estimated 60 per cent were owned by people of Indian origin. Thousands lost their property and livelihood and during the four-year period spanning 1964–68 some 150,000 Indo-Burmese left the country.[33]

Many leaders of the formerly democratic Burma also fled, among them the deposed prime minister U Nu, who went into exile in India. The Indian government put him up in a stately residence in Bhopal, where he remained for well over a decade before returning to Burma under a general amnesty in 1980. Bilateral relations between India and Burma remained more or less stagnant until Burma's 1988 uprising for democracy.

After the uprising was brutally crushed by the Burmese military, India received a stream of refugees. They were not as many as the thousands of pro-democracy activists escaping to Thailand, but many young Burmese managed to cross the border into Manipur, and were later allowed to stay in New Delhi under the protection of the United Nations High Commissioner for Refugees.

In an official statement issued in the wake of the violence, India expressed its support for the 'undaunted resolve of the Burmese people to achieve their democracy.'[34] The Burmese-language service of the state-sponsored All-India Radio, AIR, became even more outspoken in its criticism of Burma's new military government, which made it immensely popular with the population at large.

In response, Burma's state-run *Working People's Daily* newspaper began publishing outright racist articles and cartoons against AIR and ethnic Indians in general, attempting to revive the anti-kala xenophobia of the 1930s. But even then it was clear that India's hard diplomatic stand was not driven by illusions of serving as a regional guardian or promoter of democracy. It was never overlooked that India shares a 1,371-km frontier with Burma and that ethnic insurgents fighting against New Delhi had long used under-administered territories in Burma as sanctuaries to conduct cross-border raids into India's sensitive north-eastern areas. Since the 1960s, Burma's only reaction to this situation had been to mount half-hearted and essentially futile military operations against the insurgents, mainly the Nagas.

It was widely believed in New Delhi in the late 1980s and early 1990s that a new democratic government in Burma would likely take a more tactful approach. India's sympathy for Burma's pro-democracy movement was further strengthened by the fact that its prime minister until December 1989, Rajiv Gandhi, was a personal friend of pro-democracy leader Aung San Suu Kyi.

Their acquaintance dated to the early 1960s, when her mother, Daw Khin Kyi, served as Burma's ambassador to India. Suu Kyi's father, national independence hero Aung San, had also known Rajiv's grandfather, Nehru, personally. But it was also clear that India's support for Burma's pro-democracy forces was also guided by an Indian desire to counter its main regional rival, China, whose influence with Burma's internationally isolated generals was growing after 1988. Around 1993, India began to re-evaluate its strategy due to concerns that its policies had achieved little except to push Burma closer to Beijing. The result was a dramatic policy shift aimed at improving relations with Burma's generals, as it was also becoming clear that the pro-democracy movement would not achieve power in the foreseeable future.

At that time, Burma's military government had effectively cowed Suu Kyi's party, National League for Democracy, once a mighty mass movement, into submission. Nor did the exiled community seem to have any impact on political developments inside the country – even as some of them actually stayed in the personal residence in New Delhi of senior Indian politician George Fernandes, who served as defence minister from 1998 through 2004. It was during his time as defence minister that Indian concerns over China's alleged designs for the Coco Islands reached their crescendo. Fernandes was the first to claim, wrongly, that the islands had been part of India until they were donated to Burma by Nehru.[35] Fernandes, who once openly branded China as India's 'enemy no 1', was also an ardent supporter of the Tibetan government in exile as well as Burma's pro-democracy students.[36]

But India's security apparatus had another approach to the 'Chinese problem' in Burma. In January 2000, chief of the Indian Army, General Ved Prakash Malik, paid a two-day visit to Burma, which was followed by a reciprocal visit by his Burmese counterpart, General Maung Aye, to the north-east Indian city of Shillong. The unusual nature of this visit – by a foreign leader to a provincial capital – was accentuated by the arrival of a group of senior Indian officials from the trade, energy, defence, home and foreign affairs ministries to hold talks with the Burmese general.

In the aftermath of those meetings, India began to provide non-lethal military support to Burmese troops along their common border. Most of the Burmese troops' uniforms and some other combat gear now originate from India, as do the leased helicopters Burma uses to combat the ethnic insurgents who operate from sanctuaries along the two sides' common border. In November 2000, the Indian government (the Bharatiya Janata Party-led National Democratic Alliance, not the Congress) felt confident enough about the improvement in bilateral relations to invite Maung Aye to New Delhi, where he headed a delegation that included several other high-ranking junta members and cabinet ministers. Defence Minister Fernandes, however, pointedly did not meet the Burmese delegation.[37]

In 2004, junta chief, General Than Shwe, also visited India, followed in December 2006 by the then third-highest-ranking officer in Burma's military hierarchy, General Thura Shwe Mann, who toured the National Defence Academy in Khadakvasla, India's premier officer-training school, as well as the Tata Motors plant in Pune, which manufactures vehicles for the Indian military.

Around the mid-1990s, AIR's Burmese-language service conspicuously ceased broadcasting its anti-junta rhetoric; it is still on air today, but programming consists almost exclusively of Burmese pop music. A strange kind of 'cultural diplomacy' followed. In the early 2000s, the Indian right-wing Hindu organization, Rashtriya Swayamsevak Sangh, RSS, renewed its presence in Burma.[38] The RSS first came to Burma in the 1940s to provide social and religious services to the country's ethnic Indian minority, but it lay dormant after the military took over in 1962 and commenced nationalizing Indian private companies.

The renewed effort to build up the RSS's Rangoon branch was made apparently with the blessings of Maung Aye, a staunch Burmese nationalist who has been reported to frown on the country's recent economic and military reliance on China. The RSS, which in Burma is referred to as the Sanatan Dharma Swayamsevak Sangh, appears to have convinced some of the Burmese generals that Hinduism and Buddhism are 'branches of the same tree' and that 'the best guard against China is culture', to quote a Kolkata-based RSS official.[39]

Although the RSS is the parent organization of the Hindu nationalist Bharatiya Janata Party, which in alliance with several other parties led the Indian coalition government from between 1998 to 2004, it is not certain that the Hindu fundamentalists' new mission in Burma had the blessings of the Indian government. But cultural ties between the two countries have definitely strengthened in recent years.

So, too, has cross-border trade. Before 1988, there was scant commercial activity along the two countries' shared border, apart from smuggling. In February 2007, Sanjay Budhia, vice-president of the Indian Chamber of Commerce and Industries, said in a speech in Kolkata that India and Burma 'have set a 1 billion US dollar trade target in 2006–07, up from 557 million dollars in 2004–05.'[40]

He noted that principal exports from Burma to India include 'rice, maize, pulses, beans, sesame seeds, fish and prawns, timber, plywood and raw rubber, base metals and castor seeds.' In return, India exports machinery and industrial equipment, dairy products, textiles, pharmaceutical products and consumer goods. The India–Burma trade now rivals that of the booming cross-border trade with China, which has been brisk for almost two decades.

India has also shown a competitive interest in purchasing natural gas from Burma and to build a 1,200 megawatt hydroelectric power station on the Chindwin River across from India's north-eastern region. New Delhi is also actively involved in several infrastructure projects inside Burma, including major road construction projects. It was becoming clearer that Burma is viewed from India's perspective as a 'land bridge' to South-east Asia and as such a vital link in its new business-driven 'Look East' policy. By the turn of the new millennium, India's old policy of covert support for Burmese rebels and dissidents had definitely been buried.

In January 2007, Indian foreign minister Pranab Mukherjee became the first senior leader from a major democracy to visit Burma's new capital Naypyitaw, where the junta moved its administrative offices in November 2005. Even in the midst of the tumultuous anti-government demonstrations led by Buddhist monks in late 2007, senior officials from the Indian state-owned Oil and Natural Gas Corporation, led by Petroleum and Natural Gas Minister

Murli Deora, flew to Naypyitaw to sign an agreement to explore for gas in three new blocks in the Bay of Bengal off Burma's south-western Arakan coast.[41]

India has successfully weaned Burma from its near-total dependence on China for economic and military support by resisting the strong position taken by the US and the European Union against the generals in Naypyitaw. While still allowing Burmese dissidents to operate openly in New Delhi, it was becoming clear that India would not risk – to China's benefit – the precious foothold it has achieved in Burma since the policy changed in the 1990s. The West–East corridor India wanted to open through Burma served a double purpose: to establish direct trade with the booming economies in South-east Asia and to keep China at bay in Burma.

In September 2010, the New Delhi ambassadors of the member countries of the Association of South-East Asian Nations, ASEAN, were invited to Manipur. They travelled down to Moreh on the Burmese border. A group of businessmen from Tamu on the other side of the border came across to Moreh to welcome the ambassadors, who 'expressed confidence that trade and commerce between India and ASEAN countries through Moreh would be feasible'.[42]

But for that to materialize, it would be necessary to repair and upgrade not only the potholed road that leads from Imphal to Moreh, but the highways to and from Assam as well – not to mention Burma's hopelessly inadequate road network and other infrastructure. And before anyone can even think of a highway from India through Burma to Bangkok and Singapore, a lasting solution must be found to the ethnic problems and insurgencies in India's north-east.

The ceasefire deal the Indian government entered into with the NSCN (IM) in July 1997 seems to be holding – but it is also becoming clear that Thuingaleng Muivah is not going to become a state politician like Laldenga, once the leader of the Mizo rebels. While talking to Indian diplomats abroad and other government representatives, Muivah and his men have not given up their old ties to Pakistan and China. And they are still looking for weapons to arm their men who, since their truce with India was agreed upon, have been encamped at a place in the forest near Dimapur, which they had given the Biblical name 'Camp Hebron'.[43]

This became obvious when, on 19 January 2000, a man carrying a South Korean passport issued to a person called Hwan Soo Chung arrived at Bangkok's international airport. The Thai immigration officer was not impressed. The bearer did not look South Korean, and he had arrived on a flight from Karachi – without any Pakistani stamps in the passport. He was pulled aside, and a check proved that the passport was a fake. In no time it was established that 'Hwan' was in fact Thuingaleng Muivah. He claimed that he was on his way to attend an NGO conference in the Netherlands, but that did not make any difference. Muivah was arrested on the charge of possessing a false passport and kept in the lock-up for illegal immigrants for about a week until his nephew Apam Muivah, who lived in Thailand, raised 200,000 Thai Baht, or 230,000 Indian rupees, for bail.[44]

Muivah was released and ordered to appear in court on 1 February. Then he made another, far more serious mistake: on 30 January, he jumped bail and tried to escape to Malaysia via the small Hat Yai airport in southern Thailand, using a false Singaporean passport. The police caught him again and a Hat Yai court sentenced him to a year in prison for attempting to leave the country on a false passport. After nine months in jail, his sentence was commuted, and peace talks with the Indian government were resumed.

But some disturbing questions remained: what had Muivah been doing in Pakistan? It has obviously been a secret meeting because he had no entry and exit stamps in his fake passport. Intelligence sources in Bangkok claimed that he was in the process of working out a major arms deal with Pakistan's security services. It was also known that the Bangkok station of Pakistan's Inter-Services Intelligence had been in touch with the NSCN (IM)'s local contacts in Thailand.[45] Thailand became a haven for Naga rebels and other activists when, in April 1992, Luingam Luithui, a Tangkhul Naga from Manipur with close links to the NSCN (IM), established the Asia Indigenous People's Pact (AIPP) in Bangkok. The grouping brought together indigenous peoples from various parts of Asia and later established a regional headquarters at Chiang Mai in northern Thailand. Thuingaleng Muivah and NSCN (IM) chairman, Isak Chishi Swu, attended 'capacity building seminars' and similar events organized by the AIPP as late as in November 1999, just before his clandestine trip to Pakistan.

The actual status of the AIPP has long been a matter of conjecture. Jayanta Sarkar wrote in the *Far Eastern Economic Review* in 1994 that 'the NSCN already runs an organisation called the Asian Indigenous Peoples Pact in Bangkok. Security forces suspect it of funnelling arms to northeast militants.'[46] *BurmaNet News*, an online news service edited by Burmese exiles, criticized this assumption in a press brief in August 1990: 'Even if there is a connection between Luithui and the NSCN, the Review may be overreaching to state that the AIPP itself is an NSCN front. BurmaNet to date has seen no evidence to support or deny the Review's claims concerning AIPP.'[47]

Although the AIPP comprised representatives of more than a dozen ethnic minorities in Asia, not everyone was convinced that the AIPP did not function as a vehicle for the NSCN (IM)'s activities in Thailand. The organization soon came under surveillance by Thai security agencies in Chiang Mai and special attention was being paid to air tickets members of the organization had arranged for Naga militants using various phoney names and passports from different countries. In particular, flights from Thailand to China were being scrutinized.[48]

That a link did exist between the AIPP and the militants became obvious when NSCN (IM) stalwart Anthony Shimray was apprehended at Kathmandu's airport on 27 September 2010, and subsequently spirited off to India. An 'urgent appeal' from the Naga Movement for Human Rights, which appeared on the AIPP's website shortly after the arrest, described Shimray as a father of three children who was 'on his way to India to attend the next round of peace talks' with the government in New Delhi. Shimray was 'a well know [sic] leader of the Nagas and this incident has deeply affected the sentiments of the Naga people. We fear that if the Government[s] of India and Nepal [do] not take the responsibility and disclose his whereabouts immediately, the anger of the people will grow and threaten the peace process itself.'[49]

While Shimray may be a father of three children, he was also the NSCN (IM)'s main arms procurer – and he was not on his way to Delhi to attend some 'peace talks'. According to Indian court documents, Shimray had for years been busy creating a network of contacts in Bangladesh, Thailand, the Philippines and China for the purpose of acquiring weapons for his organization. A down payment of US$100,000 on a total of an initial US$700,000 worth of weapons was made in May 2009 to 'a foreign company selling arms and ammunition.'[50] The final list of what the NSCN (IM) wanted to buy is said to have included 600 AK-style assault rifles, nearly 600,000 rounds of ammunition, 200 sub-machine guns, light machine guns, and 200 kg of RDX explosives worth a total of 1.2 million dollars. An additional million would have to be paid for shipping the weapons from Beihai, a small port in the southern Chinese autonomous region of Guangxi, to Cox's Bazar in Bangladesh.[51]

Shimray had originally turned to the United Wa State Army for cooperation. Because Chinese arms dealers in Yunnan only deal in quantities worth at least one million US dollars, he had wanted the two organizations, the UWSA and the NSCN (IM), to make a joint order. But the UWSA began to drag their feet, and Shimray continued to negotiate alone with a middleman in Bangkok. Well aware of what happened in Chittagong in April 2004, he was also looking for a possible land route as an alternative to the long and risky sea route to deliver arms to the NSCN (IM). In December 2009, he visited Yunnan and the Laiza headquarters of the Kachin Independence Army to ask for help to send weapons through northern Burma to Nagaland. While there, he was in constant touch on his mobile phone with some members of a Naga group on a visit to South Africa.[52] The KIA, however, was unwilling and unable to provide him with any assistance.

Shimray also made several other trips to Yunnan, where he had been received by Chinese intelligence officers. The Chinese, Shimray later confessed, wanted the NSCN (IM) to help them get information about the activities of the Dalai Lama in India, and Indian troop movements in Arunachal Pradesh. The busy arms procurer also set up a company in Dhaka, the Correction Computers Bangladesh Limited, as a cover for his activities. He even had had visiting cards printed, identifying him as a representative of that 'computer service'.[53]

Shimray had left Thailand for Nepal to have his Thai visa renewed, and he also planned to sneak into India to visit his comrades in Nagaland and Manipur to inform them about the deal he had just struck in China. New Delhi was not on his itinerary. If the arms shipment had gone through, it would have been the biggest destined for India's north-eastern rebels since the aborted delivery of weapons to Chittagong in April 2004. And no one in Thailand doubted that India had had a hand in his arrest at Kathmandu airport. Shimray's movements in Thailand, and in and out Bangkok's airport, had been closely monitored by Indian intelligence for months before he left for Nepal. How he eventually ended up in custody in India is not entirely clear, but it is believed that RAW agents had him whisked out of Nepal and then interrogated him at secret locations in India.

Only a few days after Shimray's arrest, Indian intelligence pulled off another major coup: Sana Yaima, the leader of Manipur's United National Liberation Front, was apprehended in Dhaka by a joint team of Bangladeshi intelligence officers and RAW operatives.[54] He was also extradited to India – and it was clear that Bangladesh, at least under its new Awami League government, no longer was a haven for insurgents from India's north-east.

But subsequent confessions by Sana Yaima showed that Manipuri and some other rebels were still frequent visitors to China. He reportedly told his Indian interrogators that he had met Paresh Barua, the elusive commander-in-chief of the United Liberation Front of Asom, 'at the 2010 Shanghai World Expo'.[55] Evidently, Sana Yaima had been there as well. Before and after Sana Yaima's arrest, several of his close associates had been arrested in Manipur and Assam, dealing a crippling blow to the UNLF. The organization's vice-chairman, K.S. Tomba, was detained in Guwahati in April 2010, followed by more UNLF cadres in sweeps throughout Manipur. Despite the setbacks, the Manipuri rebels put on a brave face and remained defiant: 'The abduction of our honourable Chairman invigorates our party men to continue the fight against India with more urgency and intensity,' UNLF said in a statement sent to the press in Imphal in November 2010.[56] And in January 2011, a delegation from the National Investigation Agency arrived in Manipur to look into their 'tax' collection, monetary transactions through internet banking and the use of credit cards.

Many of the surrenders reported from the north-east turned out to be only plays for the gallery. In June 2011, several reports appearing on *Tehelka*'s website revealed that men who had supposedly surrendered, and guns they were said to have handed over to the security forces, were not real, but staged for propaganda purposes. Some had been recruited for the purpose and the guns obtained from a variety of sources.[57] But the writing is nevertheless on the wall after several real arrests of Naga, Manipuri and Assamese rebels and the crackdown on their financial dealings: India is determined to wipe out the north-eastern insurgencies once and for all to clear the area for trade.

In December 2009, I visited Mission Hill in Kohima, the Nagaland capital. There, remnants of the Naga National Council have what is called a 'peace camp'. Barracks, meeting halls and a church are neatly laid out on the slope of the hill, and the Naga independence flag flutters over the buildings. A few soldiers in smart uniforms clutching old rifles, which I assumed were not loaded, guarded the gate to the camp. I was received by some old NNC kilonsers, or ministers, in their version of the Naga rebel government. They courteously answered all my questions and gave me a stack of publications they had had printed in Kohima. An outline of the history of Nagaland, a booklet about the life of their late leader Angami Zapu Phizo, and another containing lists of names of hundreds of Nagas they claimed had been killed by the NNC's rivals, the NSCN (IM).

They insisted that some day India would have to recognize the 'uniqueness' of the Nagas and their history, and give them independence. I did not want to offend them by questioning what incentive New Delhi could possibly have to grant such a request, so I asked them how long they had been at the camp. Since the Shillong peace accord, they replied. That was in November 1975. It was difficult not to arrive at the conclusion that this arrangement was what suited New Delhi the best: let them stay in their camp, have their meetings and distribute their pamphlets – and ignore them.

I did not visit the NSCN (IM)'s equivalent at Camp Hebron outside Dimapur. But I am convinced that ten years from now, it will resemble the NNC's camp on Mission Hill. Endless peace talks have been held since the 1997 ceasefire with no concessions in sight from the government's side. In 2012, Muivah will turn seventy-six and Isak eighty-three. India is playing a waiting game, wearing them down and hoping that there will be no next generation of insurgent leaders among the Nagas. And, after more than a decade of ceasefire and fairly comfortable camp life at Hebron, the NSCN (IM)'s younger soldiers may not be overly eager to take on the Indian Army. The only action they have seen in recent years has been against rival Naga factions and the Kukis in Manipur.

All the insurgent groups have also been hurt financially. Following the arrest of Anthony Shimray, all the remaining NSCN (IM) cadres in Thailand returned to India, where they had to surrender their Bangladeshi passports. Whatever funds they may have had in Thai bank accounts under those names or through proxies may have been lost as well. That could have been the reason why the NSCN (IM) in June 2011 sent a note to Oil India Limited in Assam, demanding tens of millions of rupees in 'tax'.[58]

But it was ULFA that suffered the most after the 2009 expulsion from Bangladesh of almost its entire leadership. Subir Bhaumik estimates that ULFA funds frozen in Bangladesh amount to '3,990 crore Bangladeshi *takas* in 42 bank accounts', or nearly 40 billion *taka* or US$532 million, a staggering sum by any standards which, if correct, shows how effective the group's collection of 'revolutionary taxes' must have been.[59] In addition, ULFA ran its own businesses in Bangladesh until 2009 and, before 2003, in Bhutan as well. In Bhutan, ULFA was engaged in the construction business; in Bangladesh in a number of sectors: garments, real estate, the media, transport businesses and computers – the last also serving as a cover for their own procurement of electronic equipment. Paresh Barua, still at large in China or South-east Asia, may be trying to regain the losses and reassemble his scattered forces. But what sources of income does he have now and where are his men going to be based?

Despite several successful and unsuccessful arms deals with the rebels, China these days seems to be more interested in intelligence gathering than supporting armed insurrections – and to curb Chinese espionage in the north-east is no doubt another objective for India's massive crackdown on the insurgents. This time, it seems that China is sending its own pundits into this sensitive area. The mysterious training of Manipuri rebels by the KIA in the 1980s may have been part of these new Chinese designs for India's north-east. After the Kachin ceasefire with the Burmese government in 1993–94, some of those Manipuris moved to Ruili in Yunnan, where they established an unofficial liaison post and, according to a local source, 'had an excellent relationship with the Chinese.'[60] This lasted until about 2002–03, when the Manipuris who remained on the Sino-Burmese frontier settled down to fairly ordinary family life in border towns on the Chinese side. At about the same time, if Anthony Shimray is to be believed, the Chinese approached him and his men with requests to conduct espionage in India.

Chinese nationals have also been caught suspected of spying in North-east India. In May 2010, a twenty-eight-year-old Chinese national was apprehended in the Lohit area in eastern Arunachal Pradesh. He admitted to having sneaked into India through Kibithu, a remote area in north-easternmost Arunachal bordering Tibet as well as Burma.[61] During the 1962 war, Kibithu served as a launching point for deeper attacks into Arunachal by the Chinese. A fierce battle was fought at Walong – near Kibithu district in today's Anjaw district, which was carved out of Lohit in 2004 – and many Chinese soldiers were killed there. Prior to the war, the area supplied rice to Tibetan villages on the other side. It was never clear what the Chinese man was doing there. But in 1999, another Chinese had been arrested in Namsai further to the south in Arunachal on suspicion of being a spy. And in June 2010, two Chinese were picked up in a valley where Arunachal meets Nagaland. They had allegedly spent some time in a Naga rebel camp and were caught when heading for the Burmese border. The camp belonged to the NSCN (K), the Khaplang faction of the NSCN.

In another, even more curious incident in January 2011, a young Chinese woman was detained after entering Nagaland without a permit, which then was required for foreign nationals. (It has now been, at least temporarily, suspended.) She had arrived from China on 1 January, introducing herself as a 'timber company employee' and then posed as a Hong Kong-based TV reporter when she sought to meet Thuingaleng Muivah, who at that time was staying in a government bungalow in New Delhi's Lodhi Estate.[62] From there, she travelled to Dimapur in Nagaland by train under a false name, posing as a Naga student. She attracted the attention of local authorities when she was found taking pictures at the NSCN (IM)'s Camp Hebron and other areas which could be regarded as sensitive. Rather than creating a diplomatic incident, she was deported from India.

Whoever these people were, the Chinese are foolish enough to believe that they would be able to assert their claims to Arunachal and 'retake' the area. And relations between the Indian and Chinese armies at the actual border have improved considerably since the 1962 war. It is not unusual that they attend each other's national day celebrations, and exchange gifts and greetings. But China is certainly interested in knowing what kind military installations India has south of that border.

This may have become especially important for the Chinese since it became known that India will deploy six of the first eight squadrons of its new Akash air defence system in Arunachal. The *Strategy Page* reported on 9 March 2010: 'Akash is Indian designed, developed and manufactured, and is modeled on the older, but successful, Russian SA-6 system. Akash is meant to replace some very old Russian air defence systems India is still using. Each 1,543 pound Akash missile has a 132 pound warhead, a range of 27 kilometers and can kill targets as high as 49,000 feet, or as low as 66 feet.'[63] Each squadron has eight launchers, each carrying three missiles. Evidently, army commanders in the north-east are not going to be caught in a bathtub the next time the Chinese up the ante along the Sino-Indian border.

In addition, China is certainly suspicious of India's increasingly closer ties with Burma, which, as far as the Chinese are concerned, is within Beijing's sphere of interest. The country provides China with an access to the Indian Ocean. China does not look kindly at attempts by other countries to gain influence there. China certainly wants to keep an eye on India's plans for a West–East trade corridor through Burma to South-east Asia.

I visited Tawang in December 2009, shortly after the Dalai Lama had been there to commemorate the fiftieth anniversary of his flight to India. China had protested and the Indian media made it seem as if another war with China was imminent. There were reports of a massive military build-up in Arunachal. But I saw little evidence of that, or any unusual military activity. The area is heavily militarized – but it has been this since the 1962 war. 'If fighting were to break out, my unit would be the first to be hit by bullets. But do I look worried?' an Indian Army officer told me, speaking strictly off the record.[64]

I found an abundance of Chinese products in Tawang's markets: electronic goods, clothes, bedding, cutlery and the ubiquitous Chinese-made thermos flask, which are popular throughout the Himalayan region. But there is yet no direct border trade at Tawang. Chinese goods are brought into India via Nathu La in Sikkim, and then transported by road through northern West Bengal and Assam to Arunachal. Nathu La, a pass along the old Silk Road, was closed after the 1962 border war and officially reopened for cross-border trade in 2006.[65] Trade in a restricted number of items also takes place at two other points along the Sino-Indian frontier: at Shipki La, where the Sutlej River enters India in Himachal Pradesh, and Lipulekh in the Kumaon region of Uttarakhand.

Tawang, of course, is the place where the Dalai Lama crossed the border into India in 1959. And his presence in India since then remains a major worry for the Chinese. When Rajiv Gandhi visited China in December 1988 as the first Indian prime minister to do so in thirty-four years, he held talks with all the top leaders in Beijing at the time: Premier Li Peng, President Yang Shangkun and the actual strongman, Deng Xiaoping, chairman of the Central Military Commission. The visit was seen as a breakthrough in Sino-Indian relations – but the main issue the Chinese wanted to discuss with the Indian prime minister was the Dalai Lama, the Tibetan exiles in India, and what they were doing.

After decades of occupation, the Tibetans have still not accepted that they are 'Chinese', and they continue to look up to the Dalai Lama for spiritual and even political leadership. The Tibetans may be few in number but they live in a huge, strategically important area and they, more than any other nationality, remain the main threat to the unity of today's People's Republic of China. In March 2008, the Tibetan capital was rocked by massive anti-Chinese protests which shocked the establishment in Beijing. The Chinese authorities say that twenty-two people died during the rioting, but Tibetans in exile claim many times that number were killed in the protests and subsequent crackdown. Hundreds were arrested and scores received long prison sentences.[66]

China punishes and even executes 'enemies of the state' – not like India which turns them into state politicians, as seen in Mizoram, and with the surrendered Nagas, Manipuris and Assamese. This difference in political system makes authoritarian China more fragile than democratic India when it comes to internal strife, be it ethnic or political. Given the absence of outlets for the public to vent their discontent, it is not surprising that China experiences wave after wave of civic unrest – which it always blames on 'Western forces' scheming to 'split' China.[67] Cynics would claim that present income disparities, which are widening ominously, and the inflexibility on the part of the Beijing authorities may even make China ripe for a Maoist revolution.

Unrest in Tibet and occasional tensions along the Sino-Indian border are likely to remain issues that will attract the attention of security planners in New Delhi as well as Beijing. And India will have to continue seeking a solution to the ethnic problems in the north-east, and is likely to do so in accordance with Kautilya's principles of reconciliation mixed with monetary incentives, more direct force and attempts at splitting the rebel forces. In June 2011, Burmese Naga veteran fighter S.S. Khaplang was rather unexpectedly ousted from his own organization which was even named after him, the National Socialist Council of Nagaland (Khaplang). His commander-in-chief, Kholi, expelled him and announced his willingness to engage in talks with the Indian government. Kholi, a Naga from the Konyak tribe in Nagaland's Mon district, joined the old NNC in 1956 when Phizo was still in the field. Kholi had also been a member of the second Naga group that Muivah led to China in 1975, and became the undivided NSCN's commander-in-chief in 1980. Khaplang and Kholi later reconciled their differences, but the group hardly pose any challenge to India's security interests in the north-eastern border areas.

At the same time, Nagas in the four districts of Mon, Tuensang, Kiphire and Longleng have declared that they are not interested in some greater 'Nagalim' that, if it ever materialized, may be dominated by Tangkhuls from Manipur. They want to have their own state, arguing that before Nagaland was created, they did not even belong to the Naga Hills district but the then North-East Frontier Agency.[68]

At the same time, it is clear that the new focus of attention – the Indian Ocean – is much more than a tale of military developments on two former penal colonies: the Andamans and the Cocos. It could be argued that a wider new cold war is brewing in the Indian Ocean and, indirectly, China's links to the sea through Burma. Apart from India and its new partner in the Indian Ocean, the United States, some other major powers also have possessions in that maritime region. Australian-held Christmas Island, only 360 kilometres south of the Indonesian island of Java is better known as home to Australia's detention centre for illegal immigrants and asylum seekers. But it also has a major airport – and so does the nearby Cocos (Keeling) Islands, which also belong to Australia.

'Cocos' seems to be a convenient name for any islands where the coconut is to be seen. So to differentiate these from the Burmese Cocos, they are officially named the Cocos (Keeling) Islands after Captain William Keeling, who discovered them in 1609.[69] But they were not inhabited until the nineteenth century, when they became the private property of the Scottish Clunies-Ross family who brought Malays there to work on their coconut plantations. The islands were, however, annexed to the British Empire in 1857, when Britain wanted to secure its hold on the Indian Ocean as the colonial power was establishing its penal colony in the Andamans. Ten years later, the Cocos were placed under the administration of the Straits Settlements, which also included Singapore, Malacca, Penang and later Labuan. Christmas Island, where a phosphate mine was established, also came under the Straits Settlements and as such was governed from Singapore.

The strategic importance of the Australian Cocos and the Christmas Island became apparent during the two World Wars. One of the first naval battles of World War I was fought in 1914 near the Cocos Islands between the British and the Germans, resulting famously in the sinking of the German cruiser *SMS Emden*.[70] Guns from the *Emden* were later out on display in Sydney and Canberra. During World War II, Japan invaded Christmas Island, assisted by mutineers from a contingent of Indian troops, abetted by Sikh policemen who had been stationed there by the British. Five British soldiers were killed and the surviving twenty-one Europeans on the island were detained by the occupying power.

Both Cocos Islands and Christmas Island were restored to British rule after the war, but with independence for Singapore on the horizon, Britain began making preparations to transfer the small but strategically important islands to Australian sovereignty. In

1955, the Cocos Islands officially became Australian, but were still ruled in a feudal manner by the Clunies-Ross family. It was not until 1978 that Australia forced them to sell the islands and in 1983 the last so-called 'King of the Cocos', John Clunies-Ross, was told by the government in Canberra to leave and endorse full integration. Most of the 600 people who live on the Cocos Islands are ethnically Malay and Muslim, and live on Home Island, one of only two inhabited islets in the atoll. West Island remains predominantly Caucasian. In 1957, the administration of Christmas Island, whose population of about 2,000 consisted mainly of ethnic Chinese and a few Malays and Caucasians, was also transferred to Australia.

This development was not unlike the fate of the Chagos Archipelago south-west of India, which was separated from the old British colony of Mauritius when it was going to become independent in 1965, and transformed into a separate entity – the British Indian Ocean Territory. The entire native population was transferred to Mauritius and, in 1971, Britain agreed to lease until 2016 the territory's main island Diego Garcia to the United States. Air and naval bases were then built there and the US Air Force has used the facilities to refuel planes and base aircraft carriers during the 1991 Gulf War and ongoing war campaigns in Iraq and Afghanistan. The Chagos islanders, claiming they were forcefully and unlawfully evicted from their homes, are still fighting for their right to return.[71]

Although the question of Australia's sovereignty over its Indian Ocean territories is not in dispute and no one was forced to leave those islands, Britain's decision to hand them over to Canberra in the 1950s was not well received in Singapore. In June 1957, Lee Kuan Yew, then the main leader of the colony's independence movement and later prime minister, stated: 'To give away all the appurtenances of Singapore before we take over is downright swindle. A few years ago they [the British] gave away the Cocos Islands, now it's Christmas Island.'[72]

At around the same time, Devan Nair, a leading Singaporean trade unionist, wrote an open letter to the British governor strongly opposing the transfer and pointed out that in future Singapore might find the islands 'useful for defence and security' purposes.[73] His assessment was prophetic – but for Australia, not Singapore. Tiny West Island in the Cocos boasts a 2,440-metre-long runway, far too big for the needs of the territory's inhabitants. It was built after World War II, and the airport on Christmas Island is shorter but still capable of receiving more than tourist flights – and transfering illegal immigrants to the Australian mainland.

There are currently no military bases on either the Cocos Islands or Christmas Island. But as Australian defence analyst Ross Babbage wrote in a paper on his country's Indian Ocean territories, in case of an emergency, access to these would 'extend Australia's reach into the surrounding region for surveillance, air defence and maritime and ground strike operations. The islands could, in effect, serve as unsinkable aircraft carriers and resupply ships.'[74] Like the Andamans and the Burmese Cocos, the Australian islands are also ideally located to collect intelligence on Middle Eastern oil shipments destined for China, Japan and other fuel importing Asian countries. More precisely, the Cocos Islands and Christmas Island give Australia – and indirectly its Western allies, including the United States – a strategic advantage in an increasingly important maritime area. And today it is not, as it had been in the twentieth century, Germany and Japan that are of strategic concern; China's rising presence, however, is – even more so for India.[75] While no one envisages a tanker war in the Indian Ocean, it is becoming increasingly clear that this will become the main theatre of the Great Game East rather than the Sino-Indian border, or traditional flashpoints in India's north-east.

There is also a school of thought that wants to downplay the 'String of Pearls' scenario. Others dismiss the Chinese presence in Burma as more or less irrelevant, as Australian academic Andrew Selth did in his paper 'Chinese Military Bases in Burma: The Explosion of a Myth'.[76] Billy Tea, a Malaysian strategic analyst with a clear Chinese bias, argues that 'there are currently no signs whatsoever of any developments for future military purposes' in the Indian Ocean ports that China is showing an interest in, and Gwadar in Pakistan is 'actually run by the Port of Singapore Authority.' There is nothing to worry about on the Burmese Coco Islands, Tea asserts, and if one were to string together 'the current status of China's involvement at each of the Indian Ocean port facilities in question, the "String of Pearls" theory quickly becomes undone.'[77]

The fact remains that China is involved in upgrading ports in Pakistan, Bangladesh, Sri Lanka and Burma. Tea does not deny that, but argues that it is for trade purposes only. And China's project in Burma is just to build some pipelines. But any security planner in a country involved in projects like these would be foolish not to have an extensive intelligence network, and some military muscle, to ensure the safety of such an important lifeline for future oil supplies from the Middle East through Burma to China – and the sea lanes that come with it, quite apart from existing routes through the Indian Ocean and the Strait of Malacca. China has become a player in power politics in the Indian Ocean, and it is there to stay.

At the same time, the United States is rethinking its policy towards Burma. Since the 1988 massacres of pro-democracy demonstrators in Rangoon and elsewhere, Washington had been the Burmese generals' fiercest critic. But when Barack Obama took over the US presidency in January 2009, he initiated a new policy of 'engagement' with Burma's military regime. In April that same year, US senator Jim Webb, who is considered close to Obama, became the first top-level American politician to visit Burma in years. While paying lip service to 'democracy' and 'human rights' during talks with the head of the Burmese military, Gen. Than Shwe, and others – and allowed to have a meeting with the then detained pro-democracy leader Aung San Suu Kyi – Webb, a former US Navy secretary, revealed his real motives at a breakfast meeting with defence reporters in Washington after his trip to Burma: 'We are in a situation where if we do not push some kind of constructive engagement, Burma is going to basically become a province of China . . . we all respect Aung San Suu Kyi and the sacrifices she has made. On the other hand, how does the US develop a relationship that could increase stability in the region and not allow China to have dominance in a country that has strategic importance in the region?'[78]

When it was revealed that Burma even had a strategic partnership with North Korea, Washington was alarmed. In the early 2000s, it became known that North Korea was providing Burma with tunnelling expertise, heavy weapons, radar and air defence systems, and – it is alleged by Western and Asian intelligence agencies – even missile and possibly also nuclear-related technology. It was high time for Washington to shift tracks and start to 'engage' the Burmese leadership, which anyway seemed bent on clinging on to power at any cost, no matter the consequences.[79]

In March 1989, a senior US diplomat in Rangoon had told the *Washington Post*: 'Since there are no US bases and very little strategic interest, Burma is one place where the United States has the luxury of living up to its principles.'[80] That, evidently, is no longer the case. In early December 2011, US Secretary of State Hillary Clinton paid a visit to Burma, the first by a high-level American official in more than half a century. While paying lip service to democracy and human rights, it was clear that China's growing influence in Burma was a major concern. Hillary raised Burma's ties with China – and North Korea – in her talks with the new Burmese president, Thein Sein, and strategic interests have now returned to the forefront of Washington's Burma policy.

Burma is also in the process of rebalancing its foreign relations to ensure the regime's survival and future cohesion of the armed forces. The close relationship with China has not gone down well with many fiercely nationalistic Burmese Army officers, who, over the past few years, have expressed their opposition to Burma's becoming a Chinese colony. Hence, better relations with the West have to be established. But Thein Sein and the powerful military forces that back him also realized that there must be some icing on the cake for the US and the European Union to accept his nominally civilian regime and consider lifting sanctions; hence talks with pro-democracy icon Aung San Suu Kyi and the release of some, but far from all, political prisoners.[81] On 1 April 2012, Suu Kyi's National League for Democracy won a landslide victory in a by-election to forty-five seats in the national parliament and local assemblies, capturing forty-three of the forty-four seats it contested. Shortly afterwards, the EU decided to suspend – but not abolish – its sanctions against Burma, awaiting further 'positive developments'. The United States also pledged to reconsider its sanctions policy, although that will be a more complicated procedure since it involves acts passed by Congress.

It is highly unlikely that China will quietly accept the new-found rapprochement between Burma and the West. China is in Burma to stay, and there is little the country's power holders can do about it. The United States is far away whereas China is an immediate neighbour, which time and again has interfered in Burma's internal affairs. Nor is it hardly surprising that a rising economic superpower and trading nation like China is making its army leaner and meaner – and, more importantly – strengthening and expanding its navy to safeguard its own strategic interests in that region. During the military parade on 1 October 2009 – to celebrate the sixtieth anniversary of the People's Republic – a new, sophisticated naval cruise missile was displayed for the first time. In 2011, China made it public that it is building an aircraft carrier. The US Congressional Research Service identifies three objectives behind China's naval expansion: China believes it needs to defend its maritime claims in the South China Sea, and to encourage other states in the region to align their policies with Beijing's rather than remaining allies of the

United States. But first and foremost, China wants to defend vital sea lines of communications to the Persian Gulf, on which it relies for much of its energy imports.[82]

China may still be interested in destabilizing India by permitting Naga procurement officer Anthony Shimray and others access to its so-called 'black' market in arms. Paresh Barua, the militant leader of the Assamese rebels, spends most of his time in China's Yunnan province and, as late as December 2011, he supervised the delivery of a large consignment of Thailand-made automatic weapons that had been smuggled through China to north-western Burma. China has not given up its claims to Arunachal Pradesh, and the conflict in Tibet is not forgotten. Nor is the Dalai Lama's presence in India. There may be no end to the perennial turmoil in Burma, and India and China will continue to compete for influence over that buffer state between Asia's two giants. But it is in the seas where the rise of China, and its need to defend its economic interests, will be felt the strongest in South Asia. And India will be faced with a situation where the Indian Ocean may be stormier than the heights of the Himalayas and the turbulent north-east.

POSTSCRIPT

It is not every day a presidential jet lands at Rangoon's still fairly small Mingaladon airport, so 19 November 2012 was a very special day – and it was not 'any' president who came calling. The plane carried US president Barack Obama and his entourage. The visit lasted only for half a day, but it was the first ever to Burma by a serving US president. Like Secretary of State Hillary Clinton in December the year before, Obama stressed the importance of democracy and human rights, and US commitment to promoting those values in Burma and the rest of Asia. He even had a meeting with pro-democracy leader Aung San Suu Kyi, embraced her and kissed her on the cheek for the benefit of the assembled photographers. On 20 May 2013, Burma's new president, Thein Sein, was received in the White House by Obama. He was the first Burmese head of state to visit the United States since General Ne Win met then president Lyndon Johnson in Washington in September 1966.

But there is much more to the newly found cordial relations between Burma and the United States than sweet talks about human rights and democracy indicate. Obama's so-called 'pivot' in Asia has seen Washington reaffirming alliances with Japan, South Korea, the Philippines, Indonesia, Thailand and Australia – all of them traditional strategic partners in the Asia-Pacific region. The US has also been strengthening ties with its old foe Vietnam, but given that the US and Vietnam are on the same side in the new Cold War in Asia, this is not surprising.

Burma, however, is the only example of how the US has managed to expand its influence at the expense of China's. The turning point came in September 2011, when Thein Sein announced that his government had suspended a US$3.6 billion hydroelectric power project in Kachin State. The dam, to have been built at Myitsone where the Mali Hka and Nmai Hka rivers converge to form the Irrawaddy, would have been the world's fifteenth tallest and submerged 766 square kilometers of forestland, an area bigger than the Republic of Singapore. Under the 2006 deal, 90 per cent of power generated from Myitsone would have gone to China.[1]

Burma has depended on its powerful northern neighbour for trade, political support and arms deliveries since the West shunned the Burmese regime following massacres of pro-democracy demonstrators in 1988. Now it became clearer than ever before that Burma really wanted to improve relations with the West –hence the many 'democratic' reforms we have seen since Thein Sein became president in early 2011.

The strategic change in Burma didn't happen overnight. As early as 2004, an important document was compiled by Lt. Col. Aung Kyaw Hla, a researcher at Burma's Defence Services Academy in Pyin Oo Lwin, or Maymyo as it was called in the past, an old British hill station in the highlands northeast of Mandalay. His 346-page top-secret thesis, titled *A Study of Myanmar [Burma]-US Relations*, was leaked to me by a trusted source in the military.[2] 'Read this, and you'll understand why all these changes are happening,' he told me. I did, and it was astonishing reading. The Burmese-language document outlined the policies aimed at improving relations with Washington and to lessen dependence on Beijing.

Aung Kyaw Hla's thesis states quite bluntly that having China as a diplomatic ally and economic patron has created a 'national emergency', which threatens the country's independence. 'Aung Kyaw Hla', probably a committee of army strategists rather than one single person, goes on to argue that although human rights are a concern in the West, the US would be willing to modify its policy to suit 'strategic interests'. Although the author does not specify those interests, it is clear from the thesis that he is thinking of common ground with the US vis-à-vis China. The author cites Vietnam and Indonesia under former dictator Suharto as examples of US foreign-policy flexibility in weighing strategic interests against democratization.

If bilateral relations with the US were improved, the master plan suggests, Burma would also get access to badly needed funds from the World Bank, the International Monetary Fund and other global financial institutions. The country would then emerge from 'regionalism', where it currently depends on the goodwill and trade of its immediate neighbours, including China, and enter a new era of 'globalization'.

The master plan is acutely aware of the problems that must be addressed before Burma can lessen its reliance on China and become a trusted partner with the West. The main issue at the time of writing was the detention of Aung San Suu Kyi, who Aung Kyaw Hla wrote was a key 'focal point': 'Whenever she is under detention pressure increases, but when she is not, there is less pressure.' While the report implies Aung San Suu Kyi's release would improve ties with the West, the plan's ultimate aim – which it spells out clearly – is to 'crush' the opposition. The dossier also identifies individuals, mostly Western academics, known for their opposition to the West's sanctions policy, and somewhat curiously suggests that 'friendly' Indian diplomats could be helpful in providing background information about influential US congressmen.

The dossier concludes that the regime cannot compete with the media and non-governmental organizations run by Burmese exiles, but if US politicians and lawmakers were invited to visit the country they could help to sway international opinion in the regime's favour. Over the years, many Americans have visited Burma and are often left less critical of the regime than they were previously. In the end, it seems that Burma has successfully managed to engage the US rather than vice versa. As everyone can see, relations with the United States are indeed improving, exactly along the lines suggested by Aung Kyaw Hla in 2004.

In May 2008, a fraudulent 'referendum' was held to approve a new constitution which, the military said, would ensure the creation of a 'discipline-flourishing democracy'. The then ruling junta announced that the constitution had been approved by 92.4 per cent of voters, claiming a 99 per cent turnout in the regions where they had held the vote. However, in some constituencies, it was reported that more than 100 per cent of the voters had approved of the new constitution – which had to be corrected to give the referendum at least a semblance of credibility.[3]

After the referendum, a general election followed in November 2010, which everyone agrees was blatantly rigged. The military-backed Union Solidarity and Development Party, USDP, 'won' a landslide victory, capturing a solid majority in both the upper and the lower houses of the new parliament. In addition, a quarter of all seats in both chambers were reserved for the military, and thus not even elected. A new 'civilian' government was formed – consisting mainly of military officers who had replaced their uniforms with civilian clothes. The new president, Thein Sein, is a former general and so are most of his ministers.

But then changes began to occur. Hundreds of political prisoners were set free, press censorship was relaxed – and Aung San Suu Kyi, the Nobel Peace Prize laureate who had been under house arrest, was released and allowed to re-register her party, the National League for Democracy, NLD. The establishment of a more acceptable regime than the old junta provided has made it easier for the Burmese military to launch its new policies, and to have those taken seriously by the international community.

The US would, of course, deny that its new Burma policy has anything to do with regional power politics. But in late 2010,

Washington insiders say, the Obama administration decided that a fundamental policy shift was needed. Diplomats began actively to engage Burma with the aim of pulling it away from China's embrace, and making sure that North Korea did not have a military ally and partner smack in the middle of South and Southeast Asia. Thwarting the alliance with North Korea may have been the main issue in the immediate term, but longer term there is little doubt that the rise of China was the main concern.

On a visit to Canberra in November 2011, President Obama stated that, 'with my visit to the region, I am making it clear that the United States is stepping up its commitment to the entire Asia-Pacific region. The United States is a Pacific power,' Obama said, and 'we are here to stay.' But he was quick to add: 'The notion that we fear China is mistaken. The notion that we are looking to exclude China is mistaken.'[4]

That statement was about as convincing as Thein Sein's assurance that he had suspended the Myitsone dam project in the north because he was concerned about 'the wishes of the people' – which he said at the time in a speech before the Burmese parliament. At the same time, a popular campaign against the Myitsone dam had indeed been launched – and it was quietly supported by the US embassy in Rangoon. A 4 January 2010 cable from the embassy, made public by Wikileaks, stated: 'An unusual aspect of this case is the role grassroots organizations have played in opposing the dam, which speaks to the growing strength of civil society groups in Kachin State, including recipients of Embassy small grants.'[5]

The two old adversaries, Burma and the United States, may have ended up on the same side of the fence in the struggle for power and influence in Southeast Asia. Frictions, and perhaps even hostility, can certainly be expected in future relations between China and Burma. And Burma will no longer be seen by the United States and elsewhere in the West as a pariah state that has to be condemned and isolated.

But some signs of reform were needed before Washington could justify its new Burma policies, and a degree of liberalization came after what was by any measure a blatantly fraudulent general election in November 2010. Nevertheless, a quasi-civilian government took over, and that was enough – at least for the time being. But a major hurdle remained: the iconic pro-democracy leader Aung San Suu Kyi. She was released from house arrest a few days after the 2010 election and immediately embarked on a campaign to solve Burma's ethnic crisis. She called for a 'second Panglong' – a reference to a series of meetings between the majority Burmans and some of the leaders of the ethnic minorities that her father, Aung San, initiated half a year before he was assassinated and nearly a year before Burma became independent. For that, she was attacked by bloggers close to the government as a 'traitor'.[6]

Her party, the NLD, then won a landslide victory in April 2012 by-elections, capturing forty-three out of forty-four seats it contested. Tens of thousands of people rallied to hear her speak and people were jubilant. But then, she began praising the military, which had kept her under house arrest for most of the time since 1989 and, as she herself had stated on numerous occasions, was responsible for heinous human rights abuses.

On January 2013, she told the British Broadcasting Corporation, BBC, that, 'It's genuine, I'm fond of the army. People don't like me for saying that. There are many who have criticized me for being what they call a poster girl for the army – very flattering to be seen as a poster girl for anything at this time of life – but I think the truth is I am very fond of the army, because I always thought of it as my father's army.'[7] On Armed Forces Day that year, March 27, she, as the only woman among uniformed generals, was given a seat in the front row, where she could watch the Burmese military display its latest hardware.

It was soon becoming clear that Suu Kyi had reached an agreement with the military – and that there has been considerable outside, read US, pressure on her to come to terms with the country's rulers. A politically divided Burma would not serve America's purposes; an alliance between Thein Sein's government and the popular Suu Kyi would.

NLD activists admit in private that Suu Kyi and the party leadership were told by the US that they could count on continued support from Washington if they could reach an understanding with Thein Sein and the de facto ruling military. On 19 August 2011, Suu Kyi met Thein Sein at the presidential palace in the new capital Naypyidaw. Since then, she has generally not said anything critical of the government or the military. Nor has she said anything meaningful about the country's ethnic conflicts, which are considered a question of national security and, therefore, the responsibility of the military. The astounding election victory for her NLD party in the November 2015 election, in which it won an overwhelming majority of seats in both the upper as well as the lower house of the national parliament could be the beginning of a slow process towards change, but it is too early to speculate how the powerful military will react when a new government takes over. A partial ceasefire agreement between the central government and three ethnic armies and five very minor groups, which was signed in the new capital Naypyitaw on 15 October 2015, is unlikely to have any real impact on the country's decades-long civil war.

None of the major major groups – the Kachin Independence Army, the United Wa State Army, the Shan State Army (North), and ethnic armies in the Kokang, Mong La and Palaung areas – were signatories to that agreement.

It is not going to be an easy path forward – and the US as well as China is prepared for more conflicts over their divergent interest in Burma. Burma has to tread carefully; China is and will always be a powerful neighbour and any more moves similar to the suspension of the Myitsone project would have serious repercussions on the relationship between the two countries. For China, Burma remains of vital economic and strategic importance. Apart from the Myitsone project, China has substantial investments in other hydroelectric power schemes and mineral extraction, including mining for copper and rare earth minerals. The country is also a significant trade outlet for China's landlocked south-western provinces. Moreover, China is building gas and oil pipelines that will facilitate the import of energy from the Bay of Bengal and the Middle East, bypassing the potential strategic chokepoint of the Strait of Malacca. In other words, China cannot just 'hand over' Burma to the US.

Then there is the India factor. It is obvious that Burma's drift away from China is welcome in New Delhi, and Burma remains a vital link in India's business-driven 'Look East' policy, a gambit aimed at expanding trade, investment and influence to Southeast Asia. But before that can succeed, India has to find a lasting solution to the ethnic insurgencies and other security problems in its northeastern hinterlands. To India's chagrin, many of those rebels, ethnic Nagas, Manipuris and Kukis, still maintain sanctuaries in remote areas on the Burmese side of the border. These rebel forces are also known to have obtained weapons from various clandestine sources on the Sino-Burmese border even recently. Some of these weapons originate in China while others are made in secret gun factories in areas in northeastern Burma not controlled by the Central government at Naypyidaw.

Despite these difficulties, trade between India and Burma is booming, and India is busy opening its west–east corridor through Burma to protect its economic as well as strategic interests. And, not surprisingly, the Obama administration has expressed its support for India's 'Look East' policy. On 22 November 2011, US Deputy National Security Advisor for Strategic Communication, Ben Rhodes said: 'The president very much welcomes India's Look East approach. We believe that just as the United States, a Pacific Ocean power, is going to be deeply engaged in the future of East Asia, so should India as an Indian Ocean power and as an Asian nation.'[8]

As a result, China is playing a complex diplomatic game with Naypyidaw to counter American as well as Indian influence. China's double game has become clearer after the Myitsone dam controversy – and the resumption of hostilities in the far north between Burmese government forces and the Kachin Independence Army, KIA. For seventeen years, from 1994 to 2011, the KIA enjoyed a ceasefire agreement with the Central government. But in June 2011, government forces began attacking KIA strongholds on the border with China. The reason for the attacks is not clear, but it is plausible to assume that the government wanted to clear the area for trade with China. Kachin State is one of the country's resource-richest areas with large deposits of jade, gold, rare earth and other minerals.

But the KIA put up an unusually stiff resistance. Casualties on the government's side were extremely heavy, with thousands of dead and wounded. In December 2012, the government brought in Russian-made Hind helicopter gunships and Chinese-supplied attack aircraft. But even that did not cow the Kachins into submission.[9] China then decided to intervene in the conflict, which was also affecting cross-border trade. Mediation efforts began in earnest when, on 19 January 2013, then Chinese Vice Foreign Minister Fu Ying visited Burma and met with Thein Sein, as well as General Min Aung Hlaing, Commander-in-Chief of the armed forces. Several rounds of Chinese-sponsored peace talks were also held at the Chinese border town of Ruili, and Chinese officials have reportedly told the Kachin rebels, who are eager to have foreign observers present, that 'outside' participation is needed. China, the go-betweens said, will 'solve the problem'. Presumably, the Chinese have sent a similar message to the government.[10]

While waving a carrot in front of the Burmese government – a promise to solve the bloody conflict in Kachin State and, in January 2013, pledges of generous loans in the order of US$527 million for infrastructure development and other projects – China is also waving a big stick: support for the United Wa State Army, the UWSA, the successor to the Communist Party of Burma and the country's most powerful ethnic army. The UWSA may have had a ceasefire agreement with the government since 1989, but it has continued to acquire, without difficulty it seems, sophisticated weaponry from China. In 2012, Chinese arms dealers supplied the UWSA with not only assault rifles, machine-guns, rocket launchers and the HN-5 series man-portable air defence systems, or MANPADS, but also PTL-02 6x6 wheeled 'tank destroyers' and another armoured combat vehicle identified as Chinese 4x4 ZFB-05s. And if armoured vehicles were not enough, China supplied the UWSA with several Mi-17 medium-transport helicopters armed with TY-90 air-to-air missiles, *HIS Jane's Defence Weekly* reported in its 29 April 2013 issue.

'The provision of a range of new weapons systems – surface-to-air missiles, armoured vehicles and now helicopters – appears effectively to be turning the UWSA into a cross-border extension of the PLA,' one of the authors of the article, Anthony Davis of *IHS Jane's*, told me at the time, referring to the Chinese People's Liberation Army. 'Even in the context of China's large-scale military support for the Communist Party of Burma in the late 1960s and 1970s, what is happening today is unprecedented.'[11] And all of this comes in the wake of a remarkable thaw in relations between Washington and Naypyidaw.

Few observers believe that China would want the UWSA to actually go to war against the government, but the MANPADs, armoured vehicles and now missile-equipped helicopters supplied to the UWSA serve as a deterrent that will make the Burmese military hesitate to launch an offensive against the Wa. They also serve as a reminder that China, unlike the US, is Burma's immediate neighbour and has the means to interfere in its internal conflicts – that it can and is willing to step up the pressure if Naypyidaw moves too close to Washington.

Local sources living in Sino-Burmese border areas said that Chinese authorities increased security all along the frontier during Obama's one-day visit to Burma in November 2012. This was, of course, not necessary from a security point of view, but, as one source put it, the gesture was another way of reminding the Burmese government that China will always be there, while the US is far away. Burma, in other words, is caught in the middle and is now finding out that its engagement with the West has a price if it affects the interests of its powerful neighbour. According to *Jane's*: 'The acquisition of helicopters marks the latest step in a significant upgrade for the UWSA, which has emerged as the largest and best-equipped non-state military force in Asia and, arguably, the world.'

It remains to be seen what China's next step will be and if the US is prepared to counter it with increased support, including possible military-to-military engagement, for the Burmese government. But whatever those moves may be, Burma has been dragged into a superpower rivalry that it may not be able to handle as the competition for influence intensifies. It is already the country where Obama's pivot comes into greatest contact with China's own strategic designs for the region. And the turmoil in India's northeast, which for decades have been a cockpit of anarchy, only adds to the uncertainty of what no doubt has become Asia's most volatile frontier.

CHRONOLOGY OF EVENTS

1946

2 February: The Naga National Council, NNC, is formed in Kohima.

1947

19 July: A.Z. Phizo and a delegation of NNC leaders meet Mahatma Gandhi at Bhangi Colony in Delhi.

14 August: The NNC declares independence for the Naga Hills.

15 August: India becomes independent from British rule.

1949

21 September: The maharaja of Manipur signs an agreement merging his state with India.

1 October: Mao Zedong declares victory in the Chinese Civil War and proclaims the People's Republic of China at a ceremony at the Gate of Heavenly Peace, or Tiananmen, in Beijing. The remnants of the old regime, the Kuomintang (Guomindang)-led Republic of China, retreat and regroup on the island of Taiwan.

15 October: The princely states of Manipur and Tripura formally join the Indian Union.

1950

26 January: Assam becomes a state within the Indian Union, and India becomes a republic under the new constitution that is adopted on this day.

March: Hijam Irabot, a Manipuri revolutionary, sets up Red Guards to fight for an independent socialist republic in Manipur.

1 April: India and the People's Republic of China establish diplomatic relations.

May: China begins to move troops into Tibetan-inhabited areas.

25 June: The North Korean army crosses the 38th parallel and marches into South Korea. The three-year Korean War begins, as do US-sponsored covert operations on the Chinese mainland and, in 1955, in Tibet.

19 October: The tiny and ill-equipped Tibetan army surrenders to invading Chinese forces. The Chinese invasion begins in earnest.

9 December: A.Z. Phizo becomes president of the NNC.

1951

16 May: The NNC organizes a plebiscite in the Naga Hills. Thumbprints are collected and 99.9 per cent are said to vote for independence.

23 May: Representatives of the fourteenth Dalai Lama and China sign the 'Seventeen Point Agreement for the Peaceful Liberation of Tibet' in Beijing, recognizing Tibet as part of China but also guaranteeing it autonomy and that 'the central authorities will not alter the existing political system in Tibet. The authorities will also not alter the established status, functions and powers of the Dalai Lama ... the religious beliefs, customs and lama monasteries shall be protected.'

1952

25 January: Most Nagas boycott independent India's first free election.

21 July: Indian authorities issue an arrest warrant for A.Z. Phizo.

1953

30 March: The prime ministers of India and Burma, Jawaharlal Nehru and U Nu, visit Kohima.

1954

26 January: The North-East Frontier Agency, NEFA, which was established in 1951, is more formally constituted and divided into six frontier divisions, comprising the present state of Arunachal Pradesh and Tuensang and Mon districts in today's Nagaland.

29 April: Representatives of China and India sign an Agreement on 'Trade and Intercourse Between the Tibet Region of China and India'.

11 September: The Dalai Lama and the Panchen Lama on a visit to Beijing hold talks with Mao Zedong. The Dalai Lama also meets other Chinese leaders, including Deng Xiaoping and Zhou Enlai.

1955

May: A.Z. Phizo forms the 'Hong King Government' in the Naga Hills.

October: Indian troops move into Tuensang in the Naga Hills.

December: An anti-Chinese rebellion breaks out among the Khampas of eastern Tibet. The US Central Intelligence Agency (CIA) begins to take an interest in the Tibetan resistance against the Chinese invaders.

1956

January: Chinese outposts are attacked, communications cut off and Chinese garrisons stationed in several provinces in Kham are completely wiped out by Khampa guerrillas.

27 February: The first encounter between the Indian Army and Naga militants, called the Naga Safe Guards, takes place at Mima village in the Angami region.

22 March: The NNC establishes the Federal Government of Nagaland, FGN, and the Naga Safe Guards become the Naga Home Guards, a more properly organized armed wing of the movement.

11 June: Battle between the Indian Army and the Naga Home Guards near Kohima. War breaks out in the Naga Hills.

13 August: NNC leader A.Z. Phizo leaves the country, finds sanctuary, first in East then West Pakistan.

1 November: The Andaman and Nicobar Islands become a Union Territory.

November: The Dalai Lama travels to India to celebrate the Buddha's birthday. He asks Nehru whether India would grant him asylum should he have to leave his homeland. Nehru encouraged him to stay in Tibet.

1957

January: The Dalai Lama returns to Tibet via Kalimpong.

1958

11 September: The Armed Forces (Special Powers) Act is enacted in the Naga Hills.

29 October: The Mizo Hills District Council issues a statement warning of an impending mautam, or 'bamboo death'. The bamboo flowers and rats invade. A severe famine breaks out in the Mizo Hills.

1959

10 March: An anti-Chinese uprising breaks out in Lhasa. 10,000 to 15,000 Tibetans are killed in three days. The Dalai Lama escapes from the Tibetan capital.

26 March: The Dalai Lama arrives at Lhuntse Dzong in Bhutan where he repudiates the 1951 'Seventeen Point Agreement for the Peaceful Liberation of Tibet'.

30 March: The Dalai Lama crosses the border into exile in India, arriving at Tawang, a Tibetan Buddhist monastery in the northwestern corner of today's Arunachal Pradesh.

1960

Between 1960 and 1962, over 150 Tibetans were sent to the United States for training. The first American arms drop into Tibet occurs in 1960. The CIA works with Tibetan exiles in Kalimpong, northern West Bengal.

12 June: NNC leader A.Z. Phizo arrives in London, where he settles and begins to propagate the Naga cause.

1961

26 January: A combined force of three divisions, or 20,000 men, of regulars from the Chinese People's Liberation Army, PLA, and 5,000 Burmese troops attack Guomindang bases in eastern Shan State, Burma. The operation is code-named 'the Mekong River Operation'.

5 February: The Kachin Independence Army, KIA, is formed in northeastern Shan State of Burma. The rebellion spreads to Kachin State proper, and within a couple of years, most of northernmost Burma is controlled by the insurgents.

April: Naga militants establish camps in East Pakistan (now Bangladesh), which becomes an important 'foreign' base for the Naga independence movement.

22 October: The Mizo National Famine Front becomes the Mizo National Front, led by Laldenga. The formal announcement was made on 28 October, declaring the MNF a political party.

1962

2 March: The military led by Gen. Ne Win seizes power in Burma. The Chinese begin to support the Communist Party of Burma, CPB, then in exile in China.

30 March: East Pakistan inaugurates a new hydropower station with a huge dam at Kaptai in the Chittagong Hill Tracts. The project, which lasted from 1957 to 1962, caused the displacement of 100,000 tribal people in the area. Thousands of them flee to India, where they are resettled in NEFA (the North East Frontier Agency, now Arunachal Pradesh). In 1962, Pakistan's constitution also changes the status of the Chittagong Hill Tracts from an 'excluded area' to a 'tribal area'.

20 October: Thousands of Chinese troops cross the McMahon Line, attacking army posts all over NEFA. The Indian army suffers a humiliating defeat.

21 November: China declares a unilateral ceasefire after reaching the foothills of Assam, and begins to withdraw across the McMahon Line.

1963

June: Training of Tibetan guerrillas in Fort Hail, Colorado, concludes. A few dozen Tibetan fighters return to India.

November: The first batch of Mizo militants cross over into East Pakistan to get arms and military training.

1 December: The Naga Hills become Nagaland, a state within the Indian Union.

1964

3 January: The Naga Home Guards become the Naga Army.

January–February: A 'Peace Mission' is set up in Nagaland comprising the Rev. Michael Scott, a British church worker, Jayaprakash Narayan, an Indian grass-roots community leader, and Assam chief minister Bimala Prasad Chaliha.

April: More Naga rebel camps and training facilities are established in East Pakistan.

6 September: A ceasefire agreement is agreed upon between Indian authorities and the Naga rebel movement.

24 November: The United National Liberation Front, UNLF, is formed in Manipur.

1965

7 April: The Eastern Naga Revolutionary Council, ENRC, is formed in

Somra, a Tangkhul Naga-inhabited area in Burma, opposite northern Manipur.

1966

1 March: Fighting breaks out all over the Mizo Hills as the Mizo National Front, MNF, launches 'Operation Jericho'. MNF declares independence from India.

4 March: Indian Air Force jets strafe Aizawl, capital of the Mizo Hills District.

16 May: Mao Zedong launches the Great Proletarian Cultural Revolution, plunging China into turmoil. It officially ends in 1969, but lasts until Lin Biao dies in a plane crash in 1971. The power struggles and political instability between 1969 and the arrest of Mao's widow and the so-called 'Gang of Four' in 1976 are now also widely regarded as part of the Cultural Revolution. Monasteries and sacred buildings in Tibet are ransacked by Red Guards, monks are slaughtered and religious books and artifacts destroyed. Of the 6,259 monasteries in Tibet before the Chinese occupation, only eight remained in 1976.

May: The Rev. Michael Scott is arrested in Shillong and deported from India. The 'Peace Mission' to which be belonged collapses.

5 June: Brig. Neidelie of the Naga Army sets up base in East Pakistan. He resides most of the time in Dhaka.

24 October: The first contingent of 132 Naga rebels start trekking through northern Burma to China. The group is led by Thinoselie M. Keyho and Thuingaleng Muivah.

1967

4 January–23 February: More than 45,000 people from the villages in the Mizo Hills are relocated in eighteen so-called group centres on the main road through the Mizo Hills.

27 January: The 123-strong Naga group led by Thinoselie and Muivah reach the Chinese border at Pangwa Pass. Muivah remains in Beijing as a representative of the Naga National Council until November 1970. The other Nagas receive military and political training in Yunnan. They return to Nagaland with Chinese-made assault rifles, machine guns and rocket launchers. Over the next decade, more than 900 Nagas receive similar training in China (for a complete list of Naga missions to China, see Appendix III).

22 June: The Naga National Council/Federal Government splits as Semas led by Kaito Sukhai break away from the movement. He is executed by former Naga comrades on 3 August.

1968

1 January: Several hundred heavily armed CPB troops, many of them Chinese 'volunteers', cross the border from China into north-eastern Burma. Within five years, the China-supported CPB has wrested control over a 20,000 square kilometer-area along the Chinese border in north-eastern Burma.

April: Sapzova of the Mizo National Front travels through Burma to the Thai border to contact Western powers.

1 June: Mizo National Front guerrillas overrun Falam, Tiddim and Tuibual in Burma's Chin State.

June: Vanlalngaia of the Mizo National Front travels through Burma to China and spends five months with the Chinese People's Liberation Army in Yunnan.

2 November: Scato Swu and Kughato Sukhai, 'president' and 'prime minister' respectively of the Naga Federal Government break away to form the Naga Revolutionary Government.

1969

March: A group of Nagas who have returned from training in China are captured along with their Chinese-made guns. The Indian government issues a formal protest to the Chinese.

1971

26 March: Sheikh Mujibur Rahman declares East Pakistan independent, and named Bangladesh.

9–11 July: Henry Kissinger, President Richard Nixon's assistant for security affairs, visits China. The United States begins a process of normalization with Beijing. America agrees to end support for the Tibetan resistance.

July: The Mizo Hills, still a hill district of Assam, is offered status as the separate Union Territory of Mizoram. Mizo leaders accept the proposal on condition that statehood would be granted later.

25 October: The United Nations General Assembly adopts a resolution declaring that the People's Republic of China will replace the Republic of China as China's representative in the United Nations, including its Security Council. Bhutan also becomes a member of the United Nations.

16 December: Victory day in Bangladesh. Pakistan surrenders to the 'Mitro Bahini', a combined force of East Pakistani Mukti Bahini (Liberation Forces) and the Indian Army. Two Naga rebel officers, Thinoselie and Neidelie, are arrested by Indian troops in Dhaka. Laldenga and other leaders of the Mizo National Front escape to Burma. Several Manipuri rebels who also try to escape are apprehended by Indian security forces

1972

21 January: NEFA becomes the Union Territory of Arunachal Pradesh. The old princely state of Manipur, a Union Territory since November 1, 1956, becomes a state, as does the old princely state of Tripura. Meghalaya also becomes a separate state. Mizoram becomes a Union Territory.

21–28 February: US President Richard Nixon visits China.

Through 1972: Inspired by the Nagas, the Mizo National Front begins to send groups of soldiers to China for training. A group of thirty-nine leave the Mizo Hills in 1972 and reach China in 1973.

1973

16 August: The Sema-led Naga Revolutionary Government surrenders to Indian authorities and become a unit of the Border Security Forces under the Indian army.

1974

July: 10,000 Nepalese troops seal off the southern approaches to Mustang, Nepal. The Dalai Lama sends a taped message to Tibetan resistance fighters there urging them to surrender. Resistance officers and soldiers commit suicide rather than complying with the order. Armed resistance in Tibet comes to an end.

1975

20 January: A second contingent of Mizo rebels begins trekking through northern Burma, reaching China in August.

27 March: Nagaland comes under presidential rule, i.e. direct rule from New Delhi.

April: The Indian Army takes over Sikkim, then an Indian protectorate squeezed between independent Bhutan and Nepal.

16 May: Sikkim becomes an Indian state after a referendum.

June: First talks between Mizo rebels and Indian government representatives take place in Bangkok, Thailand.

15 August: Sheikh Mujibur Rahman, president of Bangladesh, is killed as a group of junior officers storm the presidential palace in Dhaka.

11 November: Representatives of the Naga underground sign an accord with the Government of India. Known as 'the Shillong Accord' after the place where it was signed, Meghalaya's state capital Shillong, it causes serious rifts within the Naga movement.

1976

April: A group of sixteen or eighteen Manipuri militants known as ojas ('teachers') reach Tibet via Nepal. They remain for two years in Lhasa where they receive military training. On their return to India in 1979, the PLA launches attacks all over the Imphal valley.

9 September: Mao Zedong dies. A more moderate Chinese leadership under Deng Xiaoping takes over.

6 October: The new Chinese government officially led by Hua Guofeng has the 'The Gang of Four' arrested. China embarks on the road to capitalism. Exporting revolution no longer is the hallmark of Chinese foreign policy.

1978

16 December: China and the United States establish diplomatic relations. The United States derecognizes the Republic of China (Taiwan).

1979

10 March: The Eastern Naga Revolutionary Council, led by Shangwang Shangyung Khaplang, merges with the Naga National Council.

7 April: The United Liberation Front of Asom, ULFA, is formed at Rang Ghar in Sibsagar.

November–December: Bloody infighting erupts in the Naga Army's base area and cross-border sanctuaries in the Naga Hills of Burma. Scores of Naga rebels are killed. Fifteen NNC leaders are executed by a militant faction led by Isak Chishi Swu and Thuingaleng Muivah.

1980

31 January: The National Socialist Council of Nagaland, NSCN, is set up in the Naga Hills of northwestern Burma. Isak Chishi Swu becomes its chairman, S.S. Khaplang vice-chairman, and Thuingaleng Muivah general secretary. It establishes a base area in the Burmese Naga Hills, from where it launches armed forays into Nagaland and Manipur.

2 February: The newly formed NSCN sets up the 'Government of the People's Republic of Nagaland' with its main base in the Naga Hills of Burma.

8 September: The entire state of Manipur is brought under the Armed Forces (Special Powers) Act.

1981

February: Manipuri rebel leader Temba Singh makes it to Ruili in Yunnan and established contacts with the KIA and the CPB. Most of them return to Manipur in early 1986, equipped with Chinese-made automatic rifles.

1982

November: More than eighty Manipuri rebels from the PLA reach Kachin State, where they receive military training from the KIA.

1983

January–February: Agitation against 'foreigners' begins in Assam. Hundreds of Muslim villagers are killed by rampaging mobs.

1985

15 February: Mizo rebel leader Laldenga meets India's Prime Minister Rajiv Gandhi. Formal peace talks begin.

15 August: An accord is signed between the Indian government and representatives of the Assamese student movement. Hardline elements from the ULFA cross the border into Burma where they receive training in camps controlled by the NSCN.

1986

30 June: An accord is signed between the Mizo National Front and the Government of India, paving the way for statehood for Mizoram.

21 September: Former rebel chief Laldenga is installed as head of the interim government of Mizoram.

1987

20 February: Mizoram become a full-fledged state within the Union of India with Laldenga as chief minister. China protests against the decision to elevate the status of Arunachal Pradesh from a union territory to that of a state on the same day.

October: Anti-Chinese riots rock Lhasa. Demonstrators demand independence for Tibet. Six people are killed and nineteen seriously injured in the most serious outbreak of violence in the Tibetan capital since the suppression of the 1959 revolt.

1988

20 March: The Chin National Front is formed in Burma. A movement is launched to merge Burma's China State with Mizoram and become part of India.

April–May: The Burmese Nagas, led by S.S. Khaplang, break with the Nagas from the Indian side. Dozens of Indian Nagas are killed, and Isak Chishi Swu and Thuingaleng Muivah flee to the border areas opposite Manipur. The National Socialist Council of Nagaland splits into two factions, NSCN (Isak-Muivah; IM) and NSCN (K; Khaplang).

August–September: A massive pro-democracy uprising takes place in Burma. Hundreds of thousands of people march in the capital Rangoon and in cities and towns across the country. Burmese troops fire on the demonstrators, killing thousands. A junta called the State Law and Order Restoration Council, SLORC, takes over on 18 September. In the wake of the crackdown, thousands of pro-democracy activists flee to the Thai border areas, but also Manipur.

6 August: China and Burma sign a border-trade agreement, for the first time opening the area for free trade.

18 November: Two Chin organizations in Burma issue a joint declaration saying that Chin State has joined the Indian Union.

19–23 December: Rajiv Gandhi pays an official visit to China, the first by an Indian Prime Minister in thirty-four years.

1989

March–April: A mutiny breaks out among the hill-tribe rank-and-file of the CPB's rebel army. The Burman top leaders are forced into exile in China, and the former communist army is divided into four regional armies based on ethnic lines, of which the United Wa State Army, UWSA, is the strongest. The CPB mutineers make peace with the Burmese government, and are allowed to retain their weapons and control of their respective areas – and to engage in any kind of business to sustain themselves – in exchange for not fighting government troops. The CPB mutineers immediately increase the production of heroin as well as methamphetamines, which begin to pour across Burma's borders in all directions.

10 December: The Dalai Lama receives the Nobel Peace Prize in Oslo, Norway.

1990

30 April: A.Z. Phizo passes away in London. His daughter Adinno Phizo is sworn in as acting president of the Naga National Council (NNC).

11 May: A grand funeral service is held for A.Z. Phizo in Kohima, attended by thousands of Nagas from all walks of life.

27 May: A general election is held in Burma. The National League for democracy wins a landslide victory but is prevented from forming a new government.

1991

The UNLF in Manipur forms the Manipur People's Army and begins attacking Indian security forces.

All rebels from India's northeast, mainly Assamese and Manipuri, are told to leave KIA-controlled areas in northern Burma.

1992

April: Luingam Luithui, a Tangkhul Naga from Manipur with close links to the NSCN (IM), establishes the Asia Indigenous People's Pact, AIPP, in Bangkok, Thailand. The AIPP is widely suspected of being a cover for the NSCN (IM) and, as such, comes under surveillance by Thailand's security agencies. Thailand is being used increasingly as a base for NSCN (IM) militants, among them Thuingaleng Muivah and Isak Chishi Swu. Later, peace talks between the NSCN (IM) and Indian authorities are held in Chiang Mai. The NSCN (IM)'s main arms procurer, Anthony Shimray, also sets up base in Thailand from where he frequently travels to China.

May: Ethnic clashes break out between ethnic Nagas and ethnic Kukis in Manipur. Hundreds are killed on both sides, but the Kukis suffer the most as NSCN (IM) rebels ransack Kuki villages in Chandel, Tamenglong, Senapati and Churachandpur districts, butchering men, women and children. The killings reach a peak in 1992-1993 and continue until 1996.

5 June: Rebels from the KIA, heavily armed with weapons supplied by elements within India's security services, attack and capture Pangsau on the Indo-Burmese border and the nearby township centre of Namyung. Burmese government soldiers flee across the border to India, but reinforcements arrive from other garrisons in the area. On 15 June, the KIA is forced to withdraw from Pangsau and, on 2 July, government forces recapture Namyung.

1993

24 January: The NSCN (IM) joins the Unrepresented Nations and Peoples Organization, UNPO, a Dutch NGO that brings together separatist movements from all over the world. At about the same time, the NSCN becomes the 'National Socialist Council of Nagalim'. ('Nagalim' refers to a 'greater Nagaland' encompassing the state of Nagaland, most of Manipur, parts of Arunachal Pradesh and Assam, and the Naga Hills of Burma.)

6–8 April: The KIA and the Burmese government agree on a ceasefire on the same terms as the peace deals with the former CPB forces.

November: Detained Burmese pro-democracy leader Aung San Suu Kyi receives the 1993 Jawaharlal Nehru award, which is presented by the Government of India and administered by the Indian Council for Cultural Relations.

1994

21 January: India and Burma sign a border-trade agreement. Official trade begins at Moreh in Manipur, opposite Tamu in Burma.

24 February: The KIA signs a formal peace agreement with the Burmese government.

9–13 May: Gen. Bipin Chandra Joshi visits Burma. It is the first such visit by an Indian army chief.

1995

12 April: A customs station is opened at Moreh, Manipur, to collect revenue on the cross-border trade with Burma.

1997

19 February: Deng Xiaoping dies. A new China combining capitalism and authoritarianism has emerged. Communism remains in name only.

27 July: A ceasefire agreement is agreed upon between the NSCN (IM) and the Government of India. The ceasefire is then extended several times.

2 December: The Awami League government in Bangladesh finalizes a peace deal with Shanti Bahini rebels in the Chittagong Hill Tracts. Chakma and other tribal refugees in camps in Tripura begin to return to Bangladesh.

1998

16 March–27 April: NSCN (IM) leaders Isak Chishi Swu and Thuingaleng Muivah are allowed to attend and address the 54th session of the United Nations Commission of Human Rights in Geneva.

2000

7–8 January: The second-in-command in Burma's military hierarchy, Gen. Maung Aye, travels Shillong in the first such visit to India in years by a high-ranking Burmese army officer.

19 January: NSCN (IM) leader Thuingaleng Muivah, travelling on a South Korean passport, is arrested at Bangkok airport on his way back from a secret visit to Pakistan. He is released on bail, tries to escape to Malaysia on a false Singaporean passport, but is rearrested and interned in Thailand.

13 September: Thuingaleng Muivah is released on bail.

17–24 November: Gen. Maung Aye, pays a week-long visit to India, including New Delhi.

2001

11 May: The Government of India approves the establishment of the Andaman and Nicobar Command as an integrated command encompassing all three services of the Armed Forces.

8 October: The Chairman Chiefs of Staff Committee formally announces the formation of the Andaman and Nicobar Command with its headquarters at Port Blair.

2002

December: Manipuri rebel leader Sana Yaima is arrested in Burma with a large consignment of guns. He is later released after bribes have been paid to the Burmese military.

2003

December: The Bhutanese Army, assisted by the Indian military, launches 'Operation All Clear' and drives out ULFA, the National Democratic Front of Bodoland, NDFB, and the Kamtapur Liberation Organization, KLO, from their sanctuaries in the hills and jungles of southeastern Bhutan.

2004

2 April: A huge consignment of mainly Chinese weapons are seized in Chittagong, Bangladesh. The munitions are destined for Assamese and other insurgents in northeastern India.

2006

6 July: Closed since the 1962 war, the border crossing at Nathu La in Sikkim is opened for trade between India and China. This came after several meetings between Indian and Chinese representatives. On December 1991, India and China signed an initial agreement, the Memorandum on the Resumption of Border Trade, which was followed in July 1992 by the Protocol on Entry and Exit Procedures for Border Trade was signed. On 23 June 2003, India and China signed an additional Memorandum on Expanding Border Trade, which removed the final hurdles for the opening of Nathu La. In April 2003, Indian Defence Minister George Fernandes – otherwise an anti-Chinese hawk – visited China, followed by a return visit to India by Chinese Defence Minister Gen. Cao Gangchuan in March 2004. A thaw in Sino-Indian relations can be seen, but major problems and mutual distrust remain.

2007

November: A mautam famine breaks out in Burma's Chin State. Thousands of Chins flee to India.

2008

11–25 March: Sponsored by the Dutch NGO Kreddha, a group of Naga activists visit Bougainville, an island that attempted to break away from Papua New Guinea but later settled for an autonomy deal. The trip is meant to show the Naga activists an example of a successful peace and reconciliation process.

14 March: Anti-Chinese riots break out in Tibet's capital Lhasa. Scores of people are killed as Chinese security forces crack down on the protests.

November: Gen. Shwe Mann, joint chief of staff of Burma's Armed Forces and number three in the ruling junta, pays a secret visit to North Korea, where he inspects air defence systems and missile factories. Burma and North Korea sign an agreement that mentions joint military training programs, air defence schemes, joint efforts in building tunnels and language training.

2009

March: China signs an agreement with Burma in to build a natural gas pipeline from the coast to Yunnan.

June: China and Burma sign an agreement to build a 771-kilometre long crude oil pipeline from the new deep-water port of Kyaukphyu near Sittwe in Arakan State to Kunming in Yunnan.

June: Rival Naga factions meet for reconciliation talks in the northern Thai city of Chiang Mai. A 'Joint Working Group' is formed.

30 November: ULFA chairman Arabinda *Rajkhowa* and its deputy commander-in-chief Raju Baruah along with eight other Assamese militants are arrested in Bangladesh, now run by an Indian-friendly Awami League-led government. They are extradited to India and produced before the chief judicial magistrate in Kamrup, Assam, on December 5.

4–17 December: A group of eleven Nagas visits South Africa in another arrangement sponsored by Kreddha. The group includes student leaders and other civil society activists. They first visit Johannesburg with the aim of learning more about reconciliation efforts between different warring factions of a resistance movement, in the case of South Africa the Xhosa-dominated African National Congress and the Zulu-based Inkhata Freedom Party. They then visit to Durban, where they address a gathering of the city's ethnic Indian community. At the same time, NSCN (IM)'s chief arms procurer, Anthony Shimray, visits Yunnan and the Laiza headquarters of the KIA near the Chinese border to secure arms shipments through northern Burma to Nagaland. He fails, but is in constant touch with some members of the Naga group in South Africa.

2010

18 May: A suspected Chinese spy is arrested in a remote corner of Arunachal Pradesh. He is subsequently expelled from India.

27 September: NSCN (IM)'s chief arms procurer, Anthony Shimray, is arrested at Kathmandu airport in Nepal and extradited to India.

29 September: Rajkumar Meghen *a.k.a.* Sana Yaima, the leader of the UNLF (Manipur), is arrested in Dhaka and bundled off to India.

7 November: An election is held in Burma. The military controlled Union Solidarity and Development Party, USDP, secures most parliamentary seats. Most outside observers dismiss the election as blatantly rigged.

13 November: Burmese pro-democracy icon Aung San Suu Kyi is released from house arrest in Rangoon.

2011

January: A suspected Chinese spy is apprehended in Nagaland and expelled from India after a visit to the NSCM (IM)'s Hebron Camp near Dimapur.

March 20: Elections are held among Tibetans in exile. A layman born in exile in India, Lobsang Sangay, becomes head of the Tibetan government in exile. The Chinese protest.

March 30: A new government takes over in Burma. It consists mainly of army officers who have donned their uniforms for civilian clothes.

June: Fighting breaks out in northern Burma between the KIA and government troops, effectively ending the ceasefire agreement that had been in place since 1994.

June: The NSCN (K) splits. Burmese Naga leader Khaplang is ousted by India-based commander Khole Konyak who expresses willingness to participate in talks with the Indian government. The two factions are later reunited.

30 September: Burma's new president, Thein Sein, announces that his government has decided to suspend a US$3.6 million joint-venture project with China. The dam would have flooded 600 square kilometers of land, and 90 per cent of the electricity was earmarked for export to China. This move comes as a total surprise to China, and is seen as a first major step by the Burmese government to distance itself from Beijing and forge closer ties with the West, especially the United States.

2 November: Manipuri peace activist Irom Sharmila Chanu has been on a hunger strike for eleven years to demand that the Indian government repeal the Armed Forces (Special Powers) Act, 1958, which she blames for violence in Manipur and other parts of India's northeast.

30 November–2 December: US Secretary of State, Hillary Clinton pays an official visit to Burma. Burma's relations with China are high on her agenda.

12 December: The weekly *Myanmar Times* reports that the Burmese government has reassured China that its recent diplomatic overtures to the United States 'would not affect relations with its traditional ally.' Thure Shwe Mann, the speaker of the Lower House of the Burmese parliament (and a former general) told China's ambassador to Burma, Li Junhua, in Rangoon after China donated computers to Burma's new parliament, that Burma 'is a good neighbor of China. We are also a true friend.'

December: ULFA, now led by Paresh Barua, takes delivery of a large consignment of Thailand-made automatic weapons smuggled through China to north-western Burma.

2012

January–March: Fierce fighting continues between Burmese government forces and the KIA in the northernmost part of the country.

23 February: Thura Shwe Mann pays a visit to China where he meets Chen Bingde, chief of the General Staff of the People's Liberation Army and a member of the Central Military Commission. A Chinese government website quotes Chen as saying: 'No matter how the international situation changes, our faith in consolidating and promoting China-Myanmar [Burma] relations will not change.'

1 April: By-elections are held in Burma. Aung San Suu Kyi's National League for Democracy, NLD, wins in forty-three of the forty-four seats it contested (out of forty-six). The NLD's by-election victory comes at a time when the Burmese government has released hundreds of political prisoners and eased censorship of the media.

9 April: NSCN (K) concludes a ceasefire agreement with the Burmese government.

28 May: Indian prime minister Manmohan Singh pays an official visit to Burma.

19 November: Barack Obama pays an historic visit to Burma, the first ever by a sitting US president.

24 December: The Burmese government launches a major offensive against the KIA. The KIA captures Swedish-made 84mm Carl Gustaf rocket launchers, supplied to the Burmese Army by India in violation of the end-user agreement with Sweden. The rocket launchers were most probably supplied by India to be used against ULFA and PLA (Manipur) bases on the Burmese side of the border, not the KIA.

2013

January: Heavy fighting rages in Kachin State for several weeks. The Burmese government uses Russian-supplied Hind helicopter gunships and Chinese-made attack aircraft against the KIA.

20 May: Burmese president Thein Sein is received in the White House by US president Barack Obama, the first Burmese head of state to visit the United States since September 1966, when Gen. Ne Win met then US president Lyndon Johnson in Washington.

27 May: KIA commander Gen. Gun Maw is greeted by tens of thousands of Kachin civilians as he arrives in the state capital of Myitkyina for peace talks with the government. Both sides agree to de-escalate the fighting, but no ceasefire agreement is reached.

29 August–3 September: A Chinese hospital ship visits Rangoon to provide free medical services to civilians as well as Burmese military personnel, indicating that China is launching a charm offensive to shore up its tattered image in Burma.

8–10 October: Another round of peace talks are held in Myitkyina. The KIA and the Burmese government sign a new agreement aimed at reducing hostilities and laying the groundwork for political dialogue, but fail to reach a permanent ceasefire agreement.

13 October: Vice chairman of China's Central Military Commission Fan Changlong pledges during a meeting with Burma's Commander-in-Chief of the Defence Services Gen. Min Aung Hlaing that 'China will work with Burma to further improve military ties and jointly safeguard border stability.'

MAJOR ARMED NON-STATE ACTORS IN NORTH-EASTERN INDIA, THE CHITTAGONG HILL TRACTS AND NORTHERN BURMA

NAGALAND

NNC (Naga National Council): Formed in 1946, it led the Nagas into open rebellion against the Government of India in the 1950s. In 1956, it established the 'Federal Government of Nagaland' (FGN). Two years later, its main leader at the time, Angami Zapu Phizo, escaped to East Pakistan (now Bangladesh) and continued to Karachi (West Pakistan), Switzerland and the UK. He died in Bromley, Kent, near London, in 1990. During his years in exile, the NNC/FGN continued to fight for Naga independence. It maintained sanctuaries in East Pakistan and was, at least until the mid-1970s, supported militarily by China. A radical faction led by Thuingaleng Muivah broke away in 1980 and formed the NSCN (described next). Following the death of Phizo, the remnants of the NNC/FGN split up into several factions, the main one being led by Phizo's daughter, Adinno Phizo. No longer a viable fighting force, it nevertheless has a following especially among the tribes that led the struggle in the 1950s and 1960s: the Angamis, the Chakhesangs and the Aos.

NSCN (IM) (National Socialist Council of Nagaland [Isak-Muivah]): Formed in 1980 by Thingaleng Muivah (a Tangkhul from Manipur), Isak Chishi Swu (a Sema from Nagaland) and Shangwang Shangyung Khaplang (from the Burmese Naga Hills), it quickly became the main insurgent group among the Nagas and was, thanks to the alliance with Khaplang, able to establish bases on the Burmese side of the border. But, in 1988, the Burmese Nagas rose up in rebellion against the Nagas from the Indian side and drove them out. Hence, there are two groups claiming the same name although the Isak-Muivah faction now uses 'Nagalim' instead of 'Nagaland' (so the name of the organisation now is the 'National Socialist Council of Nagalim'). Its administrative arm is called the GPRN (the Government of the People's Republic of Nagalim.) In 1997, the NSCN (IM) entered into a ceasefire agreement with the Government of India. It now maintains a base near Dimapur called Camp Hebron and can, if necessary, mobilize several thousand fighters and activists. It collects 'taxes' from businesses and individuals in Nagaland as well as Manipur. It has a comparatively large following among the Tangkhuls in Manipur's Ukhrul district, and in pockets of Nagaland. It demands the inclusion of the Naga-inhabited areas of Manipur, south-eastern Arunachal Pradesh, parts of Assam, and north-western Burma into the proposed 'Nagalim' ('Greater Nagaland').

NSCN (K) (National Socialist Council of Nagaland [Khaplang]): It became a separate organization when S.S. Khaplang broke with Isak and Muivah in 1988. It entered into a ceasefire agreement with the Government of India in 2001, but formal peace talks are yet to begin. The NSCN (K) advocate independence for Nagaland and the Naga Hills of Burma, but not necessarily including other Naga-inhabited areas. It may have about 2,000 fighters and activists and maintains bases on the Burmese side of the border. The NSCN (K) also collects 'taxes' from businesses and individuals in Nagaland. Its main following is among Nagas from Burma, the Konyaks of Nagaland's Mon District, with some cadres from the Sema and the Ao, and smaller Naga tribes whose territories straddle the Indo-Burmese border. The NSCN (K), in turn, split in June 2011.

NSCN-U (National Socialist Council of Nagaland – Unification): In November 2007, several NSCN (IM) cadres led by its one-time 'home minister' Azheto Chopey broke away and formed this group, the stated aim of which is to reunite the two NSCN factions. In 2008, at least fourteen of its cadres were killed by the NSCN (IM) near Dimapur. Since then, the group appears to be dormant, but is believed to be loosely allied with the NSCN (K).

MANIPUR

UNLF (United National Liberation Front): Formed in 1964, it is the oldest of Manipur's militant groups. Its leader, Rajkumar Meghen aka Sana Yaima, is a distant descendant of the ancient Manipuri royalty, but also a leftist revolutionary. Once allied with the undivided NSCN, Sana Yaima fell out with Muivah in 1990. The armed strength of UNLF is estimated at 1,500–1,700. It maintains a strong presence in the Imphal Valley and around Moreh on the Burmese border, and Tamu on the opposite side inside Burma. On 29 September 2010, Sana Yaima was arrested in Bangladesh and bundled off to India, where he remains in the custody of the Indian authorities. The UNLF refers to its army as MPA (the Manipur People's Army).

RPF/PLA (Revolutionary People's Front/People's Liberation Army): Formed in 1978 and for many years the main insurgent group among the majority Meiteis of Manipur, its fighters were trained in the 1980s by the Kachin Independence Army, KIA, in northern Burma. In the late 1980s and early 1990s, it also had a presence in Bangladesh. The current president of the RPF is Irengbam Charoen and the strength of the PLA is estimated at 1,500. It is active in the Imphal Valley and other Meitei-inhabited areas. It follows a revolutionary Marxist ideology and, in 2007, entered into an agreement with the Communist Party of India (Maoist). The Maoists recognized Manipur's right to self-determination, while the PLA pledged not to attack 'the Indian proletariat' in Manipur, i.e., labourers who have migrated from the plains in the west to find work in the state.

PREPAK (People's Revolutionary Party of Kangleipak): Formed in 1977, it is also a revolutionary Marxist outfit. Since then, it has split into five or six different factions all demanding an independent Manipur

('Kangleipak') that again regrouped and reunited to being just three groups. The combined strength of these groups is estimated at 600–650 fighters. Some of the factions are reported to have camps in Burma and Bangladesh. In 2008, yet another faction of PREPAK broke away and formed the UPPK (United People's Party of Kangleipak) with an armed wing called KPA (the Kangleipak People's Army).

KCP (Kangleipak Communist Party): Established in the mid-1950s, it traces its origin from the movement of Hijam Irabot Singh, Manipur's first leftist revolutionary who died in 1951. The KCP raised its first armed units in the 1970s, but most of its leaders were arrested during an Indian government offensive in 2009 ('Operation Grand Slam'). At least until then, it had an estimated strength of 350–400 and was active in the Imphal valley and parts of Thoubal district. In 2010, a breakaway KCP faction led by Sapamacha Kangleipal, formed the Maoist Communist Party of Manipur, a militant group that has led a campaign against 'religion-based education' in the state, forcing the closure of several schools run by Roman Catholics.

KYKL (Kanglei Yawol Kanba Lup): Formed in 1994 by Meiteis who in 1989 had broken away from the UNLF, its purported aim is an independent 'Kangleipak' ('Greater Manipur') but, even so, it is reported to maintain links with NSCN(IM), which is active in the Naga-inhabited areas of Manipur (especially the Tangkhul-dominated Ukhrul district, where Muivah was born). It may have an armed strength of 950-1,000 and has camps on the Burmese side of the border, opposite Moreh. It operates mainly in the Imphal Valley, Bishnupur and Thoubal, where it collects 'taxes' from businesses and individuals. It is known for violent campaigns against drug traffickers and even addicts, for imposing certain dress codes on women and for opposing all 'foreign' (i.e. Indian) influences on Meitei culture.

PULF (People's United Liberation Front): A Meitei Pangal (Muslim) group, it was formed in 1993 following communal clashes between Hindu Meiteis and Muslims, which began in Thoubal district and then spread to parts of the Imphal Valley. Its aim is to establish an independent Islamic state in north-eastern India and, to achieve that objective, it has reportedly established alliances with other Islamic groups in the region, among them

MLF, the Muslim Liberation Front, MULFA, the Muslim United Liberation Front of Assam, MULTA, the Muslim United Liberation Tigers of Assam, and ILAA, the Islamic Liberation Army of Assam. It is also suspected to have links with Islamic groups in other parts of India, such as Harkat-ul Mujahideen and Lashkar-e-Taiba. However, its armed strength is limited to between eighty to a hundred men and several of its leaders were either killed or captured during government operations in 2008 and 2009.

Kuki Groups: About a dozen different Kuki militant groups are active in southern and south-eastern Manipur. In 1987, the KNF (Kuki National Front) was formed, demanding a separate homeland for the Kukis on both sides of the Indo-Burmese border, but it soon split into several rival factions. The combined strength of these groups is believed to be 500–600, the main one being the KNO (the Kuki National Organization) led by P. Soyang Haokip. The original KNF also exists as well as various groups calling themselves KNA (the Kuki National Army) and KRA (the Kuki Revolutionary Army). The KNO/KNA's relationship with other Kuki groups is described as hostile. On 29 December 2005, three Kuki rebel groups, KRA, UKLF (the United Kuki Liberation Front) and KNF-S (Kuki National Front-Samuel), merged under the banner of KNC (the Kuki National Council) to fight the KNA.

Other Groups Ethnically Related to the Kuki-Chins: UKRA (United Komrem Revolutionary Army) was formed in 2004 and has no more than forty to fifty armed cadres. Its stated aim is to protect the interests of the Komrem community in Manipur. Similar groups with communal aims exist among the Hmars, such as HNA (the Hmar National Army), HPC (the Hmar People's Convention – various factions) and the ZDV (the Zou Defence Volunteers – several factions).

Naga Groups: Apart from the NSCN (IM), there is also the much smaller MNRF (Manipur Naga Revolutionary Front), formed in 2008 under the leadership of Allen Siro and with the aim of saving 'the territorial integrity' of Manipur; and UNPC (the United Naga People's Council), which was also formed in 2008 and consists of a splinter group from NSCN (IM). Its leader, S.S. Max, is also said to be in favour of 'safeguarding the territorial integrity of Manipur'.

ASSAM

The South Asia Terrorism Portal (http://www.satp.org/satporgtp/countries/india/terroristoutfits/index.html) lists no less than eighteen militant groups operating in Assam. However, of these only the following are of any actual significance:

ULFA (United Liberation Front of Asom [Assam]): Founded on 7 April 1979 and led by Arabinda Rajkhowa (the political wing) and Paresh Barua (military commander-in-chief), it wants Assam to become an independent republic. During its heyday in the 1980s, it had base areas in Upper Assam, and camps in Bhutan, Bangladesh and the Burmese Naga Hills. It was driven out of Bhutan in December 2003 and, in late 2009, most of its leaders – including Rajkhowa – were arrested in Bangladesh and handed over to the Indian authorities. Barua is the only main leader who remains at large. He is said to be based near the Burmese border in China's Yunnan province.

KLO (Kamtapur Liberation Organization): This was set up on 28 December 1995 with the objective of carving out a separate 'Kamtapur' state comprising six districts in northern West Bengal and four in western Assam, which would include the narrow and strategically sensitive 'Siliguri Neck' connecting north-eastern India with the rest of the country. The group is known to have had links with ULFA and other militant groups in the north-east. Its chairman, Tamir Das aka Jibon Singha, was arrested in October 1999 but later released in a bid to persuade the group's cadres to surrender.

NDFB (National Democratic Front of Bodoland): Formed on 3 October 1986 with the objective of securing a 'homeland' for the Bodo plains tribals north of the Brahmaputra River, it shared bases with ULFA in Bhutan until December 2003 and, since May 2005, has a ceasefire agreement with the Indian government. Its present leaders are B. Sungthagra aka Dhiren Boro (president) and Govinda Basumatary (general secretary).

BLTF (Bodo Liberation Tiger Force): Another Bodo group, which was established on 18 June 1996 under the leadership of Prem Singh

Brahma, it entered into a formal ceasefire agreement with the Indian government in March 2000. Hagrama Basumatary is its present 'chairman-cum-commander-in-chief'.

KNV (Karbi National Volunteers): A militant organization among the Karbi tribe in the hills of Karbi Anglong, Assam, it became active in the 1980s and established links with Isak Chishi Swu's and Thuingaleng Muivah's faction of the NSCN. In early 2000, the KNV merged with another Karbi militant group, the Karbi People's Front, KPF, to form a new organization called the United People's Democratic Solidarity, UPDS.

HPC (Hmar People's Convention): It was formed in 1986 as a political party advocating self-government for the Hmars of the northern and north-eastern Mizoram, Manipur's Churachandpur district and the North Cachar Hills of Assam. On 27 July 1994, the HPC reached an agreement with the Indian authorities, which led to the formation of a splinter group, the Hmar People's Convention (Democracy), led by Lalrupui and Laltuolien Hmar. Its is active mainly in the North Cachar Hills.

MEGHALAYA

HNLC (Hynniewtrep National Liberation Council): One of half a dozen small insurgent outfits in Meghalaya, it was set up in 1992 to fight for Meghalaya as a state exclusively for the Khasi tribe and free it from 'domination' by the Garos. Is also wants 'outsiders', i.e., other Indian citizens, to leave the state. It operates in Khasi areas of Meghalaya and has underground cells in the state capital Shillong. Its chairman is Julius K. Dorphang and commander-in-chief Bobby Marwein.

ANVC (Achik National Volunteer Council): It was formed in December 1995 to establish a homeland called 'Achikland" in the areas of Garo Hills of Meghalaya with Dilash R. Marak as chairman and Jerome Momin as commander-in-chief. It is mainly active in extorting money from the local business community. After it entered into a ceasfire agreement with the Indian government in July 2004, a new, more militant outfit called the Garo National Liberation Army, GNLA, was formed. But neither of these groups or other smaller outfits in Meghalaya and the nearby

'Kamtapur' in Assam ever became really powerful. The main task of the Garo and Kampatur 'liberation armies' was to facilitate the movement of ULFA militants and their equipment between their bases in Bhutan and Bangladesh.

PLF-M (People's Liberation Front of Meghalaya): Allied with ANVC and led by Vincent Sangma and Nimush Marak, it is primarily active in Dainadubi and Williamnagar, in East Garo Hills, and Dalu in West Garo Hills. Like other groups in the region, it collects 'revolutionary tax' from local businesses and individuals.

TRIPURA

There are more than two dozen militant outfits in Tripura claiming to represent the state's tribal population or local political interests. The most significant are the Tripura Tribal Volunteer Force, TTVF, the National Liberation Front of Tripura, NLFT, the All Tripura Tiger Force, ATTF, and the Tripura Liberation Organization Front, TLOF. The United Bengali Liberation Front, UBLF, claims to represent the state's Bengali population. Most tribal outfits trace their origin to the former Tripura National Volunteers, TNV. The tribal groups want to deprive all Bengali settlers who entered Tripura after 1956 of their voting rights and restore land to the tribal population. The ultimate aim is to expel all Bengalis who settled in the state after 1956 and their descendants.

NORTHERN BURMA

KIO/KIA (Kachin Independence Organization/Army): It was set up in the Kachin-inhabited areas of north-eastern Shan state on 5 February 1961. Later, it seized control over most of Kachin state and is known to have had links with Naga, Mizo, Manipuri and Assamese rebels from north-eastern India. It made peace with the Burmese government in April 1993 and signed a formal ceasefire agreement on 24 February 1994. Since then, the group has lost most of its former strength which at its peak in the late 1980s, then led by the late Brang Seng, numbered nearly 8,000 well-equipped fighters. In 2010–11, the KIA came under pressure to become a government-commanded Border Guard Force, but refused. In June 2011, the ceasefire agreement with the government collapsed and hostilities broke out once again. Its present chairman is Lanyaw Zawng Hra and the chief of staff of the KIA is Lt Gen. Gam Shawng Gunthang. But the military strongman is Gen. N'Ban La.

KDA (Kachin Democratic Army): Formerly the 4th Brigade of the KIA in north-eastern Shan state, it broke away and entered into a ceasefire agreement with the Burmese government on 11 January 1991. It is led by Mahtu Naw, former commander of the KIA's 4th Brigade. Sometimes, it is erroneously referred to as the Kachin Defence Army.

NDA-K (New Democratic Army-Kachin): This organization is led by Zahkung Ting Ying, a Kachin of Ngochan tribe from the Yunnan frontier who broke with the KIA in 1968 and joined the Communist Party of Burma together with another KIA defector, Zalum. Together, they established the 101 War Zone of the CPB encompassing areas around the mountain passes of Kambaiti, Pangwa and Hpimaw on the Yunnan frontier. Ting Ying and Zalum joined the 1989 CPB mutiny and transformed its 101 War Zone into the NDA-K. On 15 December 1989, it entered into a formal ceasefire agreement with the Burmese government. Unlike most other former rebel armies, the NDA-K agreed in 2011 to become a Border Guard Force commanded by the Burmese army.

CPB (Communist Party of Burma): It was set up in 1939 and went underground shortly after Burma's independence from Britain in 1948. It established base areas in central and northern Burma in the 1950s. The CPB received massive support from China during the decade 1968–78, when it also built up a 20,000 sq. km base area along the Chinese border. In March–April 1989, the hill-tribe rank and file of the CPB's army rose in mutiny against the ageing, predominantly Burman Maoist leadership and drove them into exile in China. The CPB subsequently split up into four different ethnic armies, of which the 20,000-strong United Wa State Army (UWSA) is by far the biggest. The others are the NDA-K, the Myanmar National Democratic Alliance Army in the Kokang area in north-eastern Shan state, and the National Democratic Alliance Army-Eastern Shan State in the east. All four groups entered into ceasefire agreements with the Burmese government in 1989, which enabled them to engage in any kind of business. The UWSA assumed control over the lucrative drug trade – opium, heroin and methamphetamines – in the Burmese sector of the Golden Triangle. It has also been engaged in smuggling Chinese-made weapons to India's north-east as well as assault rifles manufactured in its own gun factories. The UWSA maintains close links with China's security services, as do the three other former CPB forces.

CHITTAGONG HILL TRACTS OF BANGLADESH

The ethnic conflict in the Chittagong Hill Tracts of Bangladesh, CHT, where local tribals fought the government's army and Bengali settlers for decades, officially ended when a peace accord was signed on 2 December 1997, recognizing the special status of the hill peoples. In 1973, Manabendra Narayan Larma founded the Parbatya Chattagram Jana Shanghati Samiti (PCJSS) as a political organization, and its armed wing was known as the Shanti Bahini. While East Pakistan and later Bangladesh gave shelter to insurgents from India's north-east, India's security services maintained close links with the Shanti Bahini, which had a presence in the state of Tripura. The 1997 accord has established peace in the CHT – at least temporarily. If the issue of autonomy for the tribals is not resolved, it is likely that hostilities may break out again.

REBEL MISSIONS TO CHINA

NAGAS

1. The first Naga mission to China left Nagaland on 24 October 1966 and, after trekking through Sagaing division and Kachin state in northern Burma, they reached the Chinese frontier on 27 January 1967. The political leader of the 132-strong group was Thuingaleng Muivah, and the military commander General Thinoselie M. Keyho. Thinoselie left China in November 1967 and reached Nagaland two months later. Muivah remained in Beijing as the unofficial representative of the Naga National Council (NNC) and its 'Federal Government of Nagaland' until November 1970. He returned to Nagaland in December 1971 after spending a year in Kachin state. The Naga soldiers received military and political training at Tengchong, and returned with modern Chinese-made assault rifles, machine guns and rocket launchers.

2. Isak Chishi Swu of the NNC's political leadership and General Mowu Gwizan from the Naga Army led the second Naga mission to China. They left along with 330 men in December 1967 and reached China in March 1968. They also received training and equipment at Tengchong.

3. Ngasating Shimray and Lt Col. Taka with 100 men left Nagaland in January 1968 and reached the headquarters of the 6th Battalion of the Kachin Independence Army (KIA) in western Kachin state in February.

The KIA refused to let them proceed; the Nagas were disarmed by the Kachins and sent back to Nagaland.

4. Major Vesai and Jonathan led a 275-man contingent (which also included Lieutenant General Dusoi, a prominent Naga rebel leader) that left for China in February 1968. On their way through northern Sagaing division in Burma, they were ambushed by the Burmese army. Many Naga rebels from India were also killed by hostile Burmese Nagas (eastern Konyaks). The survivors, seventy-six men including Dusoi, were captured by Burmese government troops on 18 June 1968.

5. S. Angam and Brigadier Koshang left in March 1968 with 150 men. They were ambushed by the Burmese army while attempting to cross the Chindwin River in northern Sagaing division. Angam and three of his men were captured alive; the rest retreated to Nagaland.

6. General Thungti and 200 of his men left later in 1968. They reached Chindwin, but had to return since the Kachins beyond the river were unwilling to escort them any further.

7. Lieutenant General Thinoselie M. Keyho, who had returned to Nagaland in January 1968, went to China by air from East Pakistan (now Bangladesh) in 1969. He was accompanied by Brigadier Neidelie. In Beijing they met Muivah before returning to Dhaka in November 1970. East Pakistan remained a major foreign base for the Nagas until the creation of Bangladesh in 1971.

8. Major Vedayi Moire left with fifty-eight men in December 1971 to receive Muivah who was on his way from China. They missed him, however, and Moire and his men continued to China. They returned to Nagaland in 1973.

9. Muivah left for a second mission to China in September 1974, escorted by 130 men. Isak Chishi Swu and 146 Naga rebels followed on 15 December. Only eleven men from Isak's group made it to China. They reached Tengchong in Yunnan on 14 August 1975, and stayed there until November 1975. They were back in Nagaland in February 1976. This was the last contingent of Nagas that received free arms and ammunition from the Chinese.

10. 'The Lhasa 27' became the nickname for a group of young Nagas who reached Lhasa via Nepal in September 1976. They remained in Tibet until March–April 1977, when they started to trickle back into India. Several of them were apprehended by the Indian police on their way back. Although they did attend some political seminars in Lhasa, they were given no support or military training.

11. Muivah and 200 of his men left for China a third time in October 1976. They reached China in March 1977. Colonel Ashiho with 100 men caught up with them at the general headquarters of the KIA near the Yunnan frontier. This was Muivah's last mission to China, and although he was allowed to stay in China for almost a year, he was told that no more aid would be forthcoming from the Chinese. He left China in November and reached Nagaland in February 1978. The Naga rebel movement split shortly afterwards.

12. Colonel Abam Shimray and S. Angam left in September 1977 as leaders of a 140-man contingent (mostly Tangkhul Nagas from Manipur), but they were turned back at the 2nd Brigade headquarters of the KIA. Abam Shimray died in Kachin state. Ten stragglers, including Angam, remained at the 2nd Brigade headquarters until Muivah arrived there from China in December 1977. Angam, Muivah and all the other Nagas returned to Nagaland in January 1978.

13. Shortly after the formation of the National Socialist Council of Nagaland (NSCN) on 31 January 1980, Muivah decided to send a new delegation to China. They left in June 1980 and the delegation was led by Isak Chisi Swu and included Angam and Khui Khip, a Naga from the Burmese side. The entire delegation was refused entry to China; they returned to Nagaland in December 1981.

14. NSCN officer Haw, one of Muivah's closest associates, left with ten to fifteen troops in September 1982 and reached KIA general headquarters (GHQ) in March 1983. They were not allowed to proceed to China although the Kachins introduced them to a Chinese liaison officer on the border. The Nagas had blamed the Kachins for preventing them from proceeding to China and the Kachins, in turn, wanted the Chinese officer

to explain to the Nagas that it was Chinese policy not to accept any more Nagas in China. However, Haw delivered a letter to the Chinese requesting support; the letter was signed by the NSCN, the ULFA (Assam) and the UNLF (Manipur). The Chinese returned the envelope unopened.

15. Small groups of NNC members also reached Kachin GHQ during 1983, including one delegation led by Tubu Kevichusa. He stayed at the Kachin headquarters from July to November 1983, but was unable to make contact with the Chinese. Tubu returned to Nagland, where he was killed by the NSCN (IM) on 4 June 1996.

16. Muivah made his last attempt to reach China via northern Burma in 1986–87. He reached the Kachin headquarters, but had to retreat when it was attacked by Burmese government troops in May 1987. He then returned to Nagaland.

17. In the 1990s, the NSCN (IM), using the cover of NGOs purportedly working for the rights of indigenous people, established a presence in the Thai capital Bangkok as well as in the northern city of Chiang Mai. The NSCN (IM)'s chief arms procurer, Anthony Shimray, was based in Thailand until he flew to Nepal in October 2010, where he was arrested at Kathmandu airport and extradited to India. While based in Thailand, Shimray and other Naga militants were frequent visitors to China (by air from Bangkok or Chiang Mai). An unofficial 'office' was also established in China's Yunnan province to coordinate their arms procurement activities. Following his arrest, Shimray reportedly told the National Investigation Agency (NIA) that he paid an advance of several hundred thousand US dollars in 2009 to a Bangkok-based company to procure rocket launchers, grenades, assault rifles and ammunition for the Naga and other insurgent groups in Assam and Manipur from a weapons supplier in China.

MIZOS

Inspired by the Nagas, the Mizo National Front (MNF) also began to send groups of soldiers and political cadres to China in the early 1970s. Damkhosiaka and thirty-eight of his men left Mizoram in 1972 and reached China early the following year. They received military training in

China at Kotong post opposite Panwa Pass, on the Yunnan frontier with Burma's Kachin state. A second delegation left its hideout in Burma's Arakan state (opposite Mizoram) in November 1974, returned to Mizoram to collect more recruits, and then set off for China on 20 January 1975. They trekked through northern Burma for seven months, reaching China in August. The leader of the group was a Mizo commander called Biakvela, and his 108 soldiers received military training in Meng Hai, Xishuangbanna (Sipsongpanna), in southern Yunnan. They left China on 4 January 1976 and returned via Kachin state to Mizoram. The MNF overlord, Laldenga, his foreign secretary, Lalhmingthanga, and a few others also visited China, including Beijing, but they went by air from East Pakistan (now Bangladesh) and did not trek through the Burmese jungles.

MANIPURIS

1. In April 1976, sixteen, some claim eighteen, Manipuri militants went to Tibet via Nepal. They received political training, and some military instruction, in Lhasa. They returned to Manipur in 1979, where they became known as *ojas* (master or teacher in the Meitei language). The People's Liberation Army, PLA, of Manipur was formed, and later the 'army' also set up a political wing, the Revolutionary People's Front, RPF. On their return, they launched a number of attacks in the Imphal Valley, but the Indian authorities managed to capture several of the ojas, including their overall leader, Bisheswar Singh. The acting chairman of the RPF, Soibam Temba Singh, left for Kachin state in 1983. The Kachins promised him training and equipment; so he returned to Manipur to collect his followers. Subsequently, eighty-seven PLA activists received training by the KIA in Kachin state. The KIA agreed to arm them as well, but when they were about to leave for Manipur, a split occurred. Temba was ousted and remained at Kachin headquarters at Pa Jau, near the Yunnan frontier. In the end, only fifty-one PLA soldiers, led by a commander whose *nom de guerre* was Dina, returned to Manipur. Another fifty RPF/PLA cadres arrived in the Kachin area in July 1986, led by Manikanta (aka Laiba). About a dozen of them defected to the Communist Party of Burma, CPB, in late 1986. All Manipuri insurgents undergoing training by the KIA were

told to leave its area in 1991. The majority went back to Manipur, while some remained behind at Panwa Pass in Ting Ying's former CPB area in Kachin state. A group of former Manipuri militants, including some of those who defected to the CPB in 1986, have settled in Tengchong, Yunnan. Some sources have suggested that RPF/PLA cadres have been used for intelligence purposes by the Chinese, through the KIA until 1991, and, perhaps more importantly, through the former CPB.

2. The United National Liberation Front, UNLF, another Manipuri rebel group, sent their chairman, Rajkumar Meghen aka Sana Yaima, to Kachin state in 1985, to unite with the RPF/PLA. That failed, however, and he returned to Manipur in early 1986. Both the RPF/PLA and the UNLF tried to contact the Chinese authorities in Yunnan, but were unsuccessful. However, the UNLF has managed to buy Chinese-made weapons through intermediaries in northern Burma. The identities of those remain obscure, but they are believed to be weapons dealers connected with the United Wa State Army, UWSA.

ASSAMESE

The United Liberation Front of Asom, ULFA, sent delegations to Kachin state in 1986 and 1987. For more than a year, its chairman, Arabindra Rajkhowa, remained at the Pa Jau headquarters of the Kachin Independence Organization, KIO, where 300 of his men received military training from its military wing, the Kachin Independence Army, KIA. China's attitude is uncertain; some reports suggest that they were discreetly debriefed by Chinese intermediaries about the situation in India's north-east. But there is little evidence to support the suggestion that the Chinese gave them any direct assistance. However, the ULFA (like the UNLF, the NSCN and the RPF before them) tried to buy arms from the black market in Yunnan, which, in the beginning, was only partly successful; at the time, most ULFA weapons were obtained from Pakistan (the Afghan border) and through contacts in Bangladesh. All ULFA activists were ordered out of the KIA-held areas in Kachin state in 1991. However, the massive April 2004 arms haul in Chittagong was arranged through Chinese contacts in Yunnan, and then shipped out from Hong Kong to Bangladesh. While emissaries from the NSCN (IM) travel to Yunnan frequently from Thailand, ULFA's military commander, Paresh Barua, and his men opened an unofficial 'office' in the Chinese frontier town of Ruili in the early 1990s. They maintained a presence there until 2007 and managed to buy weapons from Chinese dealers as well as former rebel groups that had made peace with the Burmese government, mainly the UWSA, the main component of the former CPB. Barua reportedly spends most of his time in China, from where he travels to the Philippines, Thailand and other countries in the region, mostly using his Bangladeshi passport.

NAXALITES

China's interest in India's Maoist movement was potentially even more dangerous for India's security than support for the ethnic insurgents in the north-east. In September 1967, a few months after a peasant rebellion in Naxalbari in northern West Bengal, a group of twelve Indian Maoists travelled overland through Nepal and Tibet to China where they received military and political training. Among them were several militants who had taken part in the Naxalbari uprising: Sourin Bose, Kanu Sanyal, Jangal Santhal, Dipak Biswas, Kadam Mallik, Khodan Mallik and Keshab Sarkar. While in China, they met Chairman Mao Zedong and the powerful intelligence chief Keng Sheng.

On 9 April 1970, Radio Beijing announced, 'at present, the flames of the peasants' armed struggle have spread to West Bengal, Bihar, Uttar Pradesh, Punjab, Himachal, Orissa, Assam and Tripura, and particularly Andhra Pradesh.' Later that year, the Communist Party of India (Marxist-Leninist), CPI (ML), sent Sourin Bose to Beijing, where he held talks with Zhou Enlai and Kang Sheng on 29 October. Kang Sheng reportedly told Bose that the Communist Party of China could not understand the real meaning of the Naxalite concept of 'annihilation', which he likened to the methods used in China by 'left adventurists' after the communist defeat in Shanghai in 1927.

The Indian Maoists were, however, praised in an issue of the *Beijing Review* (No. 1, 1970), which stated that Charu Mazumdar held 'correct views' and added, 'guerrilla warfare is the only way to mobilise and apply the whole strength of the people against the enemy.' The Chinese also suggested that the CPI (ML) should form a regular armed force. But little of that materialized, and the Chinese appear to have lost interest in the Naxalites when factionalism tore their tiny groups apart, and it became obvious that they were not a viable force in Indian politics.

Chinese interest in the CPI (ML) vanished altogether with Deng Xiaoping's return to power in the late 1970s. There is little evidence to suggest that the neo-Naxalites in the Communist Party of India (Maoist) have managed to get any weapons from China other than what they may have managed to procure indirectly from militants in Manipur and Assam.

THE CHITTAGONG ARMS HAUL

The arms haul at Chittagong port on 2 April 2004 was the biggest seizure of illicit arms in Bangladesh's history. The consignment of new Chinese munitions was shipped from Hong Kong, then on to Singapore where more weapons, not Chinese-made, were added. The ship then continued to Sittwe on Burma's Arakan coast of the Bay of Bengal, where the load was transferred to two smaller fishing trawlers, the *Kazaddan* and the *Amanat*, which ferried the weaponry to a jetty on the Karnapuli River, Chittagong. The shipment was destined for two insurgent movements from India's north-east – the United Liberation front of Assam and the Isak-Muivah faction of the National Socialist Council of Nagalim. The shipment was worth an estimated US$4.5–7 million.

The following is a list of the seized arms and ammunition:

1. T-56-1 7.62 mm assault rifles (with underfolding metal buttstock) (Chinese manufactured): **x** 690 in sixty-nine separate crates.
2. Magazines for the above weapons (four for each rifle: 2,760.)
3. Thirty-two separate magazines for the above rifle type in a separate crate.
4. T-56-2 7.62 mm assault rifle (side-folding butt-stock) (Chinese manufactured) **x** 600 in sixty crates.
5. Magazines for the above rifles (four for each rifle: 2, 400.)
6. Uzi 9 mm sub-machine gun **x** 400 (unclear where manufactured) in forty crates.

7. Eight hundred magazines for the above SMGs – two for each weapon.

8. T-85 7.62 mm sub-machine guns with integral silencers **X** 100 (Chinese manufactured) in ten crates.

9. Four hundred magazines for the above SMGs – four for each weapon.

10. T-69 40 mm rocket-propelled grenade launchers (Chinese manufactured) **X** 150 in thirty crates.

11. Rocket-propelled grenade tubes for above launchers **X** 2,000 (in forty crates.)

12. Optical sights for T-69 RPG launchers **X** 150 (in eight crates).

13. Ammunition in 688 crates [including 739,680 rounds of 7.62 **X** 39 mm ammunition in 512 crates (for T-56 assault rifles); and 400,000 rounds of 7.62 **X** 25 mm ammunition (for T-85 SMGs) in 176 crates: total 1, 139,680 rounds.]

14. T-82-2 hand grenades (Chinese manufactured) **X** 25,020 in 417 crates (sixty units per crate.)

15. RPG warheads **X** 840 in 210 crates.

16. Walkie-talkie communication sets **X** 2.

Source: *Jane's Intelligence Review*
1 May 2004 and 1 August 2004

NOTES

INTRODUCTION

1. Thuingaleng Muivah told me the story about his first trek to China during several interviews in October and November 1985 at the headquarters of the then undivided National Socialist Council of Nagaland (NSCN) at Kesan Chanlam, the Naga Hills of Burma. I also interviewed Thinoselie M. Keyho at Kohima on 18 October 1985 and 24 December 2009.
2. Interview with Mowu Gwizan, Kohima, 18 October 1985.
3. For a complete list of Naga 'missions' to China, see Appendix 3.
4. Amar Jasbir Singh, 'The Tibetan Problem and China's Foreign Relations', in Surjit Mansingh (ed.), *Indian and Chinese Foreign Policies in Comparative Perspective*. Delhi: Radiant Publishers, 1998, p. 266.
5. Quoted in P.C. Chakravarti, *India-China Relations*. Calcutta: Firma K.L. Mukhopadhyay, 1961, p. 53.
6. Ibid., p. 54.
7. Quoted in Yuliya Babayeva, 'The Khampa Uprising: Tibetan Resistance Against the Chinese Invasion', Honours College Theses, Paper 31, Pforzheimer Honours College, 8 January 2006. p. 15 http://digitalcommons.pace.edu/honorscollege_theses/31
8. For an account of the CIA's secret war in 'the Golden Triangle', see Bertil Lintner, *Burma in Revolt: Opium and Insurgency Since 1948*, Chiang Mai: Silkworm Books, 2000, pp. 125–62. The initial role of the US consulate in Chiang Mai as an intelligence posting has been confirmed to me by retired US government officials.

9. Carole McGranaham, *Arrested Histories: Tibet, the CIA, and Memories of a Forgotten War*, Durham and London: Duke University Press, 2010, p. 93.

10. Mikel Dunham, *Buddha's Warriors: The Story of the CIA-Backed Tibetan Freedom Fighters, the Chinese Invasion, and the Ultimate Fall of Tibet*, New York: Jeremy P. Tarcher/Penguin, 2004, p. 224.

11. For a complete list of weapons seized in Chittagong on 2 April 2004, see Appendix 4.

12. *The People's Daily Online*, 17 December 2010, at http://english.peopledaily.com.cn/90001/90776/90883/7233524.html

13. *Working People's Daily* (Rangoon), 1 October 1989.

14. *Indian Express*, 6 May 1998. See also http://cns.miis.edu/archive/country_india/china/nsacris.htm

15. Andrew Selth, 'Chinese Military Bases in Burma: The Explosion of a Myth'. The Griffith Asia Institute, Regional Outlook Paper No. 10, 2007, p. 16. Can be downloaded at www.griffith.edu.au/data/assets/pdf-file/0018/18225/regional-outlook-andrew-selth.pdf

1. WAR AND SPOOKERY IN THE HIMALAYAS

1. Brig. J.P. Dalvi, *Himalayan Blunder: The Curtain-raiser to the Sino-Indian War of 1962*, Dehra Dun: Natraj Publishers, 1969, p. 166. Kenneth Conboy and James Morrison quotes from Dalvi's book in their *The CIA's Secret War in Tibet*, Lawrence, Kansas: University Press of Kansas, 2002, p. 168.

2. Dalvi, op. cit., pp. 167–68.

3. Ibid., p. 170.

4. See http://www.dhapa.com/chinese-seek-china-india-1962-war-memorial/ Dhapa is a community blog for the Chinese in Kolkata.

5. Utpal Borpujari, 'Chowdhury hopes her work will garner support for the hapless Assamese-Chinese community,' *The Times of India*, 29 November 2010, available at http://indianchinese.blogspot.com/

6. George N. Patterson, *Peking Versus Delhi*. London, Faber and Faber, 1963, p. 95.

7. *Concerning the Question of Tibet*, Beijing: Foreign Language Press, 1959, quotes from pp. 187–202.

8. Ibid., p. 256.

9. Stuart and Roma Gelder, *The Timely Rain: Travels in New Tibet*, London: Monthly Review Press, 1964.

10. Anna Louise Strong, *When Serfs Stood Up in Tibet*, Beijing: Foreign Languages Press, 2003 (first published by New World Press, Beijing, 1960).

11. Israel Epstein, *Tibet Transformed*, Beijing: New World Press, 1983.

12. Han Suyin, *Lhasa, the Open City: A Journey to Tibet*, New York: G.P. Putman's Sons, 1977.

13. Ratne Deshapriya Senanayake, *Inside Story of Tibet*, Colombo: The Afro-Asian Writers' Bureau, 1967, pp. ii–iii.

14. *The Sino-Indian Boundary Question*, Beijing: Foreign Languages Press, 1962, p. 39.

15. For the full text of the 1914 Shimla Accord, see http://en.wikisource.org/wiki/Simla_Accord_%281914%29

16. *The Sino-Indian Boundary Question*, pp. 10–11.

17. Ibid., p. 11.

18. For an overview of all these proposals, see http://www.fnsr.org/Backgrounders/back_india1.htm

19. Tsepon W.D. Shakabpa, *Tibet: A Political History*, New Delhi: Paljor Publications, 2010 (first published by Yale University Press, New Haven, 1967), pp. 337–40. The declaration is available online at http://www.tibetjustice.org/materials/tibet/tibet1.html

20. Alex McKay (ed.), *The History of Tibet: The Modern Period: 1895, The Encounter with Modernity*, London: Routledge Curzon, 2003, p. 269.

21. Quoted in Patrick French's excellent biography of Francis Yonghusband, *Younghusband: The Last Imperial Adventurer*, London: Penguin Books, 2011, p. 220.

22. Ibid., p. 226.

23. For another vivid account of Francis Yonghusband's 'expedition' to Lhasa, see Peter Hopkirk, *Trespassers on the Roof of the World: The Race for Lhasa*, Oxford: Oxford University Press, 1982, pp. 159–83.

24. French, op. cit., p. xx.

25. See http://www.lostintibet.com/britishmission.html

26. Melvyn Goldtsein, *A History of Modern Tibet: 1913-1951*. New Delhi: Munshiram Manoharlal Publishers, 2007 (first published by University of California Press, 1989), pp. 391–92.

27. Quoted in http://en.wikipedia.org/wiki/Tibetan_sovereignty_ debate

28. Quoted in Goldstein, op. cit., p. 607.

29. The full text of the seventeen-point agreement is available at http:/ /www.friends-of-tibet.org.nz/17-point-agreement.html Ngapoi Ngawang Jigme, who passed away in Beijing in 2009 at the age of ninety-nine, became the first president of the newly established Tibet Autonomous Region in 1964. In an interview with *Asiaweek* (20 October 2000), he predicted that 'nothing will change' when the present Dalai Lama dies. 'Without a Dalai Lama for 40 years, we've done quite well.' Many Tibetan exiles condemned Jigme as a traitor and collaborator, see http://www.tibetinfonet.net/content/update/ 152. His name is often spelt Ngapo Ngawang Jigme in English texts.

30. *Concerning the Question of Tibet*, pp. 17–18.

31. For a detailed account of the two Sikkimese princesses and their CIA contacts, see Conboy and Morrison, op. cit. pp. 21–23.

32. Ibid., p. 23.

33. Ibid., p. 35.

34. Ibid., pp. 91–92.

35. Melinda Liu, 'When Heaven Shed Blood', *Newsweek*, 19 April 1999.

36. Conboy and Morrison, op. cit., p. 61.

37. Ibid., p. 103.

38. *Newsweek*, 19 April 1999.

39. John Kenneth Knaus, *Orphans of the Cold War: America and the Tibetan Struggle for Survival*, New York: Public Affairs, 1999, p. 325.

40. Richard Ehrlich, 'Death of a dirty fighter', *Asia Times Online*, 8 July 2003, at http://www.atimes.com/atimes/Southeast_Asia/ EG08Ae02.html

41. Tsering Shakya, *The Dragon in the Land of Snows: A History of Modern Tibet Since 1947*, London: Pimlico, 1999, p. 359.

42. Carole McGranahan, 'Truth, Fear, and Lies: Exile Politics and Arrested Histories of the Tibetan Resistance', *Cultural Anthropology*, 20/4, 2005, p. 593, available at www.colorado.edu/Anthropology/ people/bios/documents/TruthFearandLiesPDF.pdf

43. This account of the 'Raid into Tibet' is based on an interview with Adrian Cowell, Bangkok, 5 July 2011.

44. Interview with Lhasang Tsering, McLeodganj, 20 April 2011.

45. Bernardo Cervellera, 'Beijing wants to destroy the Dalai Lama but without him there will be no peace in Tibet', *AsiaNews.it*, 10 March 2009, at http://www.asianews.it/news-en/Beijing-wants-to-destroy-the-Dalai-Lama-but-without-him-there-will-be-no-peace-in-Tibet-14683.html

46. Tomas Laird, *Into Tibet: The CIA's First Atomic Spy and His Secret Expedition to Lhasa*, New York: Grove Press, 2002.

47. Ibid., p. 240.

48. The remarkable story about this expedition is told by Sydney Wignall himself in his book *Spy on the Roof of the World: A True Story of Espionage and Survival in the Himalayas*, New York: Lyons & Burford Publishers, 1996.

49. There is a good account of the mission in Vinod K. Jose's cover story for *The Caravan*, December 2010: 'Spies in the Snow: How the CIA and Indian Intelligence Lost a Nuclear Device in the Himalayas'. There is also an excellent and more detailed account of the attempt to place a nuclear-powered detection device on Nanda Devi in M.S. Kohli and Kenneth Conboy, *Spies in the Himalayas: Secret Missions & Perilous Climbs*, Lawrence, Kansas: University Press of Kansas, 2002.

50. *The Caravan*, December 2010, p. 35.

51. Ibid., p. 32.

52. Thongchai Winichakul, *Siam Mapped: A History of the Geo-Body of a Nation*, Chiang Mai: Silkworm Books, 1994, p. 77.

53. Dr N.N. Osik, *Modern History of Arunachal Pradesh (1825-1997)*, Itanagar and New Delhi: Himalayan Publishers, 1999, p. 2.

54. Neville Maxwell, *India's China War*, London: Penguin Books, 1970; and Dehra Dun: Natraj Publishers (reprint), 2010. Alistair Lamb wrote several books about the Sino-Indian border. One of the most detailed of these is *The McMahon Line: A Study in Relations between India, China and Tibet, 1904 to 1914* (two volumes), London: Routledge and Kegan Paul, 1966.

55. Neville Maxwell, *India and the Nagas*, London: Minority Rights Group Report No. 17, 1973.

56. Quoted in Ramachandra Guha, 'Verdicts on India', *The Hindu*, 17 July 2005, at http://www.hindu.com/mag/2005/07/17/stories/2005071700140300.htm

57. For instance, 'Postal map of China 1917', in *The Chinese Threat*, New Delhi: Publications Division, Ministry of Information and Broadcasting, Government of India, 1963.

58. Verrier Elwin, *The Tribal World of Verrier Elwin*, New York and Bombay: Oxford University Press, 1964, p. 240.

59. Verrier Elwin, *A Philosophy for NEFA*, Delhi: Isha Books, 2009 (reprint). Nehru's foreword outlined his five principles of tribal administration, which sought to combine respect for local culture with the need to establish a functioning administration.

60. Nari Rustomji, *Imperilled Frontiers: India's North-Eastern Borderlands*, Delhi: Oxford University Press, 1983, p. 97.

61. Ibid., p. 107.

62. Press Trust of India, 'China "strongly" protests PM's visit to Arunachal Pradesh', 13 October 2009, at http://www.hindustantimes.com/ China-strongly-protests-PM-s-visit-to-Arunachal-Pradesh/Article1-464632.aspx

63. Indo-Asian News Service, Itanagar, 'Arunachal MPs furious, slam China for protesting PM's visit', 13 October 2009.

2. THE NAGAS: CHALLENGING THE IDEA OF INDIA

1. This account of Muivah's first trip to China and his stay there is based on my extensive interviews with him at Kesan Chanlam, the Burmese Naga Hills, during 5–9 and 21 November 1985.

2. Interview with Muivah, Kesan Chanlam, 5 November 1985.

3. Interview with Muivah, Kesan Chanlam, 21 Novmeber 1985.

4. Interviews with Thinoselie M. Keyho, Kohima, 18 October 1985 and 24 December 2009.

5. Interviews with Thinoselie, Kohima, 24 December 2009 and Muivah, Kesan Chanlam, November 1985.

6. Interview with Isak Chishi Swu, Kesan Chanlam, 11 November 1985, and Mowu Gwizan, Kohima, 18 October 1985.

7. Nirmal Nibedon, *Nagaland: The Night of the Guerrillas*, New Delhi: Lancers Publishers, 1983, p. 212.

8. Interview with Muivah, 21 November 1985.

9. Interview with Thinoselie, Kohima 24 December 2009. Muivah

also told me about the same journey from Beijing to Dhaka when I interviewed him at Kesan Chanlam in October–November 1985.

10. 'Manifesto of the National Socialist Council of Nagaland', 31 January 1980 (printed by the NSCN). The manifesto is also reproduced in Luingam Luithui and Nandita Haksar, *Nagaland File: A Question of Human Rights*, New Delhi: Lancer International, 1984, pp. 111–38.

11. Interview with Thuingaleng Muivah in *Tehelka*, 9 February 2011. Available at http://www.tehelka.com/story_main48.asp?filename=Ws100211Muivah2.asp

12. Verrier Elwin, *Nagaland*, Shillong: Adviser's Secretariat, 1961, p. 22, quoted in Puthuvail Thomas Philip, *The Growth of Baptist Churches in Nagaland*, Guwahati: Christian Literature Centre, 1983, p. 14. Also quoted in verbatim in S.K. Sharma and Usha Sharma, *Discovery of Northeast India, Vol. 9, Nagaland*, New Delhi: Mittal Publications, 2005, p. 143.

13. Visier Sanyu, *A History of Nagas and Nagaland*, New Delhi: Commonwealth Publishers, 1996, pp. 15–17.

14. Ibid., p. 21.

15. M. Alemchiba, *A Brief Historical Account of Nagaland*, Kohima: Naga Institute of Culture, 1970, p. 30. See also Jogesh Das, *Folklore of Assam*, New Delhi: National Book Trust, 1972, p. 8, and http://taiahominternational.org/

16. L.W. Shakespear, *History of Upper Assam, Upper Burmah and North-Eastern Frontier*, London: McMillan & Co, 1914, pp. 198–99.

17. Asoso Yonuo, *The Rising Nagas*, Delhi: Manas Publications, 1984, p. 25.

18. Mashangthei Horam, *Naga Polity*, Delhi: Low Price Publications, 1992, p. 112,

19. This description of the ordination of America's first missionaries comes from Courtney Anderson, *To The Golden Shore: The Life of Adoniram Judson*, Boston: Little, Brown and Company, 1956, pp. 106–14. See also Bertil Lintner, 'Praise the Lord and pass the ammunition', *Far Eastern Economic Review*, 21 January 1988.

20. P.T. Philip, op. cit., pp. 47–48. 'Tai' is what these people call themselves; in Burma they are referred to as 'Shan' which is actually a corruption of 'Syam' or 'Siam'.

21. Cited by Verrier Elwin (ed.) in *The Nagas in the Nineteenth Century*, Bombay: Oxford University Press, 1969, pp. 114.

22. For the growth of the Church in Nagaland, see P.T. Philip, op. cit, and Dr Joseph Puthenpurakal, *Baptist Missions in Nagaland*, Shillong: Vendrame Missiological Institute, 1984.

23. Verrier Elwin, *Nagaland*, Guwahati and Delhi: Spectrum Publications, 1997 (reprint), p. 4. For the origin of the word 'Naga' see also P.T. Philip, op. cit., pp. 4–5, and Yonuo, op. cit., pp. 41–42, and M. Horam, op. cit., pp. 21–23.

24. Elwin, *Nagaland*, p. 26

25. Ibid., p. 44

26. Yonuo, op. cit., p. 133.

27. Elwin, *Nagaland*, p. 36. He continues: 'Instead of "backward tracts" . . . the commission proposed the establishment of "excluded areas", of which there were two categories: Excluded and Partially Excluded. The principle of their selection was partly "backwardness" but, even more, administrative convenience. There was a general feeling that that all tribal people needed some kind of protection but, as many of them lived mixed up and in close contact with other populations, this would not be practicable. But where there was an enclave or a definite tract of country inhabited by a compact tribal population it was classified as an Excluded Area. Where the tribal population was less homogeneous, but still undeveloped and substantial in number it was classified as Partially Excluded . . . the administration of the Excluded Areas was vested in the Governors acting in their discretion and that of the Partially Excluded Areas in the control of the Ministers subject, however, to the Governor exercising his individual judgment.'

28. See Sir Ribert Reid, 'The Excluded Areas of Assam', *The Geographical Journal*, Vol. 103, No. 1/2, January–February 1944.

29. See Christoph von Fürer-Haimendorf, *The Naked Nagas*, Calcutta: Thacker Spink & Co, Private Ltd, 1933 (reprint 1968). He later wrote *Return to the Naked Nagas: An Anthropologist's View of Nagaland 1936-1970*, London: John Murray, 1976.

30. P.T. Philip, op. cit., p. 62.

31. Quoted in Yonuo, op. cit., p. 120 and originally appeared in 'The Aboriginals', *Oxford Pamphlets on Indian Affairs*, Bombay, 1944, p. 14.

32. Narola Rivenburg, 'The Star of Naga Hills', Unpublished private circulation, Chicago, 1941, p. 82, quoted in P.T. Philip, op. cit., pp. 62–63.

33. See Yonuo, op. cit., pp. 125–26, and M. Horam, *Naga Insurgency*, New Delhi: Cosmo Publications, 1988, p. 37.

34. Elwin, *Nagaland*, p. 49, and Yonuo, op. cit., p. 126.

35. Yonuo, op. cit., p. 132, and M. Alemchiba, op. cit., pp. 162–64.

36. Yonuo, op.cit., pp. 132–33.

37. Ibid., pp. 126-129.

38. Quoted in ibid., p. 129. For a comprehensive account of 'the Mystic Rani' see also S.C. Dev, *Nagaland: The Untold Story*, Calcutta: Gouri Dev, 1988, pp. 68–79.

39. Frank Owen, *The Campaign in Burma*, Dehra Dun: Natraj Publishers, 1974 (reprint), p. 76.

40. Subhas Chandra Bose at a rally of Indians in Burma, 4 July 1911, at http://www.scribd.com/doc/19855244/Speech-of-Subhas-Chandra-Bose

41. Quoted in Sisir K. Bose (ed.), *A Beacon Across Asia: A Biography of Subhas Chandra Bose*, Hyderabad: Orient Longman, 1996, p. 167.

42. Ibid., p. 169.

43. Ibid., p. 171.

44. Quoted in M. Alemchiba, op. cit., p. 152.

45. Quoted in M. Alemchiba, op. cit., pp. 139–40.

46. Viscount Slim, *Defeat Into Victory*, Dehra Dun: Natraj Publishers, 1981, pp. 334–35.

47. This version was given to me at the NSCN's headquarters in November 1985. There is a slightly different version of this memorandum in Yonuo, op. cit., pp. 161–63.

48. Interview with A.Z. Phizo, London, 8 June 1989. For a detailed biography of Phizo, see Pieter Steyn, *Zapuphizo: Voice of the Nagas*, London: Kegan Paul, 2002.

49. Yonuo, op. cit., p. 171. See also 'Golden Jubilee: Federal Republic of Nagaland 1956-2006', published by the pro-Phizo NNC, Kohima,

2006, p. 15: 'May 21 (1947): Naga National Council called upon Assam to form a Sovereign state of Assam.'

50. Yonuo, op. cit,. p. 172. For a fuller extract of Sakhrie's speech, see Charles Chasie, *The Naga Imbroglio: A Personal Perspective*, Guwahati: United Publishers, 1999, pp. 168–69.

51. For the full text of the Hydari Agreement, see Yonuo, op. cit., pp. 173–74, and Chasie, op. cit. pp. 170–72.

52. This version of Gandhi's alleged promise can be found in many books and articles written by Nagas, for instance M. Alemchiba, op. cit., p. 173, Yonuo, op. cit., pp. 180–82. Even Neville Maxwell writes in his report *India and the Nagas* (Minority Rights Group, Report No. 17, November 1973), p. 8: 'Two days later (July 19, 1947), they saw Gandhi: Phizo reported that Gandhi said, "Nagas have every right to be independent. We don't want to live under the domination of the British and they are now leaving us. I want you to feel that India is yours. I feel that the Naga Hills are mine just as they are yours. But if you say they are not mine, the mater must stop there. I believe in the brotherhood of man, but I do not believe in force or forced unions. If you do not wish to join the Union of India nobody will force you do do that." There is no reason to doubt Phizo's account (of the meeting with Gandhi); any other response from Gandhi would have been uncharacteristic.'

53. Nibedon, op. cit., pp. 34–35.

54. M. Alemchiba, op. cit., p. 174.

55. Yonuo, op. cit., p. 202, and A. Lanunugsang Ao, *From Phizo to Muivah: The Naga National Question in North East India*, New Delhi: Mittal Publications, 2002. p. 49.

56. *Assam Tribune*, 3 December 1953. Quoted in 'Naga Goodwill Mission to Assam: Report (30 November to 15 December 1953)', Naga National Council, Kohima, 1984, pp. 36–37, and in M. Alemchiba, op. cit., p. 175.

57. Nibedon, op. cit., pp. 71–72. Nibedon also writes: 'The subject of Sakhrie's death is a taboo in the Angami Naga country. Both the Phizo group as well as Sakhrie's clansmen refrain from giving details. The latter say it was Phizo who signed the Azha (order),

while the former say Phizo was not in the know of it and it was perpetrated by overzealous followers of the movement. The NNC had ordered the detention of Sakhrie, but one of the guerrillas had a personal grudge against the singer. Phizo lamented the death of his friend. Authorities, however, believed Phizo was responsible and issued an arrest warrant against him and some other close followers.'

58. Maxwell, *India and the Nagas*, p. 11. This is the same Neville Maxwell who wrote *India's China War* (London: Pelican Books, 1972), a pro-Chinese account of the 1962 border war between India and China.

59. Ibid., p. 12.

60. B.N. Mullik, *My Years With Nehru: 1948-1964*, Bombay: Allied Publishers, 1972, p. 313.

61. V.K. Anand, *Conflict in Nagaland: A Study of Insurgency and Counter-insurgency*, Delhi: Chanakya Publications, 1980, p. 232.

62. Ibid., p. 140.

63. Mullik, op. cit., pp. 313–14.

64. Ib id., pp. 300 and 315–16.

65. Ibid., p. 316.

66. Ibid., p. 317.

67. Yonuo, op. cit., p. 222.

68. Mullik, op. cit. p. 317.

69. Ibid., p. 319.

70. According to 'Historical Events of Nagaland' (NNC mimeograph), a 'farewell service' was held for Phizo on 13 August 1956, for his departure for abroad. The decision to send him abroad was taken 'at Sanis, on 12 July 1956 . . . to put forward the Naga cause before the UNO.' ('Phizo Souvenir: Angami Zapu Phizo, President, Naga National Council from 28th December 1950–30th April 1990', prepared by the Funeral Organizing Committee, Kohima, April 1991.) Steyn (op. cit., p. 100) erroneously claims that Phizo left Nagaland in December 1957, a year later after the convention in Kohima.

71. See 'The Nagas: India's Problem – or the World's? The Search for Peace', by the Rev. Michael Scott, a forty-seven-page booklet published by Scott in Great Britain in 1967.

72. Ibid. pp. 4–6.

73. Ibid., p. 6.

74. For Gavin Young's account of his visit to the Naga Hills in 1961, see 'The Nagas: an unknown war, India's threat to peace', reprinted from *The Observer*, NNC, London, 1962, and also available at http://www.nagajournal.tk/publ/others/achan/8-1-0-6

75. Ibid., p. 25.

76. Ibid., p. 15.

77. Ibid., p. 17.

78. Ibid., p. 16.

79. These terms appear in most writings about the Naga national movement, but the meanings and origin were recorded by me when I stayed at the NSCN's headquarters from October to December 1985.

80. See M. Alemchiba, op. cit., pp. 197–200 and Yonuo, op. cit. pp. 229–30.

81. See Mullik, op. cit., p. 331 and Yonuo, op. cit., p. 244: 'Dr. Imkongliba was shot dead by a rebel Naga in contempt of his stand against . . . Naga independence on August 22, while returning home from his dispensary, after the previous attempt on his life foiled in December 1960.'

82. Hokishe Sema, *Emergence of Nagaland: Socio-Economic and Political Transformation and the Future*, New Delhi: Vikas Publishing House, pp. 99–100.

83. Interviews with Isak and Muivah, Kesan Chanlam, November 1985. See also Subir Bhaumik, 'The External Linkages in Insurgency in India's Northeast', in B. Pakem (ed.), *Insurgency in Northeast India*, New Delhi: Omsons Publications, 1997, p. 94.

84. Interview with Mowu Gwizan, Kohima, 18 October 1985.

85. Lawrence E. Cline, 'The Insurgency Environment in Northeast India', *Small Wars and Insurgency*, Vol. 17, No. 2, June 2006, pp. 126–47.

86. For Scott's account of the peace mission, see his own account in 'The Nagas: India's Problem or the World's?', and Yonuo, op. cit., pp. 254–96.

87. Yonuo, op. cit., p. 294.
88. Ibid., p. 384.
89. For a detailed account of the infighting in the Naga movement at this time, see Nibedon, op. cit., pp. 217–19 and 267–78.
90. Ibid., pp. 304–05. Also interview with Thinoselie M. Keyho, Kohima, 18 October 1985 and 24 December 2009.
91. Nibedon, op.cit., pp. 339–40. For the full text of the accord, see http://www.satp.org/satporgtp/countries/india/states/nagaland/documents/papers/nagaland_accord_the_shillong_nov_11_1975.htm
92. 'Report on Naga Political Affairs From 1978 to 1981', by W. Shapwon Heimi, Chaplee Kilonser, Federal Government of Nagaland, Eastern Oking, and 'Nagaland and Th. Muivah's Terrorist Activities', published by the NNC, Kohima, 28 April 2005, p. 20. Isak and Muivah also talked openly about the purges, including the executions, when I interviewed them at Kesan Chanlam on 6 November 1985.

3. THE MIZOS: FROM FAMINE TO STATEHOOD

1. Brig. C.G. Verghese and R.L. Thanzawna, *A History of the Mizos*, Volume 1, New Delhi: Vikas Publishing House, 1997, p. 313.
2. Lt Col. J. Shakespear, *The Lushei Kuki Clans*, Guwahati: Spectrum Publications, 1994 (reprint, first published in Great Britain in 1912), p. 43.
3. Verghese and Thanzawna, op. cit., p. 101.
4. Suhas Chatterjee, *Mizo Chiefs and the Chiefdom*, New Delhi: M.D. Publications, 1995, p. 130.
5. Ibid., p. 130.
6. Ibid., p. 130.
7. Col. E.B. Elly, *Military Report on The Chin-Lushai Country*, Aizawl: Tribal Research Institute, 1978 (reprint, originally published in Shimla, 1893), p. 2.
8. Vumson, *Zo History*, Aizawl, published by the author, undated but most probably published in the early 1990s, p. 143.
9. Shakespear, op. cit., p 62. See also P. Lalnithanga, *Emergence of*

Mizoram, Aizawl: Lengchhawn Press, 2010, p. 19: 'Mizos believed in a supreme God called *Pathian* who was the creator of the world. They also believed in life after death. All people after death would go to *Mitthikhua*, dead men's village on the other side of which is situated *Pialral*, the abode of bliss.'

10. Shakespear, op. cit., p. 22.
11. Quoted in Sajal Nag, *Pied Pipers in North-East India: Bamboo-flowers, Rat-famine and the Politics of Philanthropy*. New Delhi: Manohar, 2008, pp. 199–200.
12. Verghese and Thanzawna, op. cit., p. 336. See also http://mizoram.nic.in/more/yma.htm
13. Suhas Chatterjee, 'Autonomy Movements in Mizoram: A Historical Analysis', in R.N. Prasad (ed.), *Autonomy Movements in Mizoram*, New Delhi: Vikas Publishing House, 1994, pp 81-82.
14. Ibid., p 82.
15. See http://www.zogam.org/history.asp?article=history_1921, and C.G. Verghese and R. L. Thanzawna, *A History of the Mizos*, Volume II. New Delhi: Vikas Publishing House, 1997, p. 6.
16. Ibid., p. 8.
17. 'Mi' means people and 'Zo' hill or mountain. According to more recent research by a team at Mizoram's Art and Culture Department, the term has a deeper meaning. The department argues that 'Mizo' is the name of an old nation which may have existed somewhere in Central Asia in 'ancient times', consisting of eleven tribes: the Aso, Chho, Halam, Hmar, Lai (Pawi), Lusei, Mara, Miu-Khumi, Paite (Zomi), Ralte and Thado (Kuki). Each of them is supposed to have had numerous clans, among them Sailo, Chhakchhuak, Kawlni, Khupchawng, Thiak and Chawngthu, and each clan contained at least five sub-clans. The veracity of this research is impossible to ascertain.
18. From the website http://www.mizostory.org/mizostory/Mizo_Story_7.html
19. V. Venkata Rao, *Century of Government and Politics in North East India: Mizoram*, Vol. 3, New Delhi, 1991, p. 235.
20. See *shodhganga*.inflibnet.ac.in/bitstream/10603/1883/7/07_chapter3.pdf

21. Nag, op. cit., p. 243.
22. Ibid., p. 252. Nag's account of the 1958–59 famine, and previous mautams as well, is the best study of famine politics in Mizoram.
23. Nag, op. cit., p. 253 and Lalnithanga, op. cit., p. 171.
24. Lalnithanga, op. cit., p. 171.
25. Nag, op. cit., p. 260.
26. Ibid., p. 262.
27. The name 'Pakistan' was coined by a group of Indian Muslim students in Cambridge led by Choudhary Rahmat Ali, who in 1933 issued a pamphlet called *Now or Never*. They came up with the term 'Pakistan' which was actually an acronym composed of letters taken from the various Indian provinces with sizeable Muslim populations: **P**unjab, **A**fghania (i.e., the North-West Frontier Province), **K**ashmir, **S**indh and Baluchi**stan**. 'I' was added to make it easier to pronounce. Rahmat Ali in his 1947 book *Pakistan: The Fatherland of the Pak Nation*, stated that the acronym stands for **P**unjab, **A**fghania, **K**ashmir, the **I**ndus Valley, **S**indh, **T**urkharistan (modern Central Asia), **A**fghanistan and Baluchista**N**. Whichever way one prefers, the name is Persian for 'the Land of the Pure'. But neither includes one of the most populous Muslim provinces of erstwhile British India: East Bengal, which after 1947 became East Pakistan and, in 1971, the independent nation of Bangladesh.
28. Verghese and Thanzawna, *A History of the Mizos*, Vol. II, p. 21.
29. Ibid., pp. 22–23. See also Lt Col. Vivek Chadha, *Low Intensity Conflicts in India: An Analysis*. New Delhi: Sage Publications, 2005, pp. 335–36.
30. Chadha, op. cit., p. 336.
31. Interview with Peter Sapzova, Chiang Mai, 29 January 2011.
32. C. Chawngkunga, *Important Documents of Mizoram*, Aizawl: R.T.M. Press, 1998, pp. 314–19. The memorandum is dated 30 October 1965, and signed by 'S. Lianzuala, General Secretary, and Laldenga, President, Mizo National Front'.
33. Quoted in Subir Bhaumik, *Insurgent Crossfire: North-East India*, New Delhi: Lancers Publishers, 1996, p. 151.
34. Verghese and Thanzawna, *A History of the Mizos*, Vol. II, pp. 59–69.

35. Interview with Lalchamliana, Aizawl, 14 November 2010.

36. For the full text of the Mizo declaration of independence, see Suresh K. Sharma, *Documents on North-East India, Vol 8: Mizoram,* New Delhi: Mittal Publications, 2006, pp. 100–02.

37. Verghese and Thanzawna, *A History of the Mizos,* Vol. II, pp. 29–30.

38. Vijendra Singh Jafa, 'Grouping of Villages in Mizoram (1968-1970)', undated mimeograph in the author's possession, pp. 5–6.

39. Ibid., p. 17.

40. Ibid., p. 16.

41. Nirmal Nibedon, *Mizoram: The Dagger Brigade,* New Delhi: Lancers Publishers, 1983, p. 109, and *The Mizo Heroes,* Aizawl: Tribal Research Institute, 2003, which contains biographies of famous Mizo heroes.

42. Interview with Lalchamliana, Aizawl, 14 November 2010.

43. This account of Sapzova's travels is based on interviews with him in Chiang Mai, 29 January 2011. For an obituary of William Young, see Bertil Lintner, 'Wise man on the hill', *Asia Times Online,* 8 April 2008, at http://www.atimes.com/atimes/Southeast_Asia/MD08Ae01.html

44. Interview with Vanlalngaia, Aizawl, 9 September 2010.

45. Interview with Kyaw Mya, then a member of the Central Committee of the Communist Party of Burma, Panghsang, 29 December 1986.

46. Bhaumik, op. cit., p. 172.

47. Interview with Rama, Danai Yang, Kachin State, 3 February 1986.

48. Chaitanya Kalbag, 'The Art of Survival', *India Today,* 15 November 1982.

49. Interview with Vanlalngaia, Aizawl, 9 September 2010.

50. For a brief biography of Brig. T. Sailo, see Lalnithanga, op. cit., pp. 169–170.

51. Verghese and Thanzawna, *A History of the Mizos,* Volume II, pp. 164–165.

52. See Nirmal Nibedon, *Northeast India: The Ethnic Explosion,* New Delhi: Lancers Publishers, 1981, p. 127.

53. Ibid., pp. 166–67.

54. Ibid., pp. 28–29.

55. For the full text of the accord, see Lalnithanga, op. cit., pp. 530–34.

56. George A. Theodorson, 'Minority Peoples in the Union of Burma', paper presented at the First International Conference of South-East Asian historians, Singapore, January 1961; see also Bertil Lintner, *Burma in Revolt: Opium and Insurgency since 1948*, Chiang Mai: Silkworm Books, 2003 (third edition), pp. 63–64.

57. Interviews with John Khaw Kim Thang, the Indian-educated chairman of the CNF, Bangkok, July 1989.

58. A copy of the declaration is in my possession.

59. A copy of that letter is also in my possession.

60. See 'Unsafe State: State-sanctioned sexual violence against Chin women in Burma', the Women's League of Chinland, March 2007.

61. See Namrata Goswami, 'Mizoram on the Verge of Another Mautam?', Institute for Defence Studies and Analyses, 1 April 2008. Retrieved from http://www.idsa.in/idsastrategiccomments/ MizoramontheVergeofAnotherMautam_NGoswami_010408

62. For an account of the food crisis in Chin state, see also http:// www.projectmaje.org/mautam.htm

63. Quoted in Human Rights Watch, 'We Are Like Forgotten People: The Chin People of Burma, Unsafe in Burma, Unprotected in India', January 2009, p. 32.

64. The full report can be downloaded from www.burmacampaign. org.uk/reports/HRW_we_are_forgotten_people.pdf See also http:/ /www.hrw.org/en/node/79892/section/1 (follow arrows to read the report).

65. J.H. Hre Mang, *Report on the Chin Refugees in Mizoram State of India*, New Delhi: Other Media Communications, 2000, p. 78.

66. 'We Are Like Forgotten People', pp. 77–78.

67. For an account of the controversy, see http://www.bnionline.net/ news/mizzima/5933-report-not-aimed-at-chin-mizo-confusion-hrw.html

68. Frank K. Lehman, *The Structure of Chin Society*, Urbana, Illinois Studies in Anthropology, 1963, p. 177. Quoted in Shalva Weil, 'Lost Israelites From the Indo-Burmese Borderlands: Re-Traditionalisation and Conversion Among the Shinlung or Bene Menasseh', *Anthropologist*, Vol. 6, No. 3, 2004, pp. 219–33, available at http:// www.scribd.com/doc/22147803/Burmese-Jews

69. Verghese and Thanzawna, *A History of the Mizos*, Volume I, p. 78.

70. Weil, 'Lost Israelites From the Indo-Burmese Borderlands', p. 223.

71. Hillel Halkin, *Across the Sabbath River: In Search of the Lost Tribe of Israel*, Boston and New York: Houghton Mifflin Company, 2002.

72. 'Indian converts to Judaism: lost tribes of Israel or economic migrants?', *AsiaNews.it* at http://www.asianews.it/index.php?art= 4148&l=en

73. http://www.e-pao.net/epSubPageExtractor.asp?src= leisure.essays. Isaac_Hmar.The_Jewish_Connection_Myth_or_Reality

74. 'Indian converts to Judaism: lost tribes of Israel or economic migrants?'

75. Quoted in Wikipedia, http://en.wikipedia.org/wiki/Bnei_Menashe

4. MANIPUR: THE ETERNAL IMBROGLIO

1. For the full text of the Armed Forces (Special Powers) Act (1958), see http://www.satp.org/satporgtp/countries/india/document/ actandordinances/armed_forces_special_power_act_1958.htm In July 1990, it was extended to Jammu and Kashmir as The Armed Forces (Jammu and Kashmir) Special Powers Act (1990).

2. 'Irom Sharmila awarded Tagore peace prize', *The Hindu*, 12 September 2010, at http://www.thehindu.com/news/national/article627268. ece For a biography of Sharmila Irom, see Deepti Priya Mehrotra, *Burning Bright: Irom Sharmila and the Struggle for Peace in Manipur*, New Delhi: Penguin Books, 2009.

3. 'Manipur Rebels: Child's Play', by Wasbir Hussain, director of the Centre for Development and Peace Studies, at http://cdpsindia.org/ point-of-view14.asp

4. http://manipursacs.nic.in/

5. http://wikileaks.tetalab.org/mobile/cables/06CALCUTTA389. html. See also http://www.thehindu.com/news/the-india-cables/ the-cables/article1556742.ece

6. Ibid.

7. Romesh Bhattacharji, *Lands of Early Dawn: Northeast of India*, New Delhi: Rupa & Co., 2002, p. 203.

8. Neelesh Misra and Rahul Pandita, *The Absent State: Insurgency as an Excuse for Misgovernance*, Gurgaon: Hachette India, 2010, p. 235.

9. Quoted in T. Hemo Singh, *Manipur Imbroglio*, New Delhi: Akansha Publishing House, 2009, p. 12.
10. See http://www.chinahistoryforum.com/index.php?/topic/27570-chinese-people-living-in-manipur/
11. Hemo Singh, op. cit., p. 14.
12. There are various accounts of how long Garibnawaz's reign lasted. According to Manipur Wiki, he became king in 1709 and was murdered by one of his sons in 1748. See http://www.manipurwiki.com/index.php?title=Meidingu_Pamheiba Other sources say that he died in 1749 or 1751.
13. P.B. Pemberton, *The Eastern Frontier of India*, New Delhi: Mittal Publications, 1979 (reprint, first published in 1835), p. 46. Also quoted in Rajendra Kshetri, *The Emergence of Meitei Nationalism*, New Delhi: Mittal Publications, 2006, p. 30.
14. Kshetri, op. cit., p. 30.
15. Ibid., p. 48.
16. Mehrotra, op. cit., p. 19.
17. Kshetri, op. cit., p. 58.
18. The text of the merger agreement is available at http://manipuri.itgo.com/archives/the_manipur_merger_agreement.html
19. Ibid., p. 62.
20. See 'Annual Statement of the Central Committee, UNLF: 31st Anniversary, November 24, 1995', a twenty-one-page pamphlet published by the United National Liberation Front.
21. Ibid., p. 2.
22. See http://www.satp.org/satporgtp/countries/india/states/manipur/terrorist_outfits/unlf.htm
23. *Manipur Online*, http://manipuronline.com/features/the-lake-on-fire-manipur-burns-delhi-bungles/2010/09/15
24. Kshetri, op. cit., p. 121 and 125.
25. Interview with Temba Singh, Pa Jau (headquarters of the Kachin Independence Organization, KIO, northern Burma), 22 April 1986.
26. Quoted from *Dawn*, a PLA publication, Volume I, 1979, p. 3. The modern Pinyin spelling of Mao's name is Mao Zedong.
27. Ibid., p. 10.

28. Ibid., p. 11.
29. Ibid., p. 10.
30. Interview with KIO chairman Brang Seng, Pa Jau, 1 May 1986, and Kam Htoi, local commander, the Kachin Independence Army, western Kachin state, 26 January 1986.
31. Suniti Kumar Ghosh, *Naxalbari Before and After: Reminiscences and Appraisal*, Kolkata: New Age Publishers, 2009, p. 124.
32. Ibid., pp. 121–27.
33. http://www.bannedthought.net/India/PeoplesMarch/PM1999-2006/publications/30%20years/part1.htm
34. Sumanta Banerjee, *In the Wake of Naxalbari*, Calcutta: Subarnarekha, 1980, p. 118.
35. The full text of the *People's Daily* editorial is available at http://www.marxists.org/subject/china/documents/peoples-daily/1967/07/05.htm
36. Banerjee, op. cit., p. 223.
37. Ibid., pp. 125–26.
38. Ibid., p. 166.
39. Ghosh, op. cit., p. 270.
40. Banerjee, op. cit., p. 264, and Ghosh, op. cit., p 271 and 332.
41. Ghosh, op.cit., p. 272.
42. This account of Temba's trips to Burma's Kachin state is based on my interviews with him at Pa Jau, Kachin rebel headquarters, 22 April 1986.
43. I met a group of about forty PLA guerillas led by a young commander called Dina, near the Chindwin River in early January 1986, as they were on their way back to Manipur to fight.
44. T. Hemo Singh, op. cit., p. 78.
45. Ibid., p. 87.
46. This and other details about the UNLF can be found on Global Security's website, http://www.globalsecurity.org/military/world/para/unlf.htm
47. 'Getting Away With Murder: 50 Years of the Armed Forces Special Powers Act', Human Rights Watch, August 2008, p. 4. Available at http://www.hrw.org/legacy/backgrounder/2008/india0808/

48. I met and interviewed Yumnam Shinnaba at the NSCN's Kesam Chanlam headquarters on 29 November 1985.

49. For a history of the CPB and an account of the 1989 mutiny, see Bertil Lintner, *The Rise and Fall of the Communist Party of Burma*, Ithaca, New York: Cornell University South-east Asia Programme, 1990.

50. *International Narcotics Control Strategy Report*, Washington: US Department of State, Bureau for International Narcotics and Law Enforcement, 1987, 1989, 1995.

51. *Foreign Economic Trends Report: Burma*, Rangoon: US embassy, 1996.

52. 'Burma-India: A Fourth Side to the Golden Triangle', *Geopolitical Drug Dispatch, Observatoire Geopolitical Des Drogues*, Paris, No. 14, December 1992.

53. *Report on Trip to Northeast India*, Chiang Mai: Southeast Asian Information Network, 1997.

54. 'On the move', *Far Eastern Economic Review*, 13 January 2000.

55. 'India-Burma: The Burmese Generals Add a String to Their Bow', *Geopolitical Drug Dispatch, Observatoire Geopolitical Des Drogues*, Paris, No. 14, April 1999.

56. Michael Black, 'UWSA: From Drugs to Guns', unpublished paper. See also Subir Bhaumik, 'Where do "Chinese" guns arming rebels really come from?' BBC News, South Asia, 3 August 2010, available at http://www.bbc.co.uk/news/world-south-asia-10626034

57. 'Manipuri militant held in Delhi', *Midday*, 10 May 2011, at http://www.mid-day.com/news/2011/may/100511-news-delhi-Manipuri-militant-arrested-a-militant-Special-Cell-banned-terrorist.htm

58. Rakhee Bhattacharya, *Development Disparities in Northeast India*, New Delhi: Foundation Books (an imprint of Cambridge University Press, India), 2011, pp. 91–125.

59. Ibid., p. 114.

60. Ibid., p. 96.

61. Ibid.

62. Ibid., p. 117.

63. Ibid., p. 91.

64. Ibid., p. 121.

65. http://manipurassembly.nic.in/html/resolutions/r120602.htm
66. http://www.hindu.com/2007/02/06/stories/2007020603711100.htm
67. For a comprehensive background to the conflict, see http://manipurcomments.com/understanding-historical-background-of-kuki-and-naga-relations/
68. P.S. Haokip, *Zale'n-Gam: The Kuki Nation*, Kuki National Organization, June 2008, p. 373ff.
69. According to an email I received from P.S. Haokip on 5 March 2010.
70. For the *Telegraph* report, see http://.www.telegraphindia.com/1100509/jsp/northeast/story_12427001.jsp
71. http://www.manipuronline.com/Features/Dec2001/meirapaibi23.htm
72. Quoted from http://www.telegraphindia.com/1040725/asp/look/story_3533201.asp
73. 'Insurgency: The Long Way Down', at http://www.boloji.com/wfs5/wfs680.htm
74. The French press agency Agence France-Presse ran a feature about this in May 2011, which was picked up by some local newspapers in Imphal. It also appeared in the Thai daily *Bangkok Post* on July 11, 2011: 'K-pop elbows Bollywood out of Indian northeast'.

5. ASSAM AND BANGLADESH: FOREIGNERS? WHAT FOREIGNERS?

1. See, for instance, http://www.satp.org/satporgtp/countries/india/states/assam/timelines/Year1996.htm
2. For a complete list of what was seized in Chittagong on 2 April 2004, see Appendix 4.
3. Anthony Davis, 'New Details Emerge on Bangladesh Arms Haul', *Jane's Intelligence Review*, August 2004, posted on the Internet on 6 July 2004.
4. Ibid.
5. Ibid.
6. Subir Bhaumik, *Troubled Periphery: Crisis of India's Northeast*. New Delhi: Sage Publishers, 2009, pp. 189–90.

7. *Jane's Intelligence Review*, August 2004.
8. Ibid., p. 191.
9. *Small Arms Survey: Profiling the Problem*, Oxford: Oxford University Press (and Small Arms Survey, Geneva), 2001, p. 181.
10. 'China supplying arms to N-E militants?', *The Hindu*, 19 August 2000, available at http://www.hinduonnet.com/thehindu/2000/08/19/stories/0219000p.htm
11. *Jane's Intelligence Review*, August 2004.
12. 'Rahim, Sahab tell of ISI link', *The Daily Star*, 31 May 2009, at http://www.thedailystar.net/newDesign/news-details.php?nid =90552 See also 'Rahim tells of ARY meeting, a foreign embassy link', *Bangladesh News*, 28 May 2009, at http://www.bangladeshnews.com.bd/2009/05/28/rahim-tells-of-ary-meeting-a-foreign-embassy-link/
13. Ahmede Hussain, 'Selling their souls to the devil', *Star Weekend Magazine*, 22 May 2009.
14. Muhammad Ghulam Kabir, *Changing Face of Nationalism: The Case of Bangladesh*, New Delhi: South Asian Publishers, 1994, p. 189.
15. *Patterns of Global Terrorism 2001*, Washington: The Office of the Coordinator of Counterterrorism, 21 May 2002.
16. Bhaumik, op. cit., p. 169.
17. Bertil Lintner, 'Sinister Links', *India Today*, 31 March 1992.
18. Bertil Lintner, 'Northeast India: Boiling Pot of International Rivalry – Part I', *YaleGlobal Online*, 17 February 2010, available at http://yaleglobal.yale.edu/content/northeast-india-boiling-pot-international-rivalry-part-i
19. Abdul Barkat (ed.), *An Enquiry into Causes and Consequences of Deprivation of Hindu Minorities in Bangladesh through the Vested Property Act*, Dhaka: Prip Trust, 2000.
20. Saleem Samad, 'State of Minorities in Bangladesh: From Secular to Islamic Hegemony', paper which previously was available at http://www.mnet.fr/aiindex/ssamad_Bangladesh.html but then was attacked by hackers and is no longer available.
21. Abdul Barkat, op. cit., p. 20.
22. *Crisis in South Asia: A Report by Senator Edward Kennedy to the Subcommittee Investigating the Problem of Refugees and Their Settlement, Submitted to the*

US Senate Judiciary Committee, November 1, 1971, US Government Press, p. 66.

23. In China, the Tais are called Dai and live in the Ruili area and Sipsongpanna (which the Chinese corrupt to Xishuangbanna) in Yunnan. 'Shan' is actually the way the Burmese pronounce 'Siam': 'm' as final consonant in Burmese becomes a nasal 'n'. Siam, of course, is an old name for Thailand. To the Burmese, there is no difference betweens the Thais and the Shans.

24. For a detailed account of the Tai Khamtis, their language and history, see Lila Gogoi (ed.), *The Tai Khamtis*, published by Chowkhamoon Gohain, ex-MP, NEFA, and printed by Nabajiban Press, Calcutta, 1971.

25. See 'Fire in Assam: South Asia's Arc of Crisis', (cover story), *Asiaweek*, 4 March 1983.

26. Ibid.

27. Ibid.

28. Interview with Arabinda Rajkhowa, NSCN headquarters at Kesan Chanlam, north-western Burma, 16 December 1985.

29. Based on interviews with Arabinda Rajkhowa, Pradip Gogoi, Paresh Barua and other ULFA leaders, Kesan Chanlam, November–December 1985.

30. For an account of Sanjoy Ghose's life and disappearance, see Sumita Ghose (ed.), *Sanjoy's Assam: Diaries and Writings of Sanjoy Ghose*, New Delhi: Penguin Books, 1998.

31. Interview with Arabinda Rajkhowa, Kesan Chanlam, 29 November 1985.

32. Bhaumik, op. cit., pp. 169–70.

33. Ibid., pp. 107–08.

34. For a complete list of militant groups in India's north-east, see Appendix 2.

35. Asoka Raina, *Inside RAW: The Story of India's Secret Service*, New Delhi: Vikas Publishing House, 1981, p. 1.

36. Ibid., p. 5.

37. Ibid., pp. 4–5, and Kautilya, *The Arthashastra*, New Delhi: Penguin Books, 1992, p. 463.

38. Raina, op, cit., p. 5; *The Arthashastra*, pp. 468–70.

39. Bhaumik, op. cit., p. 90.

40. Bhaumik uses 'dam' but the correct term is, of course, 'dan'.

41. Ibid., p. 90.

42. Peter Hopkirk, *Trespassers on the Roof of the World: The Race for Lhasa*, Oxford: Oxford University Press, 1982, pp. 25–26.

43. Ibid., pp. 26–27.

44. Ibid., p. 27.

45. Quoted in Raina, op. cit., pp. 48–49.

46. Bertil Lintner, 'Isolated Force', *Far Eastern Economic Review*, 5 April 1990.

47. Exact figures are difficult to come by, but some statistics can be found at the website of Bangladesh's ministry of Hill Tracts Affairs, http://www.mochta.gov.bd/

48. Subir Bhaumik, Meghna Guhathakurta, Sabyasachi Basu Ray Chaudhury, *Living on the Edge: Essays on the Chittagong Hill Tracts*, Kolkata: South Asia Forum for Human Rights, 1997, pp. 48–49.

49. Wolfgang Mey (ed.), *Genocide in the Chittagong Hill Tracts, Bangladesh*, Copenhagen: International Working Group for Indigenous Affairs, 1984, pp. 27–28.

50. *Life is not Ours: Land and Human Rights in the Chittagong Hill Tracts of Bangladesh, Update 4*, Amsterdam: The Chittagong Hill Tracts Commission, 2000, pp. 17–18

51. Ibid., p. 18.

52. 'Bangladesh: Country Report on Human Rights Practices – 2001', Washington: US Department of State, 4 March 2002, p. 27.

53. Bertil Lintner, 'Intractable Hills/Isolated Force/Tribal Turmoil', *Far Eastern Economic Review*, 5 April 1990. I visited the Chittagong Hill Tracts, and the refugee camps in Tripura, in January–February 1990. The estimate of the number of Shanti Bahini fighters comes from an interview with Maj. Gen. Abdus Salam, the Chittagong commander of the Bangladesh army, Chittagong, 22 January 1990.

54. See 'South Asia Terrorism Portal; Countries; Bangladesh; Terrorist Groups; HuJI'; www.satp.org

55. For the full text of the fatwa, see http://www.mideastweb.org/osamabinladen2.htm

56. 'Patterns of Global Terrorism 2001, the Office of the Coordinator for Counterterrorism, 21 May 2002'. See http://www.state.gov/s/ct/rls/crt/2001/

57. Email from a local NGO activist in the area who requested anonymity, 25 September 2002.

58. An attempt on the life of Rahman was made on 18 January 1999. After the police arrested ten HuJI activists and sealed its office in the Dhaka suburb of Khilgaon, interrogations revealed that they planned to kill twenty-eight prominent intellectuals including National Professor Kabir Choudhury, writer Taslima Nasreen and the director general of the Islamic Foundation, Maulana Abdul Awal. See 'South Asia Terrorism Portal; Countries; Bangladesh; Assessment 2000;' www.satp.org

59. 'Patterns of Global Terrorism, 2001'.

60. *The Eighth Parliamentary Elections 2001*, Dhaka: Society for Environment and Human Development for Coordinating Council for Human Rights in Bangladesh, March 2002, p. 2.

61. Ibid.

62. *Bangladesh: Attacks on Members of the Hindu Minority*, London: Amnesty International, December 2001.

63. *The Hindu*, Chennai, 23 January 2002. Also see Subir Bhaumik, 'The Second Front of Islamic Terror in South Asia', paper presented at an international seminar on terrorism and low intensity conflict, Jadavpur University, Kolkata, 6–8 March 2002.

64. *Far Eastern Economic Review*, Hong Kong, 11 July 2002.

65. Ryan Clarke, *Lashkar-i-Taiba: The Fallacy of Subservient Proxies and the Future of Islamist Terrorism in India*, US Army War College, Strategic Studies Institute, March 2010, p. 64.

66. Ibid.

67. 'IDSA Comment: LeT finds a new base in Manipur', at http://www.idsa.in/idsastrategiccomments/LeTfindsanewbaseinManipur_TKSingh_220107

68. Bertil Lintner, 'Beware of Bangladesh'/'Bangladesh: A Cocoon of Terror', *Far Eastern Economic Review*, 4 April 2002.

69. That picture appeared together with another story I did for *Jane's*

Intelligence Review, 'Is religious extremism on the rise in Bangladesh?', *JIR*, May 2002, p. 12.

70. 'Bombs explode across Bangladesh', *BBC News*, 17 August 2005, at http://news.bbc.co.uk/2/hi/south_asia/4158478.stm

71. Bertil Lintner, 'Northeast India: Boiling Pot Of International Rivalry – Part I', *Yale Global Online*, 17 February 2010, at http://yaleglobal.yale.edu/content/northeast-india-boiling-pot-international-rivalry-part-i

72. Sanjoy Hazarika, *Strangers in the Mist: Tales of War and Peace from India's Northeast*, New Delhi: Viking and Penguin Books, 1994, p. 169.

73. Quoted in 'Northeast India: Boiling Pot Of International Rivalry – Part I.'

74. According to an email I received from a trusted source in Ruili on 26 January 2010, Barua had been spotted in Yingjiang in 'the last week of November 2009'.

6. BURMA: A STATE OF REVOLT

1. My wife, our daughter and I stayed in Panghsang from 18 December 1986 to 22 March 1987. I also walked through the entire CPB-controlled area, from Kyuhkok/Panghsai in the north to the Mekong River in the east. After spending six months in areas controlled by the Kachin Independence Army, we entered CPB-held territory on 14 November 1986 and crossed illegally into China on 18 April 1987. From there, we were deported to Hong Kong. I describe those events in *Land of Jade: A Journey from India through Northern Burma to China*, Bangkok: Orchid Books, 1996 and 2011. The description of post-mutiny Panghsang comes mainly from Michael Black, an American researcher who has visited the town on a number of occasions. Together, we wrote *Merchants of Madness: The Methamphetamine Explosion in the Golden Triangle*, Chiang Mai: Silkworm Books, 2009.

2. For an account of the CPB mutiny and its aftermath, see Lintner and Black, *Merchants of Madness*, pp. 17–35.

3. For an overview of the drug problem in China, see

http://en.wikipedia.org/wiki/Illegal_drug_trade_in_the_People
%27s_ Republic_of_China

4. Interview with a former CPB cadre who requested anonymity, Ruili, Yunnan, 7 January 1991.

5. For a comprehensive account of Chinese arms deliveries to the UWSA since the 1990s, see Michael Black and Anthony Davis, 'Wa and Peace – The UWSA and Tensions in Myanmar', *Jane's Intelligence Review*, March 2008; posted on the Internet, 14 February 2008.

6. See http://en.wikipedia.org/wiki/Illegal_drug_trade_in_the_ People%27s_Republic_of_China (information from Chinese government sources and the International Narcotics Strategy Report, US Department of State, 2002).

7. See http://factsanddetails.com/china.php?itemid=298&catid= 8&subcatid=50

8. For a detailed account of the Indian community in twentieth-century Burma, see N.R. Chakravarty, *The Indian Minority in Burma: The Rise and Decline of an Immigrant Community*, London: Oxford University Press, 1971.

9. *Communism in India: Unpublished Documents 1925-1934*, Calcutta: National Book Agency, 1980, pp. 177–78.

10. For a complete list of the Thirty Comrades and their fates, see Bertil Lintner, *Burma in Revolt: Opium and Insurgency Since 1948*, Chiang Mai: Silkworm Books, 2003, pp. 527–29.

11. *Thakin* is a Burmese title which means 'master' and was once reserved for the British. In the 1930s, the Burmese nationalists started to call themselves thakins to demonstrate that they were the real masters of the country. Thakin Thein Pe later dropped that title and became known as Thein Pe Myint. *Yebaw* means 'comrade' and is an honorific used by Burmese communists and socialists.

12. Col. Henry Yule and A.C. Burnell, new edition edited by William Crooke, *Hobson-Jobson: A Glossary of Colloquial Anglo-Indian Words and Phrases, and of Kindred Terms, Etymological, Historical, Geographical Discursive*, New Delhi: Munshiram Manoharlal Publishers, 1979 (originally published in 1903), p. 131.

13. *Myanmar-English Dictionary* by Myanmar Language Commission,

Ministry of Education, Union of Myanmar, Kensington, Maryland, US: Dunwoody Press, 1996.

14. *A Brief History of the Dobbama Asiayone* (in Burmese), Rangoon: Sarpay Beikman, 1976, p. 215,

15. Gustaaf Houtman, *Mental Culture in Burmese Crisis Politics: Aung San Suu Kyi and the National League for Democracy*, Tokyo: Tokyo University of Foreign Studies, 1999, pp. 15ff.

16. See, for instance, Charles B. McLane, *Soviet Strategies in Southeast Asia*, Princeton, New Jersey: Princeton University Press, 1966, p. 352.

17. Ruth McVey, *The Calcutta Conference and the Southeast Asian Uprisings*, Ithaca, New York: Cornell Modern Indonesia Project, Interim Report Series, 1958, p. 8.

18. J.H. Brimmell, *Communism in Southeast Asia*, London: Oxford University Press, 1959, p. 257.

19. See, for instance, Victor Purcell, *Malaya: Communist or Free?*, Stanford, California: Stanford University Press, 1954, pp. 60–61; and Aleksandr Kaznacheev, *Inside a Soviet Embassy: Experiences of a Russian Diplomat in Burma*, London: Robert Hale, 1962, p. 160. The latter book is ostensibly written by a defector from the Soviet embassy in Rangoon, but in reality ghosted by writers from *Reader's Digest*.

20. McVey, op. cit., pp. 7 and 9.

21. Interview with Baladas Ghoshal, Bangkok, 7 March 1993.

22. See for instance John F. Cady, *A History of Modern Burma*, Ithaca and London: Cornell University Press, 1978, p. 582. Thakin Ba Thein Tin provided a detailed account of the youth conference and the CPI's second congress when I interviewed him at Panghsang in December 1986. No other foreign journalist or writer has ever interviewed the late chairman of the CPB.

23. Sumanta Banerjee, *In the Wake of Naxalbari*, Calcutta: Subarnarekha, 1980, p. 82.

24. Interview with Thakin Ba Thein Tin, Panghsang, 23 December 1986.

25. Among them the German scholar Klaus Fleischmann, *Documents on Communism in Burma 1945-1977*, Hamburg: Institut für Asienkunde,

1989, p. 123. Fleichmann's book also contains the full text of the so-called 'Ghoshal thesis'.

26. Martin Smith, *Burma: Insurgency and the Politics of Ethnicity.*, London and New Jersey: Zed Press, 1991, p., 446, and second updated edition, 1999, p. 464. This is just one of many factual errors in Smith's book, which has excellent accounts of smaller rebel armies in Burma such as those among the Karennis and the Pa-Os, but it is considerably weaker when it comes to the CPB, the Kachin and the Shans.

27. Letter from Khin Maung Gyi, dated 14 April 1992, is in my possession.

28. This was acknowledged by U Nu himself in his autobiography *Saturday's Son*, New Haven and London: Yale University Press, 1975, p. 227: '[In the hour of my need] I found in Premier Nehru a friend and a saviour. Without the prompt support in arms and ammunition from India, Burma might have suffered the worst fate imaginable.'

29. Robert Taylor, *The State of Burma*, London: Hurst & Company, 1987, p. 262.

30. Josef Silverstein, *Burma: Military Rule and the Politics of Stagnation*, Ithaca and London: Cornell University Press, 1977, n. 6, p. 181.

31. Interview with Aye Ngwe, Panghsang, 4 January 1987.

32. A copy of the brochure is in my possession.

33. Ian Fellowes-Gordon, *The Battle for Naw Seng's Kingdom*, London: Leo Cooper, 1971, p. ix.

34. Interview with Zau Mai, Panghsang, 3 January 1987. This Zau Mai should not be confused with Malizup Zau Mai, chief of staff of the KIA throughout the 1980s and 1990s.

35. Silvertstein, op. cit. pp. 161–62. From interviews with residents in Rangoon, held less than a year after the affair, Silverstein learned that the shortages in the spring of 1967 were so severe that people were near revolt; the Red Badge affair, however, deflected their rage from their own leaders to the Chinese. When tempers finally cooled, towards the end of the year, the new harvest was beginning to enter the market, and shortages began to disappear; the government

quietly repaired the Chinese restaurants, and communal tensions diminished.

36. Bertil Lintner, *The Rise and Fall of the Communist Party of Burma*, Ithaca, New York: Cornell University South-east Asia Programme, 1990, p. 26. My account of the CPB's expansion at this time is based on extensive interviews with all the CPB leaders who were alive when I visited Panghsang during 1986–87.

37. Interview with ex-colonel Khin Maung Soe, a retired Burmese artillery officer, Bangkok, 1 May 1992. CPB commanders I interviewed in Panghsang during 1986–87 also admitted that the bulk of their fighting force at Kunlong was actually Chinese.

38. Interview with Thuingaleng Muivah, Kesan Chanlam, 21 November 1985. Thakin Pe Tint stayed in China with chairman Thakin Ba Thein Tin until 1978, when the CPB's central office moved to Panghsang headquarters. Pe Tint left for China for medical treatment in 1986, so I never met him when I was in Panghsang. He died in Beijing on 5 July 1990. Thakin Ba Thein Tin died in Changsha in Hunan province in 1995 and Khin Maung Gyi in 2007 in Kunming.

39. The events on the Thai border in August 1976 are still sensitive topics among the Kachin. But according to transcripts of internal radio messages which I read when I was at the KIO's Pa Jau headquarters in 1986, there seems to be little doubt that the junior officer, who carried out the killings and then was himself executed, acted on orders from the north.

40. See Bertil Lintner, *Burma in Revolt: Opium and Insurgency Since 1948*, Chiang Mai: Silkworm Books, 2003, pp. 287–88.

41. *Beijing Review*, 30 July 1976.

42. *Beijing Review*, 30 September 1976.

43. *Beijing Review*, 26 November 1976.

44. Bertil Lintner, 'Broadening the Breach', *The Irrawaddy*, July 2000, available at http://www.irrawaddy.org/article.php?art_id=1896

45. Handwritten minutes of this meeting were passed on to me during a visit to Jinghong, Yunnan, in May 1989.

46. The Morses's escapades are described by a member of the family, Eugene Morse, in *Exodus to Hidden Valley*, London: Collins, 1975.

47. Subir Bhaumik, *Troubled Periphery: Crisis of India's North East*, New Delhi: Sage Publications, 2009, p. 175.

48. Interview with Gauri Zau Seng, a high-ranking Kachin Independence Organization official, Chiang Mai, Thailand, 2 February 2011.

49. This account of the Kachin Baptist mission to the Burmese Naga Hills is based on an interview with Labwi Hthing Nan at a KIA camp in western Kachin state, 27 January 1986.

50. See for instance http://www.myanmar-explore.com/eng/destinations/naga/index.html Indian Naga activists claim there are 500,000 Nagas in Burma living in '300 villages' in Sagaing divison and Kachin state (see http://www.facebook.com/nagayouthburma) which would make it an unrealistic average of more than 1,600 people per village, if there were as many as 300 Naga villages in Burma. There are also no Naga villages in Kachin state, or anywhere east of the Chindwin River. According to Burma News International, a pro-democracy website in exile, there are 200,000 Nagas in Burma, but even that figure is probably too high: http://www.bnionline.net/feature/kng/6193-appalling-conditions-in-naga-hills-region-under-burmese-junta.html

51. This and the following account of developments in the Naga Hills of Burma are based on interviews with S.S. Khaplang at Kesan Chanlam, 12–15 November 1985.

52. 'A Brief Account of Free Nagaland', Publicity Department, Government of the People's Republic of Nagaland, mimeograph, 1982, p. 8.

53. These events are also chronicled in my book *Land of Jade*.

54. A Naga from the Kesan Chanlam area who knew some rudimentary Burmese once asked us when 'those Indians' would 'return home'. He was talking about the Nagas from the Indian side.

55. For the Isak-Muivah faction's version of events, see 'The Joint Statement of Mr. Isak Chishi Swu, Chairman, and Mr. Th. Muivah, Secretary General, the Nationalist Socialist Council of Nagaland', mimeograph dated 7 July 1989.

56. The UNPO has its own website, http://.www.unpo.org Its members range from Tibetan organizations, the Aboriginals of Australia and

other serious parties to an organization in the southern Swedish province of Skåne which could be described as a group of jaunty students calling for 'independence' for their 'homeland.'
57. See the UNPO's website, http://www.unpo.org/members/7899

7. THE INDIAN OCEAN: A TALE OF TWO ISLANDS

1. Dinesh Kumar, 'Weapons Seized were for North-East Militants', *The Times of India*, 13 February 1998, available at http://www.burmalibrary.org/reg.burma/archives/199802/msg00355.html
2. Nandita Haksar, *Rogue Agent: How India's Military Intelligence Betrayed the Burmese Resistance*. New Delhi: Penguin Books, 2009, p. 19. Haksar's book on the case of the events contains many useful details about the case, but is riddled with inaccuracies in regard to Burmese history. The book also badly needs an editor; the narrative is both incoherent and repetitive. A better account of 'Operation Leach' is in Subir Bhaumik, 'Blood and Sand', *Sunday*, 31 May 1998.
3. Haksar, op. cit., p. 63.
4. Andrew Selth, 'Chinese Military Bases in Burma: The Explosion of a Myth', the Griffith Asia Institute, Regional Outlook Paper No. 10, 2007, p. 16, available at www.griffith.edu.au/__data/ . . . /regional-outlook-andrew-selth.pdf See also the Introduction of this book.
5. For a brief biography of B.B. Nandy, see http://en.wikipedia.org/wiki/Bibhuti_Bhusan_Nandy He is also mentioned in Haksar, op. cit., p. 141.
6. For an overview of this policy shift, see Bertil Lintner, 'China and South Asia's East', *Himal*, October 2002, and 'India Stands by Myanmar Status Quo', *Asia Times Online*, 14 November 2007, at http://www.atimes.com/atimes/South_Asia/IK14Df02.html
7. Haksar, op. cit., p. 141.
8. Brahma Chellaney, 'Promoting Political Freedoms in Burma: International Policy Options', in Johan Lagerkvist(ed.), *Between Isolation and Internationalisation: The State of Burma*, Stockholm: Swedish Institute of International Affairs, 2008, p. 167.
9. Available at http://www.strategicstudiesinstitute.army.mil/pubs/display.cfm?pubid=721 and, in full, www.strategicstudiesinstitute.army.mil/pdffiles/ pub721.pdf

10. The New China News Agency, *Xinhua*, 3 November 2009, at http://downstreamtoday.com/newsarticle.aspx?a_id=19041 &AspxAutoDetectCookieSupport=1 and Graeme Jenkins, 'Burmese Junta Profits from Chinese Pipeline', *The Telegraph*, 14 January 2008, at http://downstreamtoday.com/news/article.aspx?a_id= 19041&Aspx AutoDetectCookieSupport=1

11. Bertil Lintner, 'Arms for Eyes', *Far Eastern Economic Review*, 16 December 1993.

12. Chellaney, op.cit., p. 67.

13. For a brief history of the Coco Islands, see Andrew Selth, *Burma's Coco Islands: Rumours and Realities in the Indian Ocean*, Hong Kong: City University, South-east Asia Research Centre, 2008, available online at www6.cityu.edu.hk/searc/Data/FileUpload/294/ WP101_08_ASelth.pdf

14. Ibid., p. 6.

15. Selth writes in *Burma's Coco Islands*, p. 7. that 'Bertil Lintner has suggested that the Great Coco Island penal colony was modelled after Indonesia's Buru Island prison, but the latter facility was not opened until 1969.' But Selth himself writes that 'in 1969, it [the Great Coco penal colony] was enlarged to cater for an increased number of political prisoners.' (p. 7). The penal colony that existed on Great Coco before 1969 was small and not comparable to the Buru Island-like facility that was established later.

16. Interview with Aung Htet, Panghsang, 19 January 1987.

17. Interview with Tin Zaw, aka Hla Pe, another political prisoner who was on Great Coco from February 1969 to December 1971, Manerplaw (Karen rebel headquarters), 11 May 1991.

18. *The Daily Telegrams* (a Port Blair daily), 6 January 2011.

19. 'Patriot Arrives in Port Blair', http://www.c7f.navy.mil/news/2010/ 03-march/32.htm

20. Sudha Ramachandran, 'India Bids to Rule the Waves: From the Bay of Bengal to the Malacca Strait', *Asia Times Online*, 19 October 2005, at http://www.atimes.com/atimes/South_Asia/GJ19Df03.html

21. http://indiannavy.nic.in/Milan%202008_files/Page4063.htm

22. Balaji Chandramohan, 'US Courts India in the Indian Ocean', *Asia*

Times Online, 6 May 2010, http://www.atimes.com/atimes/South_Asia/LE06Df02.html

23. Saibal Dasgupta, 'China Gets First-Ever Chance to Enter Indian Ocean for Exploration', *Times of India*, 2 August 2011, http://articles.timesofindia.indiatimes.com/2011-08-02/china/29842183_1_ore-deposit-mineral-exploration-cnpc

24. Ibid.

25. This story is told, and refuted, in P. Mathur, *History of the Andaman and Nicobar Islands*, Delhi: Sterling Publishers, 1968, pp. 13–14.

26. Referred to at this website: http://www.esa.int/esaEO/SEMQ8L2IU7E_index_0.html

27. Mathur, op. cit. pp. 272–73.

28. Ibid., pp. 273–74. After the first Danish missionaries came Moravian Christians.

29. For a colourful description of Ross Island, see Tilak Ranjan Bera, *Andamans: The Emerald Necklace of India*, New Delhi: UBS Publishers, 2007, pp. 31–41.

30. Mathur, op. cit. pp. 221–22. For an account of the penal colony in the Andamans, see also Baban Phaley, *The Land of Martyrs: Andaman & Nicobar Islands*, Nagpur: Saraswati Prakashan, 2009.

31. Phaley, op. cit. pp. 60–61.

32. C. Uday Bhaskar, 'Rising Together', *Himal*, September 2010.

33. For an excellent account of the Indian communities in Burma, see Nalini Ranjan Chakravarti, *The Indian Minority in Burma: The Rise and Fall of an Immigrant Community*, London: Oxford University Press, 1971.

34. Quoted in Bertil Lintner, 'Different Strokes', *Far Eastern Economic Review*, 23 February 1989, available online at http://www.burmalibrary.org/reg.burma/archives/199701/msg00063.html

35. C.S. Kuppuswamy, 'Myanmar-India Cooperation', South Asia Analysis Group, 3 February 2003, http://www.southasiaanalysis.org/%5Cpapers6%5Cpaper596.html

36. Vijay Rana, 'China and India's Mutual Distrust', *BBC News*, 21 April 2003, at http://news.bbc.co.uk/2/hi/south_asia/2964195.stm

37. For Maung Aye's visits to Shillong and New Delhi in 2000, see 'Maung Aye's Itinerary in India', Mizzima News Group,

15 November 2000, at http://www.ibiblio.org/obl/reg.burma/archives/200011/msg00071.html

38. Bertil Lintner, 'India Stays by Myanmar Status Quo', *Asia Times Online*, 14 November 2007, at http://www.atimes.com/atimes/South_Asia/IK14Df02.html

39. Ibid.

40. 'India, Myanmar sets $1 bn trade target in 2006-2007', *The Economic Times*, 15 February 2007, at http://economictimes.indiatimes.com/articleshow/1619338.cms

41. Amitav Rajan, 'Myanmar Burning, MEA Told Deora: We Need to Visit But Keep it Low-key', *Indian Express*, 28 September 2007, at http://www.indianexpress.com/news/myanmar-burning-mea-told-deora-we-need-to/222028/

42. 'ASEAN Diplomats Confident Of Trade Boom', *Manipur Online*, 19 September 2010, at http://manipuronline.com/headlines/asean-diplomats-confident-of-trade-boom/2010/09/19

43. 'Hebron' was where Abraham made his first covenant, an alliance with some local clans. It is unclear why the NSCN (IM) chose this name for its camp because the original Hebron today is a major Palestinian town in the Israeli-occupied West Bank.

44. For an account of the arrest and its aftermath, see Bertil Lintner, 'Grounded', *The Week*, 5 March 2000, available at http://www.ibiblio.org/obl/reg.burma/archives/200002/msg00089.html

45. Ibid. This is based on several interviews with Thai and other intelligence operatives in January and February 2000.

46. Jayanta Sarkar, 'Tribal Trouble', *Far Eastern Economic Review*, 1 September 1994.

47. 'Some Background on the AIPP, *BurmaNet*, 30 August 1994, http://www.burmalibrary.org/reg.burma/archives/199408/msg00068.html

48. According to talks I have had with Thai travel agents in Chiang Mai, who were approached by Thai intelligence, and Thai intelligence officers who carried out the surveillance.

49. See http://www.aippnet.org/home/urgent-appeal/248-urgent-appeal.

50. See, *National Investigation Agency, Ministry of Foreign Affairs, Government of India, New Delhi, Charge Sheet U/s 173 CrPC* (in the Court of Special Judge NIA, Patiala House Courts, New Delhi, 26 March 2011).

51. Saikat Datta, 'The Great Claw of China', *Outlook*, 7 February 2011, at http://www.outlookindia.com/article.aspx?270223

52. Interview with Gauri Zau Seng, a high-ranking Kachin Independence Organization official, Chiang Mai, Thailand, 2 February 2011.

53. *Charge Sheet U/s 173 CrPC*, pp. 7–8.

54. 'UNLF Confirms Arrest of Sana Yaima', *Hueiyen News Service*, 16 October 2010.

55. 'ULFA military chief in China: Top UNLD leader', *NDTV News*, 22 June 2011, at http://www.ndtv.com/article/india/ulfa-military-chief-in-china-top-unlf-leader-78089

56. 'UNLF Vows to Continue Liberation Struggle Despite Setbacks', *Imphal Free Press* on *Kangla Online*, 24 November 2010, at http://kanglaonline.com/2010/11/unlf-vows-to-continue-liberation-struggle-despite-setback/

57. See https://mail.google.com/mail/?shva=1#search/fake+surrenders/ 1309a5b92f282fb9

58. Ratnadiop Chaudhury, 'NSCN-IM Extortion Note to OIL', *Tehelka*, 17 June 2011, at http://www.tehelka.com/story_main49.asp?filename= Ws170611NSCN.asp

59. Subir Bhaumik, 'What Next For ULFA?' 25 December 2009, at http://subirbhowmikscolumn.blogspot.com/

60. This source has requested anonymity.

61. Atonu Choudhurri, 'Espionage scare in Arunachal', *The Telegraph*, 26 May 2010, at http://www.telegraphindia.com/1100526/jsp/northeast/story_12486031.jsp

62. Nisit Dholabhai, 'Spy? She just took pictures', *The Telegraph*, 1 February 2011, at http://www.telegraphindia.com/1110201/jsp/nation/story_13519484.jsp. See also http://www.siasat.com/english/news/india-coy-over-chinese-spy

63. James Dunnigan, 'Save the New Stuff for the Chinese', The *Strategy Page*, 9 March 2010, at http://www.strategypage.com/dls/articles/Save-The-New-Stuff-For-The-Chinese-3-9-2010.asp

64. See Bertil Lintner, 'Northeast India: Boiling Pot of International Rivalry – Part II', *YaleGlobal Online*, 19 February 2010, at http://yaleglobal.yale.edu/content/northeast-india-boiling-pot-international-rivalry-part-i

65. La means 'pass' in Tibetan. Skirmishes, but no major battles, between Indian and Chinese troop occurred at Nathu La during the 1962 war.

66. See Tania Branigan, 'China sentences 76 over Tibet riots', *The Guardian*, 11 February 2009, at http://www.guardian.co.uk/world/2009/feb/11/tibet-china-riots

67. See for instance, 'China Official Warns of Domestic Unrest and "Hostile" West', *Reuters*, 22 February 2011.

68. Sudha Ramachandran, 'Naga Purge Benefits New Delhi', *Asia Times Online*, 24 June 2011, at http://www.atimes.com/atimes/South_Asia/MF24Df05.html

69. There is also a third group of islands called the Cocos, off the coast of Costa Rica in Central America.

70. SMS stands for Seiner Majestäts Schiff, His Majesty's Ship, in German.

71. An outline of the Chagos islanders' case can be found at http://business.timesonline.co.uk/tol/business/law/reports/article1862399.ece See also Duncan Campbell and Matthew Weaver, 'Chagos islanders lose battle to return', *The Guardian*, 22 October 2008, at http://www.guardian.co.uk/politics/2008/oct/22/chagos-islanders-lose

72. Ross Babbage, *Should Australia Plan to Defend Christmas and Cocos Islands?*, Canberra: Strategic and Defence Studies Centre, The Australian National University, 1988, p. 33.

73. Ibid.

74. Ibid., pp. 36 and 40.

75. See also Bertil Lintner, 'Australia's Strategic Little Dots', *Asia Times Online*, 25 June 2010, at http://www.atimes.com/atimes/China/LF25Ad01.html

76. Selth, op. cit.

77. Billy Tea, 'Unstringing China's Strategic Pearls', *Asia Times Online*,

11 March 2011, at http://www.atimes.com/atimes/China/MC11Ad02.html

78. Josh Rogin, 'Webb: We can't let Burma become a "Chinese province"', *Foreign Policy*, 27 October 2010, at http://thecable.foreignpolicy.com/posts/2010/10/27/webb_we_can_t_let_burma_become_a_chinese_province

79. See Bertil Lintner, 'Clouded Alliance: North Korea and Myanmar's Covert Ties', *Jane's Intelligence Review*, October 2009

80. Quoted in a 1989 report by Human Rights Watch. See http://www.unhcr.org/refworld/country,,HRW,,MMR,,467bb4881d,0.html

81. See Bertil Lintner, 'China Behind Myanmar's Course Shift', *Asia Times Online*, 19 October 2011, http://www.atimes.com/atimes/Southeast_Asia/MJ19Ae04.html and Bertil Lintner, 'Realpolitik and the Myanmar Spring', *Foreign Policy*, 30 November 2011, http://www.foreignpolicy.com/articles/2011/11/30/democracy_myanmar_china_clinton

82. Ronald O'Rourke, *China Naval Modernization: Implications for US Navy Capabilities – Background and Issues for Congress*, Washington: Congressional Research Service, 22 April 2010. Available at http://opencrs.com/document/RL33153/

POSTSCRIPT

1. See, for instance, *Democratic Voice of Burma*, 30 September 2011, 'China-backed Myitsone Dam Suspended', at http://www.dvb.no/news/china-backed-myitsone-dam-%E2%80%98suspended%E2%80%99/17887, and Bertil Lintner, 'Burma Delivers Its First Rebuff to China', *Yale Global Online*, 3 October 2011, at http://yaleglobal.yale.edu/content/burma-delivers-its-first-rebuff-china

2. A copy of the original document (in Burmese) is in my possession.

3. For an assessment of the 2008 referendum, see 'Burmese Constitutional Referendum: Neither Free nor Fair'. The Public International Law & Policy Group, Washington, May 2008, http://www.docshut.com/zmkkz/pilpg-report-burmese-constitutional-referendum-neither-free-nor-fair-may-2008.html and 'No Real

Choice: An Assessment of Burma's 2008 Referendum'. *Burma Institute for Political Analysis and Documentation*, Rangoon, 2009, available at http://www.burmalibrary.org/show.php?cat=595

4. Jackie Calmes, 'A US Marine Base for Australia Irritates China', *New York Times*, 16 November 2011, http://www.nytimes.com/2011/11/17/world/asia/obama-and-gillard-expand-us-australia-military-ties.html?pagewanted=all

5. https://www.wikileaks.org/plusd/cables/10RANGOON30_a.html

6. Bertil Lintner, 'Myanmar's Endless Ethnic Quagmire', *AsiaTimes Online*, 8 March 2012, http://www.atimes.com/atimes/Southeast_Asia/NC08Ae02.html

7. http://www.bbc.co.uk/news/uk-21217884

8. 'US Wants India to Play Significant Role in Asia Pacific', *Press Trust of India*, 23 November 2011, http://www.hindustantimes.com/world-news/Americas/US-wants-India-to-play-significant-role-in-Asia-Pacific/Article1-772839.aspx

9. Bertil Lintner, 'More War than Peace in Myanmar', *Asia Times Online*, 18 December 2012, http://www.atimes.com/atimes/Southeast_Asia/NL18Ae01.html

10. Bertil Lintner, 'Powers Seek Influence in Burma's Conflict', *YaleGlobal Online*, 18 March 2013, http://yaleglobal.yale.edu/content/powers-seek-influence-burmas-conflict

11. Bertil Lintner, 'Myanmar Morphs to US-China Battlefield', *Asia Times Online*, 2 May 2013, http://www.atimes.com/atimes/Southeast_Asia/SEA-01-020513.html

ANNOTATED BIBLIOGRAPHY

THE SINO-INDIAN FRONTIER, ARUNACHAL PRADESH AND TIBET

BOOKS

Ali, Mahmud S, *Cold War in the High Himalayas: The USA, China and South Asia in the 1950s*, Surrey: Curzon Press, 1999, 286 pp. By the editor of the BBC World Service's Bengali service who examines the relationships between India, Pakistan, the USA and China in the 1950s.

Avedon, John F, *In Exile from the Land of Snows*, London: Wisdom Publications, 1985, 479 pp. The story of Tibet as told to the author by Tibetans in exile, including a man who was trained by the US Central Intelligence Agency (CIA) in Colorado.

Borah, Swapnali, Deke Tourangbam, and **A.C. Meitei**, *Encyclopaedic Studies of North-Eastern States of India: Arunachal Pradesh*, New Delhi: New Academic Publishers, 2010, 251 pp. Contains information about history, anthropology, religions developments and the political situation in Arunachal Pradesh.

Barua, Lalit Kumar, *India's Northeastern Frontier: The Colonial Legacy*, Guwahati and Delhi: Spectrum Publications, 2010, 68 pp. Includes Captain St John Mitchell's 1892 report 'Notes on the North-East Frontier of Assam', which describes the political and economic situation north of the Brahmaputra plain before the McMahon Line was drawn up in 1914.

Bower, Ursula Graham, *The Hidden Land*, London: John Murray, 1953, 244 pp. The same author who wrote *Naga Path* (included in the later section) examines tribal societies in the North-East Frontier Agency (now Arunachal Pradesh).

Chandola, Harish, *The Naga Story: First Armed Struggle in India*. New Delhi and New York: Chicken Neck, an Imprint of Bibliophile South Asia, 2012, 428 pp. A comprehensive study of the Naga conflict written by an Indian journalist who has been involved in the peace process in Nagaland.

Chakravarti. P.C., *India-China Relations*, Calcutta: Firma K.L. Mukhopadhyay, 1961, 195 pp. An overview of Sino-Indian relations from 1950 to 1960, written before the 1962 war; concludes that 'the key to Sino-Indian relations lies hidden in the soil of Tibet.'

Craig, Mary, *Tears of Blood: A Cry for Tibet*, New Delhi: HarperCollins Indus, 1992, 374 pp. A very critical account of China's occupation of Tibet, which covers events from 1951 to 1991, including the 1959 uprising and the turmoil of 1990–91.

Chowdhury, J.N., *The Tribal Culture and History of Arunachal Pradesh*, Delhi: Daya Publishing House, 1990, 187 pp. A comprehensive overview of the religions and customs of the tribal population of Arunachal Pradesh.

Conboy, Ken, and **James Morrison**, *The CIA's Secret War in Tibet*, Lawrence: University Press of Kansas, 2002, 301 pp. One of the most authoritative accounts of the CIA's secret war in Tibet.

Dalai Lama, *My Land and My People: Memoirs of His Holiness the Dalai Lama of Tibet*, London: Panther Books, 1964, 254 pp. Dalai Lama's own memoirs which include glimpses of old Tibet, his dealings with China, the flight to India in 1959, and life in exile.

Dalvi, J.P., *Himalayan Blunder: The Angry Truth about India's Most Crushing Military Disaster*, Dehra Dun: Natraj Publishers, 1969 (reprinted 1997, 2010), 506 pp. An excellent account of the 1962 Sino-Indian war written by an Indian Army brigadier, who took part in the action and was held captive by the Chinese for seven months.

Das, Gautam, *China and India: The 1962 War and the Strategic Military Future*, New Delhi: Military Affairs Series, Har-Anand Publications, 2009,

340 pp. An interesting account of Sino-Indian relations by an Indian Army officer who also examines China's questionable historical claims to Tibet.

Dunham, Mikel, *Buddha's Warriors: The Story of the CIA-backed Tibetan Freedom Fighters, the Chinese Invasion, and the Ultimate Fall of Tibet*, New York: Jeremy P. Tarcher/Penguin, 2004, 434 pp. A detailed account of the CIA's secret war in Tibet, with a foreword by the Dalai Lama.

Elwin, Verrier, *A Philosophy for NEFA (North East Frontier Agency)*, Delhi: Isha Books, 2009 (reprint, first published in 1957). With a foreword by Jawaharlal Nehru; outlines Elwin's proposed policy for the integration of NEFA.

Epstein, Israel, *Tibet Transformed*, Beijing: New World Press, 1983, 566 pp. A pro-Chinese account of developments in Tibet written by a Polish-American communist who resided in Beijing until his death in 2005.

French, Patrick, *Younghusband: The Last Great Imperial Adventurer*, London: Penguin Books, 2011, 440 pp. A beautifully written and well-researched biography of Sir Francis Younghusband, the British officer who led a military expedition to Lhasa in 1904 and later became what French calls 'a premature hippy'.

Fürer-Heimendorf, Christoph von, *The Apa Tanis and Their Neighbours*, London and New York: Routledge & Kegan Paul, 1962, 166 pp. A detailed account of the Apatani tribe in Arunachal Pradesh.

Garver, John W., *Protracted Contest: Sino-Indian Rivalry in the Twentieth Century*, Seattle and London: University of Washington Press, 2001, 447 pp. The writer, an American academic, examines the two countries' actions and policy decisions over the past fifty years.

Gelder, Stuart and **Roma Gelder**, *The Timely Rain: Travels in New Tibet*, New York and London: Monthly Review Press, 1964, 248 pp. A pro-Chinese account of a journey through Tibet in the early 1960s. Stuart Gelder was also the official translator of Mao Zedong's *Selected Works* into English.

Goldstein, Melvyn C., *A History of Modern Tibet 1913-1951: The Demise of the Lamaist State*, New Delhi: Munishiram Manoharlal Publishers, 2007 (reprint; first published by University of California Press, 1989), 898 pp. A detailed history of the period in Tibet's history when it was completely free of Chinese influence.

Gupta, Karunakar, *Spotlight on Sino-Indian Frontiers,* Calcutta: New Book Centre, 1982, 178 pp. A pro-Chinese account of the Sino-Indian border dispute distributed by the Communist Party of India (Marxist)'s publishing firm.

Harrer, Heinrich, *Seven Years in Tibet,* London: Pan Books, 1956, 267 pp. A classic written by an Austrian mountaineer who escaped to Tibet from British custody in India. In Lhasa, he became a close friend of the Dalai Lama.

———,*Return to Tibet: Tibet After the Chinese Invasion,* New York: Penguin Putman, 1998, 210 pp. Harrer returns to Tibet in 1982 and witnesses the Chinese destruction of the country.

Knaus, John Kenneth, *Orphans of the Cold War: America and the Tibetan Struggle for Survival,* New York: Public Affairs, 1999, 399 pp. An excellent account of the American involvement with the Tibetan resistance by a former CIA operations officer who helped organize covert operations in the Himalayas.

Lamb, Alastair, *The McMahon Line: A Study in Relations between India, China and Tibet, 1904 to 1914,* London: Routledge and Kegan Paul, 1966, two volumes.

Kohli, M.S., and **Kenneth Conboy,** *Spies in the Himalayas: Secret Missions and Perilous Climbs,* Lawrence: University Press of Kansas, 2002, 226 pp. A very readable and authoritative account of Cold War espionage and CIA-sponsored spy missions in the Himalayas.

Laird, Thomas, *Into Tibet: The CIA's First Atomic Spy and His Secret Expedition to Lhasa,* New York: Grove Press, 2002, 364 pp. The story of an American undercover expedition into Tibet during 1949–50, months before the Chinese invaded.

Levenson, Claude B., *Dalai Lama: A Biography,* London, Sydney and Wellington: Unwin Hyman, 1988, 291 pp. A fairly romantic account of the Dalai Lama and life in Tibet before the Chinese invasion. But it also covers more recent anti-Chinese riots in Lhasa and the Dalai Lama's travels abroad where he stated his policy of a 'Middle Way', allowing for limited autonomy in Tibet rather than full independence.

Mansingh, Surjit (ed.), *Indian and Chinese Foreign Policies in Comparative Perspective*, New Delhi: Radiant Publishers, 1998, 530 pp. A collection of essays by security analysts, academics and former military officers.

McGranahan, Carole, *Arrested Histories: Tibet, the CIA, and Memories of a Forgotten War*, Durham, North Carolina: Duke University Press, 2010, 308 pp. The author examines the CIA-sponsored resistance in Tibet, and explains the ensuing repercussions for the Tibetan refugee community.

McKay, Alex, *Tibet and Her Neighbours: A History*, London: Edition Hansjörg Mayer, 2003, 240 pp. Examines Tibet's historically complex relations with the outside world, including Nepal, Bhutan, Mongolia, India, China and the United States.

Maxwell, Neville, *India's China War*, London: Penguin Books, 1972, 546 pp. A detailed account of the 1962 war which questions the belief that India was the victim of unprovoked Chinese aggression.

Noorani, A.G., *India-China Boundary Problem: History and Diplomacy 1846-1947*, New Delhi: Oxford University Press, 2011, 351 pp. A comprehensive study of the Sino-Indian border dispute with maps of the areas of conflict.

Norbu, Thubten Jigme, and **Colin Turnbull**, *Tibet: Its History, Religion and People*, London: Penguin Books, 1972, 366 pp. An account of Tibet's history and traditions by the elder brother of the fourteenth Dalai Lama and British academic.

Osik, N.N., *Modern History of Arunachal Pradesh (1825-1997)*, Itanagar and New Delhi: Himalayan Publishers, 1999, 150 pp. A rare history of Arunachal Pradesh from the early days of British colonial rule to the late 1990s by a native of the state.

Palit, D.K., *War in High Himalaya: The Indian Army in Crisis, 1962*, London: Lancer International, C. Hurst & Co. Publishers, and New York: St Martin's Press, 1991, 450 pp. A detailed account of the 1962 war by a retired brigadier general in the Indian Army. Includes some very useful maps.

Patterson, George N., *Peking Versus Delhi*, London: Faber and Faber, 1963, 310 pp. An early study of the rivalry between China and India, written a year after the Himalayan war. Includes notes on NEFA (now Arunachal Pradesh) and Nagaland.

Peissel, Michel, *The Secret War in Tibet*, Boston and Toronto: Little Brown and Company, 1972, 258 pp. A unique inside account of the Tibetan resistance written by a French author, explorer and scholar.

Sali, M.L., *India China Border Dispute*, New Delhi: 1998, 313 pp. Deals in detail India's historical claims to Aksai Chin, and the formation of the McMahon Line (which the author, an academic, unfortunately, calls the MacMohan Line).

Senanayake, Ratne Deshapriya, *Inside Story of Tibet*, Colombo: The Afro-Asian Writers' Bureau, 1967, 164 pp. A pro-Chinese account of developments in Tibet written by a Sri Lankan journalist.

Shakaba, Tsepon W.D., *Tibet: A Political History*, New Delhi: Paljor Publications, 2010 (fifth printing), 520 pp. A detailed history of Tibet, written by Tibet's secretary of finance 1930–50, and later the Dalai Lama's official representative in New Delhi. First published in 1967.

Shakya, Tsering, *The Dragon in the Land of Snows: A History of Modern Tibet Since 1947*, London: Pimlico, 1999, 574 pp. A very detailed history of modern Tibet by a Western-educated Tibetan, including a detailed account of the CIA's involvement with the resistance.

Singh, K. Natwar, *My China Diary 1956-88*, New Delhi: Rupa & Co, 2009, 206 pp. Recounts events that occurred when the author served as a diplomat in Beijing. He later became India's external affairs minister (2004–05).

Singh, K.S., *People of India Volume, XIV: Arunachal Pradesh*, Calcutta: Anthropological Survey of India, 1995, 465 pp. Describes in detail the history, cultures and social systems of all the ethnic groups in Arunachal Pradesh.

Strong, Anna Louise, *When Serfs Stood Up in Tibet*, Beijing: Foreign Languages Press, 2003, 222 pp. A pro-Chinese account of developments in Tibet since the Chinese invasion, written by an American communist.

Thant Myint-U, *Where China Meets India: Burma and the New Crossroads of Asia*, New York: Farrar, Straus and Giroux, 2011, 361 pp. About new and old links between India's north-eastern region, northern Burma, and south-western China.

Wang Lixiong and **Tsering Shakya**, *The Struggle for Tibet*, London and New York: Verso, 2009, 277 pp. Covers recent unrest in Tibet; by a Beijing-based, dissident Chinese writer who is sympathetic to the Tibetan cause, and a Tibetan historian who teaches at the University of British Columbia, Canada.

Wignall, Sydney, *Spy on the Roof of the World: A True Story of Espionage and Survival in the Himalayas*, New York: Lyons & Burford, 1996, 267 pp. A fascinating account of a British mountaineer who was assigned by Indian intelligence to investigate Chinese incursions into Tibet and Aksai Chin in the 1950s.

Ya Hanzhang, *The Biographies of the Dalai Lamas*, Beijing, Foreign Languages Press, 1991, 442 pp. The official Chinese version of the lives of the fourteen Dalai Lamas. Attempts to prove that Tibet has always been part of China.

OFFICIAL PUBLICATIONS

Concerning the Question of Tibet, Beijing: Foreign Languages Press, 1959, 276 pp. An official Chinese version of Tibetan history and the question of Tibet's sovereignty.

The Chinese Threat, New Delhi: Publications Division, Ministry of Information and Broadcasting, Government of India, 1963, 77 pp. +maps.

The Sino-Indian Boundary Question, Beijing: Foreign Languages Press, 1962, 134 pp. +maps.

The Tibetans in Exile 1959-1980, Dharamshala: Information Office, Central Tibetan Secretariat, 1981, 306 pp. Includes details about Tibetan refugee settlements in India and the government in exile's offices in the United States and Switzerland.

ARTICLES AND PAPERS

Babayeva, Yuliya, 'The Khampa Uprising: Tibetan Resistance Against the Chinese Invasion', *Honours College Theses*, Paper 31, Pforzheimer Honours College, 8 January 2006, 30 pp. Available at http://digitalcommons.pace.edu/honorscollege_theses/31

Datta, Saikat, 'The Great Claw of China', *Outlook*, 7 February 2011. Although mostly about Anthony Shimray, an arms procurer for the Naga rebels, it also contains interesting material about how Chinese companies sell arms to insurgents in the region. Available at http://www.outlookindia.com/article.aspx?270223

Deane, Hugh, 'The Cold War in Tibet'. *Covert Action Information Bulletin*, No. 29 winter 1987.

Garver, John W., and **Fei-Ling Wang**, 'China's Anti-encirclement Struggle', *Asian Survey*, Vol. 6, No. 3, 2010, pp. 238–61.

Gearing, Julian, 'Lama Wars: Can the Dalai Lama hold his divided people together – and keep China at bay?' *Asiaweek* (cover story), 20 October 2000.

———, 'The tale of two Karmapas'. *Asia Times Online*, 24 December 2003. Available at http://www.atimes.com/atimes/China/EL24Ad02.html

Jose, Vinod K., 'Spies in the Snow: How the CIA and Indian Intelligence Lost a Nuclear Device in the Himalayas', *The Caravan* (cover story), December 2010.

Liu, Melinda, 'Tibet: China's Kosovo? The Inside Story of How the CIA Helped the Dalai Lama', *Newsweek* (cover story; Asian edition), 19 April 1999.

Roy, Anirban, 'Return of the Dalai Lama', *The Northeast Today* (cover story), November 2009.

NAGALAND AND THE NAGAS

BOOKS

Allen, B.C., *Naga Hills and Manipur: Socio-Economic History*, Delhi: Gian Publications, 1980 (reprint, first published in 1905), 151 pp. An early account of the Indo-Burmese border.

Anand, V.K., *Nagaland in Transition*, New Delhi: Associated Publishing House, 1967, 144 pp. An account of the war in Nagaland from the point of view of an Indian army officer.

——, *Conflict in Nagaland: A Study of Insurgency and Counter-Insurgency*, Delhi: Chanakya Publications, 1980, 268 pp. A more detailed study of the war by the same author.

Ao, Akang (ed.)., *A Light to the Nagas*, Mokokchung: Molungkimong Baptist Church, undated, 64 pp. A drama which enacts hundred years of the Baptist church in the Ao area.

Ao, Alemchiba, *A Brief Historical Account of Nagaland*, Kohima: Naga Institute of Culture, 1970, 261 pp. One of the first attempts to make a systematic record of the history of the Naga Hills. The author is a Naga of the Ao tribe.

Ao, Lanunungsang, *From Phizo to Muivah: The Naga National Question in North East India*, New Delhi: Mittal Publications, 2002, 409 pp. A comprehensive history of modern Nagas and the problems surrounding unification of the various political factions in Nagaland.

Aram, B., *Peace in Nagaland: Eight Years Story, 1964-72*, New Delhi: Arnold-Heinemann, 1974, 335 pp. About the peace process in the Naga Hills and the emergence of Nagaland as a state within the Indian Union.

Barua, S.N., *Tribes of Indo-Burma Border*. New Delhi: Mittal Publications, 1991, 411 pp. A study of the social systems of the various tribes, mostly Naga, who inhabit the Patkai range.

Bower, Ursula Graham, *Naga Path*, London: John Murray, 1952, 238 pp. An excellent account of life among the Naga tribes of Manipur, especially the Tangkhul.

Chasie, Charles, *The Naga Imbroglio (A Personal Perspective)*, Guwahati: United Publishers, 1999, 230 pp. Written by a senior Naga journalist in the form of an informal letter to the Naga people.

Das, N.K., *Kinship Politics and Law in Naga Society*, Calcutta: Anthropological Survey of India, 1993, 183 pp. About Naga polity and social structure.

Dev, S.C., *Nagaland: The Untold Story*, Calcutta: Mrs Gouri Dev, 1988, 209 pp. One of the most authoritative accounts of the integration of Nagaland with additional notes on Assam, Meghalaya, Mizoram, Manipur and Tripura.

Elwin, Verrier, *The Nagas in the Nineteenth Century*, Oxford and Bombay: Oxford University Press, 1969, 650 pp. A thorough account of the Nagas' first contacts with the outside world written by a British administrator who was for ten years adviser for tribal affairs to the North-East Frontier Agency, now Arunachal Pradesh.

——, *Nagaland*, Shillong: the Research Department of the Adviser's Secretariat, 1961, 108 pp. A second and updated edition was published by Krishan Kumar (United Publishers) on behalf of Spectrum, 1997, 108 pp. A detailed account of how the administration of the Naga Hills changed in the late 1950s.

Fürer-Heimendorf, Christoph von, *The Naked Nagas*, Calcutta: Thacker Spink & Co., reprint 1968, 239 pp. A unique account of Naga life and society in the 1930s by a prominent anthropologist.

——, *Return to the Naked Nagas*, London: John Murray, 1976, 268 pp. The same anthropologist returns to the Naga Hills in the 1970s.

Ganguli, Milada, *A Pilgrimage to the Nagas*, New Delhi: Oxford & IBH Publishing Co., 1984, 277 pp. An account of the author's – a naturalized Indian citizen of Czech origin – experiences among the Naga tribes in the 1970s.

Ghosh, B.B., *History of Nagaland*, New Delhi: S. Chand & Company, 1982, 264 pp. A history of the area by a former editor of the *Nagaland District Gazette*.

Glancey, Jonathan, *Nagaland: A Journey to India's Forgotten Frontier*, London: Faber and Faber, 2011, 268 pp. A travelogue by a British journalist who in many ways overemphasizes the 'remoteness' of the Naga Hills.

Hodson, T.C., *The Naga Tribes of Manipur*, Delhi: Low Price Publications, 1989 (reprint, first published in 1911), 199 pp. Similar to B.C. Allen's book, but with more emphasis on the Nagas of Manipur.

Horam, Mashangthei, *Naga Insurgency*. New Delhi: Cosmo Publications, 1988, 344 pp. A Naga himself, the author examines the origin and course of the Naga insurgency.

——, *Naga Polity*, Delhi: Low Price Publications, 1992, 161 pp. The same author deals with Naga life and culture.

Hutton, J.H., *The Angami Nagas*, Bombay: Oxford University Press, 1969, 499 pp. A definitive account of the Angami tribe.

——, *The Sema Nagas*, Bombay: Oxford University Press, 1968, 467 pp. A similar book about the Sema Nagas.

——, *The Ao Nagas*, Bombay: Oxford University Press, 1973, 510 pp. The same in the series, about the Ao Nagas.

International Work Group for Indigenous Affairs, *The Naga Nation and Its Struggle Against Genocide*, Copenhagen: IWGIA Document 56, 1986, 236 pp. A general survey of the history and present conditions of the Naga tribes.

Iralu, Kaka., *Nagaland and India: The Blood and the Tears*, Kohima: Self-published, 2000, 543 pp. A personal account of Naga history from the British time to the mid-1970s, including accounts of Naga missions to Pakistan and China.

Jacobs, Julian, *The Nagas: Hill Peoples of Northeast India*, London: Thames and Hudson, 1990, 359 pp. An attractive and informative coffee-table-style book about the Nagas and their culture.

Kamei, Gangmumei, *A History of the Zeliangrong Nagas: From Makhel to Rani Gaidinliu*, Guwahati and Delhi: Spectrum Publications, 2004, 356 pp. Contains a detailed account of the Zeliangrong uprising in the 1930s led by Jadonang and Gaidinliu.

Kanwar, Randip Singh, *The Nagas of Nagaland: Desperadoes and Heroes of Peace*, New Delhi: Deep & Deep Publications, 1987, 199 pp. Written by a former police officer who organized the Naga police force in the 1950s and 1960s.

Lintner, Bertil, *Land of Jade: A Journey from India through Northern Burma to China*, Bangkok: White Lotus, 1996 and 2011, and Guwahati and Delhi: Spectrum Publications, 2011, 380 pp. Includes an account of a five-month stay in Nagaland as well as the Naga Hills of Burma in 1985. Also published in Manipuri (2006 and 2009).

Luithui, Luingam, and **Nandita Haksar**, *Nagaland File: A Question of Human Rights*, New Delhi: Lancer International, 1984, 277 pp. Includes the most important documents relating to Naga nationalism and alleged human-rights abuses in the area.

Luthra, P.N., *Nagaland: From a District to a State*, Guwahati: Tribune Press, 1974, 122 pp. A brief account of political developments in Nagaland in the 1960s.

Mankekar, D.R., *On the Slippery Slope in Nagaland*, Bombay: Maniktala, 1967, 202 pp. An account of the peace process in the 1960s from an official Indian point of view.

Maxwell, Neville, *India and the Nagas*, London: Minority Rights Group Report No 17, 1973, 32 pp. A background to the war in Nagaland by a former South Asia correspondent for *The Times*.

Mills, J.P., *The Lotha Nagas*. London: Macmillan and Company, 1922. Similar to Hutton's books about the Lotha Nagas.

———, *The Ao Nagas*. London: Macmillan and Company, 1929, 510 pp. A similar book on the Ao Nagas.

———, *The Rengma Nagas*. London: Macmillan and Company, 1937, 428 pp. A similar book about the Rengma Nagas.

Ngareophun, Ng, *Legacy of R. Suisa*, Imphal: Tarun Printing, 1977, 70 pp. A compilation of documents by and about R. Suisa, a Tangkhul Naga member of the Indian parliament in the 1960s.

Nibedon, Nirmal, *Nagaland: The Night of the Guerrillas*, New Delhi: Lancers Publishers, 1983, 404 pp. A racy account of the civil war in Nagaland written by an Indian journalist.

Nuh, V.K., *Nagaland Church and Politics*, Kohima: Vision Press, 1986, 235 pp. An account of the church in politics by a Chakhesang Naga.

Philip, Puthuvail Thomas, *The Growth of Baptist Churches in Nagaland*, Guwahati: Christian Literature Centre, 1983, 228 pp. Outlines the spread of Christianity among the Naga tribes.

Pillai, Sushil K., 'Anatomy of an Insurgency: Ethnicity and Identity in Nagaland', in K.P.S. Gill and Ajai Sahn ed., *Faultlines: Writings on Conflicts and Resolution*, Delhi: Bulwark Books, 1999 pp. 39–78. An excellent background paper on the ethnic conflict in Nagaland.

Puthenpurakal, Joseph, *Baptist Missions in Nagaland*, Shillong: Vendrame Missiological Institute, 1984, 292 pp. A study of the beginnings of the Baptist church in Nagaland.

Sanyu, Visier, *A History of Nagas and Nagaland*, New Delhi: Commonwealth Publishers, 1996, 162 pp. A history of Naga society from a Naga point of view (the author hails from the legendary Angami village of Khonoma).

Saul, J.D., *The Naga of Burma: Their Festivals, Customs and Way of Life*, Bangkok: Orchid Press, 2005, 214 pp. The result of thirty years of fieldwork among the Nagas of north-western Burma. Contains unique pictures of the Burmese Nagas.

Scott, Michael, *The Nagas: India's or the World's? The Search for Peace*, London, 1967, 47 pp. A pamphlet about the peace process in the 1960s written by a British priest who played an important role in initiating talks between the Naga rebels and the Indian government.

Sema, Hokishe, *Emergence of Nagaland: Socio-Economic and Political Transformation and the Future*, New Delhi: Vikas Publishing House, 1986,

272 pp. The author played a crucial role in establishing peace in the Naga Hills in the 1960s and later became chief minister of the state of Nagaland.

Singh, Chandrika, *Political Evolution of Nagaland*, New Delhi: Lancers Publishers, 1981, 244 pp. An account of political developments in the Naga Hills by a former instructor in the Assam Rifles.

Singh, K.S. (ed.), *The People of India Volume XXXIV: Nagaland*, Calcutta: Anthropological Survey of India, 1994, 286 pp. Detailed descriptions of the various Naga tribes of Nagaland as well as other non-Naga communities in the state.

Singh, Prakash, *Nagaland*, New Delhi: National Book Trust, 1972, 233 pp. Impressions by an author who served as a police officer in Nagaland from 1965 to 1968.

Steyn, Pieter, *Zapuphizo: Voice of the Nagas*, London, New York and Bahrain: Kegan Paul, 2002, 230 pp. A biography of A.Z. Phizo written by a British sympathizer who spent time with the Nagas during World War II.

Stracey, P.D., *Nagaland Nightmare*, Bombay: Allied Publishers, 1968, 320 pp. About war and peace in Nagaland.

Tyson, Geoffrey, *Forgotten Frontier*, Calcutta: W.H. Targett & Co., 1945. The story of the work of the Indian Tea Association in assisting the escape into India of refugees from Burma during the summer of 1942. Contains unique information about the Nagas and other frontier peoples.

Yonuo, Asoso, *The Rising Nagas*, Delhi: Manas Publications, 1984, 440 pp. A detailed account of Naga history and society by a Naga from the Nagaland–Manipur border.

Young, Gavin, *The Nagas: An unknown war. India's threat to peace*, London: the Naga National Council, 1962, 27 pp. A compilation of articles by the only Western journalist to visit the Naga war zones in the 1960s.

SELECTED REBEL PUBLICATIONS:
NAGA NATIONAL COUNCIL (NNC) AND
'THE FEDERAL GOVERNMENT OF NAGALAND'

A Brief Historical Background of Naga Independence, undated mimeograph, 68 pp. Naga history as seen by the NNC.

The Case of the Nagas, undated mimeograph, 49 pp. An outline of Naga history as seen by the NNC.

Naga Goodwill Mission to Assam: Report, Nov. 30-Dec. 15, 1953, 1984, printed in Gauhati (Guwahati), 58 pp.

Report on Naga Political Affairs From 1978 to 1981, by W. Shapwon Heimi, Chaplee Kilonser, Federal Government of Nagaland, Eastern Oking, 12 pp. Contains a list of Naga rebel leaders who were killed by the Isak-Muivah faction during the turmoil of the late 1970s.

Phizo Souvenir, printed 1991 and reprinted 2008 in Kohima, 26 pp. Published after Phizo's death in London on 30 April 1990.

A Brief Account of Nagaland, June 2000, 30 pp., printed. A collection of documents and open letters written by NNC activists.

A.Z. Phizo: Birth Centenary 1904-2004, May 2004, printed in Kohima, 42 pp. A biography of A.Z. Phizo.

Nagaland and Th. Muivah's Terrorist Activities, printed in Kohima, 28 April 2005, 108 pp. Contains lists of hundreds of Nagas who, according to the NNC, were murdered by the NSCN.

Golden Jubilee: Federal Republic of Nagaland 1956-2006, March 2006, printed in Kohima, 52 pp. Includes a chronology of events 1880–1996, and pictures of prominent Nagas.

A Collection of the Press Interviews and Statements of the Naga National Council and the Federal Government of Nagaland, Sept. 2002-May 2008, August 2008, 104 pp.

SELECTED REBEL PUBLICATIONS:
NATIONAL SOCIALIST COUNCIL OF NAGALAND
[NAGALIM] (NSCN) AND 'THE PEOPLE'S REPUBLIC OF
NAGALAND' [NAGALIM]

Manifesto of the National Socialist Council of Nagaland, 31 January 1980, printed, 42 pp. Declares the formation of the NSCN and outlines its policies, including a one-party system, 'the dictatorship of the people', socialism, 'the faith in God' and 'Nagaland for Christ'.

Statement of the National Socialist Council of Nagaland, 3 January 1984, printed, 23 pp. A policy declaration denouncing A.Z. Phizo and the Naga National Council.

Polarisation, 7 February 1985, mimeograph, 43 pp. A scathing attack on A.Z. Phizo and the Naga National Council.

The Joint Statement of Mr. Isak Chishi Swu, Chairman, and Mr. Thuingaleng Muivah, Secretary General of the National Socialist Council of Nagaland (sic). 7 July 1989, mimeograph, 26 pp. Outlines Isak and Muivah's version of the April–May 1988 uprising by S.S. Khaplang's Burmese Nagas against the Nagas from the Indian side.

A Political Account of Free Nagaland, 7 May 1992, mimeograph, 32 pp. Mentions 'miracles' and 'healing' performed by Naga activists in the Naga Hills of Burma.

MIZORAM

BOOKS

Chatterjee, Suhas, *Making of Mizoram: Role of Laldenga – Vol 1 and 2*, New Delhi: M.D. Publications, 1994, 445 pp. About the emergence of Mizoram as a state in the Indian Union and the role of former rebel chief Laldenga, who became the first chief minister of the state.

——, *Mizo Chiefs and the Chiefdom*, New Delhi: M.D. Publications, 1995, 201 pp. An excellent social history of the Mizos and their system of chiefdom.

Chawngkunga, C., *Important Documents of Mizoram*, Aizawl: Art and Culture Department, 1998, 384 pp. A collection of historical documents relating to the Mizos (Lushais) from the British time to independence in 1947, and recent state election results in Mizoram.

Elly, E.B., *Military Report on the Chin-Lushai Country*, Aizawl: Tribal Research Institute, 1978 (reprint, first published in 1893), 17 pp. An interesting account of British forays into the Lushai (Mizo) hills in the late nineteenth century by a British army officer.

Halkin, Hillel, *Across the Sabbath River: In Search of a Lost Tribe of Israel*, Boston and New York: Houghton Mifflin Company, 2002, 394 pp. Are the Mizos, as many of them believe, one of the ten lost tribes of Israel? The author, an American-Israeli Jew, travels to the Indo-Burmese border to find out.

Hre Mang, J.H., *Report on the Chin Refugees in Mizoram State of India*, New Delhi: Other Media Communications, 2000, 127 pp. About the tens of thousands of Chins (who are ethnically related to the Mizos) from Burma who have sought refuge in Mizoram.

Human Rights Watch, *'We Are Like Forgotten People': The Chin People of Burma: Unsafe in Burma, Unprotected in India*, New York: Human Rights Watch, 2009, 104 pp. A report on the situation of the Chin refugees from Burma in Mizoram. The report was criticized by Mizo community groups for being 'anti-Mizo', which Human Rights Watch denies.

Kipgen, Mangkhosat, *Christianity and Mizo Culture*, Aizawl: Mizo Theological Conference, 1997, 359 pp. An excellent account of the encounter between Christianity and Mizo culture.

Lalkhama, *A Mizo Civil Servant's Random Reflections*, Aizawl: Lalkhama, 2006, 368 pp. Memoirs of the first Mizo direct-recruit officer with the Indian Administrative Service, IAS, who is also one of the signatories of the 1986 Mizo peace accord.

Lalnithanga, P., *Emergence of Mizoram*, Aizawl: Lengchhawn Press, 2010, 555 pp. A detailed account of Mizo history from the days of British colonial rule to statehood in 1987. Also contains long lists of Mizo officials and community leaders.

Nag, Sajal, *Pied Pipers in North-East India: Bamboo-flowers, Rat-famine and the Politics of Philanthropy (1881-2007)*, New Delhi: Manohar, 2008, 307 pp. About the ecological phenomenon known as bamboo flowering, which occurs every thirty to forty years. The one in 1959 caused an uprising in the area, which broke out in the mid-1960s and continued until 1986. The author teaches modern contemporary history at Assam Central University, Silchar.

Nibedon, Nirmal, *Mizoram: The Dagger Brigade*, New Delhi: Lancers Publishers, 1980, 269 pp. A detailed, lively account of the Mizo rebellion by the author of *Nagaland: The Night of the Guerrillas*.

Prasad, R.N., (ed.), *Autonomy Movements in Mizoram*, New Delhi: Vikas Publishing House, 1994, 221 pp. A collection of essays about ethnic strife and insurgency in Mizoram.

Shakespear, J., *The Lushei Kuki Clans*, Guwahati and Delhi: Spectrum Publications, 2004 (reprint, initially published in the UK in 1912), 250 pp. The history, folklore, traditional religion, and clan system among the Lushei (Lushai) and Kukis.

Tribal Research Institute, *The Mizo Heroes*, Aizawl: The Tribal Research Institute, Government of Mizoram, 2003, 145 pp. Interesting biographies of Mizo national heroes in pre-colonial times. Later, Mizo rebel units were named after some of those heroes.

Verghese, C.G. and **R.L. Thanzawna**, *A History of the Mizos, Vols I and II*, New Delhi: Vikas Publishing House, 1997, 370 pp. and 334 pp. A detailed history of the Mizos by a retired Indian Army officer and a Mizo civil servant.

Vumson, *Zo History*, Aizawl: By the author, undated but most probably published in the early 1990s, 349 pp. A comprehensive history of the Zo (Mizo, Chin) people and their struggle to preserve their separate identity. By a Chin from Burma who later settled in the United States.

PAPERS

Jafa, Vijendra Singh, 'Grouping of Villages in Mizoram (1968-1970)', presented at a seminar on grouping of villages, Aizawl, 7–9 September 2010.

Weil, Shalva, 'Lost Israelites From the Indo-Burmese Borderlands: Re-Traditionalisation and Conversion Among the Shinlung or Bene Menasseh', *Anthropologist*, Vol. 6, No. 3, 2004, pp. 219–33. Available at http://www.scribd.com/doc/22147803/Burmese-Jews

MANIPUR

BOOKS

Chishti, S.M.A.W., *The Kuki Uprising in Manipur 1919-1920*, Guwahati and Delhi: Spectrum Publications, 2004, 84 pp. A brief but well-researched account of the 1919–20 Kuki rebellion against the British.

Grimwood, Ethel St Clair, *My Three Years in Manipur*, New Delhi: Gyan Publishing House, 2008 (reprint), 294 pp. The memoirs of the wife of the British political agent of Manipur during the close of the nineteenth century.

Haokip, P.S., *Zale'n-gam: The Land of the Kukis*, published by the Kuki National Organization in 1996 and written by its chairman, 96 pp. Gives the Kuki version of the conflict with National Socialist Council of Nagaland (Isak-Muivah) in the 1990s.

———, *Zale'n-gam: The Kuki Nation*, first published by the Kuki National Organization in 1998, 302 pp., and then a revised and expanded edition in 2008, 608 pp., by the chairman of the Kuki National Organization. The second edition contains gory pictures of Kukis killed by the NSCN(IM) in the 1990s.

Hemant, Sagolsem, *Far Beyond in the Misty Hills: An Unforgettable Trip to Meet a Rebel Leader*, Shillong: Ibohal Kshetrimayum for Eikhoigi Panthung,

2008, 167 pp. An account of a trek into the wilds of the India–Burma border, where the author met Sana Yaima, the leader of the United National Liberation Front, by the president of the All Manipur Working Journalists' Union.

Kshetri, Rajendra, *The Emergence of Meeitei Nationalism*, New Delhi: Mittal Publications, 2006, 214 pp. A history of national movements in Manipur since the days of Irawat (Irobot) by a Manipuri academic.

Ningthouja, Malem, *Freedom From India: A History of Manipur Nationalism (1947-2000)*, Guwahati and Delhi: Spectrum Publications, 2011, 362 pp. A very nationalistic account of political movements in Manipur by an academic who is also a political activist.

Parratt, John, *Wounded Land: Politics and Identity of Modern Manipur*, New Delhi: Mittal Publications, 2005, 252 pp. Covers Manipur's merger with independent India in 1947 and subsequent insurgencies, civil rights abuses and government failures to find a solution to the conflict. By a British scholar whose wife is a Manipuri academic.

Singh, K.S. (ed.), *People of India Volume XXXI: Manipur*, Calcutta: Anthropological Survey of India, 1998, 286 pp. An overview of the various peoples and tribes of Manipur in a series about India's ethnic groups.

Singh, N. Kelchandra, Sapam Bheigya and **Sorokhaibam Rupoban Singh** (eds), *Kangla: The Ancient Capital of Manipur*, Calcutta: Seagull Books (Anthropological Survey of India), 2006, 185 pp. A good overview of Manipur history and the importance of the ancient capital Kangla.

Singh, N. Joykumar, *Revolutionary Movements in Manipur*, New Delhi: Akansha Publishing House, 2005, 189 pp. Examines the genesis, nature and character, leadership and impacts of Manipur's many anti-government rebel groups. By a Manipuri academic.

Singh, T. Hemo, *Manipur Imbroglio*, New Delhi: Akansha Publishing House, 2009, 380 pp. A very good overview of Manipur's various insurgencies by a Manipuri officer in the Indian Army.

REBEL PUBLICATIONS

A Brief Introduction to Manipur and Her Liberation Struggle and General Programme of the United National Liberation Front: Manipur, mimeograph, 12 pp. The Goodwill Mission of the Central Committee of the UNLF: Manipur, Pa Jau, 9 January 1986.

ASSAM AND MEGHALAYA

BOOKS

Bhat, Anil, *Assam: Terrorism and the Demographic Challenge*, New Delhi: Centre for Land Warfare Studies, 2009, 82 pp. A brief study of illegal immigration and insurgency in Assam by an Indian Army officer who served in Assam in the 1990s.

Bora, S., *Student Revolution in Assam 1917-1947 (A Historical Survey)*, New Delhi: Mittal Publications, 1992, 388 pp. Deals with the early years of the student movement in Assam, but also provides useful information of the origin of more recent agitations in the state.

Dutta, Anuradha, *Assam in the Freedom Movement*, Calcutta: Darbari Prokashan, 1991, 372 pp. An account of the growth of the Indian independence movement in Assam.

Gait, Edward Albert, *A History of Assam*, Guwahati and Delhi: Spectrum Publications, 2011 (reprint, first published in 1905), 388 pp. A history of Assam by a senior colonial officer and ethnographer.

Ghose, Sumita (ed.), *Sanjoy's Assam: Diaries and Writings of Sanjoy Ghose*, New Delhi: Penguin Books, 1998, 258 pp. Compiled in memory of Sanjoy Ghose, who died in captivity of Assamese militants in 1997.

Gogoi, Lila (ed.), *The Tai Khamtis*, Calcutta: Nabajiban Press, 1971, 210 pp. A collection of writings about the Tai Khamtis of Assam and the closely related Hkamtis of Upper Burma, and their relations with other ethnic groups in the area.

Gogoi, Puspadhar, *Tai of North-East India*, Dhemaji, Assam: Chumra Printers and Publications, 1996, 88 pp. The history and culture of Assam's Tai peoples (Ahom, Khamti, Phake, Aiton, Turung and Khamyang) by an Assamese academic.

Gohain, Hiren, *Assam: A Burning Question*, Guwahati: Spectrum Publications, 1985, 183 pp. A collection of articles on the movement in Assam against 'foreign infiltration' from mainly Bangladesh.

Gurdon, P.R.T., *The Khasis*, Delhi: Low Price Publications, 1992 (reprint, originally published in 1903), 227 pp. A colonial account of the Khasis which describes them as 'a tribe of independent Tartars'.

Lahiri, Rebati Mohan, *The Annexation of Assam (1824-1854)*, Calcutta: Firma K.L. Mukhopadhyay, 1975 (reprint, originally published in 1954), 250 pp. It described how Assam became part of British India.

ARTICLES

Bhaumik, Subir, 'Caught in Cox's Bazar: The Inside Story of the Arrest of Arabinda Rajkhowa'. *The Week*, 20 December 2009.

Reid, Sir Robert, 'The Excluded Areas of Assam', *The Geographical Journal*, Vol. 103, Nos. 1–2 (January-February 1944), pp. 18–29.

——, 'Fire in Assam: South Asia's Arc of Crisis' (cover story), *Asiaweek*, 4 March 1983.

THE NORTH-EAST IN GENERAL, COUNTER-INSURGENCY, INTELLIGENCE AND INDIAN STATECRAFT

BOOKS

Barua, Lalit Kumar, *India's North-East Frontier: The Colonial Legacy*, Guwahati: Spectrum Publications, 2010, 68 pp. A collection of colonial writings about India's north-eastern frontier.

Baruah, Sanjib, *Durable Disorder: Understanding the Politics of Northeast India*, New Delhi: Oxford University Press, 2005, 265 pp. The author argues that prolonged counter-insurgency operations have eroded the democratic fabric of the region and institutionalized authoritarian practices.

——, (ed.), *Beyond Counterinsurgency: Breaking the Impasse in Northeast India*, New Delhi: Oxford University Press, 2009, 383 pp. Essays on the northeast, including Assam, Nagaland, Manipur and Mizoram.

Bhattacharji, Romesh, *Lands of Early Dawn: North East of India*, New Delhi: Rupa & Co., 2002, 350 pp. A personal account of travels through the northeastern states by an Indian commissioner of customs.

Bhattacharya, Rakhee, *Development Disparities in Northeast India*, Delhi, Bengaluru, Mumbai, Kolkata, Chennai, Hyderabad and Pune: Foundation Books (an imprint of Cambridge University Press), 2011, 176 pp. Mainly about recent economic developments in the north-east, it also contains interesting details about the finances of insurgent groups in India's north-east, or so-called 'revolutionary taxation'.

Bhaumik, Subir, *Insurgent Crossfire: North-East India*, New Delhi: Lancer Publishers, 1996, 360 pp. An overview of insurgency in India's north-east written by the BBC's former Kolkata correspondent.

——, *Troubled Periphery: Crisis of India's North East*, New Delhi: Sage Publications, 2009. 305p. An excellent and very detailed account of north-eastern India's ethnic problems.

Chadha, Vivek, *Low Intensity Conflicts in India*, New Delhi: Sage Publications, 2005, 515 pp. An excellent study of local insurgencies by an Indian army officer who served in the north-east (and Jammu and Kashmir).

Chaudhury, Sabyasachi Basu Ray, Samir Kumar Das, and **Ranabir Samaddar** (eds), *Indian Autonomies: Keywords and Key Texts*, Calcutta, New Delhi and London: Sampark, 2005, 465 pp. A collection of essays about various tribal areas in India, including Assam, Nagaland, Manipur and Tripura.

Chib, S.S., *Caste, Tribes and Culture of India Vol 8: North-Eastern India*, New Delhi: Ess Ess Publications, 1984, 328 pp. Deals with the historical background and sociocultural spectrum of the communities in India's north-east.

Dhar, Maloy Krishna, *Open Secrets: India's Intelligence Unveiled*, New Delhi: Manas Publications, 2005, 519 pp. This book by a former joint director of India's Intelligence Bureau (IB), this book describes intelligence operations in, among other parts of the country, the north-east.

Elwin, Verrier, *The Tribal World of Verrier Elwin: An Autobiography*, New York and Bombay: Oxford University Press, 1964, 356 pp. The autobiography of one of Jawaharlal Nehru's chief advisers on tribal affairs.

Fürer-Heimendorf, Christoph von, *Life Among Indian Tribes: The Autobiography of an Anthropologist*, Delhi: Oxford University Press, 1991, 186 pp. Von Fürer-Heimendorf's autobiography with notes about the Apatanis of Arunachal Pradesh and other tribes.

——, *The Tribes of India: The Struggle for Survival*, Delhi: Oxford University Press, 1989, 342 pp. Not only about the north-east but also about other tribal communities in India and their relations with the majority population.

Hazarika, Sanjoy, *Strangers of the Mist: Tales of War and Peace from India's Northeast*, New Delhi: Viking, 1994, 388 pp. A personal account of north-eastern India's social and political problems written by an Assamese journalist.

——, *Rites of Passage: Border Crossings, Imagined Homelands, India's East and Bangladesh*, New Delhi: Penguin Books, 2000, 347 pp. The same author writes about illegal migration from Bangladesh and other cross-border issues.

Hussain, Wasbir (ed.), *Peace Tools & Conflict Nuances in India's Northeast*, Guwahati: Worldwaves India Publications, 2010, 235 pp. A collection of essays on ethnic strife and insurgencies in India's north-east.

Intelligence Branch Division of the Chief of Staff Army Headquarters, India, *North and North-Eastern Frontier Tribes of India*, Delhi: Cultural Publishing House, 1983 (reprint; first published in 1907 by Government

Monotype Press, Simla), 249 pp. Describes the land and peoples of India's north-eastern frontier at the turn of the century.

Kautilya, *The Arthashastra*, New Delhi: Penguin Books, 1992, 819 pp. An ancient treatise on statecraft and military strategy by a Maurya Empire statesman and philosopher who lived c. 350–283 BC. The basic philosophies outlined here are still practised by India's security services.

Khanna, S.K., *Encyclopaedia of North-East India*, Delhi: Indian Publishers' Distributors, 1999, 724 pp. Contains chapters about Assam, Meghalaya, Tripura, Mizoram, Manipur, Nagaland, Arunachal Pradesh and Sikkim.

Marwah, Ved, *India in Turmoil: Jammu & Kashmir, the Northeast and Left Extremism*, New Delhi: Rupa & Co, 2009, 352 pp. Contains ninety pages on ethnic and political problems in India's north-eastern states. The author is a former member of the Indian Police Service.

Mullik, B.N., *My Years With Nehru 1948-1964*, Bombay: Allied Publishers, 1972, 474 pp. Contains a detailed account of behind-the-scenes dealings in the 1960s written by Prime Minister Jawaharlal Nehru's security adviser.

———, *My Years With Nehru: The Chinese Betrayal*, Bombay: Allied Publishers, 1971, 650 pp. The first edition of B.N. Mullik's memoirs in which he does not cover covert operations in Nagaland and other sensitive issues. The focus here is on the conflict with China.

Nepram, Binalakshmi, *South Asia's Fractured Frontier: Armed Conflicts, Narcotics and Small Arms Proliferation in India's North East*, New Delhi: Mittal Publications, 2002, 310 pp. Written by a Manipuri researcher and peace activist.

Nibedon, Nirmal, *North-East India: The Ethnic Explosion*, New Delhi: Lancers Publishers, 1981, 220 pp. The author of *Nagaland: The Night of the Guerrillas* and *Mizoram: The Dagger Brigade* looks at north-east India in a broader perspective.

Pakem, B., (ed.), *Insurgency in North-East India*, New Delhi: Omsons Publications, 1997, 375 pp. A collection of essays, including 'The External Linkages in Insurgency in India's Northeast' by Subir Bhaumik.

Raina, Asoka, *Inside RAW: The Story of India's Secret Service*, New Delhi: Vikas Publishing House, 1981, 117 pp. The first book about RAW, the Research and Analysis Wing, to appear in print in India. Describes Indian action in East Pakistan and the creation of Bangladesh in 1971.

Raman, B., *The Kaoboys of RAW: Down Memory Lane*, New Delhi: Lancers Publishers, 2007, 294 pp. Memoirs of an Indian intelligence officer with the Research and Analysis Wing (RAW) which contains notes on Assam, Manipur and Nagaland, and its capabilities for covert action relating to Pakistan and China.

Reid, Sir Robert, *History of the Frontier Areas Bordering on Assam 1883-1941*, Guwahati and Delhi: Spectrum Publications, 1997 (reprint, first published in 1942), 303 pp. Reid draws from his experience as governor of Assam 1937–42.

Rustomji, Nari, *Enchanted Frontiers*, Delhi: Oxford University Press, 1973, 333 pp. A vivid account of life and politics in India's north-east by an Indian political officer who served as prime minister of Sikkim and adviser to the king of Bhutan.

——, *Imperilled Frontiers: India's North-Eastern Borderlands*, Delhi: Oxford University Press, 1983, 160 pp. A sequel to *Enchanted Frontiers*.

Saikia, Jaideep (ed.), *Frontier in Flames: North East India in Turmoil*, New Delhi: Penguin Books/Viking, 2007, 205 pp. The authors argue that 'even after sixty years of independence, integration with the rest of India has eluded the states of the Northeast'.

——, *Documents on North East India* (Compiled by Jaideep Saikia), New Delhi: Institute for Defence Studies and Analyses, 2010, 308 pp. A useful collection of key documents relating to political developments in India's Northeast, including peace treaties with ethnic rebels.

Sarin, V.I.K., *India's Northeast in Flames*, Ghaziabad: Vikas Publishing House, 1982, 267 pp. A brief overview of ethnic issues in Assam, Nagaland, Manipur, Tripura, Mizoram and Arunachal Pradesh.

Sarma, Siddhartha, *East of the Sun: A Nearly-Stoned Walk Down the Road in a Different Land*, Chennai: Tranquebar, 2010, 249 pp. A sometimes humorous account of a young Indian's travels in the north-east.

Shakespear, L.W., *History of Upper Assam, Upper Burma, and the North-East Frontier*, London: Macmillan and Company, 1914, 264 pp. A classic history of Assam and surrounding frontier areas.

Singh, K.S. (ed.), *Tribal Movements in India*, Vol. 1, New Delhi: Manohar, 2006, 403 pp. A collection of essays on ethnic conflicts in India's northeast.

Sinha, Surajit (ed.), *Tribal Polities and State Systems in Pre-Colonial Eastern and North Eastern India*, Calcutta and New Delhi: K.P. Bagchi & Company, 1987, 366 pp. A collection of essays on pre-colonial Assam, Meghalaya, Mizoram, Sikkim and Orissa.

Tarapot, Phanjoubam, *Insurgency Movements in North Eastern India*, New Delhi: Vikas Publishing House, 1993, 254 pp. The author, a Manipuri journalist, outlines the backgrounds of the insurgencies in Assam, Nagaland and Manipur.

Thompson, Sir Robert, *Revolutionary War in World Strategy 1945-1969*, New York: Taplinger Publishing Company, 1970, 171 pp. Does not deal with India, but Indian counter-insurgency strategists used Thompson's teachings as a model for operations in Mizoram in the 1960s and 1970s.

Verghese, B.G., *India's Northeast Resurgent: Ethnicity, Insurgency, Governance, Development*, New Delhi: Konark Publishers Pvt. Ltd, 1996, 476 pp. An account of political developments in India's north-east, including Nagaland.

Vidyarthi, L.P., *Art and Culture of North East India*, New Delhi: Publications Division, Government of India, 1986, 124 pp. This book gives a fair account of the origin, history and cultural heritage of the various tribal peoples in north-eastern India.

ARTICLES

Cline, Lawrence E., 'The Insurgency Environment in Northeast India', *Small Wars and Insurgencies*, Vol. 17, No. 2, June 2006, pp.126–47.

Datta, Saikat, 'The Great Claw of China: The Confessions of NSCN (IM) leader Anthony Shimray'. *Outlook*, 7 February 2011, available at http://www.outlookindia.com/article.aspx?270223

Lintner, Bertil, 'Northeast India: Boiling Pot of International Rivalry-I', *Yale Global Online*, 17 February 2010, available at http://yaleglobal.yale.edu/content/northeast-india-boiling-pot-international-rivalry-part-i

——, 'Northeast India: Boiling Pot of International Rivalry-II', *Yale Global Online*, 19 February 2010, available at http://yaleglobal.yale.edu/content/northeast-india-boiling-pot-international-rivalry-part-ii

THE NAXALITE MOVEMENT

BOOKS

Banerjee, Sumanta, *In The Wake of Naxalbari: A History of the Naxalite Movement in India*, Calcutta: Subarnarekha, 1980, 436 pp. Probably the most accurate and detailed account of the early years of India's Maoist movement.

Chakravarti, Sudeep, *Red Sun: Travels in Naxalite Country*, New Delhi: Penguin Books, 2008, 411 pp. A personal account of travels through Naxal-influenced areas in India which also contains very useful background information about the movement.

Duyker, Edward, *Tribal Guerrillas: The Santals of West Bengal and the Naxalite Movement*, Bombay, Calcutta and Madras: Oxford University Press, 1987, 201 pp. About Naxalite-inspired movements among the tribal population of West Bengal by an Australian academic.

Ghosh, Suniti Kumar, *Naxalbari: Before and After*, Kolkata: New Age

Publishers, 2009, 350 pp. Written by a former member of the Central Committee of the Communist Party of India (Marxist-Leninist).

Mishra, Trinath, *Barrel of the Gun: The Maoist Challenge And Indian Democracy*, New Delhi: Sheriden Book Company, 2007, 372 pp. A comprehensive study of India's neo-Maoist movement by a former Indian police officer.

Roy, Asish Kumar, *Unfinished Revolution: The Spring Thunder and Beyond*, Kolkata: Minerva, 2008, 304 pp. An account of the Naxalite movement by a professor of political science and international relations in Kolkata.

Singh, Prakash, *The Naxalite Movement in India*, New Delhi: Rupa & Co., 2006, 318 pp. By a former officer in the Indian Police Service; contains useful biographical sketches of major Naxalite leaders.

ARTICLES

'Spring Thunder Over India', *People's Daily*, 5 July 1967, reproduced in *Liberation*, Vol. 1, No. 1, November 1967, available at http://www.marxists.org/subject/china/documents/peoples-daily/1967/07/05.htm

THE INDIAN OCEAN

BOOKS

Babbage, Ross, *Should Australia Plan to Defend Christmas and Cocos Islands?*, Canberra: Strategic and Defence Studies Centre, the Australian National University, 1988, 74 pp. About the strategic significance of Australia's Indian Ocean territories.

Bera, Tilak Ranjan, *Andamans: The Emerald Necklace of India*, New Delhi: UBSPD, 2002, 117 pp. A comprehensive introduction to the history, culture and geography of the Andaman and Nicobar Islands.

Dasgupta, Jayant, *Japanese in the Andaman & Nicobar Islands: Red Sun Over Black Water*, New Delhi: Manas Publications, 2002, 168 pp. A rare account of the Japanese occupation of the Andaman and Nicobar Islands during 1942–45.

Gordon, Sandy, *Security and Security Building in the Indian Ocean Region*, Canberra: Strategic and Defence Studies Centre, the Australian National University, 1996, 243 pp. An Australian study of security issues in the Indian Ocean.

Gupta, Manoj, *Indian Ocean Region: Maritime Regimes for Regional Cooperation*, London: Springer Science and Business Media, 2010, 400 pp. A detailed study of relations between the various Indian Ocean countries.

Haksar, Nandita, *Rogue Agent: How India's Military Intelligence Betrayed the Burmese Resistance*, New Delhi: Penguin Books, 2009, 242 pp. The story behind the events that led to 'Operation Leech' in 1998, when a number of Burmese rebels were apprehended in the Andamans. However, the book contains several historical inaccuracies.

Husain, Syed Anwar, *Superpowers & Security in the Indian Ocean: A South Asian Perspective*, Dhaka: Academic Publishers, 1992, 196 pp. Security issues in the Indian Ocean region as seen by a professor at the University of Dhaka.

Kaplan, Robert D., *Monsoon: The Indian Ocean and the Future of American Power*, New York: Random House, 2010, 367 pp. A thought-provoking exploration of the Indian Ocean as a strategic and demographic hub in the region by a senior American writer and academic.

Mathur, L.P., *History of the Andaman and Nicobar Islands (1756-1966)*, Delhi: Sterling Publishers, 1968, 355 pp. Probably the most detailed history of the islands that has been published in India.

Mukerjee, Madhusree, *The Land of the Naked People: Encounters with Stone Age Islanders*, New Delhi: Penguin Books, 2003, 238 pp. Provides unique insights into tribal life in the Andamans.

Phaley, Baban, *The Land of Martyrs: Andaman and Nicobar Islands*, Nagpur: Sarswati Prakashan, 2009, 136 pp. A brief introduction to the islands with notes about their past as a penal colony.

Vaidya, Suresh, *Islands of the Marigold Sun*, London: Robert Hale Limited, 1960, 192 pp. A personal account of travels to the Andamans in the 1950s.

ARTICLES AND PAPERS

Bhaskar, C. Uday, 'Rising Together', *Himal*, September 2010.

Datta, Soumen with **Anish Gupta** and **Sourabh Sen**, 'Blood and Sands', *Sunday*, 6 June 1990. A revealing account of 'Operation Leech' in the Andamans, including reproduction of documents which prove that there was a link between the so-called 'gunrunners' and Indian intelligence.

Dutta, Sanjay, 'Navy eyes Maldives-Counter to China's "String of Pearls" plan'. *The Telegraph*, 20 August 2009.

Lintner, Bertil, 'The Phuket Connection', *The Week*, 30 April 2000, available at http://www.asiapacificms.com/articles/phuket_connection/

———, 'Australia's Strategic Little Dots', *Asia Times Online*, 25 June 2010. http://www.atimes.com/atimes/China/LF25Ad01.html

Selth, Andrew, 'Burma's Coco Islands: Rumours and Realities in the Indian Ocean', City University of Hong Kong: South-east Asia Research Centre, No. 101, November 2008, 14 pp.

Tea, Billy, 'Unstringing China's Strategic Pearls', *Asia Times Online*, 11 March 2011. An attempt to prove that China has not strategic designs for the Indian Ocean. Available at http://www.atimes.com/atimes/China/MC11Ad02.html

THE CHITTAGONG HILL TRACTS
OF BANGLADESH

BOOKS

Bhaumik, Subir, Meghna Guhathakurta, and **Sabyasachi Basu Ray Chaudhury** (eds), *Living on the Edge: Essays on the Chittagong Hill Tracts*, Calcutta: South Asia Forum for Human Rights, Calcutta Research Group, 1997, 289 pp. A collection of essays by Indian and Bangladeshi academics and journalists.

Mey, Wolfgang (ed.), *Genocide on the Chittagong Hill Tracts of Bangladesh*, Copenhagen: International Work Group for Indigenous Affairs, 1984, 192 pp. A comprehensive overview of the history of the Chittagong Hill Tracts and atrocities committed there after Pakistan's independence in 1947 (and the creation of Bangladesh in 1971).

Shelley, Mizanur Rahman (ed.), *The Chittagong Hill Tracts: The Untold Story*, Dhaka: Centre for Development Research, Bangladesh (CDRB), 1992, 200 pp. An informative account of the Chittagong Hill Tracts which also reflects official views in Bangladesh.

The Chittagong Hill Tracts Commission, *Life Is Not Ours: Land and Human Rights in the Chittagong Hill Tracts, Bangladesh*, Amsterdam: the Chittagong Hill Tracts Campaign, 1991, 131 pp. A report compiled by Dutch activists, it was updated in 1992 and 2000.

ARTICLES

Chakma, Bhumitra, 'The Post-Colonial State and Minorities: Ethnocide in the Chittagong Hill Tracts, Bangladesh', *Commonwealth Comparative Politics*, 3 July 2010, pp. 281–300.

Lintner, Bertil, 'Intractable hills/Isolated force/Tribal turmoil', *Far Eastern Economic Review*, 5 April 1990.

REBEL PUBLICATIONS

Persecution of Human Rights in Chittagong Hill Tracts, Department of Information and Publicity, Parbatya Chattagram Jana Samhati Samiti, September 1987, 153 pp.

A Charter of Five Point Demands Submitted by the Parbatya Chattagram Jana Samhati Samiti (United People's Party) on Behalf of the Jumma People to the Government of the People's Republic of Bangladesh, Parbatya Chattagram Jana Samhati Samiti, December 1987, 7 pp.

INSURGENCY IN NORTHERN BURMA

BOOKS

Fellows-Gordon, Ian, *Amiable Assassins*, London: Robert Hale, 1957, 159 pp. About the Kachin resistance to the Japanese during World War II, but also gives an excellent description of living conditions in northern-most Burma.

Gibson, Richard M., with **Wen H. Chen**, *The Secret Army: Chiang Kaishek and the Drug Warlords of the Golden Triangle*, Singapore: John Wiley & Sons, 2011, 354 pp. A detailed account of America's and Taiwan's secret war in the Burmese sector of the Golden Triangle.

Gilhodes, A., *The Kachins: Religion and Customs*, Bangkok: White Lotus, 1996 (reprint, first published 1922), 243 pp. A record of the myths and tales of the Kachin peoples of northern-most Burma.

Leach, E.R., *Political Systems of Highland Burma: A Study of Kachin Social Structure*, London: G. Bell and Sons, 1964, 324 pp. Originally published in 1954, this is considered the standard work on Kachin social structure.

Lintner, Bertil, *Outrage: Burma's Struggle for Democracy*, London and Bangkok: White Lotus, 1990, 208 pp. An account of the 1988 uprising for democracy in Burma.

——, *Burma in Revolt: Opium and Insurgency Since 1948*, Chiang Mai: Silkworm Books, 1994, 558 pp. A history of Burma's various insurgencies, including the Kachin and the Naga rebellions in the north and north-west.

——, *The Rise and Fall of the Communist Party of Burma*, Ithaca, New York: Cornell University South-east Asia Program, 1990, 111 pp. A history of Burma's communist movement from 1939 to its collapse in 1989.

——, *The Kachin: Lords of Burma's Northern Frontier*, Chiang Mai: Teak House Books, 1997, 258 pp. A coffee-table-style book about the Kachins and their martial traditions.

——, (with **Michael Black**), *Merchants of Madness: The Methamphetamine Explosion in the Golden Triangle*, Chiang Mai: Silkworm Books, 2009, 180 pp. Drugs and insurgencies in Burma after the 1989 CPB mutiny.

Morse, Eugene, *Exodus to a Hidden Valley*, London: Collins, 1974, 224 pp. The story about an American missionary family who moved with their Lisu followers from the Putao area in northern Burma to Chaukan Pass, opposite Vijaynagar in Arunachal Pradesh.

Smith, Martin, *Burma: Insurgency and the Politics of Ethnicity*, London and New Jersey: Zed Books, 1991, 492 pp. A history of Burma's ethnic insurgencies but with limited and sometimes inaccurate information about the Kachins, the Nagas, and the Communist Party of Burma.

Tucker, Shelby, *Among Insurgents: Walking Through Burma*, London and New York: The Radcliffe Press, 2000, 386 pp. Describes a journey through Kachin rebel-held territories in northern Burma to Vijaynagar in India.

INDEX